D0947761

222222

Eng*ender*ing Democracy in Brazil

Eng*gender*ing Democracy in Brazil

WOMEN'S MOVEMENTS IN TRANSITION POLITICS

Sonia E. Alvarez

PRINCETON UNIVERSITY PRESS

PRINCETON, NEW JERSEY

Library of Congress Cataloging-in-Publication Data

Alvarez, Sonia E., 1956–
Engendering democracy in Brazil : women's movements in transition politics /
Sonia E. Alvarez.
p.   cm.
Includes bibliographical references.
ISBN 0-691-07856-4 (alk. paper) — ISBN 0-691-02325-5
(pbk. : alk. paper)
1. Women in politics—Brazil. 2. Feminism—Brazil. 3. Brazil—
Politics and government—1964–1985. 4. Brazil—Politics and
government—1985– 5. Democracy. I. Title.
HQ1236.5.B6A44   1990   305.42'0981—dc20   90-33837   CIP

This book has been composed in Linotron Times Roman

Princeton University Press books are printed on acid-free paper
and meet the guidelines for permanence and durability of the
Committee on Production Guidelines for Book Longevity of the
Council on Library Resources

Printed in the United States of America

10 9 8 7 6 5 4 3 2

Parts of the present work appeared in significantly different form in "Politicizing Gender and
Engendering Democracy," in *Democratizing Brazil: Problems of Transition and Consolidation*,
edited by Alfred Stepan. Copyright © 1989 by Oxford University Press, Inc. Used by arrangement with the publisher. Also published as "A Politização do Genero e a Democratização" in
Democratizando a Brasil (Paz e Terra, 1988). Copyright © 1988 by Sonia E. Alvarez. "Wom-
en's Movements and Gender Politics in the Brazilian Transition," in *The Women's Movement in
Latin America: Feminism and the Transition to Democracy*, edited by Jane S. Jaquette. Copyright © 1989 by Unwin Hyman. Used by arrangement with the publisher. "Contradictions of a
Woman's Space in a Male-Dominated State: The Political Role of the Commissions on the
Status of Women in Post-Authoritarian Brazil," in *Women, International Development and Poli-
tics: The Bureaucratic Mire*, edited by Kathleen Staudt. Copyright © 1990 Temple University
Press. Reprinted by permission of Temple University Press. "Women's Participation in the Bra-
zilian 'People's Church': A Critical Appraisal," *Feminist Studies* 16, no. 2 (Summer 1990).
Copyright © 1990 Feminist Studies. Used by arrangement with the publisher.

Contents

Acknowledgments

THIS BOOK owes its existence to the boundless generosity of dozens of Brazilian women's movement activists, who, over the course of the last decade, shared their political experiences and expertise with me and gave graciously of their time to this project. I am especially indebted to the countless women and men active in movements for social change whose vast energy and analytical acumen contributed immeasurably to my understanding of Brazilian gender politics. To refer to such folks as "interviewees" or "informants" would hardly do justice to the immense scope of their contributions to this project. Many women helped uncover obscure documents or nuggets of information essential to this study, opened their homes, their meetings, their personal archives to me, came to my rescue in times of need, and lent their infinite reserves of wisdom and patience to my efforts to understand the dynamics of the women's movements and politics in a country undergoing rapid change.

Though my debt of gratitude extends to all the movement activists and scholars I worked with in Brazil, the following people in particular made my research in Brazil both personally and intellectually rewarding: Miriam Bottassi, Maria Teresa Aarão, Vera Soares, Eliana Ferreira de Assis, Beatriz de Mattes, Maria Amelia Telles de Almeida, Regina Stella Duarte, Maria Aparecida Schumacher, Patricia Sellers, Sonia Alves Calió, Edward McRae, Silvia Artacho, Dulce Pereira, Hamilton Cardoso, Mario Rodrigues Torres, Magali Marques, Roberto Ronchezel, Atílio López, Reinaldo Gomes Silva, the women of Jardim Miriam, especially Palmira Santos Abrantes and Iraci Jesus Eugênio Vilela, and the members of Centro Informação Mulher. Ruth Cardoso and Teresa Caldeira of CEBRAP and Carmem Barroso of Fundação Carlos Chagas in São Paulo were highly supportive of my research; their work on Brazilian gender power relations and social movements served as an inspiration for my own.

My analysis benefited greatly from the lucid insights and incisive criticisms of friends and colleagues who lent a sympathetic ear to my evolving ideas about gender politics or read and commented on all or parts of the manuscript in progress. I thank Judit Moschkovich, Patricia Chuchryk, Marysa Navarro, Angela Araujo, June Hahner, Donna Rae Palmer, and Gwendolyn Mink for their wise advice. My colleagues in the Study Group on New Social Movements in Latin America, Arturo Escobar, Vivienne Bennett, Cathy Schneider, and Teresa Carrillo, furnished a supportive and stimulating intellectual environment, challenging me to refine many of my arguments about women's movements and gender politics in Brazil. I also would like to express my deep gratitude to Jane S. Jaquette and Scott Mainwaring, who reviewed the manuscript for Princeton, for their painstakingly detailed and analytically rigorous suggestions for revision. Finally, I am grateful to professors Alfred Stepan, David Cameron, and James C. Scott who provided helpful comments on how to revise my Yale University doctoral dissertation, the earlier incarnation of this book.

Over the years, I have had the good fortune of working with diligent, resourceful, and efficient research assistants at the University of California at Santa Cruz. Jennifer Terry helped with copyediting the final draft, prepared the index, and made many insightful suggestions for substantive revision. William Veiga assisted with reference checks and bibliography searches and generally helped keep me sane and organized while I wrote the final draft. Patricia Flanagan, Susana Wappenstein, Julia Sweig, Roger Frahm, and Patricia Elsea also provided invaluable research assistance at earlier stages of this project. Miriam Bottassi, the members of Centro Informação Mulher in São Paulo, and, more recently, Anne Blair, collected vital data and documents in Brazil in between my field trips, helping me stay current on developments in gender politics and policy. A competent, reliable, and endlessly patient team of folks assisted me in the intricacies of preparing an electronic manuscript at various, always critical, stages. My thanks go to Scott Brookie, Susan Szabo, Lisa Seiverts, and Pat Sanders. Anne Manuel and William Veiga proofread the manuscript.

To my friends and family who supported me intellectually and emotionally through the many ups and downs of writing this book, I owe the most profound thanks. My parents, Aramis and Sonia Alvarez, my sisters, Jennifer and Ana Maria, my friends, Gwendolyn Mink, Arturo Escobar, Lucrecia Bermudez, Bentley Alvarevich, Lizbeth Haas, Rachel Mailman, Hilda Gutiérrez-Baldoquín, Jennifer Terry, and most especially, Judit Moschkovich, all nourished my mind, boosted my spirits, provided in-house editorial assistance, coupled with chicken soup and cafezinhos in a pinch, and kept me from becoming an absentminded professor once and for all.

My early fieldwork in Brazil in 1981 was supported by a summer research grant from the Yale University Council on Latin American Studies. Research for the dissertation, conducted in 1982 and 1983, was funded by grants from Fulbright-Hays, the Inter-American Foundation, and the Social Science Research Council. The University of California at Santa Cruz generously supported further research for this book. Various UCSC Senate Committee on Research grants, Social Science Divisional grants, and the University of California Regents' Junior Faculty Research Fellowship Program provided research and clerical assistance and travel subsidies for field research conducted in the summers of 1985 and 1988, and granted me release time from teaching responsibilities at crucial moments in the preparation of this book.

Abbreviations

ARENA	Alliance for National Renovation
BEMFAM	Society for the Welfare of the Family in Brazil
BNDES	National Bank for Social Development
BNH	National Housing Bank
CAMDE	Women's Campaign for Democracy
CDMB	Center for the Development of Brazilian Women
CDS	Council on Social Development
CEBs	Christian Base Communities
CECF	State Council on the Feminine Condition
CELAM	General Conference of Latin American Bishops
CELADEC	Latin American Evangelical Commission of Christian Education
CLT	Consolidation of Brazilian Labor Laws
CMB	Brazilian Women's Center
CNBB	National Conference of Brazilian Bishops
CNDM	National Council on Women's Rights
COHAB	National Housing Company
CPI	Parliamentary Inquiry Commission
CUT	Central Union of Workers
FABES	Bureau of the Family and Social Welfare
FIESP	Federation of Industrialists of the State of São Paulo
GALF	Lesbian Feminist Action Group
GAP	Participation and Advisory Group
IMF	International Monetary Fund
IWD	International Women's Day
LIMDE	Democratic Women's League of Minas Gerais
MAF	Feminine Movement for Regimentation
MCC	Movement Against the Rising Cost of Living
MCV	Cost of Living Movement
MDB	Brazilian Democratic Movement
MFA	Feminine Amnesty Movement
MLC	Struggle for Day Care Movement
MMDS	Movement of Democratic Social Women
MNU	United Black Movement
MR-8	Eighth of October Revolutionary Movement
NSM	New Social Movement
OAS	Organization of American States

PAISM	Program for Integral Assistance to Women's Health
PCB	Brazilian Communist Party
PCdoB	Communist Party of Brazil
PDS	Democratic Social Party
PDT	Democratic Labor Party
PFL	Party of the Liberal Front
PMDB	Party of the Brazilian Democratic Movement
PP	Popular Party
PRI	Institutional Revolutionary Party (Mexico)
PSDB	Brazilian Social Democratic Party
PT	Workers' Party
PTB	Brazilian Labor Party
SAB	Society of Friends of the Neighborhood
SEBES	Bureau of Social Welfare
SNI	National Intelligence Service
UCF	Feminine Civic Union
UDR	Democratic Ruralist Union
UDR-Mulher	Democratic Ruralist Union-Women's Department
UN	United Nations
UNICEF	United Nations Children's Fund

Eng*gender*ing Democracy in Brazil

Introduction

BRAZIL has the tragic distinction of having endured the longest military authoritarian regime in South America. The regime installed by the conservative "revolution" of 1964 went through numerous institutional changes in response to sustained opposition and presided over the most protracted and tightly controlled process of transition to political democracy in the region. Yet Brazil is distinctive for another reason—in the 1970s and 1980s Brazilians witnessed the emergence and development of what is arguably the largest, most diverse, most radical, and most successful women's movement in contemporary Latin America. By the mid-1980s, tens of thousands of women had been politicized by the women's movement and core items of the feminist agenda had made their way into the platforms and programs of all major political parties and into the public policies of the New Brazilian Republic.

Unraveling this apparent paradox is the central aim of this study. My theoretical goals are threefold. First, this study seeks to explain the emergence and development of progressive women's movements amid the climate of political repression and economic crisis enveloping Brazil in the 1970s; it devotes particular attention to the gender politics of the final stages of regime transition in the 1980s. But this is not just a story about Brazil. The book also analyzes the relationship between nonrevolutionary political change and changes in women's consciousness and mobilization; it proposes a conceptual framework for understanding how regime change potentially might alter the status of women in Latin America. Finally, this is not just a story about women. By examining the articulation of gender-based political claims and women's movements within the Brazilian transition, this study enhances our understanding of democratization processes still underway in Brazil and other South American nations. This book closely examines one such process from the vantage point of women who, though largely excluded from the intraelite negotiations that ushered in Brazil's civilian regime in 1985, made important contributions to democratizing Brazilian social and political relations.

As a feminist scholar and activist, it was a commitment to expanding the narrow cultural and geographical grounding of contemporary Western feminist theory that originally inspired my inquiry into the gender politics of Brazil's transition. A wide variety of feminist problematics crosscut national boundaries. When I first learned of Brazilian feminism, I was intrigued by the fact that many of the issues raised and problems confronted by women's movements in Brazil, though emerging in social relations distinct from our own, nonetheless resonate in our own diverse feminist practices.

Yet North American feminism has paid scarce attention to the burgeoning women's movements of Brazil and other South American nations. Few are even aware of the fact that today, from Mexico to Argentina, women's movements are flourishing and are expanding the parameters of the struggle against oppression and exploitation in Latin America. As this study will reveal, such neglect not only has compromised international feminist solidarity but also has limited the generalizability of Western feminist political theory and political science.

Feminist scholars in the West too often have assumed that feminism is irrelevant to Latin American women's lives, unwittingly echoing the assumptions of antifeminist political forces in Latin America. The Right has considered "ordinary" women, who are supposedly entrenched in tradition, either to be ontologically apolitical or incapable of autonomous political thought and action. And the Left has insisted that, given the context of poverty, underdevelopment, and imperialism, economic issues and class conflict dominate politics in Latin America and organize the daily lives and political consciousness of its people, including its women. It is hardly my intention here to contest this central aspect of Latin American political life. But Latin American women have always lived out gender inequality *as well as* class exploitation in the flesh, in their "private" and "public" lives. Political and economic modernization brought them few advantages. In fact, as research on women and national development shows, dependent capitalist development often resulted in decreased status and increased inequality for poor and working-class women in Latin America and elsewhere in the Third World.[1]

Capitalist development (or even socialist transformation), in any case, will not resolve many of the problems that women confront in their day-to-day lives. Problems such as lack of access to contraception, spousal abuse in the home, or sexual violence in the streets will not simply fade away as the process of capitalist development unfolds or if women are successfully incorporated into the public worlds of work and politics. And while Latin American women of the popular classes, like their men, are exploited by the ruling classes, they have their own, "generically" distinct interests and concerns as well.[2]

[1] Feminist social scientists have produced a wealth of literature that suggests that political and economic modernization had overwhelmingly negative effects for women. For an excellent review of much of that literature see Susan C. Bourque and Kay B. Warren, *Women of the Andes: Patriarchy and Social Change in Two Peruvian Towns* (Ann Arbor: University of Michigan Press, 1981), especially chapters 2 and 3. See also Gita Sen and Caren Grown, *Development, Crises, and Alternative Visions: Third World Women's Perspectives* (New York: Monthly Review Press, 1987); and Lourdes Benería and Marta Roldan, *The Crossroads of Class and Gender: Industrial Homework, Subcontracting and Household Dynamics in Mexico City* (Chicago: University of Chicago Press, 1987), especially chapter 1.

[2] The term *gender* is preferred to *sex* in my analysis. As O'Brien explains, "The word 'sex' is avoided simply because it has too many levels of meaning. Sex can be an instinct, drive, an act in response to that drive, a gender, a role, an emotional bomb or a causal variable. . . . For the

If commonly held assumptions about the irrelevance of gender to Latin American women's lives are true, how then can we account for the massive mobilization of *women as women* in Brazil and other Latin American nations in recent years? This book analyzes how gender interests were shaped by and articulated in the Brazilian political system over the past two decades, proposing a reconceptualization of the dynamics of gender politics in the Latin American region as a whole. I examine the factors that account for the relative success of women's movements during Brazil's transition from authoritarian rule, tracing the strategies and tactics of middle-class feminist organizations and popular women's groups and focusing on their interaction with political parties and State institutions.

WOMEN AND MILITARY AUTHORITARIAN STATES IN SOUTH AMERICA

The rise of feminist activism in Latin America during the 1970s still puzzles many political observers. How could such movements formulate and advance gender-based political claims in a region where machismo is sanctioned by the State and sanctified by the Catholic church? Why, after decades of dormancy, would feminism resurface precisely during one of the most politically repressive and economically regressive periods in Latin America's history, a time when most countries in the region lived under the yoke of military rule?

The rise of progressive women's movements in the 1970s seems even more perplexing if we consider the fact that Latin American military regimes, like their conservative counterparts in the West, manipulated family values and reinforced traditional conceptions of women's "proper sphere." The men who staged the Brazilian right-wing coup of April 1964, for example, turned to women and the symbolism of the family to soften and justify their illegal seizure of State power. Appealing to women's "innate" commitment to family, morality, and social order, the Brazilian Right enjoined the "women of Brazil" to organize against the democratically elected government of João Goulart. Thousands of women heeded their call, participating in the now infamous marches of "the Family, with God, for Liberty." Goulart's radical populist reforms, claimed right-wing forces, threatened the very moral fabric of Brazilian society. Military men and their reactionary civilian allies convinced thousands of Brazilian women that the populist "communist menace" must be eradicated if the Brazilian family was to be saved.[3]

---

social relations between men and women and for the differentiation of male and female the word gender is preferred." See Mary O'Brien, *The Politics of Reproduction* (London: Routledge and Kegan Paul, 1981), p. 13. Gender, genderic, gender-based, and gender-specific are used throughout the text as a means of reinforcing the idea that men and women are social and political, not biological, categories, produced historically.

[3] For a comprehensive and compelling account of the mobilization of women against the Gou-

Inspired by the ideologues of the conservative revolution and guided by male coup conspirators, the wives and daughters of military men, industrialists, and landowners founded the Women's Campaign for Democracy (*Campanha da Mulher pela Democracia* or CAMDE) in 1962. Along with other right-wing women's groups, such as the Democratic Women's League of Minas Gerais (*Liga da Mulher Democrática* or LIMDE), the Feminine Movement for Regimentation (*Movimento de Arregimentação Feminina* or MAF), and the Feminine Civic Union (*União Cívica Feminina* or UCF), CAMDE organized massive demonstrations against the Goulart government during the months preceding the April 1964 coup. Traditional symbols of feminine piety and spiritual superiority, morality and motherhood were manipulated by the political Right to legitimize their repressive political project. Armed with crucifixes and rosaries, thousands of upper- and middle-class women paraded through the streets of Brazil's major cities, imploring the military to perform its "manly duty" and restore order and stability to the nation. The last women's march against the populist regime occurred in Rio de Janeiro on the day before the coup.

Conservative middle- and upper-class women thus served as handmaidens in the installation of Brazilian authoritarianism. On April 1, a military junta deposed the progressive populist government of João Goulart in a bloodless coup. The "women of Brazil" were initially hailed as the heroines of the new Brazilian "Revolution," a revolution that would combat the threat of communism and radical social change and set Brazil back onto the righteous path toward capitalist growth and development.

But these would-be heroines soon receded from the political scene. When the new ruling coalition doled out political power, the women of CAMDE, LIMDE, and MAF were ignored—sent "back to the kitchen." However, the traditional stock of feminine images and the full gamut of "moral, Christian, family values" that served as the foundation of the right-wing's mobilization of women against Goulart were not abandoned by the new military rulers, and in fact, became the bases for the new authoritarian regime's gender ideology. Indeed, Brazilian coup-makers established a new modal pattern for reactionary gender politics in the Southern Cone. Right-wing forces in Chile, for example, learned a valuable lesson from Brazil. In organizing against the Allende government in the early 1970s, they too mobilized women, also putatively in the defense of family and morality.[4]

Mainstream analysts overlooked this gender-based dimension of the mili-

---

lart government, see Solange de Deus Simões, *Deus, Pátria e Família: As Mulheres no Golpe de 1964* (Petrópolis: Vozes, 1985).

[4] See Michele Mattelart, "Chile: The Feminine Side of the Coup d'Etat," in *Sex and Class in Latin America*, ed. June Nash and Helen I. Safa (New York: Praeger, 1976); and María de los Angeles Crummett, "El Poder Femenino: The Mobilization of Women against Socialism in Chile," *Latin American Perspectives* 4, no. 4 (1977): 103–13.

tary authoritarian State. South American feminist scholars and activists, however, insisted that militarism and institutionalized violence rest on patriarchal foundations. Whereas most analysts stress the cultural or economic determinants of military politics,[5] feminists contend that such politics are also anchored in the patriarchal relations that nurture authoritarianism within the so-called private sphere. As Chilean feminist theorist, Julieta Kirkwood, argues:

> today it is more evident to many sectors that authoritarianism is more than an economic problem and something more than a political problem, that it has its roots and *causes* in all of the social structures, and that one must question and reject many elements and contents not previously considered "political" because they were attributed to day-to-day life, private life. Today people have begun saying that the family and the socialization of children are authoritarian—as well as rigid in the assignment of sex roles—; that education, the factories, intermediary associations, political parties, are constituted in an authoritarian fashion.[6]

Unequal gender power relations breed systemic authoritarianism; thus, gender inequality must be combated, along with class and racial oppression, if authoritarianism is to be eradicated from Latin American social, cultural, and political institutions. Just as imperialism, in a Marxist-Leninist view, is the "highest stage" of capitalist exploitation, military authoritarianism represents the purest, "highest expression" of patriarchal oppression in the eyes of Latin American feminist theorists.

The Brazilian military coup of 1964 also established a new modal pattern for South American politics in general. Military men and their capitalist allies in Chile, Argentina, and Uruguay soon followed Brazil's lead, installing exclusionary military regimes bent on restructuring the political economy of dependent capitalism. During the 1960s and 1970s, military regimes overwhelmed democratic political forces; quashed radical student, labor, and peasant movements; and decimated incipient revolutionary guerrilla movements in "dirty wars." In the name of national security and development,

---

[5] Explanatory frameworks emphasizing Latin America's "authoritarian political culture" abound. See, for example, Howard Wiarda, "Corporatism and Development in the Iberic-Latin World: Persistent Strains and New Variations," in *The New Corporatism; Social-Political Structures in the Iberian World*, ed. Frederick B. Pike and Thomas Stritch (Notre Dame: University of Notre Dame Press, 1974). Frameworks that privileged economic variables, directly linking structural or economic change (i.e., the "exhaustion of import-substitution industrialization") to regime change, predominated in North American social science in the 1970s. See for example Guillermo O'Donnell, *Modernization and Bureaucratic-Authoritarianism: Studies in South American Politics* (Berkeley: Institute for International Studies, University of California at Berkeley, 1973); and various critiques of the BA model in David Collier, ed., *The New Authoritarianism in Latin America* (Princeton, N.J.: Princeton University Press, 1979).

[6] Julieta Kirkwood, *Feminario* (Santiago: Ediciones Documentas, 1987), pp. 126–27. *Unless otherwise indicated, this and all subsequent translations from Spanish and Portuguese are my own.*

authoritarian rule and State terrorism reigned supreme throughout the Southern Cone by the late 1970s.

The military authoritarian regimes of Brazil and the Southern Cone rapidly and profoundly transformed social, economic, and political institutions.[7] In Brazil, social and cultural life were reordered in accordance with the military's new formulations of national security. The Brazilian economy was restructured in the interest of a form of dependent capitalist development that privileged foreign, State, and domestic capital at the expense of the the masses of Brazilian workers. To ensure the success of this new capitalist pact of domination, the political opposition was crushed; and representative political institutions, in the eyes of mainstream observers, were "emasculated."

This radical restructuring of Brazil's political economy also profoundly altered the social, economic, and political roles of women in Brazilian society. I will argue that these rapid changes in women's roles created new material bases for the articulation of gender-based political claims.

Traditional notions of "Family, God, and Liberty" became cornerstones of militaristic, authoritarian "order and progress." But from the outset, these cornerstones laid a shaky foundation for the Brazilian authoritarian edifice. The regime soon encountered massive resistance from organized sectors of civil society. In 1967 and 1968, workers and students rose in protest against the regime's curtailment of political rights and its regressive economic policies. The government set out to contain such "outbursts" at all costs. In 1968, women in Rio de Janeiro and São Paulo decided the costs were too high and denounced the government's mistreatment and torture of young people involved in the protest movements. The "women of Brazil" then organized the "March of the Family for Freedom and against Repression" and the "March for Freedom against Dictatorship"—thus belying the putative representativeness of the 1964 marches of the "Family, with God, for Liberty."

In late 1968, a hard-line coup within a coup signaled a decisive turn to the right by the Brazilian military regime. The repressive apparatus of the State was indiscriminately unleashed upon civil society; neither mothers nor anyone else was spared in the human rights abuses that ensued. But by 1974, the regime's coercive strategy of political domination began to falter. Military rulers and their civilian allies began loosening the reins of control over politi-

---

[7] Guillermo O'Donnell coined the term "bureaucratic authoritarian" (BA) to refer to these regimes. The classification, adopted by most North American social scientists in the 1970s, was intended to emphasize how these regimes differed from other forms of dictatorship and authoritarian rule, highlighting the crucial role played by military and civilian technocrats in policy formulation and implementation. See Guillermo O'Donnell, *Modernization and Bureaucratic-Authoritarianism*. As the term "BA" obscures the militaristic and coercive dimensions so central to strategies of political domination in Brazil and the Southern Cone, however, I prefer to refer to these regimes as "military authoritarian."

cal and civil society. And pressures from below—organized resistance from civil society—resurfaced throughout Brazil.

THE GENDER POLITICS OF TRANSITIONS FROM AUTHORITARIAN RULE

The Brazilian military regime, the first and most successful authoritarian experiment in political and economic restructuring, was also the first to show signs of breakdown. Beseiged by former allies and new enemies alike, the seemingly monolithic, omnipotent military regimes of the 1960s and 1970s crumbled during the 1980s. And in this context of regime transition, women's movements blossomed in full force.

Authoritarian policies not only engendered dramatic changes in women's social, economic, and political roles but also, ultimately, in their consciousness as women. A wide gap separated the State's national security discourse on gender and the family from the reality of women's lives. While official discourse acclaimed the virtues of traditional womanhood, for example, regressive economic policies thrust millions of women into the work force. While patriarchal ideology held women morally (if not financially) accountable for their family's survival, working-class women saw their children go hungry. And though the military exalted motherhood and femininity, women were hardly spared the ravages of State repression and female political prisoners and women victims of State terror were often subjected to sexual abuse and humiliation.

Chapters 2 and 3 analyze the dramatic changes in Brazil's political economy, social policies, and political and discursive practices that provide the backdrop to women's political mobilization. I will show that repressive social policies drew women of *all* social classes into the swelling ranks of the political opposition. However, the expansion and diversification of capitalist production during Brazil's "Economic Miracle" of 1967–1973 had markedly different effects on the roles of women of various racial groups and social classes. The stage thus was set for the differential articulation of gender-based interests among middle-class and working-class women.

On the one hand, economic growth and the expansion of higher education created new job and educational opportunities for white, middle-class women, but discrimination on the basis of sex continued unabated. As sexism severely circumscribed the professional opportunities and personal options available to women of the new middle classes, the rapid entry of white, middle-class women into academia and the professions soon fueled an inchoate debate about women's equality among Brazilian intellectuals. On the other hand, regressive wage policies simultaneously pushed millions of poor and working-class women into low-paying, low-status jobs in the least progressive, most exploitative sectors of the economy. Economic crises undermined working-class survival strategies, propelling hundreds of thousands of women to seek solutions to their families' needs by participating in the community self-help organizations and grassroots social movements that sprang up throughout Brazil in the 1960s and 1970s.

These rapid changes in women's roles helped spark a "second wave" of the women's movement in Brazil as elsewhere in the Southern Cone.[8] The multiple contradictions experienced by women active in male-dominant social movements and opposition parties, I shall argue in chapter 3, fueled women's consciousness, facilitated the formulation of gender-based political demands and stimulated the formation of autonomous women's groups.

Chapters 4 and 5 track the changing political dynamics and gender discourses of working-class feminine groups in the periphery of Brazil's major cities and middle class–based feminist organizations during the 1970s and 1980s. Both movement participants and social scientists in Latin America commonly distinguish between "feminine" and "feminist" groups and demands. Paul Singer clarifies the customary usage of these terms: "The struggles against the rising cost of living or for schools, day care centers, etc., as well as specific measures to protect women who work interest women closely and it is possible then to consider them *feminine* demands. But they are not *feminist* to the extent that they do not question the way in which women are inserted into the social context."[9]

In Brazil, hundreds of feminine groups emerged in the periphery of major cities and over four hundred self-professed feminist organizations were formed during the 1970s and 1980s. Chapters 4 and 5 elucidate the points of convergence and divergence between feminine and feminist mobilization. Women's groups of both types first mobilized hundreds of thousands to protest the detrimental effects of authoritarian development on women's lives. But by the early 1980s, many middle-class and popular women's groups also had mounted a political challenge to institutionalized sexism. My analysis centers on the gradual politicization and radicalization of gender issues, as women activists encountered relentless discrimination within the progressive opposition and saw their concerns relegated to the status of "secondary contradictions."

Over the course of the Brazilian transition, women formed their own organizations, enlisted in the opposition in unprecedented numbers, and urged op-

[8] In the 1920s and 1930s, Brazil saw the rise of a "first wave" of the women's movement, centered on women's suffrage and predominantly middle and upper class in composition. See Branca Moreira Alves, *Ideologia & Feminismo: A Luta da Mulher pelo Voto no Brasil* (Petrópolis: Vozes, 1980). For a compelling analysis of the mid–nineteenth-century Brazilian women's press and efforts to secure women's access to education that predated the suffrage movement, see June E. Hahner, *A Mulher Brasileira e suas Lutas Sociais e Políticas: 1850–1937* (São Paulo: Brasilense, 1981) and her "Feminism, Women's Rights, and the Suffrage Movement in Brazil, 1850–1932," *Latin American Research Review* 15, no. 1 (1980): 65–112.

[9] "O Feminino e O Feminismo," in *São Paulo: O Povo em Movimento*, ed. Paul J. Singer and Vinícius C. Brant (Petrópolis: Vozes, 1980), pp. 116–17, emphasis in the original.

position parties and unions to support the cause of gender equality. But the relationship between women's movements and the male-dominant opposition was always uneasy, at best. The struggle against authoritarianism was paramount and demands for women's equality were too often deemed divisive or frivolous by male opposition leaders.

Yet in the context of a military authoritarian regime, the fate of women's movement organizations remained closely wedded to that of the larger political opposition. And opposition strength grew dramatically in the mid-1970s, as military authoritarianism in Brazil began its slow but inexorable decline. Popular pressure from below combined with conservative liberalization from above to give rise to a process of regime breakdown and transition to civilian rule, commonly referred to as *abertura* or political liberalization. That process culminated in 1985 with the installation of the New Brazilian Republic, a civilian regime that initially retained many of the trappings of military authoritarianism but reestablished basic norms of procedural democracy through which those trappings, in theory, might be overcome.[10]

As the *abertura* process unfolded, the growing political clout of the opposition in Brazil, coupled with the regime's attempts to contain it through conservative political liberalization, gradually expanded the political space available to women and allowed for the articulation of gender-specific claims. In chapters 6 and 7, I show how political parties gradually came to view women's movements as a vast and untapped source of political currency. Thus, during *abertura*, the opposition actively courted women's support. And women's movement organizations overwhelmingly supported the opposition, mobilizing thousands of women for electoral participation and promoting antiregime mass rallies. Though opposition parties proved resistant to the movements' more radical claims, women activists hoped a new, democratic regime would be more supportive of gender-specific demands for equality and justice.

Some of their hopes were realized during the 1980s. As demonstrated in chapters 8 and 9, most Brazilian parties now endorse many core issues of the women's movements' political agenda and women conquered significant political space within parties and the State apparatus. Most parties formed women's divisions, and councils on the status of women were created at the municipal, state, and federal levels after 1983.

However, the incorporation of women and women's issues into Brazilian transition politics also was riddled with tensions and contradictions. Authoritarian liberalization and democratization pushed women's movements and

---

[10] See Alfred Stepan, *Rethinking Military Politics: Brazil and the Southern Cone* (Princeton: Princeton University Press, 1988); Thomas E. Skidmore, *The Politics of Military Rule in Brazil, 1964–85* (New York: Oxford University Press, 1988); and William C. Smith, "The Political Transition in Brazil: From Authoritarian Liberalization to Elite Conciliation to Democratization," in *Comparing New Democracies: Transition and Consolidation in Mediterranean Europe and the Southern Cone*, ed. Enrique A. Balorya (Boulder, Colo. Westview Press, 1987).

other organized sectors of civil society to reformulate their political strategies. During the decades of exclusionary and repressive authoritarian politics, feminists in Brazil and elsewhere in South America completely dismissed State-centered political strategies and pressure-group tactics. Indeed, during the two decades when military authoritarianism dominated South American politics, the State naturally was viewed as women's (and other oppressed groups') "worst enemy."

But the opposition political parties who courted the female electorate and appealed to organized female constituencies during the final stages of the transition to democracy are now in power. As the recently established democratic regime seeks legitimacy in redistributive policies and participation-based accountability, women's claims perilously have made their way into male-dominant policy-making arenas. Today, feminists in Brazil and other South American nations are confronted with a new conjuncture in gender politics.[11] The State, heretofore widely perceived to be women's worst enemy, is suddenly portraying itself as "women's best friend." Whether the State, the political party system, and the bureaucracy can be viable arenas for promoting improvements in the condition of women's lives is therefore an especially pressing question for Latin American feminism today. How women's movements in Brazil met this challenge in the increasingly conservative political climate of the late 1980s is the subject of chapter 10.

Through a case study of women's movements and gender politics in Brazil's transition from authoritarian rule, this book addresses vital questions concerning alternative feminist strategies vis-à-vis the dependent capitalist State in South America. To be sure, a case-specific monograph cannot yield causal theoretical explanations nor elaborate precise hypotheses. But a theoretically informed and conceptually exacting analysis of gender politics in Brazil will nevertheless allow me to present research findings that will provide a foundation for further comparative analysis of the politics of gender in Latin America today.

The theoretical and conceptual framework that informs this inquiry into Brazilian gender politics is presented in chapter 1. The book concludes with theoretical reflections on how the Brazilian findings might contribute to future comparative research in the fields of Latin American and gender politics. The final chapter identifies the macrostructural and micropolitical variables explaining the rise of women's movements in authoritarian regimes, analyzes the political articulation of gender interests, and proposes a gender-sensitive framework for understanding Latin American political change.

Over the past two decades, feminist students of Latin America have devoted

---

[11] Political conjuncture, as conceptualized by French Marxists and Latin American social scientists, refers to the correlation and articulation of social and political forces, within a given social formation, at a specific historical moment.

most of their attention to assessing the impact of dependent capitalist development on the lives of women in the region. Yet while we now have documented extensively the effects of social and economic change on women's roles, the vast literature on women and development sheds little light on the specifically political dimensions of change and their relationship to transformations in women's status in Latin America.[12]

A few recent studies analyze the gender politics of populist and nationalist regimes.[13] And some studies have examined how socialist regimes and revolutionary social policies altered women's roles in Cuba and Nicaragua. The Central American *guerrillera* in particular captured the imagination of North American leftists, feminists, and academics. We now have numerous studies of women's massive participation in the Cuban and Central American revolutions[14]; and scholars and activists extensively have debated the implications of revolutionary social change for improving the status of women in Latin America and elsewhere in the Third World.

Yet other dynamic processes of political change and rather different, though equally dramatic, forms of social struggle characterized South American politics in recent decades—the rise of popular resistance to the military authoritarian regimes during the 1960s and 1970s and the now renowned "transitions to democracy" of the 1980s. How these processes of nonrevolutionary political change affected institutionalized gender relations, women's political mobilization, and gender policy outcomes, however, has received considerably less social scientific attention.[15]

[12] Notable exceptions include Elsa M. Chaney, *Supermadre: Women in Politics in Latin America* (Austin: University of Texas Press, 1979); María Elena Valenzuela, *Todas Ibamos a Ser Reinas: La Mujer en el Chile Militar* (Santiago: Ediciones Chile y América, CESOC, ACHIP, 1987); Susan C. Bourque and Donna Robinson Divine, eds., *Women Living Change* (Philadelphia: Temple University Press, 1985); and Carmen Diana Deere and Magdalena León, eds. *Rural Women and State Policy: Feminist Perspectives on Latin American Agricultural Development* (Boulder, Colo.: Westview Press, 1987).

[13] These include Anna Macias, *Against All Odds: The Feminist Movement in Mexico to 1940* (Westport, Conn.: Greenwood Press, 1982); Marysa Navarro, *Evita* (Buenos Aires: Ediciones Corregidor, 1981); *Ideologia & Feminismo;* Julia Silvia Guivant, "O Sufragio Feminino na Argentina, 1900–1947," *Boletim das Ciências Sociais* 17 (May–July 1980); and Marifran Carlson, *¡Feminismo! The Woman's Movement in Argentina from its Beginnings to Eva Perón* (Chicago: Academy Chicago Publishers, 1988).

[14] Among the most compelling of these are Maxine Molyneux, "Socialist Societies Old and New: Progress Toward Women's Emancipation?" *Monthly Review* 34, no. 3 (July–August 1982): 56–100; Norma Chinchilla, "Women in Revolutionary Movements: The Case of Nicaragua," in *Revolution in Central America*, ed. Stanford Central American Action Network (Boulder, Colo.: Westview Press, 1982); and Jane Deighton et al., *Sweet Ramparts: Women in Revolutionary Nicaragua* (London: War on Want and the Nicaraguan Solidarity Campaign, 1982).

[15] Jane S. Jaquette's edited volume, *The Women's Movement in Latin America: Feminism and the Transition to Democracy* (Boston: Unwin Hyman, 1989), is an important recent contribution. See also works on women's movements in Brazil, Argentina, Uruguay, Peru, and Chile listed in the select bibliography.

The democratization processes still underway in Brazil and other South American nations fall far short of even the most restricted concept of "revolutionary." They nevertheless significantly transformed women's social, economic, and political roles in these societies. And gender-conscious political and social movements conquered political space during the years of authoritarian regime breakdown and transition to civilian rule.

This book is fundamentally concerned with exploring the relationship between these transitions to democracy and the emergence of new gender-related political claims among women of all social classes. It raises a number of pressing questions about the politics of gender in Brazil and in other Latin American nations where socialist transformation remains a relatively distant goal for progressive social forces. Most importantly, this study asks what political activists concerned about the transformation of oppressive and exploitative social relations in those societies can and have done *in the meantime*, while patriarchal, capitalist, and racist power relations remain entrenched in the pact of domination represented in the State.

SOCIAL MOVEMENTS IN THE BREAKDOWN OF AUTHORITARIANISM AND TRANSITIONS TO CIVILIAN RULE

Finally, this book hopes to contribute to the theoretical debate about the process of military authoritarian regime breakdown and the nature of the transitions to civilian rule in Brazil and other South American nations. Most analyses of the processes of liberalization and democratization focus on: (1) the shifting alliances among those sectors of the ruling classes represented within the military authoritarian regimes; and (2) the emergence of a hegemonic "moderate opposition" (usually elite-based) among the forces within political society that challenged authoritarianism during the 1970s and early 1980s.[16] To borrow a phrase from Alexander Wilde's "Conversations among Gentlemen: Oligarchical Democracy in Colombia,"[17] most studies of contemporary political change in Brazil and the Southern Cone focus on "conversations among gentlemen and generals" in analyzing the transition process.

But grassroots and liberation movements and other nonelite-based organi-

[16] See especially Guillermo O'Donnell, Philippe C. Schmitter, and Laurence Whitehead, eds., *Transitions from Authoritarian Rule* (Baltimore, Md.: Johns Hopkins University Press, 1986); Howard Handelman and Thomas G. Sanders, eds., *Military Government and the Movement toward Democracy in South America* (Bloomington: Indiana University Press, 1981); Paul W. Drake and Eduardo Silva, eds., *Elections and Democratization in Latin America, 1980–1985* (San Diego: Center for Iberian and Latin American Studies, Center for U.S.—Mexican Studies, Institute of the Americas, 1986); and James M. Malloy and Mitchell A. Seligson, eds., *Authoritarians and Democrats: Regime Transitions in Latin America* (Pittsburgh, Penn.: University of Pittsburgh Press, 1987).

[17] In *The Breakdown of Democracy in Latin America*, ed. Juan J. Linz and Alfred Stepan (Baltimore, Md.: Johns Hopkins University Press, 1978).

zations of civil society also played a critical role in these transition processes,[18] most especially in the case of Brazil.[19] Minimally, popular pressure- and mass-based political protests indirectly legitimated the more moderate goals of elite-based opposition sectors in the eyes of military incumbents. And the existence of social movements among the popular classes and other social groups, including women, the poor, and/or people of color, who were quintessentially excluded from the pact of domination under authoritarian rule, provided the elite opposition with an organizational base that could be mobilized in favor of democracy.[20]

The final chapters of this book address an additional and critical set of questions rarely considered by analysts of democratization: How will these social movements and their political claims fare if liberal democracy becomes the new political status quo in Brazil? Will their political raison d'être be nullified by the creation of new institutional mechanisms of political representation? Will the new democratic regimes, whose leadership is still in the hands of white, bourgeois men, create new channels for popular participation and representation? Will political democracy create the conditions within which progressive social forces can organize for social and economic democracy, as

[18] For comparative perspectives on social movements in regime transitions, see Ilse Scherer-Warren and Paulo Krischke, *Uma Revolução no Cotidiano? Os Novos Movimentos Sociais na América do Sul* (São Paulo: Brasilense, 1987); Elizabeth Jelin, ed., *Movimientos Sociales y Democracia Emergente*, 2 vols. (Buenos Aires: Centro Editor de América Latina, 1987); Elizabeth Jelin, ed., *Los Nuevos Movimientos Sociales*, 2 vols. (Buenos Aires: Centro Editor de América Latina, 1985); and Scott Mainwaring and Eduardo Viola, "New Social Movements, Political Culture and Democracy: Brazil and Argentina in the 1980's," *Telos* 17, no. 3 (Fall 1984): 17–52.

[19] Recent analyses stressing the relationship of social movements to political parties and the State in the Brazilian transition include: Renato Raul Boschi, *A Arte de Associação: Política de Base e Democracia no Brasil* (São Paulo: Vértice; Rio de Janero: IUPERJ, 1987); Pedro R. Jacobi, "Movimentos Sociais Urbanos numa Época de Transição," in *Movimentos Sociais na Transição Democrática*, ed. Emir Sader (São Paulo: Cortez, 1987); Lúcio Kowarick and Nabil Bonduki, "Espaço Urbano e Espaço Político: do Populismo à Redemocratização," in *As Lutas Sociais e a Cidade: São Paulo, Passado e Presente*, ed. Lúcio Kowarick (Rio de Janeiro: Paz e Terra, UNRISD, and CEDEC, 1988); Paulo J. Krischke, "Movimentos Sociais e Transição Política: Contribuições da Democracia de Base," in *Uma Revolução no Cotidiano?*; Ruth Corrêa Leite Cardoso, "Os Movimentos Populares no Contexto da Consolidação da Democracia," in *A Democracia no Brasil: Dilemas e Perspectivas*, ed. Fábio Wanderley Reis and Guillermo O'Donnell (São Paulo: Vértice, 1988); and Scott Mainwaring, "Urban Popular Movements, Identity and Democratization in Brazil," *Comparative Political Studies* 20, no. 2 (July 1987): 131–59.

[20] For analyses of the Brazilian transition that stress the role of both "elite calculations" and "resistance and opposition of subaltern groups," see especially, William C. Smith, "The Political Transition in Brazil"; and Eli Diniz, "A Transição Política no Brasil: A Uma Reavaliação da Dinámica da Abertura," *Dados: Revista de Ciências Sociais* 28, no. 3 (1985): 329–46. Diniz persuasively argues that the explanation for liberalization must be understood "to reside in the confluence of two basic dynamics: a dynamic of negotiation and conciliation directed by elites and a dynamic of pressure and demands triggered by society, articulated by social movements and translated by political organizations" (p. 333). This dual dialectic of elite negotiation and popular pressure is emphasized in my own ensuing analysis of the Brazilian transition process.

many analysts and activists hoped? Or will the movements merely be absorbed or co-opted into what is essentially a new strategy of political domination within a fundamentally unaltered pattern of dependent capitalist development?

FIELD RESEARCH

My discussion centers on women's movements and gender politics in Greater São Paulo where I conducted the bulk of my field research, though I also introduce data on other regions of the country, where possible. As the country's principal industrial metropolis, São Paulo has been the site of widespread mobilization throughout much of modern Brazilian history and many of the social and political movements that originally appeared there subsequently proliferated throughout urban Brazil.

The analysis presented in chapters 2 through 5 derives from over one hundred interviews with political activists and extended participant-observation in innumerable women's movement meetings, debates, events, protest actions, and other political activities during November and December of 1981, October 1982 to October 1983, July and August of 1985, and June and July of 1988. The fact that my own social status and organizing experience as a Latina in the U.S. women's movement was analogous to that of many São Paulo's feminists greatly facilitated my access to predominantly middle class–based feminist movement groups and events.

Access to poor and working-class women's groups proved somewhat more difficult as outsiders in general, let alone North American researchers, are generally mistrusted by local social movement groups. In late 1981, I visited several neighborhood women's groups in São Paulo in the company of middle-class feminists, social workers, and female charity workers and decided that the best field strategy would be to follow the activities of one such group quite closely. After explaining the purpose of my research to several such groups, the women's group in Jardim Miriam agreed to have me participate in their ongoing activities in the neighborhood.

Jardim Miriam is a socially heterogeneous neighborhood in the periphery of Greater São Paulo with an extensive organizational infrastructure and a long history of popular mobilization. The exceptionally varied trajectory of women's mobilization in the neighborhood afforded me a unique opportunity to explore the wide spectrum of forms of organization among poor and working-class women while concentrating my field research in a single community: the Jardim Miriam women's group began as an "apolitical" mothers' club in the late 1960s; it was sponsored by the church and led year-long job training courses for neighborhood women in the 1970s; and, by the early 1980s it had evolved into an autonomous women's organization explicitly focused on raising women's consciousness of their oppression as women. I attended women's group meetings on a weekly basis for over ten months during 1982–1983 and have visited the neighborhood and accompanied changing political dynamics there during each of my subsequent field trips. My participation in the Jardim Miriam group also facilitated contacts with other neighborhood women's organizations throughout São Paulo's urban periphery; I regularly traveled with local activists to other neighborhoods and sometimes attended citywide popular meetings in their company. My ongoing immersion in the activities of the Jardim Miriam group thus greatly aided my developing analyses of women's organizations among the popular classes.

During each of my field trips, I conducted extensive, open-ended formal and informal interviews with participants of both feminine and feminist groups representative of the full range of political tendencies within the Brazilian women's movement—from "apolitical" mothers' clubs led by ladies' charity organizations to Marxist women's groups with direct ties to left-wing political tendencies. All of these interviews and my countless informal conversations with movement participants focused on the evolution of women's movements' political claims over time.

Chapters 2 through 5 are also based on a systematic examination of internal organizational documents, public manifestos, movement journals and newsletters, articles on the women's movement appearing in both the mainstream and the alternative press, proceedings from movement conferences and congresses (either in printed or recorded form), and other primary sources. These documents were available to me, and to any other interested researchers, thanks to the efforts of Brazilian women's movement participants themselves to ensure that the history of their struggles is recorded. Two feminist archives in São Paulo, the extensive documents and audiovisual collection at *Centro Informação Mulher* (Women's Information Center), and the *Fundação Carlos Chagas*'s (Carlos Chagas Foundation) comprehensive research library provided invaluable sources of data for the analysis presented here. Also, several individual women made their personal archives of the movement available to me.

Chapters 6 through 10 draw on over forty formal and numerous informal conversations with political party leadership, feminist party militants and candidates, government bureaucrats, and policy makers conducted between 1981 and 1988. I also surveyed local, state, and national government documents and publications concerning gender-specific and gender-related issues and observed political party events and organizational meetings and government-sponsored forums and debates about women and public policy.

Comparative insights into other contemporary women's movements and the dynamics of gender politics elsewhere in Latin America introduced throughout the text draw on field research conducted in Argentina (July 1985 and July 1988), Mexico (October 1987), Cuba (July 1979 and June 1981), and Nicaragua (November-December 1980 and December 1983). Comparative observations also rely on movement documents and publications collected during three Latin American and Caribbean Feminist Meetings I attended in Lima, Peru (1983), Bertioga, Brazil (1985), and Taxco, Mexico (1987).[21]

Finally, the ensuing analysis owes a great deal to existing secondary sources on the development of feminine and feminist movements in Brazil.[22] I can only hope that the analysis presented here will further the understanding of the complexities that characterized the relationship between women's movements, political parties, and the State in transitional Brazilian politics.

[21] For an analysis of the debates and events that took place during the four Latin American and Caribbean Feminist Encuentros, the last of which was attended by over fifteen hundred feminist activists from all countries in the region, see Nancy Saporta Sternbach, Marysa Navarro, Patricia Chuchryk, and Sonia E. Alvarez, "Feminisms in Latin America: From Bogotá to Taxco," forthcoming.

[22] The secondary sources on Brazilian gender politics most central to my own analysis are included in the select bibliography. My theoretical approach to contemporary women's movements in Brazil is especially indebted to the work of Ruth Cardoso and Teresa Caldeira of CEBRAP, in São Paulo. Cardoso's "Movimentos Sociais Urbanos: Balanço Crítico," in *Sociedade e Política no Brasil Pós-64*, ed. Bernard Sorj and Maria Hermínia Tavares de Almeida (São Paulo: Brasilense, 1983) and Caldeira's *A Política dos Outros: O Cotidiano dos Moradores de Periferia e o que Pensam do Poder e dos Poderosos* (São Paulo: Brasilense, 1984) as well as numerous conversations with each of these women were extremely influential in my own developing analyses of feminist and feminine movements in contemporary Brazil.

CHAPTER ONE

Theoretical and Comparative Perspectives on Women's Movements and the State

MOST conventional approaches to the study of women and politics provide few insights into the critical strategic dilemmas confronting Latin American women's movements in the 1980s and 1990s. Many studies of gender politics conducted in the United States, for example, implicitly embrace the liberal premise that women's claims can and should be advanced through the State and the party system.[1] Moreover, many analyses of women and politics treat "sex" as merely another variable to be quantified. That is, much of the literature examines micropolitical or individual variables that affect women's political participation, socialization, and so on, and does not afford much analytical significance to the historically specific, male-dominant, racist, and class-based institutional contexts within which "female political behavior" takes place.[2]

A comparative inquiry into the dynamics of women's movements' interaction with the State, however, must pay particular attention to those very contexts. Latin America is a region historically beseiged by State repression; shaped by political and economic dependency on core capitalist nations; and marked by rigid racial, sexual, gendered, and class-based hierarchies. Therefore, before the story of contemporary women's movements in Brazilian transition politics can be told, we must map out a theoretical terrain that will enable us to apprehend the structural-historical specificity of gender politics in Latin America. This chapter, then, lays out the conceptual apparatus that frames my Brazilian case study.

HISTORICAL PERSPECTIVES ON WOMEN'S MOVEMENTS AND GENDER POLITICS IN LATIN AMERICA

Social movements aimed at the vindication of women's rights are not new to Latin America. By the 1920s and 1930s, upper- and middle-class women in countries as diverse as Argentina, Cuba, Nicaragua, Mexico, Chile, Colom-

---

[1] See, for example, Virginia Sapiro, *The Political Integration of Women: Roles, Socialization, and Politics* (Urbana: University of Illinois Press, 1983); Ethel Klein, *Gender Politics: From Consciousness to Mass Politics* (Cambridge, Mass.: Harvard University Press, 1984); Barbara Ehrenreich and Frances Fox Piven, "Women and the Welfare State," in *Alternatives: Proposals for America from the Democratic Left*, ed. Irving Howe (New York: Pantheon, 1984).

[2] For the most comprehensive critical review of this literature, see Vicky Randall, *Women and Politics: An International Perspective*, 2d ed. (Chicago: University of Chicago Press, 1987).

bia, the Dominican Republic, and Brazil had organized to exact their demands for civil and political rights from male-dominated political systems. Historical analyses of the politics of gender in Latin America suggest that the incorporation of women and gender-specific issues into institutional arenas in Latin America most often led to the reinforcement of existing gender power arrangements. Women's claims and movement organizations were co-opted or manipulated by elites and institutions to serve the needs of the prevailing pact of domination represented in the State.[3] In contemporary Latin America, political regimes, parties, and organized sectors of civil society have reacted to today's women's movements much as they responded to their elite-based predecessors: by harnessing women's political activity into "auxiliary" women's organizations, co-opting women's movement organizations and/or appropriating their political discourses, acquiescing to limited demands through public policy making, or suppressing women's movement demands altogether.

Though rarely reflected in the mainstream literature on Latin American political systems, historical and contemporary examples of the political manipulation of autonomous female mobilization by Latin American power holders abound. Juan Perón structurally and ideologically co-opted the decades-old Argentine women's movement, creating the Peronist Feminine Party in 1949 and thus redirecting women's political activity into his ruling populist coalition. In Colombia, Rojas Pinilla made women an integral pillar of his "Third Force." Vargas in Brazil, Somoza in Nicaragua, Batista in Cuba, and Trujillo in the Dominican Republic simply bought off the more reformist strand of the women's movements in the 1930s and 1940s by promoting "progressive" legislation, such as protective labor laws and maternity benefits, that remained largely in the books and changed little in the lives of the majority of women in their countries.

In Chile and Peru until the 1950s, progressive political parties suppressed the women's movements' demands for female suffrage, fearing that women's "conservative nature" would incline them to vote for clerical or conservative parties. The same assumption kept the "revolutionary" PRI (*Partido Revolucionario Institucional* or Institutional Revolutionary Party) in Mexico from enfranchising women until 1953.

In Latin America today, many regime opposition parties as well as political incumbents are actively courting organized women's support. In Mexico, for example, the Communist Party and the Revolutionary Worker's Party took up work on women's issues and joined the Mexican Women's Front in 1980. In Argentina, women's groups were an integral part of the broad-based oppo-

---

[3] The structural-historical framework proposed in this section is elaborated more fully in my doctoral dissertation entitled, *The Politics of Gender in Latin America: Comparative Perspectives on Women in the Brazilian Abertura Process* (Ann Arbor, Mich.: University Microfilms, 1987). The historical and comparative data presented here are discussed in detail in Part I of that larger work.

sition that successfully displaced the authoritarian military regime in 1983. In Chile and Brazil, the political opposition actively enlisted organized women in its various causes. In Guatemala and El Salvador, women are fully integrated into the ranks of the armed opposition and organized into opposition-linked civilian organizations that address the specificity of women's subordination within the larger struggle for national liberation. And in Cuba and Nicaragua, socialist political regimes linked the women's movements to the State by channeling women's political activity into regime-linked mass organizations.

In some cases, the incorporation of women's organizations and women's issues into institutional political arenas resulted in concrete improvements in the condition of women's lives. In both Peronist Argentina and socialist Cuba, for example, such incorporation or institutionalization of gender-based political claims led to increased job opportunities for women, improved conditions for women workers, decreased pay differentials between men and women, and greater civil and political rights for women citizens. In both cases, gender-specific issues were ideologically politicized as well—the proper role of women in social, economic, and political life became the subject of national debate and the object of legitimate political conflict.

Significantly, both these regimes radically restructured the relationship between State and society. Both sought new social bases of support among the previously politically excluded and disenfranchised. In both countries, autonomous women's movement organizations had been mobilizing women around gender-specific political demands for several decades prior to the installation of the new regimes. This autonomous mobilization increased political elites' awareness of women as a group, as a potentially mobilizable constituency. This awareness, coupled with the need to mobilize new social sectors for economic participation, led both Perón and Castro to target women as a group for support and to champion legislative reforms in women's status that would further such support.

However, in many cases, the politicization and institutionalization of gender had less desirable outcomes for women and women's movement organizations. Women's issues, introduced into institutional arenas by women's rights organizations, often were manipulated once they entered those male-dominated arenas. And most frequently, progressive gender ideologies were co-opted by dominant political and economic interests. Political elites responded selectively to those women's issues and women's organizations that were least disruptive to the status quo while successfully excluding or actively repressing those most threatening to the contemporary pact of domination.

A closer look at the politics of gender in Peronist Argentina, for example, reveals that the Peronist Feminine Party drew support only from the most reformist and opportunistic strand of the women's movement and repressed women's rights organizations with solid historical ties to Argentine socialists and anarchists. And while Eva Perón became the self-proclaimed champion of women's rights, the ideology of gender that the Peróns propounded projected an image of women as the selfless "helpmates" of the Justicialist revolution rather than as autonomous, active participants in social change.[4] Similarly, while the Cuban revolution unquestionably brought about extraordinary improvements in the concrete condition of women's lives, political discourse on gender power relations and their relative autonomy from economic power relations, other than as conceived by dominant Marxist-Leninist ideology, has been precluded. The Cuban regime selectively mobilized women in keeping with political and economic goals that were sometimes less than self-evidently in women's interest and male party leadership often clashed with the Federation of Cuban Women in the definition of those goals.[5]

My point is that the incorporation of women and women's issues into Latin American institutional politics is hardly an absolute good; at best, it is a mixed blessing. While during the last decade feminist political scientists, sociologists, and historians have produced an extensive literature on female political participation, women's political attitudes and behavior, and female political elites in Latin America and elsewhere, this literature does not explain adequately the impact of women's organized political activity on institutional arenas or vice versa. The analytical neglect of the linkages between women's movements and government policy has resulted in both "selective omission" and "theoretical distortion" in our present understanding of women and politics in Latin America.[6]

As an analyst of Latin American political systems, I believe that our neglect of the linkages between women's movements and government policy has compromised our understanding of how State power is structured in Latin American societies. A regime's policies concerning gender form part of the structural and ideological grid upon which State power is based. That grid has a class, a racial/ethnic, and a gendered content, and is not fixed, but rather constantly in flux, reflecting the class, race, and gender struggles that take place both within and outside the State. In exploring the relationship between institutionalized political power and the continued subordination of women, then, the present project departs significantly from much of the ever-expanding literature on women and politics. That literature too often fails to explore, either theoretically or empirically, *why* political arenas are so resistant to the entry

[4] See Julia Silvia Guivant, "O Sufragio Femenino na Argentina, 1900–1947," *Boletím de Ciências Sociais* 17 (May–July 1980): 1–27; Marysa Navarro, *Evita* (Buenos Aires: Corregidor, 1984).

[5] Muriel Nazzari, "The 'Woman Question' in Cuba: An Analysis of the Constraints to Its Resolution," In *Promissory Notes: Women in the Transition to Socialism*, ed. Sonia Kruks, Rayna Rapp, and Marilyn B. Young (New York: Monthly Review Press, 1989).

[6] Morris J. Blachman, "Selective Omission and Theoretical Distortion in Studying the Political Activity of Women in Brazil," in *Sex and Class in Latin America*, ed. June Nash and Helen I. Safa (New York: Praeger, 1976).

of women and of issues that might promote changes in the status of women (whereas, for example, women entered the formal labor market arena in ever-increasing numbers).

CONTEMPORARY LATIN AMERICAN WOMEN'S MOVEMENTS AND GENDER INTERESTS

Much of the literature on women and politics in the United States, instead, focuses on how political institutions do or do not "represent women's interests."[7] But "women's interests" are no more analytically useful as a conceptual category than "men's interests." When one considers that women span all social classes, races, ethnicities, religions, nationalities, political ideologies, and so on, then an infinite array of interests could be construed as women's interests. Gender, class, race, ethnicity, sexual preference, and other social characteristics determine women's social positioning and shape women's interests.

In exploring the relationship between women's movements, political parties, and the State in Brazil, I will focus instead on the political articulation of *gender interests*. Gender interests, according to Maxine Molyneux, "are those that women (or men, for that matter) may develop by virtue of their social positioning through gender attributes."[8]

Women's movements give social and political expression to women's gender interests. Brazilian women's movements are therefore central protagonists in the story that unfolds in the ensuing chapters. Women's movements can be defined as those sociopolitical movements, composed primarily but not necessarily exclusively of female participants, that make claims on cultural and political systems on the basis of women's historically ascribed gender roles.[9]

Women's movements constitute deliberate attempts to push, redefine, or reconstitute the boundary between the public and the private, the political and the personal, the "natural" and the "artificial"[10]—a boundary that is institu-

[7] See, for example, Virginia Sapiro, "When Are Interests Interesting? The Problem of Political Representation of Women," *American Political Science Review* 75, no. 3 (September 1981): 701–16.

[8] Maxine Molyneux, "Mobilization Without Emancipation? Women's Interests, State, and Revolution," in *Transition and Development: Problems of Third World Socialism*, ed. Richard R. Fagen, Carmen Diana Deere, and José Luis Coraggio (New York: Monthly Review Press; Berkeley, Calif.: Center for the Study of the Americas, 1986), pp. 283–84.

[9] Women's movements pursue women's gender interests. Excluded from this definition, then, are State-linked mass organizations for women, women's branches of political parties, trade unions, and other organizations of civil society that are not primarily organized to advance women's gender-specific concerns. Though women's movement activists frequently work within such "women's auxiliaries," these are afforded separate treatment in my analysis.

[10] For an excellent discussion of women's "claims" and their confinement to the "natural" and the "artificial" realms, see Lisa Peattie and Martin Rein, *Women's Claims: A Study in Political Economy* (Oxford: Oxford University Press, 1983).

tionalized by the modern State. At specific historical conjunctures, women's movements successfully can and have challenged that boundary, as it is socially constructed and conjuncturally determined.

Women's movements can be seen as proactive or reactive.[11] That is, women organize to challenge or to protect their socially ascribed roles. Female gender roles give rise to two basic forms of politicization: one that grows out of and accepts prevailing feminine roles and asserts rights on the basis of those roles; another that seeks to transform the roles society assigns to women, challenges existing gender power arrangements, and claims women's rights to personal autonomy and equality.

In her analysis of women's mobilization in revolutionary Nicaragua, Molyneux makes a similiar distinction. She argues that "gender interests can be either strategic or practical, each being derived in a different way and each involving differing implications for women's subjectivity."[12] What Molyneux terms strategic gender interests

> are derived . . . deductively, i.e., from the analysis of women's subordination and from the formulation of an alternative, more satisfactory set of arrangements to those that exist. These ethical and theoretical criteria assist in the formulation of strategic objectives to overcome women's subordination, such as the abolition of the sexual division of labor, the alleviation of the burden of domestic labor and childcare, the removal of institutionalized forms of discrimination, the attainment of political equality, freedom of choice over childbearing, and the adoption of adequate measures against male violence and control over women.[13]

In this study, women's organizations that seek to advance *strategic* gender interests are conceptualized as *feminist*. Feminism is itself, of course, a highly contested concept. In terms of feminist praxis, little consensus exists as to the causes of and remedies for women's oppression, the relationship of women's subordination to other forms of exploitation and oppression (i.e., based on class, race, sexuality), the nature of the "enemy" (i.e., patriarchy or capitalism or imperialism or all of the above), and the appropriate arena of feminist struggle (i.e., the parliament or the bedroom). The fact that feminism is a partial ideology that can prove compatible with liberal, conservative, radical, and socialist ideologies compounds the controversy over which strategies would be most effective in combating women's oppression. Debates surrounding the various dimensions and forms of feminist political practice fostered considerable conflict among Brazilian feminist organizations and will be of central concern to my analysis.

Contemporary Brazilian feminists do agree that the roles assigned to all

---

[11] Charles Tilly, Louise Tilly, and Richard Tilly, *The Rebellious Century, 1830–1930* (Cambridge, Mass.: Harvard University Press, 1975), pp. 252–53.

[12] Maxine Molyneux, "Mobilization without Emancipation," p. 284.

[13] Ibid.

women by the dominant ideology are oppressive; the fact that gender is central to the distribution of economic and political power is a further point of consensus. Like their early twentieth-century predecessors, feminist movement organizations today are predominantly, but not exclusively, middle class in composition. Yet unlike many of their feminist foremothers, contemporary Brazilian feminists are overwhelmingly aligned with other progressive movements for social, economic, and political transformation of their society and formed part of the broad-based opposition to authoritarian rule.

Feminist groups are but one segment of a politically and socially heterogeneous Brazilian women's movement. That larger movement includes a wide variety of organizations, ranging from community mothers' clubs or housewives associations, to cost-of-living movements, to women's groups seeking neighborhood day-care centers.

Women's groups such as these, which advance *practical* gender interests, are conceptualized as *feminine* organizations in this study. Practical gender interests, according to Molyneux, are "given inductively and arise from the concrete conditions of women's positioning by virtue of their gender within the division of labor. In contrast to strategic gender interests, these are formulated by the women themselves who are within these positions rather than through external interventions. Practical interests are usually a response to an immediate perceived need, and they do not generally entail a strategic goal such as women's emancipation or gender equality."[14]

Whereas feminist organizations focus on issues *specific* to the female condition (i.e., reproductive rights), feminine groups mobilize women around gender-*related* issues and concerns. The cost of living, for example, is one such issue. The sexual division of labor in most societies holds women responsible for managing family budgets and allocating family incomes to provide for basic necessities. Women, then, may organize to protest the rising cost of living because inflation undermines their ability to adequately feed, clothe, or house their families.

In Brazil during the 1970s and 1980s, poor and working-class women joined community survival struggles in unprecedented numbers, seeking improvements in urban services, health care, and education, improvements that would facilitate the work they are expected to perform within the prevailing sexual division of labor. Middle- and lower middle-class women also organized movements, such as mothers' movements for human rights, whose goals similarly originated in their socially ascribed maternal roles. These women mobilized to defend their rights as wives and mothers, rights that the dominant ideology assures them in theory, but that dominant political and economic institutions deny them in practice.

A further point about gender interests needs to be emphasized at this junc-

[14] Ibid.

ture. Given the rigidity of class structures and racial hierarchies and the severity of income disparities and power imbalances in Brazil, we also must pay specific attention to the ways in which class and race are constitutive of gender interests. That is, a woman's gendered experience in the world cannot be separated out from her experience as a member of a specific racial-ethnic group or social class. Thus, a woman is not Brazilian and Black and working-class and female; she is a Brazilian working-class Black woman. Class- and race-specific gender attributes determine one's social positioning as a woman. Class and race therefore must be viewed as integral components of one's gendered identity—not additional or adjunctive characteristics—which crucially shape women's practical and strategic gender interests.

Because women as women are also members of other social groups and classes, their gender interests will encompass class- or race-specific dimensions. For example, in pointing to the representation of the *mulata*, marketed to tourists as the ultimate symbol of Brazilian sensuality, Black feminists in Brazil stress the ways in which racism shapes Black women's gendered oppression. This raises several critical questions about how sex, race, and class affect the content and scope of gender-based demands. Does the elimination of sexploitation of Black women require an end to racism or sexism or both? Is it not in the strategic interest of Black women as women to overcome racism in order to eradicate race-specific sexual discrimination?

Moreover, one woman's strategic gender interests might threaten another's practical gender interests. A Latin American white, middle-class, university-educated woman's practical gender interests, for example, might include the continuation of domestic service as an occupational category and could therefore come into direct conflict with the strategic gender interests of the dark-skinned, working-class, illiterate woman who is her would-be domestic servant. Similarly, whereas bourgeois women might be able to envision practical alternatives to existing gender power arrangements (e.g., for university-educated women in most contemporary Latin American societies, financial independence from a man is not inconceivable), for many poor and working-class women such alternatives are limited not only by their gender but also by their class position in society. This is particularly true in Latin America, where class differences are *overdetermined* by the international division of labor. And though this fact does not negate that women of the popular classes share some strategic gender interests with middle- and upper-class women, it does explain the reluctance of many poor and working-class women to accept some of the fundamental premises of feminism as it developed in the West. That reluctance is in part the result of the lack of survival alternatives outside the patriarchal family structure.

Women of all social groups and classes *potentially* share some strategic gender interests. For example, in theory, all women would be equally interested in the eradication of sexual abuse and violence against women that occurs in all classes, cultures, and nationalities. And many Latin American feminists also argue that, given the interdependence of capitalism and male domination, the eradication of class exploitation would be of strategic interest to all women. However, the rigid class structures and the elite-based political systems that prevail throughout Latin America often present formidable obstacles to the common pursuit of gender-based interests within cross-class political movements. For poor and working-class women and women of color, strategic gender interests would encompass the elimination of class and racial oppression as well as gender oppression. As the "women at the bottom of the bottom," their strategic gender interests are necessarily far broader.

However, the political expression of gender interests by a particular feminine or feminist group does not "naturally" or automatically arise out of the race or class status of its members. Rather, different conceptions of what is in "the interest of women" are always constructed politically and discursively.

This study elucidates how practical and strategic gender interests are shaped by social class; by social, political, and discursive practices; and by structural-historical forces specific to Brazil. Do Brazilian women make gender-based political demands distinct from those advanced by women's movements in the West? What factors give rise to gender-related claims in the context of repressive or exclusionary politics and societies rent by deep social cleavages and riddled by racial injustice, class exploitation, and economic dependency?

FEMINIST PERSPECTIVES ON GENDER AND THE STATE

What happens to women's varied gender interests when these are articulated in the context of the Brazilian political system? Since at least the early 1980s, when opposition parties gained control of eleven state governments, Brazilian women have been attempting to advance their interests in the sphere of formal institutional politics. In the mid-to-late 1980s, Brazilian feminists, like their counterparts in the postauthoritarian regimes of Argentina, Uruguay, and Peru, increasingly pressed new demands on male-dominant parties and policy-making arenas.

For feminist activists and all those concerned with eradicating enduring patterns of inequality in Brazil and the Latin American region as a whole, then, understanding the masculinist dimensions of the dependent capitalist State is today an especially pressing task. Feminist theories of the State are important because theories of the State are ultimately theories of politics: "different views of the State imply different politics of social change, in both their means and ends."[15] Theories of politics cannot be separated from the practice of politics. Therefore, feminist theoretical insights into the structure and function of

[15] Martin Carnoy, *The State and Political Theory* (Princeton, N.J.: Princeton University Press, 1984), p. 4.

State power potentially could inform feminist political practice as well as our theoretical understanding of the State, and are thus crucial areas for feminist research.

Latin American women's movements, like women's movements everywhere, have multiple cultural and social goals that cannot be pursued solely through the policy process; they seek attitudinal, behavioral, and normative changes that must be pursued both within and outside the State and political society. But there are many changes in women's subordinate status that must be pursued primarily, if not exclusively, within the confines of formal (male-dominant and sexist) political institutions—changes in the laws governing marriage, the family, conception and contraception, women's work, women's sexuality, women's education, and so on. These kinds of changes constitute the focus of the ensuing chapters.

As democratization progresses in Brazil and the Southern Cone, women's movement activists are confronted with "the dilemma that feminists have faced for generations: is the state a potential force for greater equality or an instrument of patriarchal oppression?"[16] And the fundamental contradiction that women's movements have encountered, in past and present times, is that the very institutional arenas in which many such changes must be sought are fundamentally premised upon the continued confinement of women to the private sphere, the sphere that is the structural foundation of both politics and production.

Moreover, while all movements for social change confront similar strategic dilemmas, feminist political science must grapple with the fact that women, as women, have a unique relationship to the State. That is, social movement activists are always faced with choices concerning whether and when to channel their demands through the institutions of the State or political society (e.g., political parties). Feminist theoretical insights, however, suggest that the modern State represents the quintessential institutional separation of the public or political from the private or personal domains of human activity. The State institutionalizes gender power relations by circumscribing the female gender to the latter domain, politically reinforcing the boundaries that confine women socially. The political, then, becomes the domain of men and male issues, and issues that directly affect the lives of women as women, like reproduction, contraception, child care, rape, sexual abuse and battery, and so on, are predefined as outside the "proper" realm of politics.[17] The "classical social

---

[16] Jane Jenson, "Both Friend and Foe: Women and State Welfare," in *Becoming Visible: Women in European History*, 2d ed., ed. Renate Bridenthal, Claudia Koonz, and Susan Stuard (Boston: Houghton Mifflin, 1987), p. 535.

[17] For a sampling on the feminist theoretical debate on the gendered content of State power, see Zillah R. Eisenstein, *Feminism and Sexual Equality: Crisis in Liberal America* (New York: Monthly Review Press, 1984); Irene Diamond, ed., *Families, Politics and Public Policy: A Feminist Dialogue on Women and the State* (New York: Longman, 1983); Mary McIntosh, "The State

movement dilemma," then, becomes a particularly poignant one when the movement in question is composed of women and advances claims considered to be, by definition, outside the legitimate reach of State intervention—for example, claims concerning women's rights in marriage and the patriarchal family.

The strategic dilemma faced by feminists is further complicated by the fact that the boundary between the public and the private is not static. Feminist theorists maintain that the female gender role, largely bounded by the private sphere and grounded in the biological and daily reproduction of the human species, serves as the foundation of the public sphere, facilitates capitalist accumulation, and frees men to engage in politics and production.[18] But because masculinity and femininity are socially and historically contingent categories, the State must regulate and delimit personal power relations in order to guarantee the smooth functioning of the public sphere; hence, the State constantly decrees changes in marriage, divorce, and inheritance laws, rape and pornography laws, population policies, family wage policies, protective labor laws, and all other political mechanisms that structure gender power relationships. That is, what is considered the legitimate realm of State intervention in the private sphere itself varies over time and across nations. Contingent upon shifting social relations of production and reproduction, the institutionalized separation between public and private is constantly redefined ideologically and new definitions are coercively enforced by the State.

---

and the Oppression of Women," in *Feminism and Materialism*, ed. Annette Kuhn and Ann Marie Wolpe (London: Routledge and Kegan Paul, 1979); Michèle Barrett, *Women's Oppression Today: Problems in Marxist Feminist Analysis* (London: Verso, 1980); Mary Fainsod Katzenstein and Carol MaClung Mueller, eds., *The Women's Movements of the United States and Western Europe: Consciousness, Political Opportunity and Public Policy* (Philadelphia: Temple University Press, 1987); Jennifer Dale and Peggy Foster, *Feminists and State Welfare* (London: Routledge and Kegan Paul, 1986); and Michèle Barrett and Mary McIntosh, *The Anti-Social Family* (London: NLB, 1982). For a stimulating discussion of how four distinct dimensions of male power are inscribed in advanced capitalist States, see Wendy Brown, "Finding the Man in the State: A Theoretical Inquiry into the Masculinist Powers of Postindustrial Liberal Capitalist States," July 1989 (Mimeograph). These and other Western feminist theories of the State, however, rarely consider the relationship between gender, class, race, and imperialism in the context of dependent capitalist states.

[18] For a discussion of the relationship between the public and the private, and production and reproduction, see Maríarosa Dalla Costa and Selma James, *The Power of Women and the Subversion of the Community*, 3d ed. (Bristol: Falling Wall Press, 1975); Michele Barrett, *Women's Oppression Today*; Susan Moller Okin, *Women in Western Political Thought* (Princeton, N.J.: Princeton University Press, 1979); Jean Bethke Elshtain, *Public Man, Private Woman: Women in Social and Political Thought* (Princeton, N.J.: Princeton University Press, 1981); and Mary O'Brien, *The Politics of Reproduction* (London: Routledge and Kegan Paul, 1983). For a Brazilian perspective on this "split," see Madel T. Luz, "O Lar e a Maternidade," in *O Lugar da Mulher*, ed. Madel T. Luz (Rio de Janeiro: Graal, 1982); and Maria Lygia Quartim de Moraes Nehring, "Familia e Feminismo: Reflexões sobre Papeis Femininos na Imprensa para Mulheres" (Ph.D. diss., University of São Paulo, 1981), part I.

States, then, mediate changes in gender power relations, as well as in class and race relations. But a crucial quesition confounds feminist practice—do capitalist, patriarchal States always act in the interests of men and private capital? Socialist feminist theory suggests that capitalism and patriarchy are interdependent systems of exploitation and domination. Though interdependent, capitalism and patriarchy do not necessarily change in synchrony with one another. That is, the changing needs of capital accumulation, on both a national and an international scale, may at times conflict with the needs of patriarchal domination or may threaten existing social relations of reproduction.

Yet the State represents *both* class and patriarchal interests. And it must mediate these distinct, and sometimes competing, interests when they come into conflict with one another. Thus, one of the central functions of the State is to promote changes in the one system of exploitation (patriarchy or capitalism) to suit the needs of the other. That is, the State may intervene to promote changes in social relations of reproduction to accommodate changes in social relations of production or vice versa.

For example, both early industrial capitalism and current transnational capitalism relied heavily on a "reserve army" of female labor. By drawing women out of the home and into the work force, these changes in social relations of production challenged male supremacy and disrupted prevailing social relations of reproduction. "The vanguard of industrial investment in the world capitalist system is in the lowest paid segment of those countries paying the lowest wages. Young women in developing countries are the labor force on this frontier just as women and children were in the industrialization of England and Europe in the nineteenth century."[19] At such historical conjunctures, the State may intervene to adjust social relations of reproduction— which may be threatened by the incorporation of women into paid labor—by assuming some of the tasks of reproduction itself.[20] States also sometimes promote changes in women's legal status, enabling them to act as "freer agents" in the sale of their labor (i.e., protective labor laws, changes in women's civil or political status).

However, because the State remains male-dominant, State-promoted changes in women's status will seldom significantly alter existing gender power arrangements. Instead, State gender-related reforms will tend to "modernize" or update existing patterns of gender inequality—that is, preserving male supremacy while providing capital with greater access to female labor. In undertaking the "modernization of gender relations," the State typically

[19] June Nash, "Introduction," in *Women, Men and The International Division of Labor*, ed. June Nash and María Patricia Fernández-Kelly (Albany: State University of New York Press, 1983), p. x.

[20] For an incisive analysis of the State's role in the transformation of familial to "social" or State patriarchy in the United States, see Eileen Boris and Peter Bardaglio, "The Transformation of Patriarchy: The Historic Role of the State," in *Families, Politics, and Public Policy: A Feminist Dialogue on Women and the State*, ed. Irene Diamond (New York: Longman, 1983), pp. 70–93.

assigns women a gender-specific place within political institutions and restructures gender difference through official ideology and policy.

Thus, contradictory policies often characterize the State's mediation of class and gender interests. That is, though genderic, as well as economic and racial, power relations find their expression and articulation within the pact of domination represented by the State, the State does not monolithically represent male interests.[21] In this study, the State is conceived of as relatively autonomous of patriarchal interests. To paraphrase Martin Carnoy's interpretation of Marxian "class struggle" theories of the State as represented in the work of authors such as Manuel Castells and the later Nicos Poulantzas: the dominant gender is conscious of its interests and attempts to influence and control the State as an object of its socioeconomic and gender-based power, but at the same time, because of the existence of class and gender struggle, the State must appear to be autonomous of existing genderic, class, and racial power arrangements in order to retain its very legitimacy as a State.[22] Thus, the State is relatively autonomous of patriarchal or male interests not because it is independent of those interests but because its legitimacy is partially derived from its ability to conceal the genderic, racial, and class interests represented within the pact of domination by granting some concessions to the subordinate groups and classes that increasingly press their political claims upon it.[23]

To coin a phrase, the State is *not* the executive committee of men, and therefore may act in the interest of particular groups of women (e.g., women of specific racial groups and classes) at a given historical conjuncture. Moreover, if State mediation of the conflicting interests of capitalism and patriarchy is sometimes contradictory, then gender-based social struggles can potentially exacerbate those contradictions. This feminist perspective on the relative autonomy of the State thus implies that class-based, racially based, *and* gender-based political struggles, led by social movements, can and *must* take place both within and outside the political apparatuses of the State.

[21] For an opposing argument, see Catherine A. MacKinnon, "Feminism, Marxism, Method, and the State: Toward a Feminist Jurisprudence," *Signs* 8, no. 4 (Summer 1983): 635–58; and her "Feminism, Marxism, Method and the State: An Agenda for Theory," *Signs* 7, no. 3 (Spring 1982): 515–44. MacKinnon argues that "however autonomous of class the liberal state may appear, it is not autonomous of sex" (1983, p. 658). This perspective leaves a crucial question of political praxis unanswered—if the State *is*, and is *always* male, then what are people concerned about gender-specific social change to do in the meantime? In my view, the State is *male-dominant*, rather than male (an argument analogous to that of poststructuralist and neo-Marxian theories that suggest that the State is bourgeois-dominant rather than bourgeois).

[22] Carnoy, *The State and Political Theory*, p. 253.

[23] Zillah Eisenstein argues that the relative autonomy of the State from male interests in late capitalist society derives from the conflicting and even contradictory needs of capitalism and patriarchy. See *Feminism and Sexual Equality*, especially pp. 87–113. See also, Jane Jenson, "Both Friend and Foe: Women and State Welfare" and her "Gender and Reproduction, or Babies and the State," *Studies in Political Economy* 20 (Summer 1986): 9–46.

Again, drawing from Carnoy, in this "gender struggle" view of the State, the "white, male, capitalist" State can be moved against dominant interests by the

> development of movements inside and outside the State to force it to move against its fundamental role as reproducer of [gender, race, and] class relations. . . . The capitalist [patriarchal and racist] State will not reform in a progressive direction without such movements pressing it. In other words, the capitalist [patriarchal and racist] State is inherently class-based [gender-based and racially-based] and will act in that way unless pressured by mass organizations. The correct political strategy is to organize at the base, both outside and inside the State, bringing those organizations to bear on society's dominant institutions to reform them.[24]

As several critical studies of social movements show, it is crucial to examine how State policies shape, and sometimes determine, the strategies and dynamics of social movement organizations and vice versa.[25] Women, in this view, are not the passive objects of State policy. Instead, women are, and have always been, active subjects in politics and, as such, historically influenced State gender-specific policy outputs, even when their political participation was largely confined to noninstitutional political arenas. The analysis that follows therefore examines the effect of State policy outputs on women's movements' political strategies and discourses and the movements' impact on State discourses and public policies. My inquiry into the relationship between women's movements and the State therefore conceptualizes that relationship as a dynamic and dialectical one rather than a linear one involving simply movement input ⎯⎯⎯→ policy process ⎯⎯⎯→ State output.

"ENGENDERING" POLITICAL CHANGE: POLITICAL TRANSFORMATIONS AND TRANSFORMATIONS IN WOMEN'S LIVES IN LATIN AMERICA

In analyzing the dialectical relationship between women's movement claims and State policies in Brazil, we must further take account of the fact that gen-

---

[24] Carnoy, *The State and Political Theory*, p. 259.

[25] For a similar perspective on the relationship between the State and the "new social movements" in Brazil, see Ruth Corrêa Leite Cardoso, "Movimentos Sociais Urbanos: Balanço Crítico," in *Sociedade e Política no Brasil Pós-64*, ed. Bernard Sorj and Maria Hermínia Tavares de Almeida (São Paulo: Brasilense, 1983); Renato Raul Boschi and Lícia do Prado Vallardes, "Movimentos Associativos de Camadas Populares Urbanas: Analise Comparativo de Seis Casos," and Pedro R. Jacobi, "Movimentos Populares Urbanos e Resposta do Estado: Autonomia e Controle vs. Cooptação e Clientelismo," both in *Movimentos Coletivos no Brasil Urbano*, ed. Renato Raul Boschi (Rio de Janeiro: Zahar, 1983). Studies of social movements in the United States also point to a dynamic interrelationship between State and civil society. See Luther P. Gerlach and Virginia H. Hine, *People, Power and Change: Movements of Social Transformation* (New York: Bobbs-Merrill, 1970); Frances Fox Piven and Richard A. Cloward, *Poor People's Movements: Why They Succeed, How They Fail* (New York: Vintage, 1977); and Doug McAdam, *Political Process and the Development of Black Insurgency, 1930–1970* (Chicago: University of Chicago, 1982).

der power relations and women's political claims are differentially articulated in contemporary dependent capitalist States when compared to advanced capitalist States. Dependent capitalism, for example, obstructs the development of social welfare policies and makes the peripheral State more reliant on the family and the private sphere for ensuring the reproduction of class, racial, and gender power relations; the dependent State therefore will prove relatively more impervious to political claims that call for a reordering of gender power arrangements. Furthermore, Third World nations' peripheral position in the world capitalist system significantly constrains State autonomy and deeply influences public policy; hence, national women's movements must not only make political claims on the national State but also, indirectly, on the international capitalist system and its regulatory institutions.[26]

But these constraints on the articulation of women's political claims in Third World countries themselves change over time, reflecting the varying needs of international capitalist patriarchy and the shifting alliances among social forces within Third World nations. Changing macro and microeconomic and political variables determine the degree of peripheral nations' dependence on core nations and shape (and reshape) public policies and dominant ideologies within Third World nations. And, as this study will show, such changes have profound consequences for women's movements and gender politics in the context of dependent societies.

On the surface, a feminist view of the State as the ultimate patriarch—the quintessential institutional expression of male domination—would appear to be consistent with the dynamics of gender politics in the military authoritarian States of Brazil and the Southern Cone. If the State, especially the dependent, militaristic State, is always the ultimate patriarch, then feminists, especially Latin American and other Third World feminists, should certainly eschew State-centered strategies for advancing the status of women.

But, as mentioned above, State structures are hardly static or immutable. The Latin American State in particular is highly politicized, constantly in flux;[27] even the powerful military regimes of the 1960s and 1970s proved vul-

---

[26] Institutions such as the United Nations and the International Monetary Fund, for example, have profound consequences for gender-specific policy outcomes in Third World nations (i.e., population policy, women and development policy, and so on). See Bonnie Mass, *Population Target: The Political Economy of Population Control in Latin America* (Toronto: L.A. Working Group and Women's Educational Press, 1976); Gita Sen and Karen Grown, *Development, Crises and Alternative Visions: Third World Women's Prespectives* (New York: Monthly Review Press, 1987); Kathleen Staudt, *Women, Foreign Assistance, and Advocacy Administration* (New York: Praeger, 1985); Kathleen Staudt, ed., *Women, International Development and Politics: The Bureaucratic Mire* (Philadelphia: Temple University Press, 1990); and, Arvonne S. Fraser, *The U.N. Decade for Women: Documents and Dialogue* (Boulder, Colo.: Westview Press, 1987).

[27] See Douglas A. Chalmers, "The Politicized State in Latin America," in *Authoritarianism and Corporatism in Latin America*, ed. James A. Malloy (Pittsburgh, Penn.: University of Pittsburgh Press, 1977).

nerable to international economic pressures and domestic oppositions. The pact of domination represented in the State changes periodically, in response to changes in the world system and concomitant realignments among domestic social groups and classes. These realignments frequently are manifest in changes in *political regime*, in the institutional arrangements that structure the relationship between State and society. And if the State institutionalizes male domination, then regime change might also alter the relationship between women and the male-dominant State. This might account for the apparent complimentarity between the process of democratization and the process of politicization of gender in contemporary Brazilian politics.

In the early years of the recent wave of authoritarian rule in Latin America, most women's groups, like other opposition organizations in civil society, engaged exclusively in the politics of protest and in promoting critical consciousness and aiding grassroots survival efforts. Absolute autonomy from regime-sanctioned parties and State-controlled labor unions was seen to be necessary for advancing radical social change; working for change outside established institutions was equated with "freedom" by all social movements emerging in military authoritarian contexts. Any State concession to movement demands tended to be viewed as co-optative and any institutionalization of the movements or absorption of their demands by the State was equated with "unfreedom."

But as authoritarianism began to crumble in the late 1970s and the military ushered in political liberalization schemes of various types and duration, the terms of this political equation began to be altered. Women's movements began making gender-based claims on the State and political society. The return of civilian rule and political efforts to consolidate precarious democracies in South America in the 1980s posed new challenges for feminist theory and practice in the region.[28] The democratization process, however restricted, in theory opens up new possibilities for nonco-optative institutional mediation of movement demands, channels through which women's movements and other movements seeking social change could impact existing structures of domination. As Renato Raul Boschi persuasively argues:

> [A]nalyses overestimate contemporary social movements, seeing in them a radical break with the sphere of liberal democratic institutions. The emphasis on innovation and discontinuity, in turn, presupposes such a degree of autonomy of those forms of collective action that change would purportedly occur without reproducing existing [social and political] conditions. Yet the impact of social movements, especially in

[28] Latin American feminist social scientists have begun exploring the relationship between feminism and the new democratic States. For an excellent sampling of the Latin American debate, see "As Mulheres e os Novos Espaços Democráticos na América Latina," special issue of *Revista de Ciências Sociais* 1, no. 2 (1987). See also Jane S. Jaquette, ed., *The Women's Movement in Latin America: Feminism and the Transition to Democracy* (Boston: Unwin Hyman, 1989).

the long run, will only be realized if there is some sort of institutional mediation, even at the cost of having dominant norms and values mold [or restrict] a large part of [the movements'] innovative potential.[29]

Since the installation of a civilian, nominally democratic regime in Brazil, women's movements activists have had to weigh the costs and benefits of seeking such institutional mediation from a still bourgeois- and male-dominant State.

Even before the advent of civilian rule, women's movements had to contend with advancing their claims in the complex and dynamic context of transition politics. As Jane S. Jaquette suggests,

> The period of transition from military dictatorship to democratic government is not politics as usual; it offers new opportunities and sets different constraints. . . . [S]ocial movements—including the women's movement—have an advantage during the transition because they can mobilize followers and bring people into the streets. Transitions are political "openings" in the broadest sense; there is a general willingness to rethink the bases of social consensus and revise the rules of the game. This gives social movements an extraordinary opportunity to raise new issues and to influence popular expectations.[30]

In Brazil, as the ensuing chapters will reveal, women's movements took full advantage of these expanding opportunities to advance a relatively successful policy agenda, even as the transition was still underway.

From a socialist feminist perspective, regime transitions also represent State attempts at restructuring class *and* gender relations. That is, political regimes have offensive and defensive policy agendas that reorder social relations of production and reproduction, reorganizing relations between capital and labor, State and family, the public and the private, women and men. This is clearly evident in military authoritarian regimes; the National Security State delineated a sharpened separation between the public world of ruthless military men and the private world of self-sacrificing, motherly women.

Today, the democratizing regimes of Brazil and the Southern Cone are once again in the process of restructuring class and gender relations. If women's movement activists successfully adapt their strategies to the more democratic political context, they could make important contributions to the consolidation of democracy by undermining the patriarchal foundations that fostered Brazilian authoritarianism. However, as the dust settles on the new democracies and the social consensus built around the defeat of the military becomes a thing of the past, the return to politics as usual could well erode some of the gains made by women during the transition. Alternatively, the new democratic regimes,

[29] Renato Raul Boschi, *A Arte de Associação: Política de Base e Democracia no Brasil* (São Paulo: Vértice; Rio de Janeiro: Iuperi, 1987), p. 23.

[30] Jane S. Jaquette, "Introduction," in *The Women's Movement in Latin America*, p. 13.

it is hoped, might provide increased political space for the articulation of gender-based claims both within and outside the State. This is critical because the male-dominant State will only promote reforms that significantly alter the concrete conditions of women's lives when it is pushed to do so by organized, gender-conscious social movements that exert political pressure both within and outside the State. Thus, people concerned about redressing gender inequality must seize the changing opportunities provided by different political regimes—or else risk allowing the State to reform gender relations through policies that will merely ''modernize'' existing capitalist, racist, and patriarchal relations of power and exploitation.

A feminist theory of the State in Latin America, then, must grapple with questions of strategy. The gender struggle perspective on the relative autonomy of the State proposed here suggests that different political regimes, which represent varying schemes of class, generic, and racial domination, may also provide different *opportunity spaces* for women's movements to act both within and outside the State and thus impact State policies.[31] In the face of relatively frequent regime change, how can feminists best take advantage of shifting political opportunities?—*before* the patriarchal, capitalist State ''renormalizes'' gender power relations once a new political regime and a new strategy of dependent accumulation are firmly in place.

The following two chapters examine how the consolidation of military authoritarian rule in Brazil hermetically sealed the State off from civil society and closed off all institutional channels for the articulation of citizen demands. Yet, as will be seen in chapter 2, the military's policies had profound implications for women's roles and indirectly set the stage for the emergence of new gender-based demands among working- and middle-class women.

---

[31] In a comparative discussion of women's movements in the United States and Western Europe, Mary Fainsod Katzenstein, drawing on Sidney Tarrow, also emphasizes the importance of the ''political opportunity structure'' in determining ''what a social movement will be able to extract from the State in terms of access to State institutions, the stability of political alignments, and the relation to allies and support groups.'' See her ''Comparing the Feminist Movements of the United States and Western Europe: An Overview,'' in *The Women's Movements of the United States and Western Europe*, pp. 10–13. Sidney Tarrow defines this concept more fully in *Struggling for Reform: Social Movements and Policy Change during Cycles of Protest*, Center for International Studies, Western Societies Occasional Paper, no. 15 (Ithaca, N.Y.: Cornell University, 1983). My use of this concept draws primarily on Doug McAdam, *Political Process and the Development of Black Insurgency*, and will be discussed more fully in chapter 3.

Women in the New Social Movements of Urban Brazil

BRAZIL'S military rulers launched a full-scale offensive against the pre-1964 status quo, an offensive that also inadvertently transformed the roles of women in Brazilian society. First, the military regime aggressively pursued political and economic stabilization, quelling democratic forces, implementing drastic austerity measures, and squelching restive student, labor, and peasant movements. This frontal attack on the populist legacy was followed after 1968 by more ruthless policies aimed at thoroughly revamping Brazil's political economy, social relations, and political life. The military's development strategy rested on an accelerated industrialization drive fueled by multinational and transnationalized domestic capital investment and debt-financed State investment and supported by regressive wage policies and tight controls on labor. A policy of deliberate income concentration coupled with the systematic political exclusion and repression of those most adversely affected by these policies were the lynchpins of the military regime's development model.[1]

Yet protest and resistance remained integral and dynamic features of the Brazilian political landscape despite the military regime's relentless attempts to demobilize the population through the selective use of institutional controls and harsh repression. Civil society was not easily subjugated and resistance soon arose among workers, students, urban slumdwellers, women, and other social sectors. This chapter explores how the military's development model inadvertently fomented protest and dissent and examines why women in particular joined liberation and survival struggles in unprecedented numbers. My focus here will be on the structural factors conditioning the rise of grassroots and liberation movements in the 1960s and 1970s, triggering social struggles in which women became important participants. The discursive, micropolitical, and conjunctural factors that facilitated the rise of social movements organizations in authoritarian Brazil will be explored at length in chapter 3.

This chapter concentrates on how the military regime's economic and social policies indirectly influenced the mobilization of women. Several analysts of authoritarian politics in Brazil have called our attention to how the authoritar-

[1] For an incisive analysis of the development model adopted by Brazil's military regime, see Peter Evans, *Dependent Development: The Alliance of Multinational, State and Local Capital in Brazil* (Princeton, N.J.: Princeton University Press, 1979). See also Alfred Stepan, ed., *Authoritarian Brazil: Origins, Policies, and Future* (New Haven, Conn.: Yale University Press, 1973); and Thomas C. Bruneau and Philippe Faucher, eds., *Authoritarian Capitalism: Brazil's Contemporary Economic and Political Development* (Boulder, Colo.: Westview Press, 1981).

ian State's "offensive" and "defensive" projects "define the options and strategies of the political opposition."[2] In explaining the rise of independent labor movements in Brazil, for example, Alfred Stepan maintains that: "The Brazilian State's concern with promoting capital accumulation did more than simply leave more space in which the opposition could move without repression. It had the unintended consequence of generating conditions that promoted the development of the structural base of the opposition, most notably in its effects on the growth of the working class in São Paulo."[3] That is, the State capitalist economic strategy adopted by the Brazilian authoritarian regime increased the absolute size of the industrial work force. Its policy of industrial concentration clustered the new working class in the city of São Paulo, setting the stage for the rise of a militant trade union movement in the late 1970s.

The authoritarian State's offensive project similarly generated new structural foundations for the emergence of gender-based political claims among working-class and middle-class women in Brazil. This chapter explores the macrostructural origins of Brazilian women's political mobilization in the early-to-mid 1970s. A gender-sensitive analysis of the policies of the Brazilian military regime will provide a partial answer to one of the central theoretical puzzles that inspired this study: how progressive gender-based political claims could surface in the context of a regime in which traditional conceptions of "Family, God, and Liberty" served as the cornerstones of regressive and repressive policies designed to promote dependent capitalist, authoritarian "order and progress." The regime's own policies, I will argue, heightened the contradictions in women's roles and indirectly helped spark women's consciousness.

THE RISE OF URBAN POPULAR MOVEMENTS IN AUTHORITARIAN BRAZIL: THEORETICAL CONSIDERATIONS

Brazil's feminine movements—women's struggles against the rising cost of living, for day care, health care, for example—form part of the massive wave of urban popular mobilization that swept Latin American politics in the 1970s. Throughout Brazil and the Southern Cone, neighborhood soup kitchens, community health and consumption collectives, and slumdwellers' associations

[2] Alfred Stepan, "State Power and the Strength of Civil Society in the Southern Cone of Latin America," in *Bringing the State Back In*, ed. Peter B. Evans, Dietrich Rueschemeyer, and Theda Skocpol (New York: Cambridge University Press, 1985), p. 318. See also Maria Helena Moreira Alves, *State and Opposition in Military Brazil* (Austin: University of Texas Press, 1985); and, Sebastião C. Velasco e Cruz and Carlos Estevam Martins, "De Castelo a Figueiredo: Uma Incursão na pré-História da Abertura," in *Sociedade e Política no Brasil Pós-64*, ed. Bernard Sorj and Maria Hermínia Tavares de Almeida (São Paulo: Brasilense, 1983); and Manuel António Garretón, *The Chilean Political Process* (Boston: Unwin Hyman, 1989): 45–117.

[3] Stepan, "State Power and the Strength of Civil Society," p. 339.

sprang from the grassroots of societies beseiged by State terror and ravaged by acute economic crises. These grassroots struggles bore witness to women's and men's unyielding resistance to authoritarian policies, even as the State often fiercely repressed more institutionalized forms of opposition.

The organizational foci of grassroots survival struggles emerged primarily in poor urban neighborhoods, not in the factories or the fields. Though there unquestionably has been renewed labor activism in Latin America (and especially in Brazil) over the past decades, most of the new movements are not centered on social relations of production but rather of consumption and reproduction. People in the peripheral neighborhoods of Latin America's ever-expanding cities came together to demand improvements in urban social services and infrastructure from state and local governments. When the State proved impervious to those demands, communities organized self-help efforts to improve the quality of their tenuous urban existence.

Organizational efforts focused on mobilizing people in their places of residence to attain day-care centers, public schools, health care centers, running water, adequate sewers, better transportation, and other services. In short, the residents of the urban periphery demanded basic services that the unbridled pace of urbanization and persistent government indifference had denied them.

The new urban social movements were not initially "opposition movements," as such. Mobilization occurred as a function of perceived community needs or *carências* but did not necessarily include a critique of the larger political system. However, in the process of pressing their demands on that system, the military authoritarian regime's exclusionary and repressive character was inevitably unveiled. Thus, participants of popular movement organizations sometimes developed an oppositional consciousness and a combative political practice, as the regime's inherent contradictions and its narrow class character were laid bare in its lack of responsiveness to popular demands.

Though grassroots social movements have arisen throughout much of Latin America in recent years, in Brazil they truly have proliferated and expanded to all regions of the country. They are most numerous and most fully developed in the country's industrial triangle—in Rio de Janeiro, Belo Horizonte, and especially, São Paulo.

Many scholars point to the worsening living conditions of Brazil's working class as responsible for the emergence of grassroots organizational efforts among the popular classes. Analysts further note that the closure of institutional channels of political participation under military authoritarianism left people to devise their own collective solutions to community problems. Faced with a regime and development model premised upon the political and economic exclusion of the working classes, Brazilian citizens organized at the community level, outside regime-sanctioned political parties and corporatist institutions, to resolve their immediate survival needs. Vinícius Caldiera Brant observes, for example, that family, kinship, and friendship networks provided the principal bases for the articulation of these urban popular organizations. He suggests that:

A major portion of the contemporary popular movements was organized in a defensive fashion. After movements existing before 1964 were destroyed or subordinated, there was extreme vigilance on the government's part to avoid the resurgence of new popular organizations.

The blocking of institutional channels of popular representation—such as political parties, legislatures, unions and mass organizations—stimulated the use of primary ties of solidarity in the day-to-day survival of the population. Relationships of vicinage, parentage, compaternity, or friendship, provided immediate protection for individuals confronting a social climate of fear. It was in good part the development of those primary ties among people who trusted one another which gave rise to several grassroots movements.[4]

Other analysts privilege structural factors, explaining the rise of popular movements in terms of the "logic of (dependent) capitalism."[5] Maria da Glória Gohn, one of the principal exponents of this line of analysis, argues that the process of deformed urbanization characteristic of Brazilian capitalist development generated "new urban contradictions" that gave rise to urban social movements among the popular classes: "The model of accumulation in force is based not only on the superexploitation of the working masses of the city and countryside, but also necessarily generates a growing superpopulation whose central function is to 'permit that the reproduction of the labor force be completed with the additional work realized in the family nucleus within the non-capitalist axis of reproduction.' "[6] Deploying a conceptual framework drawn from the early work of Manuel Castells, Alain Touraine, and other Western European social theorists,[7] Gohn argues that the miserable conditions of life in the periphery of Brazil's cities grows directly out of their inhabitants' necessary "function" in capital accumulation and reproduction. The way the State responds to popular demands for urban services, in this structuralist view, also inheres in its changed role in the process of capital accumulation: "The role of the State becomes more acute because it must respond to popular

[4] Vinícius Caldeira Brant, "Da Resistência aos Movimentos Sociais: A Emergência das Classes Populares em São Paulo," in *São Paulo: O Povo em Movimento*, ed. Paul J. Singer and Vinícius Caldeira Brant (Petrópolis: Vozes, 1980), p. 13. See also Tilman Evers, "Os Movimentos Sociais Urbanos: O Caso do Movimento do Custo da Vida," in *Alternativas Populares da Democracia*, ed. José Álvaro Moisés et al. (Petrópolis: Vozes; São Paulo: CEDEC, 1982).

[5] See, for example, José Álvaro Moisés, "Contradições Urbanas, Estado e Movimentos Sociais," in *Cidade, Povo e Poder*, ed. José Álvaro Moisés et al. (Rio de Janeiro: Paz e Terra; São Paulo: CEDEC, 1982); and Maria da Glória Marcondes Gohn, *Reivindicações Populares Urbanas: Um Estudo sobre as Associações de Moradores em São Paulo* (São Paulo: Cortez, 1982).

[6] Maria da Glória Marcondes Gohn, *A Força da Periferia: A Luta das Mulheres por Creches em São Paulo* (Petrópolis: Vozes, 1985), p. 68.

[7] See especially Manuel Castells, *Movimientos Sociales Urbanos* (Madrid: Siglo XXI de España, 1974); and Alain Touraine, *Le Voix et le Regard* (Paris: Editions Seuil, 1978).

pressures and at the same time create general conditions, fundamentally for production. It is in this movement, in attending to both the dominant and the dominated, that spaces are opened for popular struggles."[8]

Still other studies of social movements combine macrostructural explanations with micropolitical or conjunctural analyses and stress the dialectical relationship between State policies and the mobilization of civil society during the *abertura* process in Brazil. The theoretical approach to social movement dynamics adopted in the present study is indebted to the work of scholars such as Alves, R. Cardoso, Stepan, Boschi, and Santos,[9] who insist that neither regime transformations nor changes within organized civil society can be fully understood without comprehending that essential dialectic. As Maria Helena Moreira Alves succinctly puts it: "the character of the National Security State can only be understood in relation to the dynamic process of its interaction with forms and structures of opposition movements within civil society. Both the structures of the State and the forms of opposition are continuously transformed in ongoing efforts of each to control, check, or modify the other. Hence, the relationship is essentially a dialectical one."[10]

In a similar vein, Ruth Corrêa Leite Cardoso argues that the gigantic expansion of the Brazilian State itself, during the late 1960s and early 1970s, sparked urban social movements in the mid-1970s: "The popular classes always demanded decent housing and urban services but the pressure mechanism was different. The existence of public policies with social ends makes contemporary states, no matter how antipopular they may be (and frequently are), implement global social policies which themselves create demand expectations."[11] Analysts such as Cardoso, Pedro Roberto Jacobi, and others further insist that while structural variables provide the backdrop for the rise of urban popular movements, these variables alone cannot explain how *carências*

[8] Gohn, *A Força da Periferia*, p. 76. For a critique of the economism inherent in this perspective, see Pedro Roberto Jacobi, "Movimentos Sociais—Teoría e Prática em Questão," in *Uma Revolução no Cotidiano? Os Novos Movimentos Sociais na América do Sul*, ed. Ilse Scherer-Warren and Paulo J. Krischke (São Paulo: Brasilense, 1987); and Ruth Corrêa Leite Cardoso, "Os Movimentos Sociais na América Latina," *Revista Brasileira das Ciências Sociais* 2, no. 5 (October 1987): 27–37. See also Sonia E. Alvarez, "Methodological Impasses in the Study of New Social Movements in Brazil and the Southern Cone" (Paper delivered at the XV International Conference of the Latin American Studies Association, Miami, Florida, December 4–6, 1989).

[9] Maria Helena Moreira Alves, *State and Opposition in Military Brazil*; Ruth Corrêa Leite Cardoso, "Movimentos Sociais Urbanos: Balanço Crítico," in *Sociedade e Política no Brasil Pós-64*, ed. Bernard Sorj and Maria Hermínia Tavares de Almeida (São Paulo: Brasilense, 1983); Stepan, "State Power and the Strength of Civil Society"; Renato Raul Boschi, ed., *Movimentos Coletivos no Brasil Urbano* (Rio de Janeiro: Zahar Editores, 1983); Renato Raul Boschi, *A Arte da Associação: Política de Base e Democracia no Brasil* (São Paulo: Vértice; Rio de Janeiro: IUPERJ, 1987); and Carlos Nelson Ferreira dos Santos, *Movimentos Urbanos no Rio de Janeiro* (Rio de Janeiro: Zahar Editores, 1981).

[10] Maria Helena Moreira Alves, *State and Opposition in Military Brazil*, p. 9.

[11] Ruth Corrêa de Leite Cardoso, "Movimentos Sociais Urbanos: Balanço Crítico," p. 229.

(needs) were translated into political *demands* that were in turn channeled through social movement *organizations*. Organizations are created by people, by conscious political actors, not abstract structural change. Thus, many studies examine the micropolitical factors that facilitate or make possible the creation of social movement organizations among the popular classes. Among those most frequently cited are: (1) the role of progressive sectors of the Brazilian Catholic church which provide an organizational umbrella and foster community participation; (2) the influence of extracommunity political actors such as liberal professionals or leftist party militants who promote organizations among the popular classes and provide material, ideological, and human resources for mobilization; and, (3) the role of State agents (such as social workers) themselves who often encourage their clients to articulate their demands in the local political system.[12]

The extent to which so-called "new" urban movements, arising under authoritarian rule, broke with historical patterns of clientelism and corporatism to foment new ways of "doing politics" and foster new sociopolitical identities is still a subject of heated debate in Brazilian social science.[13] Early analysts maintained that urban popular movements challenged the very foundations of the State's economic and political models and called into question authoritarian and hierarchical ways of doing politics. Today their novelty and potential contribution to institutional politics have been subjected to greater critical scrutiny and few analysts are as sanguine about the democratizing impact of popular struggles as they were in earlier days; instead, many scholars now contend that urban movements were ephemeral phenomena characteristic of crisis politics, that their democratizing impact beyond the community level has been minimal.[14]

The impact of urban movements on Brazilian politics and political culture will be assessed in subsequent chapters. But for purposes of the present analysis, one truly novel, if seldom noted, aspect of urban movements stands out

[12] These factors fueling the rise of actual social movement organizations will be discussed in depth in chapter 3 below.

[13] For a provocative critical review of that debate, see Ruth Corrêa de Leite Cardoso, "Os Movimentos Sociais na América Latina."

[14] The impact of new democratic practices in civil society upon political society and the State in postauthoritarian Brazil is explored by Ruth Corrêa de Leite Cardoso in "Os Movimentos Populares no Contexto da Consolidação da Democracia," in *A Democracia no Brasil: Dilemas e Perspectivas*, ed. Fábio Wanderley Reis and Guillermo O'Donnell (São Paulo: Vértice, 1988). See also Paulo J. Krischke, "Movimentos Sociais e Transição Política: Contribuições da Democracia de Base," and Pedro Roberto Jacobi, "Movimentos Sociais—Teoria e Prática em Questão," in *Uma Revolução no Cotidiano? Os Novos Movimentos Sociais na América do Sul*, ed. Ilse Scherer-Warren and Paulo J. Krischke (São Paulo: Brasilense, 1987); Lúcio Kowarick and Nabil Bonduki, "Espaço Urbano e Espaço Político: do Populismo à Redemocratização," in *As Lutas Sociais e a Cidade* (São Paulo: Paz e Terra, CEDEC, and UNRISD, 1988); and Sonia E. Alvarez, "Urban Popular Movements and the Politics of Democratic Consolidation" (Paper presented at the Annual Convention of the American Political Science Association, Washington, D.C., September 1988).

as incontrovertible: community movements brought hundreds of thousands of poor and working-class women into local political struggles. That is, many of the participants in "new urban movements" differ from their preauthoritarian predecessors in a particularly "new" way: many are female and poor or working-class, and often Black. Much of the social science literature on the new grassroots movements ignores one glaring empirical observation: the fact that the overwhelming majority of the participants of urban social movement organizations are women. Moema Viezzer, for example, estimates that of every one hundred participants in Brazil's urban movements, eighty or more are women.[15] As Teresa Caldeira notes, urban movements in São Paulo are decidedly the domain of women who make up the majority of participants, lead most community struggles, and pressure local authorities for improved social services:

> It is women who form mothers' clubs and constitute the majoritarian clientele of Christian Base Communities (CEBs) and of other demand movements such as those for day care, those for health services, or those of the *favelas* [shantytowns]. It is women who comb the peripheral neighborhoods in search of signatures in support of petitions. It was women who conceived of, carried forth, and to a significant extent, directed the Cost of Living Movement. It is basically women who make up the marches which, nearly every day, depart from some peripheral neighborhood and head for the Prefecture to express some demand relative to the precarious neighborhoods in which they live. It is women who frequent the lobbies of regional administrations to pressure and secure services for their neighborhoods.[16]

Despite the indisputably majoritarian presence of women in urban popular struggles, most analyses of urban movements do not afford much analytical significance to gender and even the sex of participants is obscured by generic references to "neighborhood residents" or sex-blind notions of "the popular classes."[17] The section that follows proposes a theoretical explanation for why women are represented disproportionately among urban popular movement participants.

WOMEN AND SURVIVAL STRUGGLES: THE (DOMESTIC) POLITICAL ECONOMY OF THE POPULAR CLASSES AND THE POLITICIZATION OF MOTHERHOOD

If each of the above-cited theoretical perspectives were to conceive of *gender*, along with class and "urban contradictions," *as a central category of analy-*

[15] See Rede Mulher, " 'Retrato' dos Clubes do Mães e Grupos de Mulheres da Zona Leste de São Paulo," Pesquisa-Avaliação dos Clubes e Grupoes de Mães da Cidade de São Paulo, Documento no. 3, June 1985, (Mimeograph).

[16] Teresa Caldeira, "Mujeres, Cotidianidad y Política," in *Ciudadanía e Identidad: Las Mujeres en los Movimientos Sociales Latino-americanos*, ed. Elizabeth Jelin (Geneva: UNRISD, 1987), p. 77.

[17] Ibid., p. 78.

sis, their explanatory power would undoubtedly be enriched. An analysis of the role of gender in popular mobilization complements both structural and conjunctural analyses of social movement emergence and development.

Each of the above-outlined theoretical approaches to urban social movements highlight social, economic, and political relations in which gender plays a fundamental role. Given women's insertion into social relations in Brazilian society, for example, they play a fundamental role in the articulation of family, kinship, and neighborhood networks (Brant); they are the primary producers and reproducers in the "non-capitalist axis of reproduction" and their domestic labor serves a necessary "function" within the "logic of capital" (Gohn); and given women's historically and structurally determined absence from formal political institutions, one would expect that their interaction with the State during the process of political liberalization would have some gender-specific content. It is these gender-related dimensions of popular mobilization to which we now turn our attention.

Gender permeates social relations in working-class families and communities and attributes particular social responsibilities to women. Women join community movements in far greater numbers than men because social norms and patriarchal ideologies hold women responsible for articulating kinship, friendship, and community networks and organizing family survival strategies. As discussed above, studies of urban movements have shown that such primary networks were essential in the articulation of urban movements and that the rapid erosion of working-class living standards provided the structural backdrop to popular mobilization.

The economic and social policies of Brazil's military rulers profoundly undermined the survival strategies of poor and working-class families and communities. This threat to the domestic political economy of the popular classes, I shall argue, propelled some women to seek collective and individual solutions to their families' immediate survival needs.

While the Brazilian GNP soared an average of 7 percent per year throughout the 1970s, the poorest sectors of the population saw a dramatic erosion in their standard of living and a sharp drop in their real wages. The percentage of GNP accruing to the poorest 50 percent of the population fell from 17.71 percent in 1960, to 14.91 percent in 1970, to 11.6 percent in 1976, while the richest 5 percent of the population reaped the benefits of the military's policy of deliberate income concentration: by 1976 they controlled 39 percent of the country's wealth, compared to 27.69 percent in 1960.[18]

The period dubbed the "Brazilian Economic Miracle," from 1967 to 1973, had less than miraculous consequences for Brazil's wage earners. The real value of the minimum wage dropped steadily, falling to approximately 80 per-

[18] Data from *Isto É*, August 9, 1979, p. 65, cited in Maria Helena Moreira Alves, *Estado e Oposição no Brasil, 1964–1984*, 2d ed. (Petrópolis: Vozes, 1984), p. 149.

cent of its 1963 value by 1971.[19] The purchasing power of workers' real wages also fell precipitously. Whereas in 1959, a Brazilian worker labored approximately 65 hours to secure a meager government-defined minimum food basket, by 1974 the equivalent nutritional ration required over 137 hours of work.[20] By 1974, 30 percent of all Brazilians lived in absolute poverty.[21]

The military's developmental offensive also had dire consequences for Brazil's skyrocketing numbers of urban residents. The rapid promotion of capital-intensive agriculture, the expansion of jobs in the urban-based manufacturing sector, and the regime-sanctioned usurpation of rural peasant lands and urban land speculation combined to produce phenomenal population growth in Brazil's urban centers. Between 1960 and 1979, Brazil's urban growth rate averaged 4.5 percent per year; 46.1 percent of the population lived in cities in 1960; by 1979, that percentage had risen to 63.1.[22] Most of the rural-urban migrants settled in what were initially suburban regions, regions without roads or urban services, plots of land often sold illegally by speculators; these regions ring all of Brazil's cities and are today referred to as the *periferia* or urban periphery.[23] Urban growth, especially in the periphery, was not accompanied by an adequate expansion of urban and social services, however, leaving many urban residents without running water, electricity, sewage, health and educational facilities, and other basic services. Still in 1980, just 58.1 percent of all urban households had adequate sewage; only 71 percent had piped water; and 22.4 percent of all urban residents over the age of five remained illiterate.[24]

All of these factors severely undermined the domestic political economy of

[19] Vilmar Faria, "Desenvolvimento, Urbanização e Mudanças na Estrutura do Emprego: A Experiência Brasileira dos Últimos Trinta Anos," in *Sociedade e Política no Brasil Pós-64*, ed. Bernard Sorj and Maria Hermínia Tavares de Almeida, p. 155.

[20] Data from Departamento Intersindical de Estatística e Estudos Sócio-Econômicos, *Separata da Revista do DIESSE*, April 1979, cited in Maria Helena Moreira Alves, *Estado e Oposição no Brasil, 1964–1984*, p. 153.

[21] Faria, "Desenvolvimento, Urbanização et Mudanças na Estrutura do Emprego," pp. 157–59.

[22] Data from Inter-American Development Bank, *Economic and Social Progress in Latin America, 1979 Report* (Washington, D.C.: IADB, 1979), p. 399, cited in John W. Sloan, *Public Policy in Latin America: A Comparative Survey* (Pittsburgh, Penn.: University of Pittsburgh Press, 1984), p. 16.

[23] On patterns of urbanization and their relationship to historical and contemporary social struggles in the city of São Paulo, see the excellent anthology edited by Lúcio Kowarick, *As Lutas Sociais e a Cidade. São Paulo: Passado e Presente* (São Paulo: Paz e Terra, CEDEC, and UNRISD, 1988). See also Teresa Caldeira, *A Política dos Outros: O Cotidiano dos Moradores da Periferia e o que Pensam do Poder e dos Poderosos* (São Paulo: Brasilense, 1984), especially chapters 1 through 3.

[24] Basic data from 1980 Census, cited in Helga Hoffman, "Poverty and Property in Brazil: What is Changing?" in *Social Change in Brazil, 1945–1985: The Incomplete Transition*, ed. Edmar L. Bacha and Herbert S. Klein (Albuquerque: University of New Mexico Press, 1989), p. 219.

Brazil's poorest communities. And women's socially ascribed responsibility for securing family and community welfare among Brazil's urban poor made them especially sensitive to broader socioeconomic and political changes in Brazilian society that led to the progressive impoverishment of the popular classes. As Ana Maria Q. Fausto Neto argues:

> [W]oman's concrete experience, even within the home (where she confronts the objective limitations of family consumption demands) and outside the home (when she experiences differential access to goods and services), makes her internalize not so much the structural conditions of the working class, but at least, the concrete life conditions of that class, within the context of larger social relations. Therefore, it may be that women do not visualize the *explanatory roots* of the class situation of their families, and that categories such as "class relations," "mechanisms of salary determination" and "production" do not make up part of their symbolic universe . . . . Nevertheless, women concretely experience a whole series of "effects" of the conditions of production, like the *exhaustion* of their husbands and children, *low wages, accidents in the workplace*, the *irritations* and *humiliations* they experience during the workday, etc. Beyond that, the *world of reproduction of the workforce* is a world very much "their own," and it is through it, that . . . working class women understand the objective historical conditions of their class.[25]

The lack of adequate social services and the deficient urban infrastructure found in peripheral neighborhoods directly affects women and their ability to perform their ascribed feminine roles. If a neighborhood does not have running water, it is women who are expected to pump it from community wells or faucets in order to wash the family's clothing or dishes. If a neighborhood does not have adequate sewage, it is women who must care for family members who fall prey to infectious diseases contracted from open sewers. If a community has no public health facilities, it is usually women who must travel long distances to seek medical attention for their children. My research among female residents of São Paulo's urban periphery suggests that it is through this "world of reproduction" that poor and working-class women understand the objective historical conditions of their gender, as well as their class. It is women who are held primarily responsible for the day-to-day planning of their families' subsistence, even if men are held socially responsible for its "provision."

Thus, sociostructural changes which undermine family subsistence, and therefore threaten women's ability to perform their socially ascribed roles as "wives, mothers and nurturers," may lead some women to take whatever actions are within their reach to normalize the situation of their households. This sometimes means engaging in waged work outside the home or in supplemen-

---

[25] Ana Maria Q. Fausto Neto, *Família Operária e Reprodução da Força de Trabalho* (Petrópolis: Vozes, 1982), p. 86, emphasis in the original.

tary/home production of goods and services. And, indeed, women's labor force participation increased dramatically in the 1960s and 1970s. In 1980, women constituted 27.4 percent of the total labor force in Brazil, as compared to 13.5 percent in 1950, and 20.8 percent in 1970. While only 18.2 percent of all women over the age of ten participated in the formal labor market in 1970, that percentage had risen to 35.6 by 1983.[26]

Women made significant inroads into secondary sector production in the 1970s, and their overall participation in the primary sector has declined steadily over the past three decades.[27] However, as of 1980, fully 70 percent of all women workers remained employed in stereotypically female jobs, primarily in the tertiary sector[28]—jobs which essentially represented extensions of their roles as mothers, nurturers, and helpmates in the private sphere.[29] In all sectors of the economy, women consistently occupied the lowest rungs of the "pyramid of occupational prestige."[30] They held the lowest paying, least skilled, and lowest status jobs in all occupational categories.

Studies confirm that the increase in female labor force participation in recent decades "can be explained much more as a function of the impoverishment of the population than as a consequence of the expansion of employment opportunities" for women.[31] The decreasing real purchasing power of Brazilian workers' wages often necessitated the introduction of other members of the family unit into the formal labor market in order to secure the unit's basic subsistence. Neto's study of family organization in a peripheral neighborhood in Belo Horizonte found that working-class families had to adjust their survival strategies to changing market conditions by adding one or more of its members to the salaried labor force.[32] Caldeira's study similarly found that in 48.2 percent of all nuclear families in Jardim das Camelias, wives and/or teenage or adult children were working to "supplement" the declining real income of the "primary breadwinner."[33]

[26] Cristina Bruschini, *Mulher e Trabalho: Uma Avaliação da Década da Mulher* (São Paulo: Nobel and Conselho Estadual da Condição Feminina, 1985), p. 92.

[27] For an analysis of women's massive entry into secondary sector production in the 1970s and 1980s, see especially John Humphrey, *Trabalho Feminino na Grande Industria Paulista* (São Paulo: CEDEC, 1984); Helena Hirata and John Humphrey, "O Emprego Industrial Feminino e a Crise Econômica Brasileira," *Revista de Economia Política* 4, no. 4 (October–December 1984): 89–107. For data on the changing structure of the female labor force in Brazil, see Maria Cristina A. Bruschini and Fulvia Rosemberg, "A Mulher e o Trabalho," in *Trabalhadoras do Brasil*, ed. Maria Cristina Aranha Bruschini and Fulvia Rosemberg (São Paulo: Brasilense, 1982).

[28] Bruschini, *Mulher e Trabalho*, p. 39.

[29] For a discussion of sex segregation and "sex-typing" within the Brazilian labor force, see especially John Humphrey, *Gender and Work in the Third World: Sexual Divisions in Brazilian Industry* (London: Tavistock, 1987).

[30] Bruschini, *Mulher e Trabalho*, p. 49.

[31] Ibid., p. 16.

[32] Neto, *Família Operária*, p. 71.

[33] Caldeira, *A Política dos Outros*, p. 92.

Since sex discrimination in the work force and the rigid sexual divisions of Brazilian labor markets keep women's wages quite low, income from women's paid employment cannot fully offset the costs incurred by working-class families when female household members enter the labor force, however.[34] Working-class families pay a significant price when women enter the paid work force, not only in terms of the frequently high cost of private day care or other child care arrangements, but also because the work that women perform at home is essential to family survival strategies. Whereas their contribution to family income can only be "supplementary," given the adverse labor market conditions faced by women, their role as producers and reproducers within the family remains central. Poor and working-class women perform the vast majority of activities linked to the production of goods and services for the internal consumption of family members. Even when they perform paid labor outside the home, it is women who clean, cook, iron, shop, care for the children, the sick, and the elderly, and perform dozens of other tasks necessary for family subsistence. Thus, working–class women who work outside the home also pay an individual price for their participation in the labor force— they work a "double shift," performing both extradomestic labor and remaining responsible for the majority of domestic tasks.

Given these conditions of work, it is not surprising that the majority of women in the above-cited studies and in many others, conceive of their work outside the home as "a help" or "an exception." "Women's work" in the paid labor market, aside from providing for only minimal increases in the family's overall standard of living, is low-paid and low-skilled, and therefore confers little status upon women workers: "That is, the reference for women's work is not the labor market, as her most valued profession is that within the home."[35]

Women who work exclusively within the home are not "merely housewives"—they are the principal architects of family survival strategies and their roles as mothers and nurturers are imbued with a good deal of *symbolic* value.[36] Women's work in the home also generates essential use values that contribute to family subsistence. Men may, in most cases, be the principal wage earners, but women are held primarily responsible for planning and implementing survival strategies based on that wage and the wages of other working family members. As one of Caldeira's interviewees neatly put it: "Mostly, I take care of the house. He brings it in; but I take care of it."[37]

The home is women's administrative domain, and family survival, given the precarious economic conditions of the popular classes, their principal pre-

---

[34] See Humphrey, *Gender and Work in the Third World.*

[35] Caldeira, *A Política dos Outros*, p. 178.

[36] Neto, *Família Operária*, pp. 84–85.

[37] Caldeira, *A Política do Outros*, p. 172.

occupation and responsibility.[38] Circulating petitions to demand a stop to spiraling consumer prices is thus consonant with the fulfillment of women's familial obligations. Attempting to secure adequate health services from local authorities similarly can be seen as an exercise of women's responsibility for securing family welfare.

Another factor explaining why women have been at the forefront of community struggles is that in most of São Paulo's peripheral neighborhoods, while the men often travel long distances to their jobs and return late in the evening, the women rule the day-to-day life of the community.[39] Thus, they not only administer family survival, they also articulate the family's relationship to its immediate neighborhood or community. Women organize much of the social interaction in the neighborhoods and the kinship and friendship networks they maintain constitute one of the major forms of communication and information among residents of the urban periphery.[40] Perceived threats to family survival may lead women to mobilize those very networks, networks that studies have shown to be at the core of urban mobilizations of various sorts.

Importantly, such mobilization is typically understood to be in keeping with women's feminine roles. As Temma Kaplan persuasively argues in a study of female collective action in Barcelona in the early twentieth century,

> recognition of what a particular class, culture, and historical period expect from women, creates a sense of rights and obligations that provides the motive force for actions different from those Marxist or feminist theory generally try to explain. Female consciousness centers upon the rights of gender, on social concerns, on survival. Those with female consciousness accept the gender system of their society; indeed, such consciousness emerges from the division of labor by sex, which assigns women the responsibility for preserving life. But accepting this task, women with female consciousness demand the rights that their obligations entail.[41]

Female consciousness contributes to women's massive participation in urban struggles against the rising cost of living, against human rights abuses, for

[38] Women's central role in family "administration" and survival does not necessarily transfer into real power or authority within the home or the larger community, however. For an excellent critique of the popular notion that Latin American women play a "behind-the-scenes" role in politics and society through their "motherly" influential roles within the family, see Susan C. Bourque and Kay B. Warren, *Sex and Power in the Andes*, especially pp. 51–54 and 59–65.

[39] Caldeira, *A Política dos Outros*, pp. 124–25.

[40] Hanna Papanek described these types of "networking" activities that women commonly perform in most cultures as a different kind of nonmaterial production process. See her "Family Status Production: The 'Work' and 'Non-Work' of Women," *Signs* 4, no. 4 (Spring 1979): 775–81.

[41] Temma Kaplan, "Female Consciousness and Collective Action: The Case of Barcelona, 1910–1918," *Signs* 7, no. 3 (Spring 1982), p. 545.

better community health and educational facilities, for better urban infrastructure and social services in their communities.

Women's majoritarian participation in urban popular movements is sometimes trivialized; some would insist that women participate more simply because, unlike men, they have nothing better to do or because they spend more "free time" in their immediate community, whereas men spend most of their day at work or in transit to and from the workplace. Yet female participation in urban social movements can be more adequately understood as something akin to what Charles Tilly, Louise Tilly, and Richard Tilly have referred to as reactive mobilization in defense of culturally ascribed feminine rights.[42] Thousands of women in Brazil organized to confront the regime's attack on the survival of working-class families.

Caldeira's study of the residents of Jardim das Camelias in São Paulo is again a case in point. Even though her female interviewees knew little about "politics" (conceived of as those activities that take place within formal political institutions), most of them had participated in local organizations that demanded a day-care center and a neighborhood health center from the São Paulo municipal government.

> The women residents of Jardim das Camelias did not see the slightest problem in demanding day-care centers or health centers, nor in attending meetings to discuss these objectives, as they interpreted all of this as "working for the welfare of their children." It was as responsible mothers that they were able to abandon their homes and invade the mayor's office, in the same way that being mothers permits them to leave their homes more easily and "confront" the world of the streets and work. . . . In sum, the discourse which was legitimating and articulating women's participation was not political citizenship, but rather another which extended their most traditional roles.[43]

"Motherhood," not citizenship, provided the principal *mobilizational referent* for women's participation in urban social movement organizations. In light of perceived *carências* in urban infrastructure and the general decline in the standard of living of the popular classes, women mobilized to defend the welfare of their families, their children, their communities. Structural changes in Brazilian society, accelerated by the military regime's developmental offensive, thus provided an important basis for the *politicization of motherhood*, as women organized to secure an adequate standard of living for their families. Women concretely felt the economic crunch experienced by urban popular classes in attempting against all odds to perform their ascribed roles within families and communities. And, as we shall see in the ensuing chapters, *mili-*

---

[42] Charles Tilly, Louise Tilly, and Richard Tilly, *The Rebellious Century, 1830–1930* (Cambridge, Mass.: Harvard University Press, 1975), p. 250.

[43] Caldeira, *A Política dos Outros*, p. 285.

tant motherhood provided the basis for several movements organized to pursue the *practical gender interests* of Brazil's poor and working-class women.

THE TRANSFORMATION OF WOMEN'S ROLES IN THE BRAZILIAN MIDDLE CLASSES

Neither securing family survival nor fulfilling traditional feminine roles were of paramount concern to the middle-class women who made up the core of the nascent Brazilian feminist movement in the 1970s. The regime's strategy of deliberate income concentration, aimed at expanding the domestic market for durable consumer goods, benefited the middle sectors of Brazilian society. Women of middle classes saw their families' standard of living increase, at least during the years of the Economic Miracle. And while the majority of middle-class women still worked in the domestic sphere, a variety of new realms of activity became available to them with the expansion of secondary and higher education and technical and professional occupations that accompanied the growth of the Brazilian State and the diversification of dependent capitalist production.

The renowned "technocratization" of the Brazilian political economy during the 1960s and early 1970s prompted the State to rapidly expand technical, scientific, and professional education.[44] Women were among the beneficiaries of this expansion. But because university education continued to be the purview of white, upper- and middle-class Brazilians, it was middle-class women who were trained to become the white collar and professional workers in the rapidly growing State bureaucracy and in the Miracle's commercial, financial, and scientific establishments.

Between 1969 and 1975 alone, for example, the numbers of women attending Brazilian universities increased five-fold, while the number of men merely doubled.[45] The number of women enrolled in master's programs rose 336.8 percent between 1971 and 1975 alone (compared to 177.8 percent for men); there was a 400 percent increase in women earning Ph.D.s during the same period (180 for men).[46] By 1980, the number of women enrolled in Brazilian universities surpassed men in absolute numbers (429,785 women and 390,142 men). Moreover, women were disproportionately represented among university students. Of all Brazilians between the ages of 18 and 24, 5.11 percent of

[44] For a comprehensive analysis of State educational policy in Brazil from the 1960s through the 1980s, see Núcleo de Estudos de Políticas Públicas and Instituto de Economia da UNICAMP, "A Política Educacional," in *Relatório sobre a Situação Social do País*, vol. 2, pp. 141–214, ed. Núcleo de Estudos de Políticas Públicas (Campinas, SP: Editora da UNICAMP, 1987). On the growth of the "new middle classes" in authoritarian Brazil and the rise of middle-class social movements, see Renato Raul Boschi, *A Arte de Associação*, especially chapter 4.

[45] Rose Marie Muraro, "O Dia da Mulher no Brasil," *Folha de São Paulo*, March 8, 1983.

[46] Data from DIEESE/IBGE, 1979, p. 331, cited in Fulvia Rosemberg, Regina P. Pinto, and Esmeralda V. Negrão, *A Educação da Mulher no Brasil* (São Paulo: Global, 1982), p. 50.

the women and 4.75 percent of the men attended the university in 1980, compared to 2.84 and 3.65 respectively in 1970.[47]

But higher education in Brazil remains highly elitist. Though admission to the federal and state university system is putatively based on merit, poor and working-class Brazilians seldom reach the upper echelons of the educational hierarchy. Family income remains a determining variable in all educational groups beyond the elementary level.

Access to higher education is further restricted by the racist structure of Brazilian society. Less than 1 percent of all Black women have acquired a university level education, compared to 4.2 percent of all white women.[48] In the state of São Paulo, the differences in educational achievement between men and women within racial/ethnic groups are far smaller than the differences between whites and people of color. That is, white, middle-class women have greater access to education than either Black women or Black men.[49]

Although female occupational ghettos persist, the increase in white women with university degrees also augmented the numbers of women in higher status occupations. As Renato Raul Boschi points out, "the female Economically Active Population went from 18.5 percent in 1970 to 26.9 percent in 1980, a proportion which accounts for 41.2 percent of the increase in the total EAP over the decade." More importantly, the occupational structure of elite women's employment also changed as "the share of female EAP increased in administrative occupations (from 8.2 percent in 1960 to 15.4 percent in 1980) and in professions of higher prestige (engineers, architects, doctors, dentists, economists, university professors and lawyers which went from 19,000 in 1970 to 95,800 in 1980)."[50] But again, Black women were underrepresented among the new female professionals. Only 2 percent of all Black women in the labor force are in high prestige occupations, whereas 69 percent work as unskilled laborers in the primary and tertiary sectors, earning an average of 68 percent less than Black men in similar occupational categories.[51]

The expansion of educational and occupational opportunities available to white, middle-class women was accompanied by the expansion of the tertiary or service sector which became the principal source of employment for poor

[47] Data from 1970 and 1980 censuses, cited in Wanderley Guilherme dos Santos, *Crise e Castigo: Partidos e Generais na Política Brasileira* (São Paulo: Vértice; Rio de Janeiro: IUPERJ, 1987), p. 144.

[48] Sueli Carneiro and Thereza Santos, *Mulher Negra* (São Paulo: Nobel and Conselho Estadual da Condição Feminina, 1985), p. 11.

[49] Ibid., pp. 8–10.

[50] Boschi, *A Arte de Associação*, p. 62. For further information on women's work and education, see Carmen Barroso, *Mulher, Sociedade e Estado no Brasil* (Brasília: UNICEF, and São Paulo: Brasilense, 1982), pp. 13–86.

[51] Lélia Gonzalez, "Mulher Negra," *Mulherio* (September–October 1981): 8–9, cited in Bruschini, *Mulher e Trabalho*, p. 70.

and working-class women.[52] Thus, middle-class women were freed from many of their roles in domestic production as the tertiary sector generated exchange values from the unwaged labor they would otherwise have performed in their own homes. Although the majority of middle-class Brazilian women may not have full-time domestic servants, for example, most can afford to pay a day worker to do bulk cleaning, can send out laundry, or purchase processed foods. Therefore, middle-class women who enter the formal labor market do not necessarily pay as high a personal price for doing so— their "double shift" is considerably alleviated by the existence of a largely female service sector that can absorb many of the necessary domestic tasks as middle-class women enter the public world of waged work.

But this is not to say that the middle-class women who entered previously male-dominated realms in higher education and the professions did so on an equal footing with men of equivalent social status. Women remained clustered in a limited number of professions (primarily in elementary and secondary education, nursing, social service, etc.) and academic disciplines. In higher education, they predominate in the social sciences (53.8 percent of all undergraduates in these fields), psychology (86.2 percent), and the humanities (84.4 percent) but remain underrepresented in the natural sciences (40.6 percent), medicine (24 percent), physical science and technology (18.2 percent), and national defense (1.1 percent).[53] And within professional occupational categories, white women earned 35 percent less than white men and Black female professionals earned 48 percent less than their white, female counterparts.[54]

Thus, even as the professional possibilities available to white, university-educated women multiplied, many avenues of socioeconomic and status advancement remained closed to them as women. The incongruity between their new occupational roles and the persistence of a male-dominated occupational hierarchy may have led some women in the new Brazilian middle classes to question their relatively "lesser" status in the public sphere. Whereas poor and working-class women organized to demand the rights to which their roles as wives and mothers entitled them, some middle-class women who entered the upper echelons of the occupational hierarchy increasingly demanded the rights to which their new *professional* roles entitled them. The mere fact of entering previously male technical and professional occupations was already

[52] In 1980, 20.6 percent of all women in the labor force worked in paid domestic occupations and 10.8 percent in other personal service jobs. Data from Funadação IBGE, Demographic Census of 1980, cited in Vilmar Faria, "Changes in the Composition of Employment and the Structure of Occupations," in *Social Change in Brazil, 1945–1985: The Incomplete Transition*, ed. Edmar L. Bacha and Herbert S. Klein (Albuquerque: University of New Mexico Press, 1989), Table 4.11, p. 159.

[53] All data for 1980; compiled from Fulvia Rosemberg and Regina Pahim Pinto, *A Educação da Mulher* (São Paulo: Nobel and Conselho Estadual da Condição Feminina, 1985), p. 71.

[54] Lélia Gonzalez, "Mulher Negra," cited in Bruschini, *Mulher e Trabalho*, p. 70.

an act of rebellion for many women and some began to view their ascribed gender roles as restrictive or confining.

Many university-educated Brazilian women became the cadres of the Brazilian feminist movement and other liberation movements in the mid-1970s. Brazil's feminist movements—struggles for sexual equality, reproductive freedom, against male violence, and so on—form part of a wave of liberation struggles that emerged as important social forces in Brazil and other Latin American nations in the 1970s and 1980s, such as the Black liberation and gay liberation movements.[55]

Although a direct causal relationship cannot be established between the rise of women in the professions or in higher education in Brazil and the emergence of feminist movements in the 1970s, some early feminist political claims did center on equality in the workplace or equal pay for equal work, for example. These would be among the claims that Molyneux classifies as reflecting *strategic gender interests*, interests which she argues derive deductively from an analysis of women's subordination rather than practical gender interests arising from the "concrete conditions of women's positioning by virtue of their gender within the division of labor."[56] However, white, middle-class women's social positioning as women was altered dramatically in the 1960s and early 1970s through their class- and race-specific access to professional roles and educational opportunities. Some of the claims articulated by middle-class feminists therefore can be seen as reflecting their transformed, *practical* gender interests; they claimed a right to be treated like men of the same professional status.

Brazilian feminists, like participants in other liberation movements, however, have been concerned primarily with expanding personal life options and transforming cultural stereotypes and discriminatory societal norms and behaviors. All Brazilian liberation movements seek profound cultural as well as political and economic transformations. And all converge upon the politici-

---

[55] On Black movements in Brazil, see especially Hamilton B. Cardoso, "Limites do Confronto Racial e Aspectos da Experiência Negra no Brasil—Reflexões," in *Movimentos Sociais na Transição Democrática*, ed. Emir Sader (São Paulo: Cortez, 1987). See also Pierre-Michel Fontaine, "Transnational Relations and Racial Mobilization: Emerging Black Movements in Brazil," in *Ethnic Identities in a Transnational World*, ed. John F. Stack, Jr. (Westport, Conn: Greenwood Press, 1986); João José Reis, ed., *Escravidão & Invenção da Liberdade: Estudos sobre o Negro no Brasil* (São Paulo: Brasilense, 1988); and Lélia Gonzalez and Carlos Hasenbalg, *Lugar do Negro* (Rio de Janeiro: Marco Zero, 1982). On the gay and lesbian movements, see Peter Fry and Edward McRae, *O Que é Homosexualidade* (São Paulo: Brasilense, 1983); and João S. Trevisan, *Perverts in Paradise* (London: GMP Publishers, 1986); and Edward McRae, "A Afiramção da Identidade Homosexual: Seus Perigos e Sua Importância," in *Foucault Vivo*, ed. I. A. Tronca (Campinas: Pontes, 1987).

[56] Maxine Molyneux, "Mobilization without Emancipation? Women's Interests, State, and Revolution," in *Transitions and Development: Problems in Third World Socialism*, ed. Richard R. Fagen, Carmen Diana Deere, and José Luis Caraggio (New York: Monthly Review Press; Berkeley, Calif.: Center for the Study of the Americas), p. 284.

zation of daily life. Power, the activists of liberation movements maintain, is not solely concentrated in formal political institutions. Informal power relations permeate all social relations between Blacks and whites, homosexuals and heterosexuals, women and men—and those power relations are formalized, structured, mediated, and modified by political institutions. Therefore, like urban popular movements, the new Brazilian liberation movements challenge the established boundaries of the political, arguing that politics can and does affect people's everyday, lived experience as members of subordinate groups (as well as social classes) in Brazilian society.

The rise of movements whose claims do not directly concern social relations of production as such defies the facile structuralist explanations for movement emergence proposed by such as Gohn or Moisés; nor are such movements self-evidently causally related to particular aspects of the Brazilian State's offensive economic project. For example, white, middle-class women's "relative deprivation" vis-à-vis similarly situated men cannot, in and of itself, explain the emergence of the contemporary feminist movement in Brazil. In the mid-to-late 1970s, as shall be seen in chapter 3, several conjunctural variables facilitated the formulation of an ideological critique of prevailing gender power arrangements and generated the mobilizational networks through which such a movement could take shape.

CONCLUSION

Though military men and their reactionary civilian allies intended to enshrine traditional womanhood—a cornerstone of authoritarian "order and progress"—the regime's economic model had the unintentional consequence of radically transforming the roles of women in Brazilian society. Defying traditional gender role expectations, middle-class women entered the universities and the professions en masse. Working-class women joined the labor force and began participating in grassroots opposition movements in unprecedented numbers.

As the "wives, mothers, and nurturers" of family and community, women are the principal architects of the domestic survival strategies of the popular classes. Poor and working-class women were thus among the most directly and significantly affected by the regressive wage policies, rises in the cost of living, cuts in social welfare and educational expenditures, and other consequences of the military authoritarian regime's strategy of dependent capitalist accumulation.

In short, the authoritarian development model, premised upon the political and economic exclusion of the popular classes, *engendered* significant changes in the domestic political economy of the lower classes. I have argued that one result of these changes was the "politicization of motherhood," a factor frequently overlooked in the analysis of women's massive participation in popular movement organizations. As shall be shown in chapter 4 below, poor and working-class women have also mobilized *as women* within their class to defend their "rights" as wives and mothers, rights which dominant ideologies of gender assured them in theory, but which dominant authoritarian political and economic institutions increasingly denied them in practice.

The authoritarian development model had a radically different impact upon the lives of the middle-class women who predominate in the feminist movement. The expansion of State sector employment and technical and professional university education, in the early years of the regime at least, actually resulted in some improvement in the status of white, middle-class women in Brazil. Women's insertion into these previously male-dominant realms seems to have led some of them to question their own status as "lesser men" within those realms, to view gender-based inequality as a *political* problem.

In sum, the differential impact of authoritarian development on middle-class and working-class women provided differing *structural bases* for the emergence of feminist and feminine political claims and social movement organizations in Brazil in the mid-1970s. The macrostructural changes that characterized Brazilian development had a profound impact on the roles of women within all social classes—the common thread of which was the politicization of their lived experience *as women*.

But women of different social classes experience gender inequality in radically different ways, especially in the context of dependent capitalism. Women of the popular classes felt the brunt of the regressive economic policies of the regime and were forced to devise new survival strategies within their family networks—a process that placed an even greater burden on their socially ascribed roles as caretakers and mothers of family and community, while simultaneously denying them the means with which to perform those roles adequately. White, middle-class Brazilian women, on the other hand, were beneficiaries of capitalist growth and development during the late 1960s and early 1970s. They gained access to educational and professional opportunities as never before, opportunities which to some extent freed them from their socially ascribed confinement to the domestic sphere. And as will be seen below, the radically different implications of authoritarian capitalist development for Brazilian women of different social classes gave rise to distinct genderic political claims during the course of the 1970s.

This chapter has identified some of the structural factors that engendered new contradictions in women's lives and thus set the stage for the expression of new practical and strategic gender interests among Brazilian women. Chapter 3 turns to the conjunctural and micropolitical factors that enabled women to articulate those interests politically.

CHAPTER THREE

Militant Mothers and Insurgent Daughters: Women in the Opposition to Authoritarian Rule

As an indirect result of the dramatic socioeconomic changes wrought by Brazilian authoritarian development in the 1960s and early 1970s, both middle- and working-class women experienced new contradictions in their socially ascribed roles as women. But such contradictions were not translated automatically into gender-based political demands nor did they naturally lead to changes in women's gender consciousness. To account fully for the emergence of progressive gender discourses and women's movements in authoritarian Brazil during the mid-1970s, then, we must explain how some women came to understand gender inequality as both unjust and amenable to change, and identify the conditions that enabled women's organizations to surface in the context of an exclusionary political system.

In the preceding chapter, I argued that rapid changes in women's roles produced potential sources of gender-based grievances among middle- and working-class women. This chapter focuses on the political developments that made it possible for those grievances to be translated into gender-based political claims and, eventually, to be articulated by women's movement organizations.

I will show that women's growing involvement in the various organizations that rose in opposition to military rule enabled them to formulate new claims on the basis of gender and, eventually, to organize politically as women. The various opposition currents afforded key ideological and organizational resources to the women who would later organize autonomous women's movements.

Many analysts of social movements note that while broad socioeconomic change may alter the objective social conditions that can generate protest, these changes do not necessarily affect people's subjective perception of those conditions.[1] Both the subjective perception of and the objective possibilities for gender-based protest were drastically altered during the 1970s as political liberalization proceeded and women joined opposition movements and militant organizations.

Opposition discourses concerning human rights, social justice, equality and liberation, coupled with the rise of feminist discourses on an international

---

[1] Doug McAdam, *Political Process and the Development of Black Insurgency, 1930–1970* (Chicago: University of Chicago Press, 1982), p. 34.

plane, implanted ideological seeds that would later be cultivated by Brazilian women to disseminate discourses about women's rights, gendered justice, equality between women and men, and ultimately, women's liberation. Moreover, because both secular and church-linked opposition groups were male-dominated, the discrimination suffered by women in many antiregime organizations triggered an incipient consciousness of gender inequality among some women active in the opposition. The new associational networks established in opposition to the regime provided critical organizational resources that women organizers later put to the service of feminine and feminist mobilization. Finally, the regime's decision to pursue a policy of political liberalization after 1974 permitted women to articulate publicly their new political claims.

The women who later organized feminine and feminist movements in Brazil first had to come to perceive their ascribed gender attributes as grounds for asserting "natural" rights (i.e., those accruing to wives and mothers) or claiming new rights (i.e., those to which all human beings, irrespective of gender, should be entitled). The new discourses about liberation and democracy developed by the church, the militant Left, and the bourgeois opposition provided women with such grounds. Some analyses of social movements tend to underplay the importance of social discourses for awakening critical political consciousness and sometimes inspiring protest actions. Yet discourses can play a crucial role in shaping the *subjective possibilities* for protest by interpellating oppressive conditions for subordinate social groups and classes, fashioning new social and political identities, and providing moral or ethical rationales for engaging in anti–status quo behavior and political action.[2] As Doug McAdam notes, "segments of society may very well submit to oppressive conditions unless that oppression is collectively defined as both unjust and *subject to change*. In the absence of these necessary attributions, oppressive conditions are likely, even in the face of increased resources, to go unchallenged."[3]

But even assuming that consciousness of gender inequality or oppression spread rapidly among Brazilian women in the 1960s and 1970s, women's movements still could not have emerged in an organizational vacuum. A minimal degree of organization and self-conscious political action was required

---

[2] See especially Ernesto Laclau and Chantal Mouffe, *Hegemony and Socialist Strategy* (London: Verso, 1985); Tilman Evers, "Identity: The Hidden Side of New Social Movements in Latin America," in *New Social Movements and the State in Latin America*, ed. David Slater (Amsterdam: CEDLA, 1985); Jean Cohen, "Strategy or Identity: New Theoretical Paradigms and Contemporary Social Movements," *Social Research* 52, no. 4 (Winter 1985): 663–716; and Arturo Escobar V., "Social Science Discourse and New Social Movements Research in Latin America: Trends and Debates" (Paper presented at the XV International Congress of the Latin American Studies Association, Miami, Florida, December 4–6, 1989).

[3] McAdam, *Political Process*, p. 34.

before generalized attitudinal change or discontent among women could spur sustained political mobilization and give rise to movements that made claims on the basis of gender.

The creation of new associational networks among women active in the opposition to military authoritarianism therefore was crucial to the development of independent women's movements in the 1970s. Social networks afford four critical resources to incipient social movements, according to McAdam: (1) members—movement participants are recruited along established lines of interaction; (2) an established structure of solidary incentives—interpersonal rewards provide a motive force for individual participation in social movement organization; (3) a communication network—the pattern, speed, and extent of movement expansion is greatly affected by the strength and breadth of such networks; and, (4) leaders—recognized leaders in existing organizations "can be called upon to lend their prestige and organizing skills to an incipient movement."[4]

In the sections below, I analyze the micropolitical and discursive developments that facilitated the formulation of an ideological critique of prevailing gender power arrangements and generated the mobilizational networks through which Brazilian women's movements could take shape. A gender-sensitive analysis of the development of regime oppositions and the liberalization policies of the military regime will further unravel the puzzle of how progressive women's movements emerged and developed in authoritarian Brazil. I will discuss the five principal factors that catalyzed women's gender consciousness and facilitated the proliferation of women's organizations.

Because of their centrality to women's mobilization in Brazil, I will discuss two developments in particular—the political and institutional transformation of the Catholic church and the rearticulation of the militant Left—in greater detail. The transformed Brazilian Catholic church developed a new egalitarian discourse and pastoral strategy that encouraged women's participation in community self-help organizations and in sex-segregated mothers' clubs and housewives' associations. The militant Left's decision to organize at the community level in the wake of the severe government repression led many former women militants, disenchanted with the sexism inherent in revolutionary theory and practice, to work with women in neighborhood feminine organiza-

[4] Ibid., pp. 45–47. Jo Freeman also stresses the importance of women's networks for the emergence of women's movements when macrostructural variables (i.e., the continued subordination of women in society) are constant rather than causal. She maintains that before such movements can develop, a communications network or infrastructure must exist. This communications network must be co-optable to the ideas of the movement. To be co-optable, the network must be composed of "like-minded people whose background, experiences, or location in the social structure make them receptive to the ideas of a specific movement." Jo Freeman, "On the Origins of Social Movements," in *Social Movements of the Sixties and Seventies,* ed. Jo Freeman (New York: Longman, 1983), pp. 10–11.

tions. Women's involvement in the church and the Left, I will suggest, had contradictory consequences for Brazilian women's movements. On the one hand, the church and the Left provided both rationales for women's participation and organizational contexts in which women could come together and begin to identify shared concerns as women. On the other hand, the limitations of secular and religious discourses on gender and the sexism operative within opposition organizations eventually led some women to form women's groups independent of the church and the progressive opposition.

I will also discuss briefly three other factors contributing to women's mobilization in the 1970s. The military regime's political "opening" after 1974 provided greater opportunities for political protest in general and women's protests in particular. Importantly, the regime seems to have conceived of women's movements as intrinsically apolitical and allowed them greater space within its policy of *distensão* or political opening. Lastly, I will argue that new international policies concerning women and development, policies advocated by newly consolidated international feminist networks, further expanded the political space available for the articulation of women's claims in Brazil.

WOMEN'S PARTICIPATION IN THE "PEOPLE'S" CHURCH

Until the 1960s, the Brazilian Catholic church, like the institutional church throughout Latin America, was a staunch supporter of the status quo, the stalwart ally of conservative social and political forces.[5] Claiming that Goulart's radical populist government would tear assunder the moral fabric of the Brazilian family, sectors of the church helped organize the marches of "the Family, with God, for Liberty," described in the introduction.

But in the 1960s, the Brazilian church began a process of institutional renovation, the origins of which can be traced to the "gradual working out" of the political, theological, and organizational reorientation of the church following the Second Vatican Council (1962–1965) and the Second General Conference of Latin American Bishops (CELAM) held in Medellín, Colombia, in 1968.[6] These innovations had important, if contradictory, consequences for the mobilization of women in Brazil as elsewhere in Latin America.

Both Vatican II and Medellín signaled the "greater integration of religious and secular values and shifted the moral weight of the church away from legitimizing the status quo toward an increased promotion of equity and free-

---

[5] For a concise political history of the Catholic church in Brazil, see Thomas C. Bruneau, *The Church in Brazil: The Politics of Religion* (Austin: University of Texas Press, 1982), pp. 11–20.

[6] Daniel H. Levine, "Religion and Politics, Politics and Religion: An Introduction," in *Churches and Politics in Latin America*, ed. Daniel H. Levine (Beverly Hills: Sage Publications, 1980), pp. 20–21. In *The Church in Brazil*, Thomas Bruneau points out that changes in the Brazilian Catholic church actually preceded Vatican II and were related to a changing "strategy of influence" pursued by the church in Brazil.

dom.''[7] The causes of these moral and political shifts within the church and in church-State relations have been discussed extensively by other authors.[8] For purposes of the present analysis, I shall concentrate on elucidating the ways in which these changes contributed to the rebirth of civil society in Brazil in the 1960s and 1970s in general, and to the emergence of women's movement organizations among the popular classes in particular.

Vatican II's reevaluation of the church's religious mission in the world blurred the distinction between the secular and the religious, the theological and the political. By redefining its role in modern society, the church was "to act as a catalytic and prophetic force, using moral rather than temporal power to promote justice at national and international levels."[9]

Proclaiming a "preferential option for the poor," the Medellín Conference transformed Vatican II's church of the "Pilgrim People of God" into Latin America's "Church of the Poor," a church that would increasingly side with the plight of the politically and economically disenfranchised. And despite contentious debates between conservative and progressive bishops during the Third CELAM Conference, held in Puebla, Mexico, in 1979, the Latin American bishops ultimately sharpened their condemnation of "institutionalized violence" in the region and committed the church to struggle against the human rights abuses of the authoritarian regimes that predominated in Latin America at that time.[10]

In Brazil, as elsewhere in Latin America, the church's critique of the military regime's National Security Doctrine[11] became more pointed as members of the institutional church themselves became victims of State repression. As priests, nuns and Catholic lay workers joined the ranks of the tortured and

[7] Brian H. Smith, *The Church and Politics in Chile: Challenges to Modern Catholicism* (Princeton, N.J.: Princeton University Press, 1982), p. 5.

[8] The three major explanations posited by this literature are: institutional renovation, theological renovation, and changing strategies of political and social influence. For the most comprehensive account of the Church's political role in post-1964 Brazil, see Scott Mainwaring, *The Catholic Church and Politics in Brazil, 1916–1985* (Stanford, Calif.: Stanford University Press, 1986); see also Paulo Krischke and Scott Mainwaring, eds., *A Igreja nas Bases em Tempo de Transição* (Porto Alegre: L and PM, 1986).

[9] Smith, *The Church and Politics in Chile*, p. 18.

[10] See Alexander Wilde, "The Years of Change in the Church: Puebla and the Future," *Journal of Interamerican Studies and World Affairs* 21 (August 1979): 299–312; CELAM, "Evangelization in Latin America's Present and Future," in *Puebla and Beyond*, ed. John Eagleson and Phillip Scharper (Maryknoll, N.Y.: Orbis Books, 1979), pp. 113–285.

[11] The National Security Doctrine (NSD) posited a "nexus between internal security and economic development." Fostered by Superior War Colleges in Latin America under the tutelage of the United States, this doctrine became the informing ideology of military regimes throughout Latin America in the 1960s and 1970s. For an in-depth discussion of military institutional development and the NSD, see Alfred Stepan, "The New Professionalism of Internal Warfare and Military Role Expansion," in *Authoritarian Brazil*, ed. Alfred Stepan (New Haven: Yale University Press, 1973).

disappeared, the Brazilian bishops publicly began denouncing the excesses of the regime. By the mid-1970s, the National Conference of Brazilian Bishops (*Conferência Nacional dos Bispos do Brasil* or CNBB) had become a major opposition force, shielding the politically persecuted and fostering community organization and mobilization among the poor.

Christian Base Communities (*Comunidades Eclesiais de Base* or CEBs) spread rapidly throughout Brazil, especially after the 1968 coup within a coup closed most other channels of political participation. The CEBs, generally made up of fifteen to forty people from a given neighborhood or parish, brought the faithful together to discuss the new social teachings of the church and to reflect upon their daily lives in light of the Gospel.

The ascent of liberation theology further transformed the relationship between religion and politics in Brazil and throughout Latin America. With the growing involvement of priests and nuns in the external work of the apostolate, many came into close day-to-day contact with the concrete conditions of people's lives in poor urban neighborhoods and rural areas. These experiences radicalized many priests and religious workers who began "to look for an inspiration in the life of Christ which would privilege the church's relationship with the poorest sectors of the population."[12] From their search arose a new body of theological thought. Liberation theologians combined an activist reading of the gospel with concrete, sociological analyses of the realities of people's lives, drawing inspiration from more secular currents of thought such as Marxism and dependency theory.[13]

The pastoral strategy developed by the new People's church drew on the work of Brazilian educator Paulo Freire.[14] Freire's work complemented the catalytic and prophetic mission of the church by suggesting a politicized pedagogy, enabling the oppressed to identify the sources of their oppression.[15]

The promotion of critical consciousness through religious teachings politicized the faithful. In military Brazil, many of the CEBs began to organize local communities in efforts to overcome the hardships imposed by authoritarian economic policies.[16] The new People's church urged laymen *and* lay-

---

[12] Candido Procôpio Ferreira de Camargo, Beatriz Munoz de Souza, and Antonio Flavio de Oliveira Pierucci, "Comunidades Eclesiais de Base," in *São Paulo: O Povo em Movimento*, ed. Paul Singer and Vinícius C. Brant (Petrópolis: Vozes, 1980), p. 60.

[13] The principal, and highly controversial, exponent of liberation theology in Brazil is Leonardo Boff. See especially his *Igreja: Carisma e Poder* (Petrópolis: Vozes, 1982).

[14] See especially Paulo Freire, *Pedagogy of the Oppressed* (New York: Herder and Herder, 1972) and Paulo Freire, *Las Iglesias, la Educación y el Proceso de Liberación Humana en la Historia* (Buenos Aires: Asociación Editorial Aurora, 1974).

[15] Levine, "Religion and Politics, Politics and Religion," p. 30.

[16] The actual activities and the political orientations of the CEBs in Brazil vary greatly. For a discussion of their diversity, see Bruneau, *The Church in Brazil*, pp. 127–46. See also Ralph Della Cava, "The People's Church, the Vatican, and Abertura," in *Democratizing Brazil*, ed. Alfred Stepan (New York: Oxford University Press, 1989).

women to join CEBs and other neighborhood organizations. Whereas historically the "old" church relegated women to subservient roles, rhetorically at least, the progressive church now invited women to participate in full equality in its new political mission.

In summoning women to join in the church's redefined pastoral mission, progressive clergy intoned a new theological vision of women's proper role in community life. Vatican II's radically revised understanding of earthly justice and human rights (summarized in the encyclical *Peace on Earth*) implied that women, too, were worthy of rights and human dignity. Calling on women "to participate as co-equals in the construction of the human community,"[17] Pope John XXIII explicitly advocated an increased public role for women:

> It is obvious to everyone that women are now taking part in public life. This is happening more rapidly perhaps in nations of Christian civilization, and, more slowly but broadly, among peoples who have inherited other traditions or cultures. Since women are becoming ever more conscious of their human dignity, they will not tolerate being treated as mere material instruments, but demand rights befitting a human person both in domestic and public life.[18]

Despite relentless pressure from women church activists and some progressive clergy, however, the church's "old" doctrines concerning the family, maternity, morality, and sexuality remained largely unaltered. At both Medellín and Puebla, the bishops endorsed the Vatican II's call for a greater public role for women (even if, in some cases, they did so begrudgingly). But the urgent need to revise church doctrine on issues like contraception—which might facilitate their exercise of such a role—was not incorporated into CELAM's final documents at either Medellín or Puebla.

At Medellín, the bishops merely echoed the pope's acknowledgment that "women [are demanding] their right to a legitimate equality with men."[19] At the Puebla meeting, according to one observer, "only 23 [of the 364 delegates] were women, mostly representing religious orders and not particularly involved in women's issues as such."[20] Catholic feminists nevertheless stepped up their efforts to influence church policy: "women . . . were present in great numbers in Puebla throughout the conference. There was a women's documentation center and a lobbying group, *Mujeres para el Dialogo* (Women

[17] Carmen Barroso, "Organizações Não-Governamentais: O Movimento de Mulheres no Brasil," 1981 (Mimeograph), pp. 8–9.

[18] *Peace on Earth, An Encyclical Letter of His Holiness Pope John XXIII* (New York: Ridge Press/Odyssey Press, 1966), p. 140.

[19] Second General Conference of Latin American Bishops, *The Church in the Present-Day Transformation of Latin America in the Light of the Council* (Washington, D.C.: Secretariat for Latin America, National Conference of Catholic Bishops, 1979), p. 32.

[20] Robert McAfee Brown, "The Significance of Puebla for the Protestant Churches in North America," in *Puebla and Beyond*, ed. John Eagleson and Phillip Scharper (Maryknoll, N.Y.: Orbis Books, 1979), pp. 333–34.

for Dialogue), that had daily meetings and conferences, but the dialogues were mostly with lay people and not very much with the bishops."[21]

At Puebla, debates centering on the status of women and their role in the church were among the most acrimonious. Nonetheless, the efforts of those advocating reform paid off: the final document speaks of the oppression and exploitation of women in public life, affirms "the equality and dignity of women in the gospel perspective"[22] and asserts that "women are doubly oppressed and marginalized."[23]

In the post–Vatican II, pre-Puebla era, the church appeared more lenient on family and reproductive issues; in several Latin American countries, it tacitly approved or at least did not actively oppose government-sponsored family planning programs, for example. Though changes instituted after the Second Vatican Council hardly revolutionized the subordinate role of women within the church, some important reforms nevertheless ensued. Nuns shed their habits, laywomen disposed of their veils. They joined men (and in most cases, in fact, outnumbered them) in implementing programs pursuant to the church's new vision of social justice. Both lay and religious women were granted more active, if still secondary, roles within the church and in the church's work with the community.

Still, these roles seldom transcended the spheres of activity which "God" and "nature" assigned to women. That is, women continued to engage in social welfare or charitable activities consistent with their traditionally defined "nurturing and mothering" roles and remained barred from positions of authority within the institutional hierarchy. Moreover, reforms did not lead to a reformulation of core church doctrines about the sanctity of motherhood and the family.

Since Puebla, and especially under the leadership of John Paul II, the church has reasserted an unyieldingly conservative stance on moral and sexual issues vital to achieving full "human dignity" for women. Though a Synod of Bishops, held in Rome in late 1987, advocated a liberalized church position on many issues crucial to women's equality, the pope remains intransigent. Pope John Paul II continually has reiterated his distaste (and therefore the institutional church's) for "unisex equality," extramarital sex, contraception, abortion, surrogate motherhood, homosexuality, divorce, and the ordination of women.[24]

---

[21] Ibid.

[22] Rosemary Ruether, "Women and the Church," *Christianity and Crisis* (April 2, 1979), pp. 78–79, cited in McAfee Brown, ibid., p. 335.

[23] As Elsa Tamez notes, "Unfortunately this expression was put in a footnote to the final edited document of the 1979 bishops' conference at Puebla, Mexico, although it had been in the main body of the approved text. But at least it is there, in paragraph 1134." In Elsa Tamez, ed., *Against Machismo. Rubem Alves, Leonardo Boff, Gustavo Gutiérrez, José Marquez Bonino, Juan Luís Segundo and Others Speak about the Struggle of Women* (Oak Park, Ill.: Meyer Stone, 1987), p. 40 fn.

[24] Recognizing the growing importance of women in the church's community work, Pope John

Ironically, liberation theologians in Brazil, including some who like Leonardo Boff and Frei Betto have been censured by the pope, share many of the Vatican's views about women's unique vocations, even as they radically expand on its 1963 call for women to become partners in the "human community." That is, male theologians of liberation adopted a largely unmodified orthodox Marxist understanding of the "woman question," while adhering fairly closely to church teachings on matters regarding the Christian family and women's special qualities as wives and mothers.

In a 1984 interview with a Brazilian feminist journalist, Frei Betto maintained that Boff's conception of women's oppression owes a great deal to contemporary Brazilian feminism. Like other liberation theologians, however, both Boff and Frei Betto's understanding of women's subordination owes more to traditional Marxism than to contemporary Brazilian socialist feminism. Feminists maintain that the realms of family and sexuality—characterized by unequal gender power relations—are central loci of women's oppression. Liberation theologians, following the Marxist tradition, situate the locus of women's oppression in capitalist power relations. Both Boff and Frei Betto, for example, adopt an essentially orthodox view that explains women's "double oppression" as "crystallized in the profound identification that exists between the relationships of production and the relationships of reproduction, both of which have the same oppressive character."[25] The solution to women's oppression, in this view, lies in increasing their participation in the public world of politics and production.

A biologically essentialist view of women's "special qualities" oddly coexists with liberation theologians' economistic view of women's oppression. Women are said to bring a unique understanding to the people's struggle, an understanding derived from their "abnegation and prayer," from the joy and sorrow they experience as mothers of the people: "There is a profound spirituality of the poor centered on the death/life dialectic. Faced with their own life/death dialectic, even in the biological sense, women experience something that men do not. And they remind all of us of its meaning; their contribution is for everyone."[26]

Boff, for example, extols the virtues of "the feminine" in his *O Rosto Materno de Deus* (The Maternal Face of God) and goes much further than traditional theologians in revaluing femininity and women's essence.

Paul II issued a long-awaited apostolic letter, "On the Dignity of Women," in September 1988. Widely viewed as a "theological response to the women's movement," the document "is unlikely to satisfy many advocates of women's rights . . . [and] makes almost no mention of work or other public activities for women in its lengthy treatment of their place in Roman Catholic thinking." Instead, while exhorting Catholics to overcome the "evil inheritance" of male domination over women, "On the Dignity of Women" again emphasizes the feminine "vocations" of motherhood and virginity, "calling on women to find themselves in their love for others." See *New York Times*, October 1, 1988.

[25] Frei Betto, in Tamez, *Against Machismo*, p. 92.

[26] "Interview with Gustavo Gutiérrez," in Tamez, *Against Machismo*, pp. 44–45.

The feminine makes us see another way of being human and civilized. The last several millenia have been marked by masculine predominance. And it gives rise to another form of being human and of relating to reality. This form is characterized, principally, by the *logos*, rationality and concept. The *logos* introduces a rupture between man and nature; we become the owners of the land, we subjugate its forces, we break various equilibriums that it maintains. . . . In this context the feminine emerges as a possibility of an alternative path; . . . Through the feminine we develop the capacity for another type of relationship, more fraternal, more tender, more solidary with our cosmic and tellural roots.[27]

This essentialist imagery is sometimes echoed by women and men church activists. Participants at a regionwide conference entitled, "Woman: The Workshop of Life, the Builder of the New Society," held in Nicaragua in May of 1983, proclaimed that "all of us are collaborating in the great birth of a new society, in the birth of new men and women, whose cradle is peace and structures of justice and fellowship." Mary, mother of God, becomes the first revolutionary mother, ennobled by her selfless devotion to her family and to the struggle: "This war of liberation also has shown us how the woman is a revolutionary mother. Instead of being a brake and an obstacle to her sons and daughters who wish to be committed, she encourages them with her words and her example of yielding herself to the many tasks which she carries out every day in order to win this totally unequal battle."[28]

Such views do not question the socially constrictive, exclusive identification of women with maternity and the family. Liberation theologians' view of women in the "personal" or private sphere, then, is in crucial respects quite compatible with that of the Vatican. Even the progressive Brazilian church, which positions itself clearly against legal discriminations suffered by women in politics and production, is considerably more conservative when it comes to issues of morality, sexuality, contraception, divorce, violence against women, or abortion—issues that became central to Brazilian feminist politics in the late 1970s and always sparked a great deal of interest among women in neighborhood groups throughout São Paulo's urban periphery. Liberation theologians, like the orthodox Left, too often assume that such issues are irrelevant to working-class women.

In 1983, for example, the progressive São Paulo archdiocese of Dom Paulo Evaristo Arns proclaimed a year-long pastoral campaign against violence and street crime. But as noted by one participant in the statewide meeting that launched the campaign, "the specific sexual violence suffered by women was

[27] *Mulherio* 4, no. 18 (September/October 1984): 10.

[28] "Woman: The Workshop of Life, the Builder of the New Society," translated from *Educación*, published by CELADEC, the Latin American Evangelical Commission of Christian Education, Lima, Peru, no. 14, December 1983, and reprinted in Latin American Documentation, *Women in the Church* (Lima: LADOC, n.d.), pp. 5–10.

never addressed."[29] Furthermore, in the early 1980s, the otherwise progressive CNBB loudly protested the proposed decriminalization of abortion in the case of a deformed fetus and argued against the decriminalization of acts of seduction or adultery (central to Brazilian feminists' mobilizations against "crimes of passion") as this, according to the bishops, would represent "a coup against the institution of marriage"—an institution dear to the hearts of even the most progressive clergy.[30]

Women of all social classes in Brazil abort—estimates place the number of illegal abortions at over 3 million per year. Thousands, some say as many as 400,000, die each year of complications resulting from back-alley abortions. Yet in an interview with *Mulherio*, Frei Betto asserted that the "direction of sexuality and the evaluation of the ethics of various types of contraceptives is up to the couple," but stated that he was "radically against abortion . . . [it] has its roots in society, that is, I think that abortion occurs because society does not offer any security in life."[31]

In sum, the Brazilian church's new message—that women should participate "as equals" in the "human community"—coexists uncomfortably with a very old message, that women's primary and unique, if no longer exclusive, vocations remain motherhood and the family. Women's oppression in the private sphere—their inability to control fertility, their subjugation to their husbands, their sole responsibility for the care and nurture of children and the elderly—seriously inhibits their ability to participate as equals in community life. Yet even the progressive church has yet to revise its position on key issues that might ameliorate women's subordinate status in marriage and the family. As we will see in the ensuing chapters, this fundamental contradiction placed explicit limits on the politicization of gender within popular women's organizations and made for an extremely uneasy relationship between the Catholic church's mothers' clubs and the feminists who in the 1970s began organizing among women in the urban periphery.

Women *nevertheless* make up the vast majority of participants in the new church community organizations. Given their traditionally greater involvement with institutional Catholicism, women may have tended to join CEBs and other church groups in greater numbers than men. Thomas C. Bruneau's survey of religious beliefs and practices among Brazilians, conducted in eight dioceses in 1975, confirmed that women outnumber men among the "faithful."[32]

Women outnumber men in most urban popular organizations found in Brazil today, both religious and secular. As shown in chapter 2, women's traditional roles as "pillars of the family" help explain their greater participation

---

[29] Woman CEB participant from Jardim Miriam, personal communication to the author.

[30] *Mulherio* 4, no. 18 (September/October 1984): 10.

[31] Ibid., p. 13.

[32] Bruneau, *The Church in Brazil*, p. 33.

in community. Moreover, the fact that the church explicitly summoned women to engage in community activism provided an ethical rationale for forms of female participation that patriarchal norms might have been deemed inappropriate for women in earlier times.

Though women's involvement in community struggles for running water or against the rising cost of living stems in part from their housekeeping and maternal roles, participation in both church-linked and secular organizations often leads women to question those very roles, heightening their consciousness as women. Mothers' club–like organizations furnished hundreds of thousands of women of the popular classes with an unprecedented opportunity for participation in community politics. And that participation in itself empowered many women activists, sometimes leading them to challenge gender power imbalances within their marriages, their families, their communities, and even their parishes.[33] As we shall see below, the church's conservative stance on women's role in the private sphere often inhibits the full articulation of this dynamic process of self-empowerment.

The Brazilian church developed a gender-specific strategy for involving women in its new pastoral mission. In keeping with the sexual division of political labor, local parishes often created mothers' clubs, which functioned alongside other church-linked community organizations. The clubs targeted housewives in the neighborhoods and organized activities consistent with women's roles in the family and the community.

Most commonly, the clubs provide sex-stereotyped courses and activities for women—such as sewing or knitting classes—as an incentive for community women to participate. By involving women in the mothers' clubs, the local church is better able to involve them in its larger pastoral mission. And, in fact, mothers' club participants often form the organizational cadre of a local parish's community initiatives. In most of the neighborhoods I visited in São Paulo, a core of ten or so women usually participated in the local mothers' club, the *favela* movement, the CEB, and most other local church initiatives, with the glaring exception of the *Pastoral Operária*, the church's community labor organization. Women nevertheless perform most of the infrastructural work for worker organizations, as well as for local youth groups, prayer groups, and other community groups. Additionally, this same core of women often was held responsible for the upkeep of church buildings and grounds. Long after the men had left community meetings, I frequently saw women cleaning up after them—sweeping the floors, clearing the dishes after refreshments, engaging in stereotypically female work. A wide gap thus separates the

---

[33] For the best analysis of this personally transformative dimension of women's participation in São Paulo's community organizations, see Teresa Caldeira, "Mujeres, Cotidianidad y Política," in *Ciudadanía e Identidad: Las Mujeres en los Movimientos Sociales Latino-americanos*, ed. Elizabeth Jelin (Geneva: UNRISD, 1987).

church's new egalitarian discourse from the reality of women's experience in São Paulo's church-linked community organizations.

In a study of dozens of mothers' clubs in São Paulo's Southern Zone, Jany Chiriac and Solange Padilha found that these performed dual and contradictory roles among women of the popular classes: "1—the positive role played by the clubs as channels which permit the participation of housewives in community life; and 2—the limits of the clubs as transmitters of Christian ideology which influence the process of women's *concientização* in a predetermined direction."[34] They conclude that whereas the progressive church promotes formal equality between men and women from a new Christian perspective, this perspective is limited to encouraging both women and men to participate (differentially) in community activities.

> [T]he equality affirmed in discourse is translated in practice into a form of female participation different from that of men. . . . Women are always called upon to perform tasks (not to make decisions) and in the case of mothers' clubs, those tasks are mere extensions of those that women execute in their own homes.[35]

Mothers' clubs function primarily as "ladies' auxiliaries" to parish organizations. In no way created with women's gender-specific needs or demands in mind, I did not see nor hear of a single club that was created with the intention of helping women gain consciousness, or act politically, *as women*. Furthermore, the strategy of *concientização*, so central to "mixed" groups, such as the CEBs, is seldom employed to promote a critical consciousness about gender power relations among participants of church-linked mothers' clubs. Relations between men and women within marriage and the family are discussed only in the context of "preparation for marriage" minicourses that are often required of couples who are to contract matrimony, or within "couples groups" designed to enhance marital harmony rather than resolve or mediate marital conflict or power differentials between men and women within the domestic sphere.

Nevertheless, the clubs do provide a much needed space for sociability among women and thus have helped break the relative isolation of the domestic sphere to which women are often confined. The clubs create an organizational context for *networking* among neighborhood women, one which builds on and extends beyond established kinship and friendship networks. Networks of mothers' clubs provided the core organizational foci for several citywide and even nationwide gender-based social movements such the Struggle for Day Care Movement, the Cost of Living Movement, and the Feminine Amnesty Movement, as will be seen in chapters 4 and 5 below.

[34] Jany Chiriac and Solange Padilha, "Características e Limites das Organizações de Base Femininas," in *Trabalhadoras do Brasil*, ed. Maria Cristina A. Bruschini and Fulvia Rosemberg (São Paulo: Brasilense, 1982), p. 195.
[35] Ibid., p. 198.

Much of the church hierarchy and some of the progressive clergy remained doctrinally opposed, if not overtly hostile, to feminist demands for sexual autonomy, changes in the family, and reproductive freedom throughout the 1970s and 1980s. The politicization of gender within some church-linked community women's groups nonetheless provided nascent Brazilian feminism with an extensive mass base not found in any other Latin American nation, with the exception of perhaps Peru and Chile. In the largest Catholic country in the world, the Brazilian church's 217 ecclesiastical divisions (32 archdioceses, 138 dioceses, 41 prelacies, and 6 miscellaneous divisions) span the entire country like no other institution, besides the modern State.[36] The church discourses about the "human dignity" of women and its efforts at mobilizing poor and working-class women were especially influential given the breadth of the church's social reach and the depth of its moral weight in Brazil. Current estimates place the number of Christian Base Communities in Brazil at over one hundred thousand, primarily concentrated in the periphery of Brazil's urban centers. The CEBs function alongside thousands of non–church-linked popular organizations which sometimes predate the authoritarian regime, but which have become increasingly politicized over the course of the last two decades. And parallel women's associations often exist alongside both of these types of community organizations, perhaps making neighborhood women's groups the most numerous among the various new forms of associability found in Brazil today.

WOMEN IN THE LEFT

Just as the church provided a context in which Brazil's feminine groups would crystallize, the rearticulation of the militant Left in the wake of the severe government repression of the late 1960s and early 1970s would galvanize nascent Brazilian feminism in the mid-1970s. Many of the women who would become the cadre of organizers of the contemporary Brazilian feminist movement were active first in militant Left organizations and student groups. And many of the feminists I interviewed discussed their experience within those organizations as having implanted the seeds of feminist consciousness within them. Their experience in the opposition also led them into increased contact with neighborhood women's groups, provided networks that could later be mobilized in the service of the feminist cause, and fueled an inchoate consciousness of gender oppression.

The revolutionary Left's discourses on social justice and liberation included only passing reference to the "woman question," as the class struggle and the armed struggle against the regime were deemed paramount after military hardliners closed off all peaceful channels of political protest in 1968. The advent

[36] Bruneau, *The Church in Brazil*, p. 93.

of socialism, moreover, ostensibly would bring with it the liberation of women; so Leftist groups and radical student movement organizations urged women to join the revolutionary struggle that would eventually bring about their emancipation as women.[37]

But for many women militants, who felt their own issues and concerns as women were not addressed by militant organizations, the radical opposition's formulation of the woman question left much to be desired. Though Guevarist revolutionary theory argued that the presence of "women and old men" among combatants could hamper guerrilla effectiveness,[38] for example, the model Brazilian revolutionary was ostensibly genderless. As one former *guerrillera* put it:

> During the clandestine phase, one had a vision of a heroic militant. The reigning theory was that men and women were the same. I was a militant, a soldier of the revolution, and a soldier has no sex! . . . But I already felt some problems as a woman, for example, the men thought that women were not suited for certain kinds of [armed] actions.
>
> In practice, the relations between men and women were very difficult. . . . The contradictions manifested themselves in unexpected ways, sometimes you felt like you had to impose yourself as a woman, as a political militant, to show the guys that you had the capacity to do whatever. Then, sometimes you were moved to do certain things, but moved more as a function of having to affirm yourself as a woman within the group rather than as a function of some political ideal.[39]

The genderic "sameness" in revolutionary theory led revolutionaries to overlook the very real differences between women and men. Abstract equality resulted in the negation of sexual difference and gender inequality—a negation that had profound implications for the women who formed part of the militant opposition to the regime. Revolutionaries were to leave their families and their pasts behind them and devote themselves entirely to the revolutinary struggle.

[37] For a description of the major guerrilla groups and their politico-military actions, see João Batista Berardo, *Guerrilhas e Guerrilheiros no Drama da América Latina* (São Paulo: Edições Populares, 1981), pp. 202–81; Peter Flynn, *Brazil: A Political Analysis* (Boulder, Colo.: Westview Press, 1979), pp. 411–18; Fernando Portela, *Guerra de Guerrilhas no Brasil* (São Paulo: Global Editora, 1979); and Antonio Caso, *A Esquerda Armada no Brasil (1967–71)* (Lisboa: Moraes Editores, 1976). For the reflections of former *guerrilleros*, see Pedro Celso Uchôa Cavalcanti and Jovelino Ramos, *Memórias do Exílio, Brasil 1964–19??* (São Paulo: Ed. Livasmento, 1978).

[38] See, for example, Che Guevara, *Guerrilla Warfare*, with an Introduction and Case Studies by Brian Loveman and Thomas M. Davies, Jr. (Lincoln: University of Nebraska Press, 1985), pp. 132–34.

[39] Testimony in *Memorias das Mulheres do Exílio* (Rio de Janeiro: Paz e Terra, 1980), p. 248, cited by Anette Goldberg, "Feminismo em Regime Autoritário: A Experiência do Movimento de Mulheres no Rio de Janeiro" (Paper presented at the XII International Congress of the International Political Science Association, Rio de Janeiro, August 9–14, 1982), pp. 10–11.

Female revolutionaries, however, were often "encumbered" by their child-bearing and childrearing responsibilities, responsibilities which, many women complained, were neither acknowledged nor shared by their male comrades in struggle. One woman told me, for example, that when a female leader in her political organization became pregnant, the central committee called an emergency meeting to vote on whether or not she should have the child.[40] Others actually had their children and raised them in the underground and received little or no support (either material or moral) from their male colleagues for doing so.

Former *guerrilheiras* and student activists I talked to also complained about the fact that women were rarely given positions of authority within the militant Left. As in traditional political parties, female militants were instead entrusted with much of the infrastructural work of the Brazilian Left—women ran safe houses, worked as messengers, cooked meals, cared for the sick and the wounded, and were sometimes called upon to use their "feminine charms" to extract information from the enemy. Many of these women resented their relegation to subordinate positions within the internal power structure of militant groups. But, as one woman suggested, they lacked a language, an analysis that would enable them to understand their resentment in political terms.

> For a long time, I was not conscious of the existence of women's oppression within the political groups. Today, I understand that that oppression existed and that it was very much marked by the type of power structure, by the power relation that existed within the political organizations in general. When these organizations assumed Leninist principles of democratic centralism, this in practice translated into highly pronounced hierarchies, where there were different scales and structures of power, where there had to be a boss. What happened was that women almost always wound up in an inferior position within that structure.[41]

The economistic orthodoxy of many Leftist organizations precluded the evolution of a critical theory or discourse on gender power relations and the rigid, hierarchical forms of organization characteristic of the Left also prevented women from assuming the direction of revolutionary theory and practice.

In the mid-1970s, following a critical reevaluation of strategies of social change pursued during the late 1960s, the militant opposition decided to increase its organizational efforts among the popular classes. The new grass-roots mobilizational strategies pursued by the Left stemmed from the fact that, following a short-lived period of political liberalization under President Costa e Silva (known as the policy of relief or *política de alívio*), the Medici administration (1970–1974)[42] ferociously repressed all student and labor movements

[40] Interview with a feminist former member of an underground group, São Paulo, March 28, 1983.

[41] Cited in Goldberg, "Feminismo em Regime Autoritário," p. 11.

[42] For a full discussion of this period, see Maria Helena Moreira Alves, *State and Opposition*

advocating radical social change.[43] And by 1973, State security forces also had crushed all opposition tendencies engaged in armed struggle.[44]

In 1968, a right-wing coup enthroned military hard-liners who opposed any concessions to the opposition and enshrined the National Security Doctrine as the regime's informing ideology. A speech by MDB (Brazilian Democratic Movement) Deputy Márcio Moreira Alves, inciting the population to boycott the September 7, 1968, military day parade, provided a pretext for the coup. In an impassioned appeal to the "women of Brazil," dubbed "Operation Lysistrata," Alves offended the military's manhood, as well as their professional pride, by entreating the wives and girlfriends of military men to withhold "sexual favors" until democracy was restored. The military responded swiftly to this affront to their corporate integrity and virility—they closed Congress and installed hard-line authoritarian rule, promulgating Institutional Act No. 5 (AI-5).

Widely regarded as the ultimate expression of Brazilian authoritarianism, AI-5 granted unlimited powers to the president, enabling him to control the opposition within both civil and political society and to suspend constitutional guarantees at will.[45] The Congress was closed indefinitely; the political stage was set for one of the most repressive periods of Brazilian political history.

AI-5 closed off all channels of peaceful opposition available to Brazilian citizens. In this repressive context, many sectors of the opposition turned to a strategy of armed struggle. As guerrilla leader Carlos Marighela would put it, "the only solution is what we are doing now: to employ violence against those who first used violence to attack the people and the country."[46] Armed resistance in Brazil, then, was a strategy of last recourse against the excesses of the regime.

Marighela's ALN (National Liberation Action) was one of twenty or more Brazilian guerrilla organizations that declared war on military authoritarianism in the late 1960s and early 1970s. Most of these organizations found their adherents among students, workers, and church activists who were forced underground due to the widespread repression that followed AI-5. Some were

in *Military Brazil* (Austin: University of Texas Press, 1985), pp. 117–32; and Peter Flynn, *Brazil: A Political Analysis*, pp. 366–417.

[43] On the 1968 student movement, see João Roberto Martins Filho, *Movimento Estudantil e Ditadura Militar 1964–1968* (Campinas, São Paulo: Papirus, 1987); and Daniel Aarão Reis Filho and Pedro Moraes, *68: A Paixão de uma Utopia* (Rio de Janeiro: Espaço e Tempo, 1988). On the 1967–1969 wave of labor mobilizations, see Francisco C. Weffort, "Participação e Conflito Industrial: Contagem e Osasco, 1969," *Cadernos de CEBRAP* 5 (1972).

[44] For a comprehensive account of guerrilla activities and government repression in Brazil, see Jacob Gorender, *Combate nas Trevas—A Esquerda Brasileira: Das Ilusões à Luta Armada* (São Paulo: Ática, 1987).

[45] For the full text of AI-5, see Maria Helena Moreira Alves, *State and Opposition in Military Brazil*, pp. 95–96.

[46] Carlos Marighela, *For the Liberation of Brazil* (Middlesex: Pelican Books, 1971), p. 21.

splinter groups from the pro-Soviet Brazilian Communist Party, which opposed armed resistance. All drew their inspiration from the Cuban revolution and the doctrine of revolutionary action that emerged from various interpretations of the Cuban revolutionary process—most notably, the guerrilla *foco* strategy developed by Ché Guevara and reinterpreted by Regis Debray in his *Revolution in the Revolution?*, a text that became a kind of "handbook" for Latin American revolutionaries.[47]

The basic idea behind the *foquista* revolutionary strategy was that a small group of committed revolutionaries could create the "subjective conditions" for a socialist revolution, as the "objective conditions" already were fully developed throughout Latin America. "This view tended to play down the role of mass organization, especially urban-based organizations, stressing rather the impact of the presence of a small group of rural guerrillas who would be the 'small motor' which would move the 'large motor' of revolution."[48]

The resounding defeat of opposition forces advocating armed resistance prompted the militant Left to reevaluate its strategy for combating authoritarianism. The failure of vanguardism and *foquismo* led many former *guerrilheiros* to rethink their approach to revolutionary transformation and privilege the role of mass organization. Many who had emphasized direct action over political work among the masses now shunned vanguardism altogether and began what many of my interviewees referred to as "'ant's labor" (*trabalho de formiginha*) among the popular classes (who had, after all, been organizing on their own since the early 1960s). Guerrilla groups that had stressed mass organization even in the late 1960s, also turned to the popular classes in search for support for their own revolutionary visions. Vanguardism was not abandoned by these groups, but rather was redefined—the initiative belonged to the people, but the revolutionary cadre would struggle along with the people and direct their struggle onto the proper revolutionary course.[49]

Though the rationales differed, the results were similar—those formerly active in urban guerrilla organizations and unarmed militant organizations began working among the people in the popular neighborhood organizations that gained strength in Brazil during the 1960s. They worked with existing church-linked and secular groups such as youth organizations, the church's pastoral groups, or other neighborhood associations.

The church's shielding of the political opposition drew middle-class, secu-

---

[47] See Ernesto "Ché" Guevara, *Guerrilla Warfare*; and Regis Debray, *Revolution in the Revolution?* (New York: Monthly Review Press, 1967). In this introduction to *Guerrilla Welfare*, Loveman and Davies provide an excellent overview of the theory and practice of guerrilla movements in Latin America. See also Richard Guillespie, "A Critique of the Urban Guerrilla: Argentina, Uruguay, and Brazil," *Conflict Quarterly* 1, no. 2 (1980): 39–53.

[48] Flynn, *Brazil: A Political Analysis*, p. 412.

[49] This analysis is partially derived from interviews with former members of underground leftist and student groups conducted in São Paulo during 1982–1983.

lar activists and intellectuals, many of them women, into Brazil's peripheral urban neighborhoods and rural areas. And when the Left turned towards organizing a "mass base" for the revolution in Brazil's urban periphery in the mid-1970s, many former *guerrilleras* and student movement activists directed their efforts at women of the popular classes. These contacts were crucial to later feminist efforts to build a cross-class, mass-based women's movement, as will be seen in chapters 4 and 5.

While it was not feminist consciousness as such that prompted many of these middle-class, university-educated women to work with the neighborhood mothers' clubs and housewives' associations discussed above, some of the women I interviewed suggested that, almost unconsciously, their experience as women in the Left led them in this particular political direction. Many began working as *assessoras* or consultants to church-linked mothers' clubs or youth groups. They helped poor and working-class women "learn the ropes" of local political institutions so they could better articulate their demands for improved urban infrastructure, schools, health care, and so on.

The experience of young, middle-class women in the Left also had more direct implications for the emergence of feminist movement organizations in contemporary Brazil. Former clandestine networks and networks established among student movement activists were remobilized around feminist issues in the mid-to-late 1970s. Former female "comrades" in the would-be Brazilian revolution became comrades in a new kind of revolutionary struggle—one that encompassed the transformation of both class and gender relations of power in Brazilian society.

Many of the women involved in the militant opposition also formed networks while in political exile in Europe and the United States in the early-to-mid-1970s. And many became involved in the feminist movements which by then were at their mobilizational peak in the West. To the extent that feminism was imported to Brazil in the 1970s, it was through the lived experience of these exiled women, within "mixed" opposition organizations in exile and within the larger feminist movements in the host countries. In Chile until 1973 and in France and Italy until the late 1970s, for example, Brazilian women associated with the Left formed their own women's groups, often joining former *montoneras, tupamaras*, and other Spanish American *guerrilleras* also in exile. Though many of these women's groups began as fronts for the political organizations in exile, some, like the *Círculo de Mulheres Brasileiras* (Brazilian Women's Circle) in Paris, developed an autonomous feminist theory and practice that they brought back to Brazil after political amnesty was conceded in the late 1970s.[50]

[50] Most of the preceding information on women in the militant left, both in Brazil and in exile, is based on extensive formal and informal interviews with former female militants who are presently active in the feminist movement. And though, therefore, they are not representative of women in the left in general, their analysis of their experience within resistance organizations was

POLITICAL LIBERALIZATION AND CHANGES IN THE STRUCTURE OF POLITICAL OPPORTUNITY IN MILITARY BRAZIL

The rearticulation of the Brazilian Left and other opposition sectors in the mid-1970s was strategically feasible due to the regime's own top-down policy of political liberalization, initiated by President Ernesto Geisel in 1974—a third factor contributing to the development of feminist and feminine activism. The policy, known as *distensão* or "decompression," largely stemmed from the regime's search for a new legitimacy formula, as other formulas were exhausted by the mid-1970s.

From 1964 to 1968, the regime relied primarily on what might be termed negative legitimation. The "Revolution" of 1964 was justified as a struggle against internal enemies—restive labor and peasant movements, the radical populism of João Goulart, and the leftist sympathies of some of his followers. That struggle was waged in the name of political order and economic development, which civilian politicians were purportedly incapable of implementing. Secure in this formula, President Costa e Silva promoted the first attempt at liberalization that, as we saw above, ended abruptly in 1968–1969.

With the security and intelligence apparatuses strengthened by AI-5 and the predominance of military hard-liners in the State, the regime embarked on a program of economic growth that relied on increased State investment, multinational capital, massive foreign financing, and, most critically, on regressive wage policies and strict government control of labor. The resulting Economic Miracle, described in chapter 2 above, served as the regime's principal new source of legitimation. With growth rates averaging over 10 percent per year between 1967 and 1973, the regime could rely on the unwavering support of large sectors of the upper and middle classes. Propounding a vision of *O Brasil Grande* (The Great Brazil), official discourse constantly reassured the Brazilian masses that the benefits of economic development would gradually "trickle down" to all Brazilian citizens.

However, by the time Gen. Ernesto Geisel came to power in 1974, the internal enemy and the economic growth legitimacy formulas were no longer viable. The populists had been banished or stripped of their political rights; the guerrillas, the student movement, and the labor opposition had been decimated by government repression under Médici; and the Economic Miracle seemed less miraculous after it was severely shaken by the 1973 oil crisis and

---

key to the development of the feminist movement. Since many of the women interviewed might be compromised politically if their names were revealed (even in the putatively democratic New Brazilian Republic), their names will not be mentioned here or hereafter. See also Angela Neves-Xavier de Brito, "Brazilian Women in Exile: The Quest for Identity," *Latin American Perspectives* 13, no. 2 (Spring 1986): 58–80.

the excessive expansion of the money supply under Minister of Planning Delfim Neto.[51]

By 1973, the elimination of the guerrilla movements and much of the radical opposition by the State security apparatus had dispelled middle-class fears of an imminent "communist threat"—the central rationale of the State's defensive project during previous administrations. The decline in the credibility of the regime's defensive project against the internal enemy and the growing ·statism of its offensive economic project led many of the regime's previous bourgeois allies in civil society to join forces with popular sectors of the opposition.[52]

Disaffected entrepreneurs, liberal professionals, and academics became more visible within the ranks of the opposition to authoritarian regime policies after 1974–1975. Professional associations such as the Brazilian Bar Association, the Brazilian Society for the Progress of Science, and the Brazilian Press Association, publicly criticized authoritarian economic policies and decried the curtailment of civil and political rights.

Though analysts differ as to the causes of Geisel's policy of political opening, most agree that a search for a new legitimacy formula and a new hegemonic strategy premised on institutionalization were its key determinants.[53] Legitimation would now be pursued through the "normalization" of politics

---

[51] See Paul J. Singer, "As Contradições do Milagre," in *Brasil: do "Milagre" à "Abertura,"* ed. Paulo J. Krischke (São Paulo: Cortez, 1983), pp. 5–22; Paul J. Singer, *A Crise do "Milagre": Interpretação Crítica da Economía Brasileira* (São Paulo: Paz e Terra, 1982); and Albert Fishlow, "Some Reflections on Post-1964 Brazilian Economic Policy," in *Authoritarian Brazil*, ed. Alfred Stepan (New Haven, Conn.: Yale University Press, 1973).

[52] Stepan, "State Power and the Strength of Civil Society in the Southern Cone of Latin America," in *Bringing the State Back In*, ed. Peter B. Evans, Dietrich Rueschemeyer, and Theda Skocpol (New York: Cambridge University Press, 1985).

[53] Among the most compelling analyses of the causes of political liberalization are Sebastião C. Velasco e Cruz and Carlos Estevam Martins, "De Castello a Figueiredo: Uma Incursão na pré-História da 'Abertura'," in *Sociedade e Política no Brasil Pós-64*, ed. Bernard Sorj and Maria Hermínia Tavares de Almeida, pp. 13–61; David V. Fleischer, "De la Distensión a la Apertura Político-Electoral en Brasil," *Revista Mexicana de Sociología* 44, no. 3 (July–September 1982): 961–98; Paulo J. Krischke, ed., *Brasil: do "Milagre" à "Abertura"* (São Paulo: Cortez, 1983); and Thomas E. Skidmore, "Brazil's Slow Road to Democratization: 1974–1985," in *Democratizing Brazil: Problems of Transition and Consolidation*, ed. Alfred Stepan (New York: Oxford University Press, 1989). Some analysts emphasize the regime's confidence rather than its crises, as the motor for *distensão*; others stress increasing tensions between military hard-liners and soft-liners; still others privilege economic determinants. The most persuasive and nuanced analyses of political liberalization examine the complex, dialectical interaction of elite negotiation and popular pressures in shaping the dynamics of the Brazilian transition. See especially Eli Diniz, "A Transição Política no Brasil: A Uma Reavaliação da Dinámica da Abertura," *Dados* 28, no. 3 (1985): 329–46; and William C. Smith, "The Political Transition in Brazil: From Authoritarian Liberalization to Elite Conciliation to Democratization," in *Comparing New Democracies: Transition and Consolidation in Mediterranean Europe and the Southern Cone*, ed. Enrique A. Balorya (Boulder, Colo.: Westview Press, 1987).

and the promise of a political "opening" which would be " 'slow and gradual and secure,' . . . and which basically would consist of substituting the discretionary powers and exceptional acts typical of a dictatorship with 'effective guarantees within a constitutional context.' "[54] In sum, the military authoritarian regime now sought legitimacy in the promise of its own demise—a promise of redemocratization, a return to procedural democracy, when and if the military deemed the Brazilian citizenry "ready" for it—hence, the process's "slow and gradual" nature.

This process of political decompression served as a catalyst for the proliferation of popular and liberation movements, the consolidation of the nascent bourgeois opposition, the remobilization of the militant Left, the crystallization of the legal political opposition, and the expansion of the church's new pastoral mission. For without the more flexible political climate of decompression, the climate of fear that reigned under Médici might have prevailed and dissipated many of the mobilizational initiatives of nascent social movements, including both feminine and feminist movements.

In short, political liberalization represented what McAdam calls a change in the "structure of political opportunities" available to sectors of civil and political society excluded from the pact of domination represented in the military authoritarian regime. According to McAdam, "[m]ovements do not emerge in a vacuum. Rather, they are profoundly shaped by a wide range of environmental factors that condition both the objective possibilities for successful protest as well as the popular perception of insurgent prospects."[55] To be sure, the objective possibilities for political protest and claim making were indeed altered under Geisel as the repressive apparatus of the State was curbed of its excesses and avenues for a would-be dialogue between State and civil society were reopened for the first time since 1968. Popular perception of the possibilities for successful protest also changed drastically with Geisel's *distensão*, as the practitioners of authoritarianism brandished a new democratic discourse. Thus, though *distensão* did not generate popular mobilization, it unquestionably fueled it.

THE PERCEPTION OF WOMEN'S MOVEMENTS AS APOLITICAL

A further consideration is key to our understanding of how conjunctural factors contributed to the emergence of feminist groups and neighborhood-based feminine associations. Within *distensão* and within the process of political liberalization in general, certain social sectors were considered more politi-

---

[54] Bernardo Kucinski, citing President Ernesto Geisel's speech of March 19, 1974, in *Abertura, a História de uma Crise* (São Paulo: Editora Brasil Debates, 1982), p. 20.

[55] McAdam, *Political Process*, p. 11.

cally problematic than others.[56] Thus, while the regime increasingly negotiated with elite sectors of the opposition (MDB politicians, the Brazilian Bar Association, and so on), it continued to repress militant Left, student, and labor organizations, which were seen as more threatening to national security. And here, an age-old stereotype seems to have worked to women's advantage.

The ingrained belief that women are indifferent to politics may have led the military rulers of Brazil to believe that anything women do is intrinsically "apolitical."[57] Thus, even when, as will be seen below, women were organizing campaigns against the rising cost of living or for human rights in Brazil, the military seems to have allowed women's associations greater political leeway than was granted to many other social movement groups.[58] The 1975 celebrations of International Women's Day were thus among the first public assemblies permitted since the mass mobilizations of 1967–1968. The Feminine Amnesty Movement was allowed to organize in the mid-1970s when a "male" movement of that sort might have been actively repressed. In sum, the institutionalized separation between the public and the private may have, in an ironic historical twist, helped propel women to the forefront of the opposition in Brazil.

INTERNATIONAL FEMINIST NETWORKS, INTERNATIONAL DEVELOPMENT
AGENCIES, AND THE GEISEL GOVERNMENT

The Percy Amendment to the U.S. Foreign Assistance Act, enacted by Congress in 1973, and the UN proclamation of the International Women's Decade in 1975, also indirectly legitimated demands for gender equality and generated greater maneuvering room for women within Geisel's policy of *distensão*. Pressured by growing international feminist networks and feminist policy ad-

[56] See Maria Helena Moreira Alves, *Estado e Oposição no Brasil (1964–1984)* 2d ed. (Petrópolis: Vozes, 1984), p. 319.

[57] This stereotypical understanding of women's political participation similarly thrust women into the forefront of opposition struggles in other Latin American authoritarian regimes. In Argentina, for example, it was the Mothers of the Plaza de Mayo, regarded as "crazy women" (*las locas*) by military rulers, who led the struggle for human rights. See Marysa Navarro, "The Personal is Political: Las Madres de Plaza de Mayo in Argentina," in *Power and Popular Protest: Latin American Social Movements*, ed. Susan Eckstein (Berkeley: University of California Press, 1989). On a similar dynamic in Chile in 1973, see Patricia Chuchryk, "Subversive Mothers: The Women's Opposition to Military Rule in Chile," in *Women, the State, and Development*, ed. Sue Ellen M. Charlton, Jane Everett, and Kathleen Standt (Albany: State University of New York Press, 1989). For a comprehensive and provocative analysis of gender politics under authoritarian rule in Chile, see Patricia Chuchryk, "Protest, Politics and Personal Life: The Emergence of Feminism in a Military Dictatorship, Chile 1973–1983" (Ph.D. diss., York University, 1984).

[58] This is not to say that women were spared the brutality of the repressive apparatus of the State. On the gender-specific aspects of State repression, see Ximena Bunster-Burroto, "Surviving Beyond Fear: Women and Torture in Latin America," in *Women and Change in Latin America*, ed. June Nash and Helen I. Sofa (South Hadley, Mass.: Bergin and Garvey, 1986).

vocates in the Third World, the international aid and development establishments began to insist on the "integration of women into development," pointing to women's inequality and "traditional values" as "obstacles" to successful capitalist growth and development.[59]

This new integrationist discourse on women and development was greatly influenced by growing feminist scholarship and by networks being established among women's organizations on a world scale. Liberal feminist studies of women in development, conducted in the early 1970s, noted that women were not reaping the benefits of capitalist development and that, indeed, such development often deprived women of traditional status and power.[60] Remaining squarely within the developmentalist paradigm, most early feminist studies did not question the prevailing assumption that development as such was a progressive process overall. They merely called for women to be integrated into the development process.

Liberal feminist policy advocates in the First World articulated this integrationist call within development foundations and bilateral and multilateral aid policy networks. As Arvonne S. Fraser points out, their lobbying efforts were largely successful.

> [The Percy Amendment] was written by Mildred Marcy, an activist in international women's organizations who was also interested in the work of the U.N. Commission on the Status of Women. It was lobbied through congressional committees by women active in domestic and international women's groups. The Amendment recognized the fact that women in developing countries play a significant role in economic production and the development process, and it required that particular attention be paid to programs, projects and activities which would integrate women into the national economics of their countries, thus improving their status and assisting their total development effort.[61]

Feminist lobbying and extrainstitutional pressures for increased attention to gender inequality on an international scale also influenced the 1967 Declaration on the Elimination of Discrimination against Women and the 1970 Programme of Concerted International Action for the Advancement of Women, both advanced by the UN Commission on the Status of Women,[62] ultimately leading to the First Women's World Conference, held in Mexico City in 1975.

[59] I am indebted to Amy Conger Lind for highlighting this international dimension of the development of women's movements in Latin America. See her "Development as if Women Mattered: The Formation of an Autonomous Women's Movement in Peru" (B.A. thesis, University of California at Santa Cruz, 1988).

[60] Ester Boserup's, *Women's Role in Economic Development* (New York: St. Martin's Press, 1970), broke new ground in the field of development studies. Since then, the study of women's changing status in the Third World has been a burgeoning subfield in development studies.

[61] Arvonne S. Fraser, *The U.N. Decade for Women: Documents and Dialogue* (Boulder, Colo.: Westview Press, 1987), p. 20.

[62] Ibid.

An additional contributing factor was the recognition of a link between women's fertility and women's status. During 1974, UN Population Year, some in the development establishment began to argue that increasing education and employment contributed to decreased fertility. Hence, the new emphasis on women in development in the 1970s was informed more by the desire to overcome "obstacles" to national development and to check the alleged "population explosion" in the Third World than by a normative commitment to gender equality in itself.

Nevertheless, these new international pressures provided women in Brazil and elsewhere in the Third World with two key political resources. New funds poured into the Third World for women's projects and a new developmentalist discourse legitimated emerging claims for increased gender equity. Thus, the international political climate was a fifth factor contributing to the growth of women's movements, even in Brazil's authoritarian context.

CONCLUSION

Changes in Brazilian relations of production and reproduction were *intervening rather than causal* variables in the politicization of gender in Brazilian society. Instead, conjunctural variables such as the redefinition of the church's political role, the rearticulation of the Brazilian Left, the emergence of a bourgeois opposition, and the regime's political liberalization policy all contributed directly to the creation of a *mobilizational infrastructure* upon which various types of women's movements could build and develop during the 1970s.

During the 1970s, moreover, the new integrationist and participatory discourses of the church, the Left, and the feminist-influenced international aid and development establishments provided new ideological rationales for women's growing participation in public life. International pressures on Latin American governments to pay greater attention to the role of women in development also served as a catalyst for women's mobilization, indirectly legitimating the incipient generic claims of early Brazilian feminists.

As we have seen, the new associational contexts in which women began to organize were themselves male-dominant and gender-biased. Thus, while both the progressive church and the militant Left encouraged women's participation and provided new, extrainstitutional networks for women's political participation, they ideologically predefined the parameters of that participation.

The church and the Left reproduced prevailing patterns of gender inequality both ideologically and organizationally. The progressive church continued to adhere to doctrinaire prescriptions about women's reproductive mission, created mothers' clubs that in no way addressed women's specific gender interests and organizationally segregated women from the pursuit of general community interests. And the militant Left largely ignored the gender-specific aspects of revolutionary struggle and also relegated female revolutionaries to a subordinate position within militant organizations. The contradictions inherent in women's participation in these sexist associational contexts eventually triggered the development of gender-conscious political discourses and strategies—providing *mobilizational referents* for the middle- and working-class women who formed the core of the Brazilian feminine and feminist movements during the latter part of the 1970s and early 1980s, as will be seen in the following two chapters.

Finally, Geisel's *distensão* provided the political opportunity space within which that nascent feminist and feminine consciousness could give rise to full-scale social movements. In 1975, Geisel decided to pay lip service to the UN's call for concerted government action toward eradicating gender-based inequality, and allowed Brazilian women to organize meetings, conferences, and demonstrations in commemoration of International Women's Day. Those commemorations, held in Rio and São Paulo in March 1975, sparked the creation of autonomous women's organizations and spurred feminist activism throughout urban Brazil in the ensuing years. Chapter 4 examines the early years of feminist and feminine organizing in authoritarian Brazil.

CHAPTER FOUR

The Genesis of Women's Movements in Authoritarian Brazil, 1964–1978

WOMEN'S organizations flourished in the more flexible political climate that prevailed in Brazil after the mid-1970s. The growing involvement of women in a variety of opposition struggles soon gave rise to new, gender-based political claims. Early organizational efforts among women in São Paulo were isolated and diffuse. The military regime's deliberate demobilization of the population placed severe constraints on their further development. However, political decompression and the proclamation of International Women's Year in 1975 (itself partially a response to the growing international women's movement) abruptly expanded the *opportunity space* available for women's mobilization even when other forms of political protest were still significantly restricted by government repression and censorship.

In the early-to-mid 1970s, when the political space available to the opposition as a whole was narrow, the demands of both feminine and feminist movement organizations were necessarily quite broadly defined. That is, women's movements not only advanced women's gender interests, they also protested the social injustice and political repression so pervasive in authoritarian Brazil. As political liberalization made a wider range of oppositional activities and discourses possible, the women's movements' demands and activities gradually narrowed—increasingly focusing on those issues that specifically concerned *women as women*.

The changing dynamics of Brazilian transition politics thus deeply affected the ways in which women articulated their gender interests. I have argued that practical and strategic gender interests are profoundly shaped by class, race, culture, and other social characteristics. How women's movements conceptualize and pursue gender interests, however, is not exclusively determined by the racial, class, or cultural attributes of movement participants. Rather, as I shall demonstrate in this chapter, the articulation of gender interests is crucially shaped by the specific political-economic environment in which women's movements arise. Women's gender interests are not given structurally; the competing class and gender ideologies and discursive practices prevailing in a given political system at a specific historical conjuncture always shape the content and political articulation of generic claims.

In the 1970s, State repression, exclusionary politics, and economic crisis led Brazilian women to formulate strategic and practical gender interests quite distinct from those advanced by second-wave women's movements in central capitalist nations. And, significantly, generic claims were couched in the language of Marxism and class struggle, then prevalent among the radical sectors of the opposition from which many women's organizations emerged.

This chapter traces the early discourses developed and strategies pursued by women of different social classes in Brazil and examines how the content and direction of gender-based claims were shaped by oppositional ideologies and the political context of authoritarianism in transition. The discussion here centers on the contours of the politicization of gender by feminine and feminist movement organizations in metropolitan São Paulo, though parallel developments elsewhere in urban Brazil will be considered tangentially.

WORKING-CLASS WOMEN AND POLITICAL MOBILIZATION

Though 1975 is frequently cited as the year that second-wave feminine and feminist groups appeared in authoritarian Brazil's major urban centers, many manifestations of gender-based organizing in fact predate that year.[1] Female domestic workers in São Paulo, for example, began organizing for increased labor benefits for their category, founding the Domestic Workers' Association in 1962. In 1964, the Housewives' Association of São Paulo's Eastern Zone, an umbrella organization of poor and working-class women's groups, was created by local women participants in the Catholic Workers' Action (*Ação Católica Operária*) and began mobilizing women to improve the quality of life in their neighborhoods. Throughout the 1960s, women staged sporadic protests against the rising cost of living and organized marches for human rights. Mothers and female relatives of political prisoners began organizing for their release as early as 1965. And during the 1960s and early 1970s, mothers' clubs were created throughout São Paulo's urban periphery as a direct outgrowth of generalized community self-help efforts promoted by development agencies and the Catholic church.

In the early 1970s, these disparate local organizing efforts began to congeal into citywide movements in defense of working-class women's practical gender interests. During 1973, mothers' clubs from the Parish of Vila Remo conducted a survey of consumer prices among local women, giving rise to one of the first contemporary manifestations of "militant motherhood" among working-class women in São Paulo. The results of neighborhood cost-of-living surveys were published in the form of open letters to local government authorities, "denouncing the miserable conditions of life in the urban periphery and demanding the freezing of prices for primary necessities, salary adjustments which would correspond to the real increases in the cost of living, an emergency salary bonus of 25 percent, municipal food distribution centers and fa-

---

[1] For a description of women's associations active in Brazil in the decades between the demise of the suffrage movement and the rise of military authoritarian rule, see Fanny Tabak, *Autoritarismo e Participação Política da Mulher* (Rio de Janeiro: Graal, 1983), pp. 113–32.

cilities for private consumer cooperatives, and day-care centers for working women."[2] The local movement's ideas spread through the urban periphery and a new, more extensive survey was conducted in 1975 (comparing prices of consumer goods in 1973 to those of 1975). These results were published in a second letter, approved by a "People's Assembly: Cost of Living x Minimum Salary," held in June of 1976, and attended by four thousand people—the largest public assembly held anywhere in Brazil since 1968.[3]

Concomittantly, other mothers' clubs in São Paulo's Southern Zone began organizing for public day care. According to one of the day-care movements' core organizers, concern for the rising cost of living went hand in hand with the heightened demand for public child care. As work outside the home became a necessity for many women, mothers' club participants began to think of alternatives that would enable them or other women to enter the paid labor force. Following a strategy similar to the early Cost of Living Movement, women conducted surveys among neighborhood residents to assess their need for child-care facilities.[4] Originally, the demand for day care was rather loosely framed—that is, "the women knew they needed a place to leave their children so they could work but they had little sense of what kind of place that should be and to whom their demands should be directed."[5]

At Jardim Miriam, the day-care movement grew directly out of the local mothers' club, founded in the late 1960s. According to one of the early participants in that club,

> the mothers' club started before any of the other church activities in the neighborhood, before there was even a church to speak of in the neighborhood. . . . The club was started at the initiative of Johnson & Johnson whose sales representatives came to the neighborhood to promote sanitary napkins, teach women to use them, etc. The sales representatives also promoted lectures on women's reproductive cycle, menstruation, and so on. After the Johnson & Johnson people left, we began holding sewing lessons for local women at the church which we combined with lectures on different subjects of interest to women.[6]

[2] Tilman Evers, "Síntesis Interpretativa del 'Movimento do Custo de Vida,' un Movimiento Urbano Brasileño," *Revista Mexicana de Sociología* 43, no. 4 (October–December 1981): 1372–73.

[3] Ibid., p. 1373.

[4] Much of the ensuing discussion of the day-care movement is derived from several formal interviews with Maria Amelia de Almeida Telles, coordinator of the São Paulo Council on the Status of Women's Day Care commission between 1984 and 1987, and one of the core organizers of early feminine and feminist movement organizations in the Greater São Paulo area, from formal and informal interviews with other core organizers of the movement, and from participant-observation at the Jardim Miriam day-care group and at several regional and citywide meetings of dozens of neighborhood-based day-care groups.

[5] Interview with Maria Amelia de Almeida Telles, São Paulo, June 22, 1983.

[6] Interview with two founding members and core organizers of both the local women's group and the day-care group in Jardim Miriam, São Paulo, December 15, 1982.

Participation in the club itself led women to formulate new, gender-related political demands. At meetings, women typically discussed problems encountered in their daily lives, in their marriages, in feeding and caring for their families. Neighborhood women began to value the ability to come together to discuss shared problems and devise collective solutions.

> The mothers' club had existed for a long time before the *creche* [day care] movement began. The women always brought their children to the club meetings and at first, we rotated taking care of them amongst ourselves. Around 1970 or so, we began to think of a place where we could leave our children to be taken care of when we had other things to do . . . discussions continued and the idea emerged to organize a group of women who would go talk to the prefecture. . . . We didn't even know what we would say there, but we went anyway, six of us, and we told them of the need for day care in our neighborhood. Two social workers appeared and suggested we circulate a petition in the neighborhood. So we did.[7]

When the women returned with the petition, signed by over one hundred local residents, the social workers told them that the *Sociedade de Amigos do Bairro* (Society of Friends of the Neighborhood or SAB)[8] was the "official" representative of neighborhood demands and that the women should therefore channel their demand for child care through that local organization.[9]

It was then that the first of several conflicts between the local women's groups and parallel, male-dominated community organizations materialized. The SAB did little to represent local women in their quest for day care—"the demand just stayed there for five whole years, and meanwhile, we were all waiting for the prefecture to come and build a day-care center because we had asked for one. . . . The women in the neighborhood don't participate much in the SAB, it only has five or six female members and they're only there to clean up for the men." Eventually the women realized that they "had been lied to" by the local SAB because, as they put it, "other things were happening in the neighborhood by then that helped us gain political consciousness."[10]

By 1975, the local Roman Catholic church had expanded its activities to include organizing the community for improved urban services. The parish priest saw the continuation of some sort of organized activity among neighborhood women as an opportunity to draw them closer to the church's new apostolic mission. As church-linked organizations blossomed in the neighbor-

---

[7] Ibid.

[8] One of hundreds of such organizations established under populist rule in the 1950s and subordinated as "clients" of local government "patrons."

[9] For a concise discussion of historical and contemporary neighborhood movements, see Paul Singer, "Movimentos de Bairro, in *São Paulo: O Povo em Movimento*, ed. Paul Singer and Vinícius C. Brant (Petrópolis: Vozes; São Paulo: CEBRAP, 1980), pp. 83–107.

[10] Interview with two local organizers of the Jardim Miriam women's group and day-care group, December 15, 1982.

hood, the women active in the mothers' club became the most fervent participants in community struggles. They mobilized around demands for elementary schools, health care facilities, and other community needs, in addition to day care.

Militant opposition groups also began doing grassroots work with these new church-linked organizations. And in response to the worsening living conditions of the popular classes, Christian charity groups also extended their work in the urban periphery. As one of the participants in the women's group explained, "the folks from [a Christian social action group] explained to us how the prefecture functions . . . that if we're there pressuring them, things will happen. If we leave it up to them or to the SAB, we'll never get anything we need in the neighborhood."[11] The women decided to press their demands themselves, without the mediation of the SAB and began organizing weekly trips to the municipal *Secretaria de Bem Estar Social* (Bureau of Social Welfare or SEBES, known as *Familia e Bem Estar Social*, Bureau of the Family and Social Welfare or FABES after 1979).

In the late 1970s, the parish, now headed by a progressive priest, organized a domestic sewing class to more aggressively recruit local women. Local daycare organizers appealed to students in the class, many of whom joined the neighborhood's Struggle for Day Care group. The day-care group also developed solid contacts with social workers at SEBES who kept them informed as to the status of their demand for a day-care center, "we would go there, 15 or 20 or more of us, whenever we thought things were being held up . . . as mothers, we demanded that we had the right to a place to leave our children . . . the folks from Cidade Adhemar [a neighboring villa where women were also organizing for day care] came to talk to us about day care and how it was every mother's right."[12]

The beginning of women's mobilization in Jardim Miriam illustrates four key characteristics shared by other women's groups in São Paulo's urban periphery. First, the women who mobilized for day care and other community improvements were usually housewives or domestic servants. Most had been employed outside the home at some point in their lives or occasionally worked as day workers in the tertiary sector. Women hoped to be freed occasionally from childcare responsibilities in order to undertake other activities, including paid employment—but "working mothers," in this and most other day-care groups in São Paulo, are in the minority in the day-care movement.[13]

Most participants I talked with at Jardim Miriam and elsewhere spoke of

[11] Ibid.

[12] Ibid.

[13] Cynthia Sarti's research on the day-care movement suggests that many movement participants see the creation of *creches* in their neighborhood as a possible source of employment close to home. See her "É Sina Que a Gente Traz (Ser Mulher na Periferia Urbana)" (Master's thesis, University of São Paulo, 1985).

their participation in day-care groups, mothers' clubs, or other women's organizations not in explicitly political terms but in terms of "personal liberation." That is, for many women, participation in community organizations is a pleasant experience, an empowering experience, one that breaks the monotony of their daily housework routines and enables them to "learn about the world" from other women and share their experiences with women whose life conditions parallel their own.[14]

Second, as in most urban neighborhoods, the mothers' club at Jardim Miriam served as the mobilizational base for other gender-related movements, such as the struggle for day care. As women came into increased, regularized contact with one another through mothers' clubs or housewives' associations, they began identifying shared concerns, common needs. Those needs were not defined in terms of the larger political-economic system nor on the basis of an articulate, theoretical, or ideological understanding of the dynamics of that system. Rather, women organized in mothers' clubs developed political claims on the basis of their day-to-day lived experience as women. As full-time residents of the urban periphery, they began to organize for urban improvements, improvements that would facilitate their jobs as wives and mothers. Hence, poor and working-class women spearheaded demands for running water, electricity, and so on in their neighborhoods while, as one woman I talked with noted, "the men were involved in the so-called 'grand' issues of union organizing, but we were around organizing for improvements in our day-to-day life in the neighborhood."[15]

Third, women's groups often lacked support from parallel community organizations, whether these were traditional, clientelistic organizations such as the SABs or male-dominated, church-linked workers' organizations. Many of the mothers' clubs and other women's groups developed a philosophy of "if we don't do it, it won't get done" and became the vanguard of local efforts to improve living conditions in the neighborhoods.

Fourth, the early organizational experience of women's groups in Jardim Miriam points to the critical role played by extracommunity actors in facilitating neighborhood-based political organizing. Popular movement participants from adjoining neighborhoods, charity workers, political activists, and state social workers all furnished key organizational resources and information to local women's self-help efforts in the urban periphery.

However, throughout much of the mid-1970s, organizational efforts among women of the popular classes remained isolated and diffuse and government response to movement demands was virtually nonexistent. As will be seen

[14] See Teresa Caldeira, "Mujeres, Cotidianidad, y Política," in *Ciudadanía a Identidad: Las Mujeres en los Movimientos Sociales Latino-americans*, ed. Elizabeth Jelin (Geneva: UNRISD, 1987) for an excellent discussion of this "personally transformative" dimension of women's participation in community organizations.

[15] Informal interview with a member of the Jardim Miriam women's group, March 20, 1983.

below, it was only after 1974–1975, with the initiation of the federal government's liberalization policies, that neighborhood women's groups proliferated throughout urban Brazil. In the early 1970s, most popular movements were still perceived as potentially subversive by local authorities.

MIDDLE-CLASS WOMEN AND EARLY FEMINIST MOBILIZATION

Parallel to the politicization of mothers' clubs in the urban periphery, signs of a budding feminist consciousness were evident among some middle-class women in São Paulo. By the late 1960s and early 1970s, female participants of student movement organizations and militant organizations of the Left began meeting in small groups, usually to discuss Marxist-feminist texts from the United States and Europe,[16] and an inchoate debate about the nature of women's oppression developed in the alternative press. Preexisting friendship networks of female militants from the days of clandestine resistance were remobilized in the early 1970s and young, university-educated women formed small consciousness-raising groups to discuss these texts and their own lived experience as women.

A few pioneering women journalists and intellectuals, such as Carmen da Silva, Heloneida Studart, Heleieth Saffioti, and Rose Marie Muraro, also began writing about women's condition.[17] Academic women and journalists were thus among the first to address systematically the "woman question." In 1972, the *Conselho Nacional de Mulheres do Brasil* (National Council of Brazilian Women), a still-active first-wave feminist organization, organized the First National Women's Congress in Rio de Janeiro, where several prominent academics presented papers on issues such as "women and work," "women and the law," and "women and development."[18]

The organizers intended to raise public consciousness about discrimination against women in all of these areas. Heleieth Saffioti pointed out that women had decreased as a proportion of the work force since the beginnings of industrialization in Brazil; Rosa Rusomano recalled the history of the suffrage

[16] Among those that received considerable attention in Brazilian Left circles were Juliet Mitchell's "Women: The Longest Revolution," first published in 1969 and then circulating in Brazil as an underground manifesto, see *Women: The Longest Revolution* (London: Virago Press, 1984); and Simone de Beauvoir's *The Second Sex* (New York: Knopf, 1953).

[17] Their early feminist works included Carmen da Silva's articles in the women's magazine, *Claudia,* and her *O Homem e a Mulher no Mundo Moderno* (Rio de Janeiro: Editora Civilização Brasileira, 1969); Rose Marie Muraro, *A Mulher na Construção do Mundo Futuro* (Petrópolis: Vozes, 1966); and Heloneida Studart, *A Mulher, Brinquedo do Homem* (Petrópolis: Vozes, 1969); Heleieth Saffioti, *A Mulher na Sociedade de Classes: Mito e Realidade* (Petrópolis: Vozes, 1976). For a discussion of the impact of these pioneer academic feminists' work, see Heleieth Iara Bongiovani Saffioti, "Feminismos e Seus Frutos no Brasil," in *Movimentos Sociais na Transição Democrática,* ed. Emir Sader (São Paulo: Cortez, 1987), pp. 117–26.

[18] *Estado de São Paulo,* April 25, 1972.

movement in Brazil and decried the fact that forty years after suffrage, women were still grossly underrepresented in the country's political institutions; others discussed the discrimination suffered by women in the liberal professions. Yet even these fairly mild manifestations of feminism aroused the military regime's suspicions of subversion. The principal organizer of the Congress, Dra. Romy Medeiros da Fonseca, a prominent attorney, was questioned by the Rio police on eight different occasions during the preparation of the Congress.[19] And Senator Eurico Resende publicly declared that he thought holding such a Congress was absurd, that he did not see "any discrimination against women in Brazilian law."[20]

Two distinct middle-class women's networks provided the organizational bases for nascent feminism in Brazil: university- and militant opposition-based networks of younger women; and academic- and professional-based networks of older women. As we shall see, both of these networks were mobilized as feminist organizations in the mid-1970s.

From these early manifestations of feminism onward, however, some Brazilians began to distinguish between a "legitimate" Brazilian feminism and that which was merely labeled as "one more instance of ideological imperialism." When noted North American feminist, Betty Friedan, visited Brazil in 1971, at the invitation of Rose Marie Muraro, managing editor of the Vozes editorial house, which published *The Feminine Mystique* in translation,[21] she was ridiculed by both the mainstream and the alternative press as an ugly, bourgeois, man-hater. In a paper delivered at the First National Women's Congress in 1972, Muraro herself denounced Friedan's brand of feminism, arguing that there are

> two types of feminism: an older one, [which is] within the system and favors the system and which pits woman against man, is a neurotic expression of resentment by the dominated—that one merely increases the existing antagonism [against feminism]. More schizophrenia! But there is another which sees women's oppression within a more global social struggle and dialectically synthesizes that struggle for justice. And it is in that sense that I position myself [as a feminist].[22]

Similarly, prominent economist Paul Singer, in an article published in the alternative press in 1973, argued that

> it is necessary that . . . we not merely transplant the feminist problematic developed in industrialized countries to our context. . . . The great majority of Brazilian

[19] Anette Goldberg, "Feminismo em Regime Autoritário: A Experiência do Movimento de Mulheres no Rio de Janeiro" (Paper presented at the XII Congress of the International Political Science Association, Rio de Janeiro, August 9–14, 1982), p. 14.

[20] *Jornal do Brasil*, October 26, 1972. That same year, a panel at the Brazilian Society for the Advancement of Science (*Sociedade Brasileira pelo Progresso da Ciência*) addressed a similar set of women's issues.

[21] Betty Friedan, *A Mística da Feminilidade* (Petrópolis: Vozes, 1971).

[22] Cited in Goldberg, "Feminismo em Regime Autoritário," pp. 14–15.

women do not have the conditions with which to free themselves from economic subjection to their husbands . . . until those conditions are radically altered (and in this men and women are equally interested), the feminist movement in Brazil will have to present itself with the vital problem of women's work, if it does not want to speak in the name of a limited group who, under current circumstances, enjoys a privileged situation.[23]

Thus, at the same time that some middle-class women were beginning to elaborate a critique of existing discrimination against women of all social classes, they were being cautioned against "imperialist feminism" by Brazilian intellectuals and activists on the Left. Muraro's notion of "two feminisms" took hold among the intellectual and political classes in the early 1970s. As Anette Goldberg argues, "the idea that there existed two feminisms began to take shape among intellectuals: one acceptable, which could be invited to take its seat among the forces of the left which attempted to reorganize the country; another, totally unacceptable, alien, the struggle of bourgeois lesbians against men."[24]

THE EXPANSION OF FEMININE AND FEMINIST MOVEMENTS, 1975–1978

When President Geisel's political decompression permitted the public commemoration of International Women's Year in São Paulo, Rio de Janeiro, and Belo Horizonte in 1975, this latter, more politically acceptable feminism (from the point of view of the left-wing political opposition) took full organizational form and came to predominate within the Brazilian feminist movement until the late 1970s. The UN's proclamation of International Women's Year in 1975 and the newly "decompressed" regime's decision to endorse its three basic goals of "Equality, Development, and Peace," enabled women who had been concerned with issues of gender inequality in Brazilian society to organize publicly for the first time. It also supplied the still-politically repressed left-wing opposition with a new "front" or forum for political action.

At the First Meeting of the Community: São Paulo, Its People, Its Problems (*I Encontro da Comunidade: São Paulo, O Povo, e Seus Problemas*) sponsored by the Catholic church and the city's *Sociedades de Amigos do Bairro* in September of 1975, participants called attention to the specific problems confronted by poor and working-class women (such as the lack of adequate maternal-infant health care, and other gender-specific needs) and decided to hold a separate meeting to honor Paulista women during International Women's Year: "the best way [to do this] would be to identify and debate [women's] lives, their problems in the home, in their workplace, their health, their

[23] Paul Singer, "Caminhos Brasileiros para o Movimento Feminista," *Opinião* 24 (April 16, 1973), cited in Goldberg, "Feminismo em Regime Autoritário," pp. 17–18.
[24] Goldberg, "Feminismo em Regime Autoritário," p. 23.

education, their participation in society, their responsibilities.''[25] Under the sponsorship of UNESCO and the Metropolitan Episcopal Tribunal of São Paulo, the *Encontro para o Diagnóstico da Mulher Paulista* (Meeting for the Diagnosis of Women in São Paulo) was held in October of 1975.

Attended by only thirty or forty people, among them members of neighborhood associations, unions, church-linked associations, political parties, research and academic institutions, the Encontro nevertheless represented the first step in the articulation of women's political claims on a citywide level. The discussions centered around five topics: "Women's Participation in Society," "Women and Work," "Women and the Law," "Women and Education," and "Women and Health."

The final document resulting from these discussions identified a set of issues for further debate, research, and political action—issues that centered on working-class women's practical gender interests. Among these were the need to promote women's greater participation in public life and in community associations because "it is necessary that we sensitize the women in our city, in our country . . . so that they will perceive that we will never be able to survive if we are not all united, men and women, those with greater consciousness, those with lesser consciousness.''[26] The final document also stressed the need to disseminate information about the discrimination suffered by women in the workplace and the legal rights of women workers and to promote job training opportunities for women:

> because only when woman gains consciousness [of these discriminations], the moment she learns to value her work outside the home, to demand increased participation in the workforce in more qualified job categories, to not be contented with salaries inferior to those of men for equal work because by doing so she is contributing to lowering the salaries of all workers, then she will be on the road to true emancipation, the emancipation of humanity.[27]

The demand for day care, heretofore voiced by isolated neighborhood women's groups, was raised as one of the proposals for action for all Paulista community associations.

> We must activate all competent channels in the sense of making society assume the responsibility for tasks that are of interest to all but which have been over-burdening working women: a) a society which wishes to reproduce itself must create the means for this. It is therefore necessary to create public *creches* (child-care centers) to attend to the needs of working-class families; b) [we call for] a new division of labor between men and women within the home.[28]

[25] Commissão Organizadora "Encontro para o Diagnóstico da Mulher Paulista," *Carta-Proposta da Mulher Paulista*, São Paulo, December 1975 (Pamphlet), p. 1.
[26] Ibid.
[27] Ibid.
[28] Ibid.

Other demands set forth during this historic meeting included: the need for research and debate to identify more adequate legislation on women's rights within marriage, the family, and the labor market; the organization of study groups, meetings, lectures, and courses that would question the discrimination between the sexes in education and propose alternatives; and the promotion of more adequate health care for pregnant women.

The list of demands emanating from this first citywide meeting of Paulista women did not depart significantly from the orthodox Marxist understanding of how the "woman question" should be addressed, an understanding shared by the progressive church activists, leftist militants, radical academics, and grassroots organizers present at the Encontro Diagnóstico and by radical sectors of the opposition in general—including many militant women. The orthodox view might be summarized as follows: inequality between the sexes originates with private ownership of the means of production and the sexual division of labor; therefore, women's subordination can only be overcome through anticapitalist struggle and socialist transformation.[29] The practical implications of this theoretical view can be characterized as *integrationist*: women must be *integrated* into the paid work force so they can gain class consciousness *and incorporated* into the revolutionary struggle so they eventually can help secure their own liberation as women.

Not surprisingly, given the authoritarian and repressive nature of the regime at this conjuncture (in spite of decompression), most demands arising from the Encontro were aimed at parallel organizations of civil society rather than at the political apparatuses of the State. And in keeping with Singer and Muraro's admonitions about "inappropriate" feminisms, all proposed areas of action and research centered on the "vital problem of women's work" and stressed the need for women to organize "within a more global social strug-

[29] In a study of several socialist states, Maxine Molyneux found remarkable uniformity in official ideology regarding the woman question. She argues that

"the uniformity in these theories of women's emancipation is to be found in the historical formation and subsequent reproduction of the orthodox communist position on women. This position was not a simple transposition from Marxist classics: the writings of Marx, Engels, and Lenin on women were fragmentary and in some ways inconsistent. What has been created is a selective canonization of their observations to produce an apparently coherent theory. Just as in the aftermath of Lenin's death an orthodox corpus called 'Marxism-Leninism' was created in Moscow and disseminated throughout the international Communist movement, so an orthodox position on women was also developed, based on an instrumental reading of the classical texts and on the official codifications of the early period of the Third International" ("Socialist Societies Old and New: Progress Toward Women's Emancipation?" *Monthly Review* 34, no. 3 (July–August 1982): 66–67).

For a critique of the orthodox view from a socialist feminist perspective, see Sheila Rowbotham, Lynne Segal, and Hilary Wainwright, *Beyond the Fragments: Feminism and the Making of Socialism* (London: Merlin Press, 1979). For a critical account of the evolution of communist thought on women's emancipation in Brazil, see Zuleika Alambert, *O Marxismo e a Questão da Mulher* (São Paulo: Nobel, 1986).

gle," thus negating any need for women to organize around both practical and strategic gender interests *as women as well as as workers*. The Christian and secular Left, then, became the silent interlocutors of the early women's movement in São Paulo. That is, women's movement activists constantly were engaged in an implicit, unspoken dialogue and debate over the church's and the militant Left's conceptions of women's proper role in politics and the primacy of class versus gender struggle.[30]

The conclusions of the Encontro centered almost exclusively on the economic dimension of the discrimination suffered by women.[31] And this dimension became the focus of the *Centro de Desenvolvimento da Mulher Brasileira* (Center for the Development of Brazilian Women or CDMB), the organization founded by some Encontro participants to advance the proposals there formulated, and of other middle-class–based feminist organizations created in the following months. The feminist label was avoided throughout the presentations and excluded from the concluding document in spite of the fact that some of the participants had begun to think of themselves as *feministas*. A few women who did not agree with this economistic focus joined women then organizing for a day-care center at the University of São Paulo to form the short-lived dissident group, *Mulheres em Questão* (Women in Question).[32]

Also in October of 1975, the first women's newspaper of the contemporary women's movement in Brazil, called *Brasil Mulher* (Brazil Woman) was founded in the city of Londrina in the state of Paraná.[33] Linked to the *Movimento Feminino pela Anistia* (Feminine Amnesty Movement or MFA) and created by recently released female political prisoners, the newspaper's first issues focused on women's insertion into movements for general social and political change, most especially on the need for women to organize at the grassroots level for political amnesty, and privileged working-class women, the "third class citizens" of Brazilian society, as their target audience.

> This is not a woman's newspaper. Its objective is to be one more voice in the search for and reconquest of lost equality. Work which is destined for both men and women. We don't want to take refuge in biological differences in order to enjoy

---

[30] I am indebted to my friend and colleague, Patricia Chuchryk for the concept of silent interlocutors. She makes a similar argument about the relationship between feminism and the Left in contemporary Chile in her "Protest, Politics and Personal Life: The Emergence of Feminism in a Military Dictatorship, Chile 1973–1983" (Ph.D. diss., York University, 1984).

[31] Moraes Nehring argues that this economistic focus was the result of the fact that the "political space [of the Encontro] was occupied by the orthodox communist political current . . . which had been saved from the repressive terror precisely because of its opposition to the armed struggle and which did not reject, as the New Left had incorrectly rejected for a period of time, the legal opportunities for political work." Maria Lygia Quartim de Moraes Nehring, "Familia e Feminismo: Reflexões sobre Papeis Femininos na Imprensa para Mulheres" (Ph.D. diss., University of São Paulo, 1981), p. 203.

[32] Moraes Nehring, "Familia e Feminismo," p. 207.

[33] According to one of my interviewees, Londrina became a kind of cultural center and political refuge for Paulista left-wing activists in the early-to-mid-1970s.

small masculine favors, at the same time that the State, constituted in masculine form, leaves us in a place comparable to that reserved for the mentally incompetent. We want to speak of the problems that are common to all the women of the world. We also want to speak of the solutions which have been found both here and in distant places; nevertheless, we want to discuss them within the context of our Brazilian and Latin American reality.[34]

During late 1975 and early 1976, the CDMB held a series of debates on the woman question at the Journalists' Union in São Paulo. A group of university women and former student movement activists who were present at those debates decided to start a women's newspaper in São Paulo, founding *Nós Mulheres* (We Women) in early 1976. *Nós Mulheres* was the first group in contemporary Brazil openly to refer to itself as feminist. They, like *Brasil Mulher*, targeted poor and working-class women as their principal readership, but from the beginning, the *Nós Mulheres'* editorials and feature stories emphasized the specificity of women's oppression within class exploitation:

WE WOMEN are oppressed because we are women. But even amongst us there exist differences. A large number of women work a double shift: they work outside the home and perform domestic labor. Others only perform domestic tasks. But even among housewives differences persist. There are those who are not obliged to spend all day doing housework because they have money to pay someone to do it for them. . . . The majority of housewives, however, are obliged to spend all day washing, ironing, cleaning, cooking, caring for children, in work that never ends. Many cannot even feed their children or educate them adequately. . . . We want to change this situation. We believe that WE WOMEN struggle so that we can prepare ourselves, like men, to confront life. So that we can earn equal pay for equal work. So that society as a whole recognizes that our children are the generation of tomorrow and that their care is the responsibility of everyone and not just of women. It is possible that we will be asked: "But if these women want all of this, who will take care of children and the home?" We will answer: Domestic labor and the care of children is necessary work, because no one eats uncooked food, goes around dirty, or can leave their children abandoned. We therefore want good *creches* and schools for our children, collective laundries and restaurants at popular prices, so that we can, together with men, undertake the responsibilities of society. . . . WE WOMEN want to struggle for a more just society, together with men, where all will be able to eat, study, work in respectable jobs, have fun, have a place to live, decent shoes and clothing. And, because of this we do not separate women's struggle from the struggle of all people, men and women, for their emancipation.[35]

And the women of *Nós Mulheres*, unlike the early organizers of *Brasil Mulher*, also stressed that women must organize their own political space within the general struggle for emancipation and stressed the need for a feminist press

---

[34] Editorial, *Brasil Mulher*, 1, no. 0 (October 1975).
[35] Editorial, *Nós Mulheres* 1 (June 1976), emphasis added.

within the alternative press that existed at that time: "WE WOMEN decided to create this feminist journal so that we can have our own space, to discuss our situation and our problems. And also, to think about solutions together. . . . There are few democratic tribunals in which women (and not just women) can express their opinions today, either in relation to the general problems of society or their specific problems as women."[36]

After 1975, these two newspapers became the principal voices of the nascent feminist movement in Brazil. Through the Feminine Amnesty Movement's political network, *Brasil Mulher* created subgroups in several major cities during the mid-to-late 1970s and later in 1976 also openly embraced the political banners of feminism. *Brasil Mulher* later moved its production headquarters to São Paulo, breaking with the Feminine Amnesty Movement,[37] and joined with *Nós Mulheres* and the CDMB, to form the core of the Paulista feminist movement until the late 1970s.

Most of the feminists I interviewed in the early 1980s recalled the years from 1975 to 1978 as a time of very elementary, undefined feminism, essentially economistic and confined to established Marxist categories of analysis. The principal question confronting the women interested in organizing women around the discriminations they suffered was how to link women's struggle to class struggle, women's *specific* needs with the need for *general* social transformation (which Brazilian feminist activists typically refer to as the tension between *o geral* and *o específico*). And the question was largely resolved either by prioritizing the general and subsuming the specific until "after the revolution" or, more commonly, by trying to "feminize" popular struggles.

[W]e thought we couldn't raise the issue of contraception, for example, and call it feminist . . . we thought the struggle was a struggle for "rights" because the women in the periphery were involved in the struggle for running water, for day care, for schools, etc., because they were working with the values they had in terms of their roles as women. So our role [in *Brasil Mulher*] in those struggles was to "feminize" them . . . that was our theory . . . our role was to reflect upon why they, [working class women], were involved in that type of struggle . . . we saw ourselves as the vanguard . . . we were the ones with the information, the ones who could reflect and theorize, and our role was to support women's organizations wherever they emerged and help women develop an analysis about why it was women who were engaged in those day-to-day survival struggles.[38]

Feminists I talked with differed in their assessment of early feminist ties to the clandestine oppositon (both the "old" Communist Party Left and the mil-

[36] Ibid.

[37] Therezinha Zerbini, the "founding mother" of the Amnesty Movement, disagreed with some of the more radical feminist issues, which she perceived to be antimale. The MFA subsequently started its own newspaper.

[38] Interview with one of the early participants of *Brasil Mulher*, São Paulo, August 18, 1983.

itant Left of the late 1960s). Some referred to the early feminist groups as mere "transmission belts" for left-wing organizations or as "screens" or "fronts" for parties still legally banned. Most suggested that the individual women who became the core organizers of early groups continued to be active in underground organizations as well as feminist groups and often "pulled their party's line" in debates about feminist organizational priorities—"those priorities, the questions of prioritizing the general over the specific or vice versa, were the ones that divided us . . . those were the sources of our disagreements and ideological and political disputes . . . our feminism was very incipient, very elementary . . . but our views on 'general' social change were ingrained through years of political practice."[39]

In fact, many feminists told me that they initially joined the early groups out of a sense "of wanting to do a different kind of political work, to work with women" or because "friends and former *companheiras* had joined" rather than as a consequence of "personal reflections about my own situation as a woman or any systematic understanding of feminism as such." Each of the early feminist organizations in São Paulo brought distinct opposition political tendencies together; two or three clandestine female opposition networks tended to predominate within a particular feminist group.

Thus, the Brazilian Left, though still underground, afforded a critical organizational base for the budding feminist movement. Friendship networks established among young women active in the underground Left during the late 1960s and early 1970s and the national organizational networks of the resistance greatly facilitated the expansion of feminist organizations in the mid-1970s. And the discourses and analyses of the Marxist Left also provided the ideological framework in which feminist claims initially were couched.

Early feminists saw themselves as the "vanguard" of what was to be a united, cross-class, mass-based women's movement in Brazil. And the prevailing conceptualization of their vanguard role grew directly out of the ideology and practice of the various ideological "tendencies" within the Brazilian Left of the 1960s and 1970s. The legacy of the Left led early feminists to concentrate on understanding women's oppression exclusively in class terms and to try to promote the expansion of the grassroots women's movement that by the mid-1970s was making its presence felt throughout the urban periphery. Nineteen seventy-five to 1978, then, was a period of feminist ideology and activism in São Paulo that Moraes Nehring termed "the other woman's feminism"—*o feminismo da outra*—a feminism deductively derived from socialist conceptualizations of the world which led middle-class movement participants to prioritize the struggles of poor and working-class women, and precluded any systematic reflection on their own lives or on the gender-specific issues they shared with working-class women (which might have constituted a more

---

[39] Interview with two early participants of *Nós Mulheres* and *Brasil Mulher*, August 18, 1983.

organic basis for cross-class alliance-building).[40] Feminist political action during this period focused on working with poor and working-class women's groups in the urban periphery, distributing and discussing the feminist newspapers with women of the popular classes, and assisting these women in their community struggles.

In fact, new feminine movement groups sprang up throughout São Paulo after 1975 and their struggles *did* center on the material conditions of women's lives in the urban periphery. After the *Encontro Diagnóstico*, the church vigorously promoted the creation of mothers' clubs or other organized activities among women of the popular classes.[41] Left-wing political organizations also became more involved in working with poor and working-class women, and with the Cost of Living Movement which, by 1976–1977, was at its mobilizational peak.

In August of 1977, the Cost of Living Movement called its first national convention, adopting the official name, *Movimento do Custo de Vida* (Cost of Living Movement or MCV). With over seven hundred representatives present, the movement elected a central coordination and elaborated an open letter to President Geisel, demanding "the freezing of prices for items of primary necessity, an increase in wages above the cost of living, and an immediate salary bonus . . . for all categories of workers."[42] In March of 1978, at a popular assembly of more than five thousand people, the MCV launched a nationwide petition drive against the rising cost of living, mobilizing tens of thousands of persons, mostly female participants in mothers' clubs and community organi-

[40] Moraes Nehring, "Família e Feminismo," provides an excellent, detailed analysis of the evolution of feminist political thought and practice in São Paulo that highlights this "other" aspect of early Brazilian feminism. Most major documents of the early years of the feminist movement in São Paulo are fully reproduced in her dissertation.

[41] *Rede Mulher*, an action-research organization created in São Paulo in 1983, has collected extensive data on mothers' clubs and housewives' associations in São Paulo's Eastern and Southern Zones, in collaboration with the women's group participants themselves. Their data suggest that whereas only a dozen or so such groups existed in the Eastern Zone before 1975, after International Women's Year and the articulation of the "woman question" at a citywide level, dozens of new groups were created in the urban periphery. The year 1979 was another big organizational "take-off" year for women's organizations among the popular classes, for reasons that will become clear below. For more specific data on women's groups in the urban periphery, see Rede Mulher, " 'Retrato' dos Clubes de Mães e Grupos de Mulheres da Zona Leste de São Paulo," Pesquisa-Avaliação dos Clubes e Grupos de Mães da Cidade de São Paulo, Documento no. 3, June 1985 (Mimeograph).

[42] Tilman Evers provides a comprehensive discussion of the cost-of-living movement, which is also unusually sensitive to its gender-specific content, in "Síntesis Interpretativa del 'Movimiento do Custo de Vida,' un Movimiento Urbano Brasileño," *Revista Mexicana de Sociología* 43, no. 4 (October-December 1981). Evers notes that after the centralization of the movement at the national level, it paid significantly less attention to the gender-specific issues, such as day care, initially raised by the mothers' clubs and housewives' associations that gave birth to the movement.

zations, throughout Brazil. The MCV collected 1.25 million signatures and delivered the petition to the president of the republic in August of 1978.[43]

Tilman Evers notes that by focusing on consumption rather than production, the MCV presented itself as "apolitical" or "above politics." Traditional symbols of "militant motherhood" such as empty pots and pans were frequently used to emphasize this tactical aspect of the movements' political mobilization. In October of 1979, the MCV organized five simultaneous regional protest actions, featuring the banging of empty pots and pans by the "mothers of Brazil who could not feed their children."[44]

The mid-to-late 1970s also saw the expansion of popular mobilization for day care. By 1975 and 1976, groups of ninety to one hundred women regularly staged protests at the *Secretaria de Bem Estar Social* (SEBES) to demand public child-care centers for their neighborhoods. The women sought and gained the support of Dom Paulo Evaristo Arns, the progressive archbishop of São Paulo. He formally agreed to present their demands to the municipal Bureau of Social Welfare. After Dom Paulo's intervention, the secretary of SEBES announced that he was willing to consider the construction of up to six hundred day-care centers in São Paulo. The official proposal was to procure material support for day-care centers that would then be run and staffed by local day-care groups.[45]

The political strategy of the day-care movement continued to be much the same as that pursued by groups in the early 1970s—"we would go directly to the SEBES or to its regional branches with dozens of women. We would always take petitions signed by neighborhood residents who needed day care so they could work, surveys identifying the number of children in each neighborhood who were in need of day care." A couple of the local day-care groups decided to accept the SEBES's proposal of administering their own day-care center through contractual agreements with local government agencies, but "it was a disaster . . . we just didn't have the resources . . . the SEBES gave us a per capita allowance for each child but the maintenance of the building was up to the community. . . . [I]t was then that we began to think that what we needed were day-care centers administered with community participation but fully financed and constructed by the State."[46]

---

[43] The Geisel administration claimed that many of the signatures were forged and that the MCV was influenced by "subversives." See Tilman Evers, "Síntesis Interpretativa," pp. 1373–75.

[44] On the strategies and tactics of the MCV, see Tilman Evers, "Síntesis Interpretativa," pp. 1374–87. He argues that with the reemergence of militant union activism in São Paulo and other major Brazilian cities after 1978, the election of two of the MCV's principal leaders to the state and federal legislatures in the November 1978 elections, and the new political conjuncture initiated by Figueiredo in 1979, the MCV gradually lost its strategic importance as a cross-class, "consumer" movement.

[45] Interview with one of the core organizers of one of the first day-care groups in São Paulo's Southern Zone, São Paulo, June 22, 1983.

[46] Ibid.

The woman who recounted the above early history of the day-care movement was also a founding member of *Brasil Mulher*. Like other women active in Paulista feminist groups during 1975 to 1978, she worked intensively with women's groups in the urban periphery, assisting them in their organizational efforts, facilitating their access to organizational resources, and educating them about the workings of the local State apparatus. As another early feminist activist put it:

> We all had contacts with women in the *periferia*, but, as an organization, we never worked jointly with popular women because our political work in the urban periphery was informed by our various ties to the organized Left . . . *Brasil Mulher was* a women's organization . . . not a left-wing front . . . but we never discussed the fact that we were a left-wing "federation" . . . that never passed through our minds . . . explicit discussions of political tendencies were not prevalent in our collective.[47]

Feminist meetings often consisted of reports on the progress of this or that day-care movement or cost of living movement group in various peripheral neighborhoods. Early feminist groups thus functioned as de facto organizational umbrellas for a wide variety of political activities, principally among women of the popular classes. Both feminist newspapers from 1975 to 1978 featured interviews with women factory workers, domestic servants, metalworkers, agricultural workers, and other "working women," in spite of the fact that, as Moraes Nehring points out, feminists' principal organizational contacts were among mothers' clubs and housewives' associations, most of whose participants did not work outside the home.[48] Issue after issue of both *Nós Mulheres* and *Brasil Mulher* recounted the "advance" of the day-care movement, the cost of living movement, and the burgeoning amnesty movement. Feminists ascribed ideological significance to popular women's struggles. As the day-care, cost of living, and feminine amnesty movements grew, so did feminist determination to capture the political significance of those struggles and to articulate them within the larger opposition.

But there was another important dimension of popular women's organizations, a dimension that some feminists began to perceive as they worked more closely with feminine groups. The rise of women's organizations in the urban periphery provided a new context within which poor and working-class women could share their experiences not only as residents of the *periferia*, but also as wives, mothers, lovers, *as women*. When given the opportunity or the ideological space, participants in feminine movement groups often discussed problems they shared about their marriages, their sexual lives, their desire to control fertility, their thirst for more information about the world outside the

---

[47] Interview with another early member of Brasil Mulher, August 18, 1983.

[48] Moraes Nehring, "Família e Feminismo," pp. 201–3. Moraes Nehring devotes a section of her dissertation to the analysis of the feminist press (see pp. 286–305).

domestic sphere to which they were usually confined, their relationships to family and community—subjects that middle-class feminists themselves initially thought would be taboo among women of the popular classes.

During meetings I witnessed at Jardim Miriam and other working-class neighborhoods, women typically would only talk about these kinds of problems when neither the priest (or in some cases, the nun) nor other men were present, when they were in their own woman's space in the neighborhood. In urban Brazil, there were and are very few places where women of the popular classes can meet for social or leisure activities. Men congregate in the corner bars that dot the urban landscape of all cities; they drink *cachaça* and *cafezinhos*, and talk about politics, work, and soccer. Outside of the church, women have no equivalent social space in the neighborhood.

Many women I talked with at Jardim Miriam and other peripheral neighborhoods told me, for example, that their husbands did not want them to participate in community activities. One woman explained to Teresa Caldeira that this was "because a woman who participates is the owner of her own nose" ("*A mulher que participa é dona de seu nariz*") and that often generated new conflicts in their marriages.[49] While the feminist press was trying to portray women's struggle as part of the "united struggle of men and women of the popular classes for a better life," the working-class women they interviewed continually demonstrated that they were fully conscious of the fact that their gender constrained their lives in ways they did not share with men of their class. When *Brasil Mulher* published the results of the First Congress of Women Metalworkers, held in 1978, for example, the interviewees themselves stressed the specificity of women's oppression within class exploitation more clearly than the feminist journalists who covered the event.

> There's no unity among the women. The men are stronger, and that's why women are on the bottom. . . . They are all men and they protect one another. . . . The owner of the factory is a man and he thinks men work more. . . . Woman works in the factory and in the home, she gets more worn out, she ages. And he sits around looking like a doll. . . . Men only do housework when they don't have a woman to do it for them. . . . I think housework should be divided between husband and wife if the woman works outside the home.[50]

By 1977 to 1978, some São Paulo feminists were also beginning to differentiate socialist feminist political analysis and practice from that of the orthodox Left, to explain women's subordination in both class- and gender-specific terms. As Moraes Nehring notes, "to the extent that our work in the distribution of the newspaper [*Nós Mulheres*] was also a moment for discussion and consciousness-raising (*conscientização*) with the women's groups with which

[49] Teresa Caldeira, personal communication to author.
[50] *Brasil Mulher* 2, no. 11 (March 1978).

we had contact, the result was that, little by little, we confirmed, in practice, the universality of certain sensations: the uneasiness or unrest of 'being female'; the feeling of suffering some injustice without necessarily exactly understanding its proportions.''[51] Feminist political practice, then, gave rise to new, inductively derived, theoretical insights, new political formulations of the woman question in Brazil, a homegrown political ideology that some feminists proudly began to defend. In a 1977 editorial, the women of *Nós Mulheres* explained how they understood feminism to be connected inextricably to the larger struggles for justice and democracy in Brazilian society.

> The following phrases are commonly heard these days from the most varied people, including some truly democratic women: "Feminism is not a struggle for underdeveloped nations like ours" or "The struggle for feminine emancipation is important, but the struggle for the emancipation of workers is much more important." . . . The tendency for all of us, feminist women, is to respond to this question in a defensive fashion: "We do not separate the struggle for women's emancipation from the broader struggle for the emancipation of humanity in general." Defensive because, in saying this, we are merely wanting to demonstrate that we are not against men, that we are not against this or that. That is, we say what we are not and what we do not think, but we do not define clearly what we mean by feminine emancipation, by the emancipation of humanity, and the connection that exists between the two. . . . [For us], struggling so that women contribute actively, together with men, to the transformation of society, is also struggling for women's emancipation. The struggle for women's emancipation then, is an integral part of the struggle for a more just, democratic society.[52]

The editorial also turned the question of "how is feminism related to the class struggle?" so prevalent among left-wing activists, intellectuals, and some feminists, *on its head*, to ask, "how is the class struggle related to the true liberation of women?"

> The fact is that the feminist struggle is not just that, it goes beyond that. Woman also suffers a specific oppression because of the simple fact of being a woman. She has more difficulty finding employment, especially if she is married and has children, she is dismissed from work if she marries or gets pregnant, when she works outside the home, she works a double shift, she is solely responsible for domestic work and for the education of her children (a task which should, in many cases, be assumed by the State, and in others, by the couple). She constantly suffers from sexual assault, in the home, in the street, in the workplace. In sum, woman is not treated as a being with the same rights and the same duties as men. . . . There are many men who think that woman is and should be treated like a being equal to men. But it is only women, because this affects them directly, organized and struggling for the

[51] Moraes Nehring, "Família e Feminismo," p. 296.
[52] Editorial, *Nós Mulheres* 6 (August–September 1977).

specific revindications, who will have the necessary strength to change this situation. . . . We know that only in a society which guarantees good conditions of existence, of work, of study, and liberty and independence to organize freely. . . . will the conditions be present to reach true emancipation for women. In that sense, it can also be said that the struggle for that type of society is an integral part of the struggle for women's emancipation.[53]

After 1975, International Women's Day (IWD) became a peak mobilizational moment for both feminine and feminist movement groups. Planned by the feminist groups in collaboration with the mothers' clubs and housewives' associations with which they had ongoing work, the March 8 commemorations, along with the feminist and the alternative press, served as the principal forums for public protests against the discriminations suffered by the "women at the bottom of the bottom" of Brazilian society. And in 1978, the International Women's Day commemorations began reflecting the changing conceptions of both feminine and feminist understandings of women's interests.

Along with the gamut of issues concerning the "feminine" side of the Brazilian class struggle (women's important role in the struggle for democracy, political amnesty, the rising cost of living, improved social services and urban infrastructure, the need for a more just distribution of income, the lack of equal pay for equal work, and so on), women's movements began calling attention to the politics of the private sphere, the politics of the family and reproduction.

> Women's principal function in the society in which we live is still the reproduction, rearing and education of their children, who will be the future workers [of Brazil]. For their domestic labor, women receive no remuneration, but that does not negate the fact that with their labor they are complementing the salary of their husband or mate. And in spite of the fact that they perform this invisible, but fundamental work for society on a daily basis, they have no legal protection nor are they protected by the State.[54]

The 1978 IWD celebrations served as the basis for an emerging women's political platform. Participants demanded changes in the laws regulating marriage; State support for female heads-of-household; the socialization of domestic labor through the creation of day-care centers, recreation centers, and schools which would operate full-time and serve meals to children; public laundries and restaurants; and State-sponsored consumer collectives. They protested the government's proposed "family planning" programs as antinatalist and claimed that population control would only result from a more just distribution of wealth in Brazilian society and improved health care for women

[53] Ibid.
[54] "Encarte Especial—Por Liberdades Democráticas," *Brasil Mulher* 3, no. 12 (May 1978).

at all stages of their lives and that "the knowledge and use of contraceptive methods should be a conquest of women themselves."[55]

New feminist groups arose throughout 1978, a reflection of the increased social and political reach of Brazilian feminism and of the diversification and expansion of prevailing definitions of the nature and content of "feminist struggle." *Nós Mulheres* split into two groups, one which retained the original name and proposed to continue publishing *Nós Mulheres*, and another, the *Associação das Mulheres* (Women's Association), which wanted to expand the earlier group's activities and social base to include greater contact with women of the popular classes.

Most of the women with whom I spoke understood this "split" in clear, political or ideological terms. The women who created the *Associação*, I was told, were more directly involved in *dupla militancia* (double militancy) in feminist groups and party organizations and insisted on the necessity for feminist "vanguardist" work among women in the urban periphery. The women who chose to stay with *Nós Mulheres* wanted to deepen their analysis of the specificity of women's oppression within all social classes, emphasizing "inward-oriented" activities centered on their own subordinate status.

Another feminist group created in São Paulo in 1978, the *Grupo Feminista 8 de Março* (March 8 Feminist Group), also wanted to redefine feminism in ways that would enhance its relevance to Brazilian society as well as highlight its specificity as a distinct form of social struggle. In a document elaborated in late 1978, the group criticized "the sexist and radical character of the first European and North American feminist movements" but argued that most contemporary Brazilian feminist groups were also misguided. They erred "in taking on the general struggles of the community (like day care, better living conditions, sewage, running water, etc.) as if they were women's specific struggles. The major problem with this attitude resides in the fact that to view these struggles as specifically feminist struggles, deprives feminism of any specific characteristics, since these struggles should be assumed by the community as a whole."[56] After arguing for a more complex understanding of the relationship between capitalism and male domination, the *Grupo Feminista* document concludes by identifying what they believed to be Brazilian feminism's key political priorities: "[T]he principal feminist struggle is to modify the distorted image of woman, helping her to gain consciousness so that she can free herself as a thinking being, who acts and produces. That she will come to 'exist'. And such existence will imply a general change in the norms and behavior of society."[57]

---

[55] Ibid. The movements' elaboration of a "reproductive rights" discourse will be discussed at length in chapter 8 below.

[56] "O Movimento de Mulheres no Brasil," *Cadernos da Associação das Mulheres*, 3 (August 1979): 74–75.

[57] Ibid., p. 82.

Another new development within the movement was the creation of a feminist organization with a service orientation and fairly specific issue-focus, in contrast to the "generic" political activities and demands of most of the groups created in 1975–1976. *Pró-Mulher* (Pro-Woman), founded in late 1977, hoped to furnish women with medical, psychological, legal, professional, and educational counseling and orientation and offer courses and lectures on these subjects to any interested organizations. It would also undertake research on women's inequality in both the private and public spheres and bring the results to the attention of public policy makers and the media.[58]

The feminine strand of the Brazilian women's movement also had greatly expanded by 1978. Women in the newly militant trade union movement held congresses for women in various occupational categories. In January of 1978, the First Congress of Women Metalworkers was held in Osasco and in June of that year, women in the chemical and pharmaceutical industries held their first congress. Like the feminist-initiated March 8 commemorations and other movement events, these congresses protested the *general* conditions of the Brazilian working class and decried the unjust and unequal *specific* conditions of women's work within the secondary sector. Union women denounced the lack of equal pay for equal work, the lack of opportunity for women to ascend the occupational ladder within their factories, the fact that women were the last hired and the first fired (especially if they married or became pregnant), and the blatant disregard of gender-specific labor legislation which established female workers' rights to paid maternity leave and *creches* in the workplace. And they called for the establishment of women's departments within the unions so that these demands could be pursued actively by women workers themselves.[59]

As we saw above, 1978 was also a peak year for the Cost of Living Movement and the Feminine Amnesty Movement. New women's groups, with a more activist orientation than the earlier mothers' clubs, were created throughout São Paulo's urban periphery. And more of those groups began demanding public day care for their neighborhoods.

The increase in feminist and feminine mobilization in São Paulo, and throughout Brazil, by 1978, is, at least in part, attributable to what was termed the rebirth of civil society during the late 1970s, which created new chains of political opportunity. Geisel's political decompression generated greater political space for the expression of opposition demands and the worsening economic crisis confronting the nation increased the militancy of Brazilian workers.

The "new trade unionism" (*novo sindicalismo*) gained center stage within

[58] *Nós Mulheres* 7 (March 1978): 4.

[59] For a description of these two congresses, see *Nós Mulheres* 7 (March 1978): 8, and 8 (June–July 1978): 10; *Brasil Mulher* 3, no. 11 (March 1978): 4–10, and 3, no. 13 (June 1978): 13.

the opposition during 1978. Auto workers staged work stoppages in the Saab-Scania plant in São Bernardo do Campo and these "cross-armed strikes" spread throughout the auto industry in the ABCD region of Greater São Paulo (composed of Santo Andre, São Bernardo, São Caetano, and Diadema, the country's industrial heartland), and soon extended into other major industrial centers.[60] The workers won only limited concessions from the government and industrial capitalists, but they gained a prominent place among the organized sectors of civil society challenging authoritarian rule. The strikes (which continued throughout 1979 and 1980) also increased the ties of solidarity between the workers' movement and the grassroots opposition, especially church-linked organizations of various types,[61] and called the attention of elite opposition sectors, such as the Brazilian Bar Association, to the plight of Brazilian workers.[62]

This generalized social and political mobilization also had important consequences for women's movement organizations and helped reshape the content of their political demands. As new organizational spaces emerged in which "general" demands for social change could be articulated, the range of activities undertaken by most women's movement organizations narrowed somewhat.

Whereas there were few organizational arenas for the expression of oppositional political claims when neighborhood women's organizations and feminist groups first arose in the early-to-mid 1970s, by the late 1970s, growing sectors of both the working class and the middle and upper-middle classes began pressuring for an end to military authoritarianism and its regressive so-

[60] On the political symbolism and significance of the São Bernardo strike, see Laís Wendel Abramo, "Greve Metalúrgica em São Bernardo: sobre a Dignidade do Trabalho," in *As Lutas Sociais e a Cidade*, ed. Lúcio Kowarick (São Paulo: Paz e Terra, CEDEC, and UNRISD, 1988), pp. 207–46.

[61] On the vital ties established between neighborhood groups and striking workers, see Silvio Caccia Bava, "A Luta nos Bairros e a Luta Sindical," in *As Lutas Sociais e a Cidade*, ed. Lúcio Kowarick (São Paulo: Paz e Terra, CEDEC, and UNRISD, 1988), pp. 287–314.

[62] For a detailed and incisive analysis of the rebirth of the Brazilian workers' movement after decades of subordination to the State, see Lúcia Lippi Oliveira, "O Movimento Operário em São Paulo—1970–1985," in *Movimentos Sociais na Transição Democrática*, ed. Emir Sader (São Paulo: Cortez, 1987). See also Margaret Keck, "The New Unionism in the Brazilian Transition," in *Democratizing Brazil*, ed. Alfred Stepan (New York: Oxford University Press, 1989); Vinícius C. Brant, "Sindicatos de Trabalhadores," in *São Paulo: O Povo em Movimento*, ed. Paul Singer and Vinícius Brant (Petrópolis: Vozes, 1980); and Maria Hermínia Tavares de Almeida, "O Sindicalismo Brasileiro entre a Conservação e a Mudança," in *Sociedade e Política no Brasil Pós-64*, ed. Bernard Sorj and Maria Hermínia Tavares de Almeida (São Paulo: Brasilense, 1983), pp. 191–214. For a comprehensive analysis of the corporatist "encapsulation" of the Brazilian labor movement under populist regimes, see Kenneth P. Erickson, *The Brazilian Corporative State and Working Class Politics* (Berkeley: University of California Press, 1977); and Youssef Cohen, *The Manipulation of Consent: The State and Working-Class Consciousness in Brazil* (Pittsburgh: University of Pittsburgh Press, 1989).

cial and economic policies. Thus, part of the reason that early women's groups, both feminine and feminist, focused on "general" as well as "gender-specific" issues (regardless of the extent of their ideological or organizational ties to the Left) was that there was an extremely limited number of public forums for protest of any sort. When International Women's Year offered the opportunity for women to organize as women, other issues of great import for Brazilian society as a whole were, of course, addressed by the new women's organizations.

In 1977–1978, most feminists still maintained that "general social transformation"[63] was essential to women's true liberation. But some feminists began insisting on the need to understand the specificity of women's oppression within class oppression. Women, they asserted, must organize independently so as to ensure gender equality in the would-be "transformed" Brazilian society.

Many neighborhood feminine groups also began zeroing in on gender-specific issues such as day care and domestic labor (rather than gender-*related* issues such as running water or sewage). As we saw above, this change resulted in part from the evolving political practice of those groups and the resistance they often encountered from parallel, male-dominated community organizations. And by 1978, the politicization of gender among popular women's groups was also attributable to their increased contact with feminist groups. Some neighborhood women's organizations, like the *Associação das Donas de Casa*, which claimed over four hundred members throughout São Paulo's Eastern Zone by the late 1970s, worked closely with feminist groups after 1975. Though class barriers prevented the consolidation of a truly cross-class women's movement, feminine organizations often found better allies in middle-class feminists than among their male "comrades" in community organizations, and surely, better allies than working-class women had found among middle-class male militants of the old and new Left.

Importantly, a specifically antifeminist reaction began to take shape among some left-wing political tendencies and sectors of the Brazilian Catholic church by 1978. The underground Left had extended its organizational efforts throughout the urban periphery since the mid-1970s, as we saw in chapter 3, and many of the more orthodox Stalinist and Trotskyist groups insisted that women must be mobilized for the "revolution," without much elaboration as to what specifically the revolution had to offer *women as women*. The official newspapers of these political organizations continued to ridicule feminism and tergiversate its meaning, claiming that it was an imperialist, bourgeois ideology developed by ladies-of-leisure that had little to offer Brazilian women and

---

[63] "General social transformation" was the standard "code word" for socialism given the regime's severe censorship laws and the ever-looming threat of AI-5 and the National Security Law even after "decompression."

would divide the workers' struggle. And though the church was an early ally of the feminist movement (having cosponsored the IWD event in 1975 that facilitated the creation of the first feminist organization in São Paulo), its overt support for the feminist movement dwindled as movement demands around women's reproductive rights and equality within the family were radicalized (see chapter 5 below).

CONCLUSION

Women's movements' political claims were deeply shaped by the changing associational structure and political discourses characteristic of the Brazilian opposition in the 1960s and 1970s. Women's groups grew out of the organizations of civil society that opposed authoritarian rule. Therefore, at first, women activists framed their political claims in the prevailing language of the opposition. As the number of oppositional arenas expanded and the *general* political claims made by the opposition were radicalized over the course of the 1970s, women's movements increasingly raised the *specific* women's banners so often ignored by the male-dominant opposition.

During the 1970s, community mothers' clubs and housewives' associations created by religious and secular opposition forces provided the organizational base and ideological rationale for several feminine movements that expanded into citywide, and even nationwide, political campaigns. As I have shown, militant motherhood provided the *mobilizational referent* for the Feminine Amnesty Movement, the Cost of Living Movement, and the Struggle for Day Care Movement.

Initially, the demands of these feminine movements did not challenge prevailing gender power arrangements. Instead, in keeping with the socially prescribed sexual division of political labor, such movements mobilized women to protest the rising cost of living and to demand community day-care centers and better health care and other services for women and children. But by the late 1970s, many feminine movement participants had begun questioning their unequal status as women. Importantly, the gradual politicization of these seemingly traditional feminine groups was often influenced by their growing contacts with more ideologically oriented, extracommunity actors, especially middle-class feminists.

Feminism in Brazil also underwent crucial political transformations during the 1970s. It began as a direct extension of the Center-Left and Left (both the "old," orthodox Left, and the militant Left of the late 1960s and early 1970s) and, thus originally couched its political claims primarily in class terms, framing generic demands in essentially unaltered orthodox Marxist categories. Given early feminists' participation in or exposure to the economism of most militant opposition groups of that era, early feminist groups centered their attention on women's role in social relations of production and paid considerably less attention to issues such as contraception, sexuality, or violence against women—issues which touched on the politics of the private sphere and women's role in social relations of reproduction, broadly defined.

Over time, most feminist groups increasingly framed their political claims in both class- *and* gender-specific terms, refusing to subordinate one struggle to the other and proclaiming that gender struggle was an integral and inseparable component of general social transformation; a struggle that, some argued, only women, the direct victims of gender oppression, could lead.

In sum, the political repression and increased social inequality wrought by military authoritarian rule led early Brazilian women's movements to focus on economic issues and to pursue working-class women's practical gender interests to a much greater extent than did the women's movements arising in advanced capitalist democracies during the 1960s. Structural-historical factors specific to Brazil account, in part, for this difference.

However, since the political fate of the women's movements was deeply wedded to that of the larger opposition, the organizational and ideological sexism prevailing within the opposition to authoritarian rule also constrained the content of gender-based claims in distinctive ways. Women's movements in Brazil not only had to contest the reactionary gender ideology of a military authoritarian regime but also had to contend with less-than-progressive gender ideologies adhered to by sectors of the radical opposition. Dependent upon the church and the Left and Center-Left for legitimacy and indispensable organizational resources, many women's movement activists intentionally refrained from addressing more radical, gender-specific issues (such as violence against women or reproductive freedom), issues that might have alienated vital allies in civil and political society.

Thus, in the early years, the Left and the church served as silent interlocutors for the women's movement, mediating the content and scope of women's demands and organizing efforts. But the sexist stereotypes operative within opposition organizations and the Left's assumption that class exploitation rather than gender oppression explained existing power imbalances between the sexes eventually led women's movements to formulate more radical genderic claims, as will be seen in chapter 5 below.

CHAPTER FIVE

The Rise and Fall of a United, Mass-Based Brazilian Women's Movement

ACCORDING to most observers and movement participants, 1979 through 1981 were *the* peak mobilizational years of the contemporary Brazilian women's movement. Feminist groups multiplied, numbering close to one hundred by 1980–1981. And dozens of new neighborhood women's associations blossomed in Brazil's urban periphery.

These were also years of acerbic conflict among diverse sectors of the growing Brazilian women's movement, a time when underlying yet unequivocal ideological differences rose to the surface among activists lumped together under the generic feminist labels of groups formed in the mid-1970s. Sharper conflicts also emerged between independent feminists and women active in women's groups tied to the larger political opposition, particularly those with links to the sectarian Left. Some neighborhood women's associations also embarked on a collision course with parallel male-domininant community organizations.

After 1979, such conflicts were exacerbated by the fact that the opposition as a whole was itself increasingly divided on strategies and tactics necessary to defeat the dictatorship and promote social justice. President Geisel's successor, General João Batista Figueiredo, expanded his predecessor's decompression strategy and initiated *abertura* (political liberalization) policies that loosened State censorship, granted a restricted amnesty to previous enemies of the regime, and considerably expanded the political space available for protest and mobilization. Figueiredo's *abertura* also made radical public discourses on gender more feasible and thus indirectly facilitated the diversification and expansion of the women's movements' mobilizational efforts.

In São Paulo, feminist and feminine groups staged citywide women's congresses in 1979 and 1980, drawing thousands of women of all social clases and political affiliations. Those congresses and other movement events drew the attention of both the mainstream and alternative media to women's mobilization and to their gender-specific claims. Rather than ridicule feminism and ignore popular women's mobilization, the media as a whole devoted a good deal of coverage to most women's movement events and protests after 1979—from feminist academic lectures or symposia to popular protests for day care at the mayor's office. Television networks and radio stations created new women's programs, which along with the traditional focus on cooking, fashion, makeup, and such, also occasionally interviewed women active in feminist groups or the day-care movement, or featured documentaries and editorials addressing such previously untouchable subjects as sexuality, virginity, contraception, divorce, and so on.[1] Even the *novela das oito* (the prime-time soap operas viewed by millions of Brazilians) began portraying women in more "liberated" roles.[2]

As the media extended its coverage of "women's issues," so the diverse sectors of the newly divided political opposition (both legal and underground) stepped up their outreach to women's organizations of all types. In large part, the military authoritarian regime's more robust offensive against the opposition's growing strength fueled these efforts to recruit women's support more actively. In late 1979, Figueiredo adopted a new divide-and-rule strategy, aimed at keeping the ruling civilian-military coalition in control of the political liberalization process. The legal opposition, previously forcibly united into a single party, the *Movimento Democrático Brasileiro* (the Brazilian Democratic Movement or MDB), was dissolved by decree and subsequently regrouped into five new parties,[3] each representing distinct strategies for completing Brazil's transition to democracy and each needing to consolidate new social bases of support. All incorporated at least some of the political banners raised by feminine and feminist movement groups and intensified their outreach to women. And some still illegal parties of the Left, harbored within these newly created parties of the opposition, sought to instrumentalize what looked to be a growing and important mass-based women's movement so as to redirect it toward their own sectarian political ends.

As the women's movements grew, so did the male-dominant opposition's determination to garner the political capital represented by organized female constituencies. This chapter examines the struggle that ensued *within* and *among* women's organizations as two ever more divergent sectors of the movement—those with continuing ties to radical sectors of the male-dominant opposition and those who insisted on developing an autonomous women's politics—battled one another over the appropriate content and site of women's struggle. Some women continued to argue that women's struggle was one and

---

[1] The heightened media attention to women is partially attributable to the efforts of Brazilian feminist journalists, such as Carmen da Silva, Irede Cardoso, and Maria Carneiro da Cunha, who pressured major newpapers and networks to grant more space to women's voices and women's issues.

[2] Teresa Caldeira brought this important example of the extensiveness of feminism's social reach to my attention.

[3] On a spectrum from Center-Right to Left, these were the *Partido Popular* (PP or Popular Party), the *Partido Trabalhista Brasileiro* (PTB or Brazilian Labor Party), the *Partido do Movimento Democrático Brasileiro* (PMDB or Party of the Brazilian Democratic Movement), the *Partido Democrático Trabalhista* (PDT or Democratic Labor Party), and the *Partido dos Trabalhadores* (PT or Workers' Party). The reform of the party system over time and its consequences for social movements will be discussed in detail in chapter 6 below.

the same as the people's struggle for a more just Brazilian society and insisted that women must therefore be mobilized primarily for participation in the struggle against the dictatorship—that is, in political parties and community organizations. Others developed more radical conceptions of gender struggle and sought to consolidate autonomous political discourses and organizational initiatives independent of the opposition as a whole.

By the early 1980s, the latter had come to view the former as female mouthpieces of a manipulative male Left and refused to recognize women's groups that continued to be organizationally tied to the Left as part of the women's movement. The women affiliated with sectarian parties of the Left, in turn, viewed autonomous feminist politics as wrongheaded, divisive, and insensitive to the real plight of poor women whose liberation, they maintained, ultimately depended on the success of the wider revolutionary struggle.

These conflicts intensified as some movement participants gained fresh insights into the specificity of women's oppression within different social groups and classes. Strategic gender interests began to feature prominently in many Brazilian feminist and feminine political platforms and agendas. Some feminists moved beyond the Marxist paradigmatic emphasis on women's insertion in social relations of production and reproduction and focused as well on the politics of the private sphere. Reproductive rights, violence against women, sexuality, and other personal issues were increasingly raised as *political* ones, and new independent feminist groups centered their organizational activities on those issues.

Similarly, an ever-growing number of neighborhood feminine groups undertook the struggle for day care, now arguing that women should not bear the sole responsibility for childrearing in Brazilian society, thus explicitly challenging the sexual division of labor. And through heightened contact with feminist organizations, some feminine groups also began centering their discussions on such issues as contraception, virginity, divorce, and abortion, bringing some groups into direct conflict with the Catholic church. These new ideological understandings of women's gender interests and the reformulation of strategies necessary to advance them were forged through political practice rather than through external ideological interventions such as heightened exposure to international feminist ideas, as some analysts have suggested.[4]

[4] See, for example, Cornelia Butler Flora, "Socialist Feminism in Latin America," *Women and Politics* 4, no. 1 (Spring 1984): 69–93; Marianne Schmink, "Women in Brazilian Abertura Politics," *Signs* 7, no. 11 (Autumn 1981): 115–34; and Jane S. Jaquette, "Introduction," in *The Women's Movement in Latin America: Feminism and the Transition to Democracy*, ed. Jane S. Jaquette (Boston: Unwin Hyman, 1989). This argument is also implicit in Molyneux's understanding of how strategic gender interests are framed. See "Mobilization without Emancipation? Women's Interest, State, and Revolution." In *Transition and Development: Problems of Third World Socialism*, ed. Richard R. Fagen, Carmen Diana Deere, and José Luis Coraggio (New York: Monthly Review Press; Berkeley, Calif.: Center for the Study of the Americas, 1986).

A Unified Women's Political Agenda? The First São Paulo Women's Congress, 1979

By 1979, women activists had sparked a burgeoning political movement that appeared to span all social classes, races, and ideologies. The 1979 International Women's Day celebrations symbolized its growing social and political reach. IWD events were held in Salvador, Rio de Janeiro, Belo Horizonte, and three events were organized in the city of São Paulo alone (other commemorations were held in Campinas and São Carlos in the state of São Paulo).

Therezinha Zerbini, who had broken with the feminist movement in 1978 over the issue of abortion,[5] staged a "feminine" event at the Municipal Legislature with the participation of the Feminine Amnesty Movement, the Human Rights Commission, the Feminine Branch of the MDB, the Mothers' Commission in Defense of Human Rights, and the Movement for Christian Renovation. At a church in São Miguel Paulista, a peripheral neighborhood in São Paulo's Southern Zone, over four hundred women from local mothers' clubs gathered to commemorate IWD.

Some of the feminist groups that had organized the 1978 citywide IWD event, discussed in chapter 4, also decided to put on a "Women's Congress" that would stimulate the creation of new women's organizations in São Paulo and promote unity among existing women's groups. Some of the organizers felt that given the rapid proliferation of feminist and feminine activities, coordinating the numerous mobilizational efforts among women was crucial to the movements' future political effectiveness. Some also hoped that a congress, in bringing together representatives from all groups working with women in São Paulo, would provide a forum for the elaboration of a consensual political agenda to be advanced jointly by all those interested in combating gender inequality. Just as workers needed to unite to extract greater concessions from management, so, some women activists argued, must women come together if they were to achieve progress in the realm of women's rights.

Coordinated by a coalition of feminine and feminist organizations and some trade unions, including the Housewives' Association, the Cost of Living Movement, the National Workers' Front, the Center for the Development of Brazilian Women (CDMB), *Brasil Mulher*, various mothers' clubs from São Paulo's Southern Zone, the *Associação das Mulheres*, trade union opposition groups, and many other organizations, the First Paulista Women's Congress drew nearly a thousand participants for two days of discussions at the Ruth Escobar Theater in downtown São Paulo. Participants broke down into small discussion groups focused on a variety of topics. And as many of my inter-

---

[5] Zerbini refused to endorse the joint feminist platform, which called for the decriminalization of abortion, that was presented to opposition candidates during the 1978 elections. This platform will be discussed in chapter 6 below.

viewees noted, the substance of some group discussions surprised even the most avid and radical of Paulista feminists.

The organizing commission's program highlighted issues of women's day-to-day lives: domestic labor, discrimination in the workplace and occupational training for women, fertility control, sexuality, the lack of day-care centers, and women's political participation. Congress participants, of course, discussed the issues that by then had become the standard banners of both feminist and feminine groups—equal pay for equal work, better schools, urban infrastructure, and so on. But many unprogrammed topics concerning the politics of the private sphere—far less acceptable to feminists' erstwhile allies in the church and on the Left—also spontaneously surfaced in the discussions. As the *Folha de São Paulo* noted, "For the first time the question of feminine sexuality was discussed, until now an issue which had taken second place as a function of problems such as work, day care, political participation."[6] And for the first time at a large public gathering, women shared feelings of dissatisfaction or lack of fulfillment in their sexual relations, discussed their common problems in controlling fertility, protested their subjugation to husbands and lovers—and they began to name unequal power relations between men and women as one of the principal causes of those "problems."

Women of the popular classes also pointed to the lack of adequate living conditions in the urban periphery and to the exhausting labor that they and their spouses performed as reasons for their lack of sexual fulfillment. But most inisisted that male and female social conditioning aggravated those material problems. The most radical gender-specific issues often were raised by women of the popular classes, the very women whom both the church and the Left always had claimed were unconcerned with such issues as sexuality or contraception.[7] Some of their declarations during the Congress were reproduced in the alternative newspaper, *Em Tempo*.

> Women suffer much more with problems of sex. I married when I was 14 years old. My father said that I was three years older on the documents. I have been living with my husband for thirty years. Sometimes I rebel and wonder why I ever got married. When the girls were born, I slept with them, after working like a dog all day long. He never helped me, slept in the other room. Then, when the girls were still, he would come and get me. He would fulfill himself and that was it. Me, never. I know I always repressed that side, sex. But because of my daughters I put up with everything. I live for them.[8]

[6] *Folha de São Paulo*, March 8, 1979.

[7] *Brasil Mulher* dedicated a special issue to the Congress that included a feature on "sexual pleasure, contraception, and marital relations" and proclaimed that "[b]esides rice, beans, day care and salaries, these things also concern working women, housewives, mothers." See *Brasil Mulher*, special issue, March 1979.

[8] *Em Tempo*, March 1979, cited in Moria Lygia Quartim de Moraes Nehring, "Família e Femi-

Em Tempo also described how other "private" issues were formulated during this historic First Women's Congress.

> Then, sexual oppression appeared. . . . the double standard of morality which allows men the practice of non-monogamy, and punishes women on the basis of the stigma of single motherhood; . . . the sadistic doctors at the Hospital das Clinicas (among others) who practice curettage in cold blood, whenever they suspect that a patient interned for hemorraging had induced an abortion. The existence of *machismo* represented in the physical violence which many women suffer and the very existence of a professional category known as prostitution—that is, in women who sell their own bodies. . . . *Machismo* which imposes the weight of contraception on women, which uses her as a sexual object, as an item for bed and table.[9]

And in summarizing the political significance of the Congress, the same article proclaimed:

> [T]he proposals presented were innumerable: they reflected the need for a cultural revolution, the inseparable complement of economic transformation. Declaring that Brazilian woman has no guarantees when she gets pregnant, given undernourishment, the lack of medical attention, many voices at the Congress declared that Brazilian woman has no right to choose and that in the face of an unwanted pregnancy, clandestine abortion is her only alternative, practiced by quacks in the case of women who lack resources (that is, the overwhelming majority of Brazilian women), or in clinics which charge exorbitant prices. . . . The capacity to create a climate of enthusiasm, solidarity, and trust, and to also touch the emotions of participants . . . led to spontaneous demands that "we cannot say good-bye now . . . we cannot wait until the next Congress: we must continue to struggle together."[10]

The 1979 Congress thus set forth one of the women's movements' most unique contributions to the struggle for a democratic Brazil, proclaiming that power relations in the family, in daily life, in civil society and not just the State and political society (i.e., parties), must also be democratized. After 1979, the movement began expanding the horizons of the feminist political project, moving beyond orthodox Marxist paradigmatic solutions to the woman question (which one of my interviewees described as a "recipe for integrating women into the revolution") and demanding a cultural as well as political and economic transformation of Brazilian society.

The First Congress further politicized other gender issues. The president of the Housewives' Association gave a speech calling for the revalorization of women's domestic labor and arguing that the government must assume greater responsibility for the essential tasks that women perform, insisting that such

---

nismo: Reflexões sobre Papeis Femininos na Imprensa para Mulheres" (Ph.D. diss., University of São Paulo, 1981), p. 246.

[9] Ibid.

[10] Ibid.

valorization of "woman as a human being must also occur at home with the division of domestic labor among husbands and children."[11] Union women reiterated the demands advanced during their own professional congresses in 1978 and enlisted the support of feminist and feminine groups in pursuing their demands within the union movement.

A Coordination of São Paulo's women's groups was formed to advance the conclusions of the First Women's Congress and consolidate the ties of solidarity established during that unprecedented event. The more radical issues raised during the Congress did not make their way into its final document, however, due to some movement participants' fear of losing important allies in the church and in the Left.[12] The principal demands advanced in that document were:

1. *Creches*—totally financed by the State and private industry, close to places of work and places of residence, which should not be mere depositories for children and must count with the participation of parents in the *creche's* pedagogical orientation.
2. For Salary Equalization, for equal pay for equal work. For better salaries for all workers.
3. Against the Program for the Prevention of High-Risk Pregnancy—for the right and the social conditions which would really permit women to opt to have or not to have children in a good state of health and other conditions for a decent life.[13]

The newly united movement's demand for day care immediately reverberated throughout São Paulo's urban periphery. Women from the new Coordination contacted all of the neighborhood women's associations that had been working for day care in an isolated fashion and called a citywide meeting, attended by hundreds of women. Regional coordinations were formed, corresponding to the principal administrative regions of the city, and weekly meetings were held to develop a united movement strategy that would strengthen the heretofore disparate local efforts to secure public day-care facilities. Middle-class feminists joined poor and working-class women in the struggle for day care and helped develop an ideological framework within which the new citywide movements' demands could be set forth. Women's confinement to the domestic sphere and their exclusive social responsibility for "caring for the workers of tomorrow" became the axis of the new united movement's political claims; and the State became the principal target for the *Movimento*

[11] *Brasil Mulher*, March 1979.

[12] Moraes Nehring argues that some of the women more directly tied to extreme-Left political tendencies "cleansed" the final document of its more radical, gender-specific content. See Moraes Nehring, "Família e Feminismo," p. 250.

[13] "I Congresso da Mulher Paulista," documento final, March 1979. Also reprinted in *Brasil Mulher*, April 1979. Women's movement political activities concerning point 3 will be discussed at length in chapters 8 and 9 below.

de Luta por Creches's (Struggle for Day Care Movement or MLC) demands.[14] The First Congress appeared to have achieved its aim of promoting concerted, unified action around shared goals.

In April of 1979, the Paulistas also took their First Congress's proposal to the First National Women's Congress, organized by Rio feminists, which drew women from over thirty groups from several major cities. The National Women's Congress endorsed the three political banners advanced during the São Paulo Congress, propelling Paulista women's organizations into the vanguard of the nascent Brazilian women's movement.

And the First Congress also fulfilled its goal of encouraging the creation of new women's organizations in São Paulo. Twenty-nine new neighborhood women's associations were formed in 1979–1980 in São Paulo's Eastern Zone alone.[15] The MLC helped new day-care groups get started in the urban periphery, and politicized the day-care issue within existing mothers' clubs and housewives' associations.

The number of core participants in existing feminist groups grew considerably in the immediate aftermath of the 1979 Congress. New feminist organizations were created as well. Among these was the *Frente de Mulheres Feministas* (Feminist Women's Front), a group growing out of women's professional and academic networks, attracting dozens of notable Paulistas such as theater arts entrepreneur and actress, Ruth Escobar; *Folha de São Paulo* journalists, Maria Carneiro da Cunha and Irede Cardoso; attorneys such as Silvia Pimentel and Floriza Verucci; and respected academics such as Ruth Cardoso, Carmen Barroso, and Christina Bruschini. The *Frente* hoped to disseminate feminist ideas through the media, the arts, and the universities. Throughout 1979 and 1980, this group promoted debates at the Ruth Escobar Theater with prominent jurists, politicians, and other experts on such controversial issues as abortion.

Alongside such respectable forms of feminist organizing, a more controversial and politically daring feminist group was formed by lesbians active in both the gay and feminist movements, *Grupo Ação Lésbica-Feminista* (Lesbian Feminist Action Group or GALF). The sexism prevailing among gay men and pervasive heterosexism and homophobia found among feminist activists convinced some lesbians in São Paulo that they needed to create an organization, independent of the male-dominated gay movement and the straight-dominated feminist movement, to advance their specific issues and concerns as lesbians. Sexuality and the right to sexual pleasure featured prominently in GALF's

---

[14] The political development of the day-care movement, in response to government initiatives in this area during the Reynaldo de Barros municipal administration will be discussed in detail in chapter 9 below.

[15] Rede Mulher, " 'Retrato' dos Clubes de Mães e Grupos de Mulheres da Zona Leste de São Paulo," Pesquisa-Avaliação das Clubes e Grupos de Mães da Cidade de São Paulo, Documento no. 3, June 1985 (Mimeograph).

political agenda, issues that early feminist groups shunned for fear of alienating working-class women and their allies in the church and on the Left.

Also in 1979, the regime's concession to opposition demands for political amnesty, spearheaded by the Feminine Amnesty Movement, and Figueiredo's *abertura* infused new political energies and discourses into all opposition currents, including the feminist movement. Thousands of exiled Brazilians returned from Europe and the United States, bringing with them new strategies for social change based on a reevaluation of their resistance activities during the 1960s and early 1970s and derived from their exposure to social movements then at their mobilizational peak in the West. Among them were women who had been involved in feminist movement organizations abroad, including Brazilian or Latin American feminist groups formed in exile.

These repatriated feminists also had struggled with the multitude of left-wing political tendencies organized in exile (which included the full range of militant organizations of the Brazilian Left, as well as Argentinian *montoneros*, Uruguayan *tupamaros*, and so on) over the primacy of class versus gender struggle. But unlike the women who stayed behind, many of the returning exiles had broken organizational, if not ideological, ties with the Left.[16] They returned to Brazil to find a sizable women's movement, but one which they perceived to be still locked into a very "elementary" or "rudimentary" conceptualization of women's struggle, a movement that had not "advanced" as far as the mass-based French or Italian feminist movements in which they had been active.[17] Some told me that they did not join Brasil Mulher or the CMDB when they returned to Brazil because they viewed them as political fronts, not feminist organizations.

But as one of the feminists who remained in Brazil put it, "the exiles literally flooded feminist groups in São Paulo." And they introduced new ideas and feminist concepts into existing groups, ideas unfamiliar to early Brazilian feminists—"We suddenly 'learned' all of these new terms . . . at every meeting, I'd come in and [one of the old members] would say, hey, we have a new term today, 'movement autonomy' . . . or 'double militancy' . . . concepts which were unknown to us at that time."[18] The feminists who stayed behind,

[16] Interview with one of the founding members of the *Círculo de Mulheres Brasileiras* in Paris, then member of *Centro Informaçao Mulher*, a women's movement information center and archive, São Paulo, March 28, 1983. According to this interviewee, Latin American and Brazilian feminist groups in exile were also direct offshoots of the left-wing opposition groups that reorganized abroad. Like the early feminist groups in São Paulo and elsewhere in Brazil, most of the participants in the exile feminist groups engaged in "double militancy" and differed among themselves as to the strategies for general social change implied by their varying commitments to party organizations.

[17] Interview with former participant of the *Círculo de Mulheres Brasileiras* in Paris and the *Associação das Mulheres*, then a member of *Sexualidade e Politica*, a feminist organization in São Paulo that focused on women's health and reproductive rights, São Paulo, April 21, 1983.

[18] Interview with early member of *Brasil Mulher*, August 18, 1983.

sometimes enduring political persecution and internal exile, expressed some resentment toward the supposedly sophisticated, "European" returnees. But resentment soon gave way to collaboration, as the *exiladas* shared their experiences in types of feminist activities unheard of in Brazil before the late 1970s. The "French" and "Italian" *exiladas*, for example, had participated in pro–reproductive choice movements in predominantly Catholic countries and successfully confronted church resistance to the more radical issues raised by feminism.

For example, returning exiles elaborated on the concept of movement autonomy, one which readily caught on among Brazilian feminists struggling to recast their relationship to the male-dominant political opposition. In a 1979 booklet, entitled *O Movimento de Mulheres no Brasil*, the *Associação das Mulheres*, a group to which many returnees flocked, explained why the women's movement's organizational autonomy came to be perceived as essential by some Brazilian feminist and feminine organizations.

> When we say that the feminist movement searches for its own organizational forms, we have in mind the articulation of two essential and inseparable initiatives. On the one hand, the discussion—among women—of questions which speak to us directly, our sexuality and the image we have constructed of ourselves, as well as our role in the family and our insertion into the process of production. On the other hand, the generalization of those discussions—and the demands that emerge from them—within society as a whole. But, above all, we believe that this movement must be autonomous, because we are certain that no form of oppression will ever be overcome unless those directly interested in overcoming it take the struggle into their own hands.[19]

But many of the Left sectarian political tendencies that survived regime repression and reorganized in exile also returned to Brazil in 1979–1980. Some, like the *Partido Comunista do Brasil* (Communist Party of Brazil or PCdoB, the Albanian-inspired splinter group of the Brazilian Communist Party), had modified significantly their political strategies and organizational objectives. And the new strategies and objectives of some of the political organizations of the sectarian Left soon directly clashed with the stance on organizational autonomy developing among some sectors of the feminist movement.

The São Paulo women's movement Coordination, established by the original sponsoring groups of the First Congress, continued meeting on a weekly

---

[19] Associação das Mulheres, in "O Movimento de Mulheres no Brasil," *Cadernos da Associação das Mulheres* 3 (August 1979): 6. Other groups also began stressing the issue of autonomy at this time. This important movement document, widely circulated among opposition sectors and movement organizations in São Paulo, contains a number of theoretical position papers on the nature, content, and direction of women's struggle as conceptualized by feminist and feminine organizations in São Paulo and Rio de Janeiro.

basis throughout 1979 to oversee the movements' political work around the three banners raised by the First Congress and to plan the Second Congress, to be held in March of 1980. At first composed of some fifteen or twenty women representing a dozen or so feminist and feminine organizations, by the beginning of 1980, the Coordination welcomed from 150 to 200 women, representing fifty-six groups.

As a direct consequence of the success of the First Congress, and as a function of the widespread political mobilization that typified most organized sectors of civil society during the early years of *abertura*, the ranks of the women's movement in São Paulo, "represented" within the Coordination, swelled virtually overnight. All groups who organized women in any type of political, union, professional, or community activities were welcome. And by early 1980, the Coordination's weekly meetings included representatives from: nine explicitly feminist organizations, twenty-one neighborhood women's associations (including organizations like the now united Struggle for Day Care Movement, the Cost of Living Movement, and the Housewives' Association, each of which represented dozens of groups throughout the city), eleven unions and union opposition groups, five professional associations, two community organizations, three student associations, two women's divisions of political parties (the only legal opposition party, the MDB, and the Trotskyist *Convergência Socialista*), two health movement groups, and the women's division of the United Black Movement.

According to one of the early members of the CDMB (renamed *Centro da Mulher Brasileira—Setor São Paulo*, the Brazilian Women's Center—São Paulo Sector, in 1980, hereafter referred to as the CMB), "The Coordination became a kind of political entity in itself. Unions, the Amnesty Movement, parties and community organizations began calling on us to 'represent' the women's movement . . . the movement was suddenly perceived as 'in vogue', politically speaking. . . . And all of a sudden, feminists became the minority [within the Coordination] even though we did the bulk of the infrastructural organizational work."[20]

Many of the union, professional, and community organizations that joined the Coordination in 1979 were directly linked (ideologically and structurally) to the various Left sectarian political groups, such as the *Movimento Revolucionario 8 de Outubro* (Eighth of October Revolutionary Movement or MR-8), the PCdoB, and others (some of which formed part of the MDB electoral front) that reemerged in full force after political amnesty was granted and the AI-5 revoked in 1979. These groups viewed the 1980 Second Women's Congress and the expanding women's movement as a whole as opportunities to

[20] Interview with founding member of CMB, participant in the Coordination for the first, second, and third Paulista Women's Congresses, and then member of *Centro Informação Mulher*, São Paulo, August 10, 1983.

recruit new militant members among a previously untapped constituency—women's organizations. Many of the feminists I talked to believed that there were several "phantom organizations" among the fifty-six represented in the Coordination, groups with no actual social base, formed with the exclusive intent of flooding the Coordination with additional members of a particular political tendency.[21]

CONFLICT AMONG "FEMINISMS": THE SECOND SÃO PAULO WOMEN'S CONGRESS, 1980

Consequently, setting the agenda for the Second Congress became a political and ideological struggle among the multitude of political tendencies and socialist and/or feminist perspectives represented on the Coordination. Independent feminists of all political stripes insisted that the Second Congress should advance on the issues raised at the First Congress and mobilize women around new issues that had surfaced within the women's movements during the course of 1979–1980.

Violence against women was one such issue. Several "crimes of passion" committed by male celebrities, assasinations of women by jealous husbands or lovers because of alleged infidelity, committed in the name of "defense of [male] honor," incited generalized outrage and vehement protests by feminist and feminine groups in São Paulo, Rio, Belo Horizonte, and other cities.[22] But other groups, like those tied to the MR-8, whose legal front was the newspaper *Hora do Povo* (HP or Hour of the People), insisted that the Congress should mobilize women around such general, pressing political issues as the convocation of a National, Sovereign Constituent Assembly to overturn authoritarian rule. In response, respresentatives of some feminine and feminist groups maintained that IWD was the only major mobilizational moment for the articulation of the women's movements' specific claims and that, moreover, by 1980, numerous political spaces existed within which women and men, together, could discuss such things as the Constituent Assembly.

It was finally agreed that the first day's agenda would center on the discus-

---

[21] The MR-8, for example, was entirely reorganized in exile and their comrades who remained in Brazil were wiped out by the military. When they returned in 1978–1979 with the intention of promoting "the unity of progressive forces" and fostering the "organization of the masses," they literally had to start from scratch and never achieved their goals of recruiting new adherents among the organizations of civil society that had developed in their absence. The PCdoB, on the other hand, did exercise a good deal of influence in some unions and numerous community organizations.

[22] For a discussion of the sanctioning of violence against women in the name of "honor" in Brazilian law and feminist mobilization around this issue, see Mariza Corrêa, *Morte em Familia: Representacões Juridícas de Papeis Sexuais* (Rio de Janeiro: Graal, 1983); Marisa Corrêa, *Crimes da Paixão* (São Paulo: Brasilense, 1981); and Heloisa Pontes, "Praticas Feministas no Brasil Contemporâneo—Um Estudo de Caso do SOS-Mulher," March 1983 (Mimeograph).

sions of the various forms of discrimination suffered by women, as "women," "mothers," "wives," and "workers," and that "women's political participation" in "the general struggle" and in "the women's movement" would be the focus of discussions on the second day, when the new, joint proposal for political action during 1980–1981 would be approved by participants. The promotional materials for the Second Congress, widely distributed throughout Greater São Paulo and some cities in the interior of the State, asked, "How Many Women Are You? One woman who works outside the home . . . a woman who takes care of the home . . . another who's a wife . . . one who conforms . . . another who rebels. . . . Let's put together the pieces, woman?"[23] To facilitate the participation of women residents of the urban periphery, organizers furnished bus transportation from several locations in the Eastern and Southern Zones of the city, day-care facilities at the Congress (which were coordinated by men), and free meals for all participants and their children during the two days of the event. The Coordination's efforts in this sense paid off—over four thousand people, including several dozen men (mostly gay movement activists), who held separate workshops on their own *machismo* and helped with day care and food preparation, and 736 children, showed up at the Catholic University of São Paulo on March 8, 1980.

The activities of the first day resembled those of the First Congress. But now women met in small groups to discuss a vastly expanded array of issues such as differential education for boys and girls, relations between men and women, sex education, the portrayal of women in the media, sexuality, violence against women, women's rights, contraception, abortion, single motherhood, day care, the economic and social functions of domestic labor, issues of concern to working women, and women's organization within unions and professional associations.

In contrast to the more unified and seemingly politically homogeneous First Congress, many of the discussions during the Second were divided along clear political lines. Members of MR-8 and other political tendencies took over the coordination of many of the discussion groups (even when group leaders had been designated by the Coordination as a whole weeks in advance of the Congress) and pushed the discussions in the direction of their predetermined partisan agendas. The church also intervened in a systematic fashion, packing the discussions on contraception and abortion with members of church-linked groups such as CEBs, mothers' clubs, and Catholic Workers' Action who adamantly opposed any form of artificial birth control.[24]

[23] "II Congresso da Mulher Paulista," promotional flyer, 1980.

[24] Interview with a feminist member of the Coordination, also cited above, São Paulo, August 10, 1983. Some of the organized Trotskyist political tendencies, like *Liberdade e Luta* and *Convergencia Socialista*, supported abortion rights at the Congress, but according to this interviewee, "still from a dogmatic point of view and only to claim one of the Congress' themes as their own

The events of the second day of the 1980 Congress distinguished the ortho-dox Left's "woman question" from the "socialist feminist question" once and for all, with lasting implications for Paulista women's movements' polit-ical strategies. The agenda set for the day was "women's political participa-tion." After the proposals of the discussion groups during the previous day were read by the chair, representatives from union groups, known to be linked to the MR-8 and other sectarian offshoots of the Brazilian Communist Party, demanded the floor. They claimed that "working women's voices had not been heard at the Congress," that "the women in the periphery are starving to death and nobody is paying any attention to that",[25] and that therefore the day's agenda should focus on the Constituent Assembly, general unemploy-ment, and other such issues (which, of course, comprised the political plat-forms of their sectarian organizations). These women were "booed" by the vast majority of the Congress participants who were anxious to get on with the preestablished agenda. Accompanied by several men from their sectarian groups, the left-wing women attempted to muscle their way toward the main microphone and mayhem struck the auditorium as other women tried to block them from doing so. The conflict escalated into outright fistfighting. Proceed-ings were temporarily halted.

In the immediate aftermath of this chaotic incident, Paulista feminist groups, including *Nós Mulheres, Brasil Mulher, Associação das Mulheres, Grupo 8 de Março, Centro da Mulher Brasileira, Pró-Mulher, Frente de Mul-heres Feministas, Grupo Ação Lésbico-Feminista*, and one feminine organi-zation, the Housewives' Association, called an emergency meeting. Some women proposed that the groups responsible for the disturbances be expelled from the Congress then and there. Instead, the feminist organizations agreed to formulate a joint resolution, to be read at the closing session, condemning the actions of those "antifeminist tendencies."[26] The motion "against at-tempts at political-partisan manipulation and distortion of the Congress's ob-jectives," repudiating the behavior of antifeminist organizations, was signed

in order to direct the movement . . . they raised it as a tactical issue, but there was no real ideo-logical support."

[25] Quoted in *Jornal do Brasil*, March 10, 1980. This claim was made, in spite of the fact that poor and working-class women constituted the majority of participants and that representatives from feminine groups and union organizations formed part of the presiding panel of the Congress. When the Domestic Workers Association and women from the United Black Movement asked for representation on the presiding panel, a representative of each was immediately invited to take seat among those presiding the Congress.

[26] Moraes Nehring, "Família e Feminismo," pp. 265–77, provides a detailed discussion of these controversial events. My own recounting of the Second Congress relies principally on in-numerable conversations with women's movement participants in São Paulo, and formal inter-views with feminists who participated in the Second Congress and women involved with one of the political tendencies held responsible for the disturbances, as well as a thorough review of media coverage of the event and of internal organizational documents of the Coordination.

by the great majority of the organizations who participated in the Coordination (including some of the ones responsible for the manipulation and distortion) and received a standing ovation at the final plenary session.[27]

Some common political banners were nevertheless approved during the closing session including: the installation of information centers on contraception in neighborhood health clinics; free, accessible, and noncoercive family planning for all women; the creation of a forum to debate the abortion issue; and, the continuation of the struggle for day care and for occupational training for women.

The major objective of the women who initiated the planning of the Second Congress had been to unify all feminine and feminist movements around gender-specific political struggles. Instead, the Congress highlighted the clear, underlying divisions within the supposed unity of purpose of an ever more ideologically diverse, politically heterogeneous, and multifaceted women's movement. As journalist María Carneiro da Cunha noted, the conflicts that surfaced during the Second Congress were in themselves evidence of the political "amplitude and importance that the event had taken on."

> The purpose of this congress was the discussion of women's specific issues. But in bringing together such a large number of people, many of them with divergent political interests, it became practically impossible to avoid that there be attempts at manipulation on the part of diverse political-partisan currents, more preoccupied with propagandizing their "slogans" than with discussing women's problematic, in spite of the efforts of various members of the coordination to impede this from happening. That is, that women serve once again as the *massa de manobra* (manipulatable mass) for interests which are not their own.[28]

The press generally began to differentiate two political currents within the "women's movement": one feminist, and the other "feminine" (in a sense different than my own usage above as it now came to connote a specific *ideological* position on gender struggle).

> [T]he divergences between the groups were many and were based principally in the definition: will the Congress be feminist or feminine? If feminist, the major preoccupation is the discussion of women's specific problems, regardless of her class or area of political action. In this case, general struggles are important and should be stimulated as areas of action for women, but only if their militancy in those struggles does not make them forget their condition as women, who are consequently doubly oppressed: as women and as a class. If feminine, its central preoccupation is to discuss the general struggles (for water, sewage, electricity, day care, etc.) and the

---

[27] Maria Carneiro da Cunha, "Tumultos e Polémica no 2.o Congresso da Mulher," *Folha de São Paulo*, March 10, 1980.

[28] Ibid.

participation of women in those struggles. The specificity of women's struggle is not important before the struggle of all of society.[29]

Many feminists, including some still active in parties of the Left, union groups, and other nonfeminist organizations of civil society, also adamantly endorsed such a distinction. Some began insisting on the need to carve out an independent feminist political project that would differ radically from the Left's formulation of women's struggle. A "true" feminist politics, some began to argue, required full organizational and ideological autonomy; feminist efforts could not or should not be sullied by the authoritarian and instrumentalist imposition of predetermined organizing agendas, so characteristic of women who called themselves women's movement activists but were in fact "mere mouthpieces" for the sectarian Left. After the Second Congress, such women were considered politically suspect by many independent feminist and feminine groups and increasingly were refused a place within what now came to be known as "the autonomous Brazilian women's movement."

CHARTING AN AUTONOMOUS WOMEN'S POLITICS, 1980–1981

The consolidation of a distinct, autonomous feminist political identity, within the larger women's movement in São Paulo, began as a direct consequence of the divisions unmistakably manifest during the Second Congress. It became increasingly clear that the so-called women's movement in fact was made up of feminist, nonfeminist, and antifeminist women's groups. Just how the lines separating such groups should be drawn continued to confound feminist politics well into the 1980s. But after the Second Congress, most feminists began redefining their relationship to male-dominant opposition forces in civil society as a whole. Whereas in the early 1970s, the Brazilian Left identified two kinds of feminism—one acceptable and one unacceptable, many Brazilian feminists now began distinguishing between two kinds of Left—one acceptable, which acknowledged the specificity of women's oppression and respected the organizational autonomy of the movement; and another unacceptable, which subsumed women's struggle within the class struggle and attempted to instrumentalize women's movement organizations.

After the Second Congress, some feminists in São Paulo also began paying closer attention to the movements' own internal political and organizational dynamics. Collective reflections on "what had gone wrong" at the 1980 Congress led to a more pointed critique of the vanguardism and "authoritarian, hierarchical ways of doing politics" that prevailed in the male-dominant Left and in traditional political parties. Other movement activists began contrasting these to "feminist ways of doing politics," emphasizing the need for nonhier-

---

[29] *Em Tempo*, 101, cited in Moraes Nehring, "Família e Feminismo," p. 268.

archical forms of decision making and participation within the feminist movement.[30]

The flooding or stacking of the 1980 Coordination by manipulative sectarian groups also led to an explicit rejection of false representational instances of the women's movement; the creation of a centralized forum such as the Coordination, some feminists now argued, left the movement more vulnerable to political manipulation and instrumentalization. Many began insisting that the movement should remain decentralized and that groups should only come together for issue-specific campaigns and other tactical purposes. Others contended that the very idea of organizing a "Congress"—where diverse sectors of the women's movement would be "represented" and priority organizing issues for the movement as a whole would be set—was in itself wrongheaded. Some advocated more loosely structured gatherings and more fluid discussions, where individual activists would come together as women, not as "representatives" of this or that group, and freely could learn from one another's organizing experiences. Others maintained that a centralized umbrella organization such as the Coordination was neither necessary nor desirable.

By 1980, the diversification of organizational activities among women in the urban periphery also testified to the growing complexity women's movement politics in São Paulo as the feminine movements' political practice gave rise to changing conceptions of working-class women's "general" and "specific" struggles. After the 1978 legislative elections (see chapter 6 below), the political demands of the Cost of Living Movement and the Feminine Amnesty Movement were absorbed by all sectors of the opposition, diluting much of the gender-related content of those movements. But new organizational initiatives, undertaken in collaboration with feminists and other extracommunity activists such as left-wing party militants, spread throughout poor and working-class neighborhoods in São Paulo.

As women participants gained consciousness of themselves as women, and therefore as second-class citizens of the community, some feminine groups assumed more explicitly feminist dimensions. In the late 1970s, for example, the church-sponsored domestic sewing class at Jardim Miriam was transformed into a "professionalization" or occupational training course for women. After months of discussion, a handful of local women in collaboration with three middle-class feminists decided that "the [domestic sewing] class that we had fell into the same old routine of showing women how to be better

---

[30] After 1980, many feminist groups professed to be promoting such alternative, nonhierarchical practices among their members. But this goal proved somewhat elusive and authoritarian practices were still in evidence within some groups in the late 1980s. A full analysis of the internal dynamics of Brazil's feminist and feminine organizations would require a separate ethnographic study. My intent in this study was to examine the evolution of feminist and feminine discourses and the movements' relationship to changing institutional politics. The enduring gap between feminist ideology and movement practice merits further analysis by feminist social scientists.

housewives . . . there was no discussion of anything, just sewing.''[31] The feminists found outside support for the installation of industrial sewing machines at the church and the course began with an enrollment of twenty to twenty-five local women.[32]

The middle-class women conceived of the course in a way that was very much in keeping with prevailing Paulista feminist political strategies before 1979–1980: ''we were going to 'develop' these women, teach them skills so that they could become incorporated in productive labor. We decided to hold discussions about why women needed to gain skills and financial independence, why working outside the home was important for women.''[33] They developed simple texts, in collaboration with the local women organizers, which were then read and discussed during the ''theoretical'' section of the professionalization course, a time when students put their sewing aside to engage in collective discussions of issues middle-class organizers assumed would be of primary interest to them as working-class women. One such early text conveys the central themes around which the course was originally structured:

> Our objective is to develop a professionalization course in industrial sewing, in which women can learn to work the machines and also learn to sew, as well as gain knowledge of what it means to be a woman worker in the society in which we live.
>
> However, in order for us to understand all of that it is necessary, first, that we understand the situation that each of us lives in today: in the family, in our work within the home, in our work outside the home (for those of us who do), in the community.
>
> From there, we will try to relate all of this with the idea of having a profession: will it change something in our lives? why have we not sought a profession until now? why do we want a profession? what type of problems do we confront?[34]

But as one of the feminist core organizers of the group put it, ''within the first three months everything we thought the course would be fell apart. . . . The course became their space. They spoke much more freely about a number of things from the beginning than we did . . . things like sexuality, their intimate relationships . . . things we hadn't anticipated discussing in the group.''[35] At

[31] Interview with two of the local core organizers of the Jardim Miriam women's group, São Paulo, December 15, 1982.

[32] Like many church-linked organizations in São Paulo, the group received funding from a Dutch Catholic charity. The grant included money for the construction of a new church and a new wing for its organizational activities. So in an unusual reversal of church support for local women's organizations, the local women's group at Jardim Miriam, in effect, supported the church.

[33] Interview with two of the middle-class core organizers of the Jardim Miriam women's group, São Paulo, August 15, 1983.

[34] Grupo de Mulheres do Jardim Miriam, ''Curso de Profissionalização em Costura Industrial,'' n.d. (Mimeograph).

[35] Interview with middle-class feminist organizers, São Paulo, August 15, 1983.

the request of students in the class, discussions gradually focused less on "women's work" and more on such topics as differential education of children, women's socialization, women in the family, and so on. A woman doctor joined the group in early 1980 and, at the behest of students in the class, began leading discussions on "woman's body" and "woman's health"; these topics became the focus of the course during its second year.

By mid-1980, the course's weekly theoretical discussions on women's health and reproduction were drawing over one hundred women so that meetings had to be held in the church itself. Topics of discussion, suggested by participants themselves, included virginity and sexual relations before marriage, unwanted pregnancy and abortion. At one discussion of reproductive rights and family planning, nearly three hundred local women flooded the church.

Core organizers had approached the parish priest on a number of occasions concerning "the limits of the women's group within the progressive discourse of the church . . . we wanted to know how far we could go in discussing the specificity of women's oppression."[36] The priest had supported the group's original proposal of developing an occupational training course for neighborhood women. But as the content of the group's discussions gradually was radicalized, challenging some of the core doctrines of the church regarding sexual norms, the family, and contraception, his support waned, eventually leading to overt conflict between the core organizers of the women's group and the local parish.

Some of the more conservative church women were scandalized by the stories of back-alley abortions, extramarital relations, and sexual relations in general that typified the course's theoretical discussions by 1980–1981. Some complained to the parish priest that the women's group had "gone too far." He then approached the core organizers, arguing that they had not "respected the limits of the parishoners" and must therefore discontinue their discussions of such controversial issues. The core organizers replied that "he thought our work was absolutely secondary within the political work of the church, [we reminded him] that the women in our group did all the support work for the church but received no support for their own issues in return. . . . The women were the foundation of the church's activities in the neighborhood . . . they cleaned, cooked . . . even did [the priest's] laundry."[37] From my own observations, women's group participants did in fact provide essential support services for other church-linked community groups and were key participants in a number of those groups. They had, for example, collected and prepared food baskets for the local campaign in solidarity with striking autoworkers during

---

[36] Interview with two of the middle-class feminist organizers of the Jardim Miriam women's group, São Paulo, August 15, 1983.

[37] Ibid.

1979–1980. And whereas the local priest, a fervent advocate of liberation theology, seemed comfortable pushing "the limits of the parishoners" on class issues and the need for "general social transformation," gender-specific issues that directly challenged church moral doctrines appear to have been a different matter altogether. As the course increasingly centered on women's oppression in the private sphere, the tenuous alliance between the women and the local male practitioners of liberation theology became ever more strained.

After several heated discussions with the priest and extensive deliberations among the core organizers of the group, the women decided to leave the church and become an autonomous women's association. They rented a separate meeting hall, retaining two of their workshop spaces in the church, but broke all organizational ties with the parish. However, individual group participants continued to be active in church-linked community organizations. And curiously, many of the men I talked to who were involved in those organizations, and the priest himself, continued to think of the women's group as a church-linked group. Others dismissed it as a "misdirected" organization of women who did not understand what was really important for people in the neighborhood, and who were dividing the community struggle.

Significant numbers of neighborhood women appear to have disagreed with this assessment. Over the course of the late 1970s and early 1980s, the women's group enrolled over 350 local residents in its professionalization course. Some became monitors in the course; they taught the basics of garment making and led new students in invariably animated discussions of domestic violence, women's legal rights, women in politics, divorce and legal separation, women's movements, feminism, and other subjects that male church activists had deemed irrelevant to working-class women. Some participants' lives were radically empowered by their experiences in the group: with the moral and material support of the group, one woman was able to leave a husband who beat her for over twenty years, for example. While some were physically prevented from attending the course because husbands thought it "made them too uppity"—a frequent subject of discussion in the course—others developed more respectful, egalitarian relationships with their spouses and children. Whereas male church activists labeled feminism a "bourgeois movement," dozens of local poor and working-class women began claiming feminism as their own.

In a 1982 survey conducted among ninety-two new student/participants by the core organizers of the women's group at Jardim Miriam, seventy-nine of the respondents said it was important to have a women's organization in the neighborhood, eleven said they did not know, and only two thought it was not important. The activies they suggested such an organization could undertake in the future were as varied as the issues that shape women's daily lives within the domestic political economy of the popular classes. Eighteen respondents suggested that the women's group should focus on "discussing and resolving neighborhood problems''; twelve wanted the organization to deal with women's problems ''as women'' within the neighborhood and eleven believed the group ought to educate local women about their ''rights as women''; still others wanted the women's association to assist indigent women and children, pressure local government authorities for more day care and public health facilities in the neighborhood, or promote leisure activities for local women ''because all women do is work all day and all night and we need a place to relax from housework.''[38]

Similar conflicts between local women's groups and the church developed in Grajaú, another popular women's organization with which I had frequent contact. A local mothers' club also served as the basis for further organizational activities for women in the neighborhood. In early 1980, a small group of women began meeting in the church and in one another's homes to discuss ''women's role in the family, in politics, women's experience of sexuality, and so on.''[39] With the help of feminists from *Sexualidade e Política* (then a subgroup of the *Associação das Mulheres* focused on women's health issues), the women organized a class on reproduction and sexuality that ran throughout 1980. As dozens of neighborhood women began attending the discussions, the group had to move to the meeting hall of the local *Partido dos Trabalhadores* (Workers' Party or PT): ''We could not return to the church because there the discussion was another one and now ours was something else altogether. . . . The priest told us that women in the *favela* don't need sex, they need bread . . . I told him that women today do need and want sex . . . and that if their husbands beat them or mistreat them, they need alternatives.''[40] Men from other community groups were also less than supportive of the women's group, ''they did not want their wives to participate . . . they said that we were being divisive . . . but we told them we needed to discuss our own issues, our own things.''[41]

With the collaboration of feminists and women PT organizers in the neighborhood, the women's group also left the PT meeting space and procured funds for the creation of a women's center in the neighborhood. As in Jardim Miriam, they obtained external funding[42] and began sponsoring a number of occupational training classes, ''consciousness'' groups, lectures, and other activities for neighborhood women. They also provided gynecological and other medical services for women as there were no health facilities in the neighborhood. By the time the center was officially inaugurated in early 1983, the *Casa*

[38] Data from a 1982 open-ended survey questionnaire designed and administered by core organizers and monitors of the Jardim Miriam group.

[39] Group interview with members of the *Casa da Mulher de Grajaú*, São Paulo, August 19, 1983.

[40] Interview with the president of the *Casa da Mulher do Grajaú*, August 19, 1983.

[41] Ibid.

[42] In this case, a grant from the Pathfinder Fund in the United States.

da Mulher do Grajaú (Grajaú Women's House) boasted over 250 local members.

Within the wide range of women's organizations found in poor and working-class neighborhoods in São Paulo, both of these groups are unusual cases. Most are restricted in their activities due to a lack of organizational resources. Others are ideologically restricted by their continuing ties to the church or antifeminist sectors of the Left.

The continued political hegemony of the church in the urban periphery in general thus severely circumscribes the nature, content, and political direction of gender- and class-based politicization among the popular classes. As Herminia Maricato puts it, "without [the church], 90 percent of the urban social movement organizations in São Paulo would not exist."[43]

The church provides an indispensable infrastructural base for local organizing efforts. Thus, as the range of secular organizational initiatives expanded in Jardim Miriam and some community groups broke away from the parish, horizontal linkages between community groups, vital to organizational survival, were considerably weakened: "In the late 70s, everything was still concentrated in the parish and you had far greater possibilities for contact with all kinds of people. . . . It wasn't like today, each [group] with its own work . . . before, there was always a minimum of [collective] discussion. . . . The activities of our day-care group, for example, always counted on some support from others."[44]

And the church's control of organizational resources, even after new institutional alternatives for popular participation emerged during the latter stages of liberalization, presents serious obstacles for social movement groups that seek political or ideological autonomy from the church. As one of the core organizers of the Jardim Miriam women's group noted: "when we were in the church, we had more women participating. The church draws people, not because it's political, but because it's church."[45]

Jardim Miriam is again a case in point. After they broke with the church, participation in the sewing course sponsored by the Jardim Miriam women's group gradually declined. In early 1983, core organizers decided to change their strategy vis-à-vis women in the neighborhood, opting to phase out the course and establish a women's center. A group of approximately ten local women began meeting weekly with a feminist organizer from *SOS-Mulher*

[43] Hermínia Maricato, *Em Tempo* 42, December 18, 1978, p. 4, cited in Tilman Evers, "Síntesis Interpretativa del 'Movimento do Custo de Vida', un Movimiento Urbano Brasileño" *Revista Mexicana de Sociología* 43, no. 4 (October–December 1981), p. 1385.

[44] Interview with the Director of the Jardim Miriam day care center, São Paulo, August 18, 1983.

[45] Interview with two middle-class core organizers of the Jardim Miriam women's group, São Paulo, August 15, 1983.

(SOS-Women), a group providing services to women victims of rape and domestic violence, hoping to create a similar organization in the neighborhood.

By late 1983, the local parish and the Jardim Miriam women's group were again at war. Rumors about the "bourgeois feminist" nature of the proposed women's center, its alleged intention to "promote lesbianism" and "tear apart our families" spread throughout the neighborhood like wildfire. The parish priest and some local male organizers fanned the flames, suggesting moreover that external monies were misused by some members of the women's group to the detriment of other parish activities. Frightened by rumors and enticed by the parish's promise of continuing its earlier activities among women, some of the core organizers broke with the women's group and returned to the church.

By mid-1985, the independent women's group had ceased to exist and neighborhood women were once again attending domestic sewing classes at the church. There were lingering signs of "consciousness." Church women still celebrated International Women's Day in the neighborhood; a woman worker was always on the roster for local May Day celebrations. But gone were the theoretical discussions that drew and inspired hundreds of women in earlier years.[46]

In the absence of space for critical ideological reflection, autonomous gender-based politicization is thus often jeopardized. Only when substantial material or organizational resources become available, as in the case of *Casa da Mulher do Grajaú*, is sustained, non–church-linked mobilization possible. In both these communities, individual feminist activists played a crucial role in procuring alternative material resources and facilitating the development of critical gender consciousness among neighborhood women. In the later 1970s and early 1980s, these kinds of concrete efforts on the part of some Paulista feminists to foster women's consciousness and build a cross-class women's movement did, importantly, furnish women of the popular classes with new ideological and organizational tools for gendered resistance.

Organizational resources are also made available to some community groups through ties established to the various left-wing political tendencies active in the urban periphery. But the ideological perspectives of those orthodox Marxist groups similarly constrain the content and direction of community movements' political claims. Other women's groups that I observed in the urban periphery, which were linked to one or another sectarian political tendency, focused on organizing women around gender-*related* issues (like running water, electricity, and other services) or "general" community activities. Reproductive issues, sexual violence against women, or issues related to women's role in marriage and the family seldom were addressed openly.

Women's groups like those in Jardim Miriam or Grajaú, then, are decidedly

---

[46] The above discussion of the downfall of the Jardim Miriam group is based on interviews conducted with participants on both sides of the split in August 1985.

the exception to the rule. The politicization of gender-specific issues, "private" issues, did not occur to anywhere near the same extent in most of the groups I visited or whose activities I learned of at regional or citywide meetings and congresses. The political trajectories of these two groups, nevertheless, highlight the fact that women of the popular classes *are* concerned with gender power relations as well as with reproduction and production and that given the organizational resources and the ideological space, they do sometimes articulate gender-specific needs and concerns. If these groups had not broken with the church or if they had been mobilized or influenced by sectarian political tendencies their organizational dynamics would undoubtedly have been rather different.

COMPETING POLITICAL DISCOURSES ON GENDER: THE EVOLUTION OF FEMININE, FEMINIST, AND ANTIFEMINIST MOVEMENTS IN BRAZIL

By 1980–1981, the so-called women's movement in São Paulo had become an organizationally complex and ideologically diverse political movement. And an ever expanding array of groups claimed a place within the ranks of that movement. After the Second Congress, a distinctive independent feminist political identity took shape and was further consolidated at a statewide feminist meeting, attended by some 150 women, held at Valinhos in June of 1980. Many Paulista women I talked with in the early and mid-1980s recalled Valinhos as a critical turning point for the São Paulo feminist movement, a watershed in their own consciousness as women, a moment when their personal understanding of feminist activism was transformed.

During a four-day retreat at a cloistered nunnery in the city of Valinhos in the interior of São Paulo state, dozens of feminist activists engaged in criticism and self-criticism of their planning and conceptualization of the Second Congress and other feminist events and activities. Many of those present argued that a clearer distinction must be made between groups organizing women for participation in community struggles or political parties and expressly feminist efforts aimed at organizing poor and middle-class women as women, directed at raising women's consciousness of their subordinate status within all social classes. Some argued that while feminists should continue to help women secure better urban services, for example, what distinguished feminist organizing efforts in the urban periphery from those led by the church or the Left was that feminists urged women to think critically about why it was community women, instead of men, who engaged in struggles over consumption and reproduction.

Others insisted, for example, that feminists must prioritize working on those issues that typically were ignored by community groups and political parties and were banned outright from the agendas of their erstwhile allies in the opposition, including women's groups with ties to the sectarian Left. Discussions centered on how independent feminists might deepen their analysis of issues such as violence against women, sexuality, and reproductive rights and on how Paulista activists would pursue new organizing initiatives around such issues.[47] The presence of a sizable openly lesbian contingent, composed mostly of women affiliated with GALF, also drew participants' attention to issues heretofore absent from most feminist platforms, issues such as sexual pleasure, interpersonal relations among women, sexual power relations, and the social construction of heterosexuality.[48]

After Valinhos, independent feminists undertook new types of political activities. The "generic" activities of earlier years gave way to more "genderic," issue-focused ones. Most women from existing feminist groups rallied around three political banners advanced at the Valinhos meeting. They created an umbrella organization that would provide counseling and social services to victims of sexual abuse and domestic violence, which later became a new feminist group, *SOS-Mulher*. A feminist commission for family planning and against population control was formed. And a new women's newspaper, *Mulherio*, reflecting the changed genderic political perspective of the feminist movement, was founded.

During 1980, Paulista feminists staged protests in support of prostitutes, in solidarity with the Mothers of the Plaza de Mayo in Argentina, and joined the gay movement and the Black movement in a protest march against the police chief's efforts to clean up the streets of downtown São Paulo of gays, Blacks, prostitutes, transvestites, and other "undesirables."

SOSs were also created in seven other major cities in subsequent years. Women in Recife organized an *SOS-Corpo* (SOS-Body), providing gynecological and contraceptive counseling to women in poor and working-class neighborhoods. And expressly feminist groups emerged in cities in the regions outside the Brazilian industrial triangle such as Goiânia, Fortaleza, Porto Alegre, Curitiba, Florianópolis, Salvador, and many others.

CONCLUSION

Though the Cost of Living and the Feminine Amnesty Movements were absorbed by the political opposition after the 1978 elections, the Struggle for

---

[47] My discussion of Valinhos is based on numerous conversations with feminists in São Paulo and on the analysis of photos and documents from the meeting collected by women present who graciously made their personal archives of the meeting available to me. I am especially grateful to Maria Teresa Aarão for granting me access to her personal files and notes on Valinhos.

[48] GALF attended this historic meeting en masse, according to several lesbian feminist activists I talked with, in order to make their presence felt among heterosexual feminists and to claim their rightful place within the ranks of the feminist movement. They led discussions on lesbian sexuality, sexual pleasure, lesbian and gay liberation, and their experience of homophobia within the feminist movement. And as many GALF activists proudly recounted to me in the mid-1980s, they also shocked some heterosexual feminists by setting up a graphic photo display on the grounds of the nunnery, featuring explicit portrayals of GALF members making love to one another.

Day Care Movement continued to grow during 1980, and won significant concessions from local government officials. Popular women's organizations also sprang up throughout urban Brazil and some initial steps were taken in the organization of rural women workers in the interior. And thanks in large part to the ideological and material resources provided by middle-class feminists, some women's groups in the urban periphery, exemplified by those found in Jardim Miriam and Grajaú, also began articulating more radical gender discourses.

In the preceding chapters, I argued that militant motherhood provided the initial rationale for and legitimation of working-class women's increased political participation. But by the late 1970s and early 1980s, as this chapter has shown, some popular women's groups began articulating their class-specific, strategic gender interests as well. The very process of claims making and organizing altered participants' self-perception and enhanced their consciousness of themselves as women, as a subset of "poor people" with particular rights and needs.

By the early 1980s, many of the women who came into the feminist movement through either academic and professional networks or through militant Left and student movement networks achieved a significant degree of ideological consensus on the fact that women's movements needed to focus on how gender power relations, as well as class relations or social relations of production and reproduction, affected women's lives in all social groups and classes.

The radicalization of feminist claims over time grew out of the political experience of some feminists within the wider opposition to authoritarian rule. Brazilian socialist feminists encountered relentless resistance from opposition groups who insisted on establishing a "hierarchy of oppressions," wherein the struggle for gender equality invariably was deemed secondary. And as feminists' work with women's groups in the urban periphery revealed that poor and working-class women *were* concerned about such "unorthodox" issues as contraception, sexuality, abortion, and so on, some feminists developed a more radical critique of gender power relations and sharpened their condemnation of the sectarian and authoritarian political practices of the male-dominant opposition that, some feminists now maintained, reinforced gender inequality. Whereas, as shown in chapter 4, the practice of early feminist groups was deductively derived from various Marxist theoretical perspectives, this chapter has revealed that as the movement developed, feminist practice gave birth to new theoretical insights about the specificity of women's oppression.

Some women's movement participants began arguing that there was no reason to organize women separately for participation in the struggle for "general social change" or in social and political causes that affect women and men equally. If a National Constituent Assembly interests women as much as men, then women should be organizing for it together with men, not in sex-segregated political organizations. Some independent feminists argued that to do so merely reinforces existing patterns of gender inequality by isolating women from the men who are often times making the ''real'' political decisions.

Women whose primary loyalties remained with militant parties of the Left, of course, disagreed with such an assessment. And not to be outdone by ever-more visible and effective organizing efforts on the part of independent sectors of the women's movement, partisan women also stepped up their recruitment efforts among women and founded their own, adamantly *non*feminist women's organizations, as will be seen in chapter 6 below.

Considered antifeminists by many of the women active in independent feminist groups, especially after Valinhos, women linked to political parties were deeply mistrusted and clearly excluded from the movements' newfound definition of autonomous feminist organizing. This vehement rejection of party activism as intrinsically inimical to the feminist cause would return to haunt ''independent'' feminists who enthusiastically joined new opposition parties after 1980–1981 and to confound the movements' incipient posture on political autonomy, as will be shown in chapters 6 and 7 below.

This chapter has demonstrated that divergent conceptions of the proper role of women in social and political change and acute conflicts over the appropriate content and context of women's struggle multiplied as independent and party-linked women's groups—feminine, nonfeminist, feminist, and antifeminist—proliferated during 1979–1981. As will be seen below, ideological and strategic differences were further accentuated during the 1981–1982 electoral conjuncture, which represented a new stage in the breakdown of authoritarianism and initiated the final stage of the process of transition to civilian rule; to more effectively advance some of their policy goals, women's movement activists were pushed to take sides.

CHAPTER SIX

Taking Sides: Women's Movements and Political Parties, 1974–1982

THE 1982 elections marked a critical turning point in Brazilian transition to civilian rule, the most significant shift in the relationship between civil society and the Brazilian "political class" since the inception of military authoritarianism in 1964. The electoral conjuncture also signaled the onset of a new stage in the relationship between women's movements and institutional politics in Brazil.

Though the two-party system decreed into existence by the military regime constituted little more than a illusion of democratic competition during the 1960s and early 1970s, by the mid-1970s, that illusion became a reality (albeit a qualified reality), as the regime's scheme of controlled elections proved to be its political Achilles' heel. Following the unexpected ascent of the opposition party in the 1974 congressional elections, the electoral process and the party system suddenly attained far greater significance in the struggle against the dictatorship.

But most social movements continued to view electoral participation as an additional form of *protest, not* an avenue through which to influence policy or achieve political *power*; in the mid-1970s, that power was still solidly and exclusively in the hands of the military and their ruling-class allies. Thus, from 1975 to 1981, women's organizations of all types mostly restricted their activities to protest actions, mobilization, and consciousness raising. And, though individual women's movement activists joined the only existing opposition party (the MDB, Brazilian Democratic Movement), most viewed the legal opposition as lacking in effective power to carry forth women's demands into legislative arenas.

But as election returns increasingly favored the opposition over the course of the 1970s, advancing a progressive women's policy agenda appeared more viable to some. Gradually, many feminists in São Paulo began arguing that women should be encouraged to participate in elections. Some also insisted that the electoral conjunctures afforded unique opportunities to spread the feminist message to regions of the state as yet untouched by feminist mobilizational efforts.

For the 1978 campaign, several feminist organizations and individual activists came together to elaborate a joint set of demands, the *Carta dos Direitos da Mulher* (Women's Rights Declaration), called the "popular" or *auténtico* (authentic) MDB candidates together, and pledged to support only those candidates who would endorse their united platform. The MDB was then an electorally fortified, if still relatively powerless, coalition of all oppositional political tendencies (from the Center-Right to Far-Left) around which the diverse strands of the women's movement could easily rally without excacerbating existing divisions within the divergent sectors of the movement. Adamantly independent feminists, neighborhood mothers' clubs, and women MR-8 (Eighth of October Revolutionary Movement) militants alike could unite in their support for the single legal party of the opposition.

After 1980, however, the opposition split into five new parties with distinct political visions. And the heightened importance of electoral competition and of conventional, institutionally based opposition highlighted the differences between feminist, feminine, and nonfeminist sectors of the women's movement in São Paulo, differences which, as we saw in the preceding chapter, rose unmistakably to the surface after the Second Congress of Paulista Women.

Differences were accentuated as each sector of the movement developed a distinctive relationship with parties of the opposition. First, for the women who so adamantly announced their intent to chart an independent path for feminist mobilization, the 1982 elections had disorienting and divisive consequences. The newly proclaimed, but still precarious, organizational and ideological autonomy of independent sectors of the Paulista feminist movement was deeply confounded as many "independents" flocked to electoral politics and engaged in pressure-group tactics. Unlike poor and working-class women's movement participants from the urban periphery, university-educated, middle-class, white feminists gained significant access to new centers of opposition "power" and the rift between feminine and feminist mobilization grew wider. Given the highly elitist nature of the Brazilian party system, popular feminine groups gained only limited access to the new partisan forums of opposition struggle. Lastly, the women who some feminists now denounced as mouthpieces of the Left, militants ostensibly beholden to sectarian parties of the Left, enthusiastically enlisted in the new opposition parties. They rushed to create mass organizations of women whose members could be mobilized more readily in support of candidates endorsed by their sectarian political organizations.

This chapter begins by examining the growing significance of elections in authoritarian Brazil and exploring the resulting changes in the relationship between political society and organized civil society during the 1970s and early 1980s. My analysis focuses on how the shift from a two-party to a multiparty system in 1979–1980 fundamentally altered the dynamics of that relationship. I examine the political debates that took place within women's movement organizations and parties as to the appropriate relationship of social movements to political-partisan electoral competition. I pay particular attention to how these debates revived many long-standing ideological and strategic differences among independent feminists as to: (1) the necessity of *dupla militancia* (women's double militancy or simultaneous participation in movement organizations and political parties); (2) the strategic importance of absolute or relative autonomy of movement organizations from parties; and (3) the relationship between general social change (as represented by alternative political party programs) and gender-specific social change (spearheaded by women's movement organizations).

I was able to trace the evolution of these debates over time as I conducted extensive interviews with movement participants and party militants in São Paulo and Rio de Janeiro during late 1981, just as these debates were assuming full shape in anticipation of the party conventions and elections to be held during 1982. When I returned to the field in early October of 1982, the campaign was in full swing and I was able to observe the practical results of the ideological and strategic struggles waged within the movement throughout the preelectoral period.

ELECTIONS UNDER AUTHORITARIAN RULE: THE REBIRTH OF POLITICAL SOCIETY IN BRAZIL

During most of the 1970s, Brazilian women's movements considered conventional parties and elections to be largely irrelevant to their generic transformational project. To understand fully why women's movement activists came to view opposition parties and electoral participation as something more than an authoritarian sham, then, we must first examine how elections gradually and unpredictably were transformed into important vehicles for undermining the military regime's hegemonic strategy.

Until 1979, the only legal opposition party was the MDB, which was "decreed into existence" by the military government in 1965. Institutional Act No. 2 dissolved all existing parties, purged the political class of all "subversives" (defined as anyone opposed to military rule or even vaguely associated with the populist politics of the 1940s to 1960s), and forced survivors of the purge to choose between the MDB or the government's own ARENA (*Aliança Renovadora Nacional* or Alliance for National Renovation). Thus, cleansed of political dissidents and deprived of all possible legislative impact by subsequent institutional acts and by a highly centralized, military-dominated executive, Brazilian authoritarianism's two-party system was born a political weakling, spawned and nurtured by a military regime that sought absolute control, neatly veiled by a pseudodemocratic facade.[1]

[1] On the creation of the two-party system and its evolution during the 1970s, see Fábio Wanderley Reis, "O Eleitorado, os Partidos, e o Regime Autoritário Brasileiro," in *Sociedade e Política no Brasil Pós-64*, ed. Bernard Sorj and Maria Hermínia Tavares de Almeida (São Paulo: Brasilense, 1983); Fernando Henrique Cardoso, "Partidos Políticos," in *São Paulo: O Povo Em*

The facade fooled few Brazilians. During the 1960s and early 1970s, Brazilians commonly referred to the government's party as the party of *SIM* (Yes) and to the opposition MDB as the party of *SIM, SENHOR* (Yes, Sir!), as citizens were fully conscious of the fact that neither party wielded political power and that the only real decision makers were the president, his immediate advisors, and the Military High Command.

Given this scenario, it is no small wonder that most nascent social movements of the late 1960s and early 1970s, including the incipient women's movements, did not actively seek the support of the MDB. Nor is it surprising that the MDB did not try to expand its power base within civil society.

However, the regime's decision to maintain a democratic facade also required that it commit to holding regular elections and observe other procedural norms, if only for purposes of internal and international political consumption. And over time, the regime's would-be Mexico-style electoral system resulted in some rather unexpected outcomes. Designed, like Mexico's Institutional Revolutionary Party (PRI), to enhance the authoritarian regime's legitimacy while ensuring its continuity, the bipartisan electoral system nonetheless provided one of the few avenues available to ordinary citizens for the expression of political dissent. The MDB came to be perceived as the "party of the people," the "party of the poor," not necessarily due to concerted efforts at political propaganda and mobilization, but because the only alternative was ARENA, widely perceived as the "party of the government," the "party of the rich."[2]

Since voting is mandatory in Brazil, many voters cast blank or null votes when they have no particular party preference. During the 1960s and early 1970s, left-wing parties (then clandestine) and social movement groups encouraged citizens to cast null or blank votes as a sign of protest against the illegitimacy of the government's controlled electoral system. This strategy began to be modified during 1973. In that year, Ulysses Guimarães, president of the MDB, ran for the presidency as an "anticandidate." Guimarães traveled throughout Brazil, using his status as a candidate to speak out against the re-

---

Movimento, ed. Paul J. Singer and Vinícuis Caldeira Brant (Petrópolis: Vozes and CEBRAP, 1981), pp. 177–205; David V. Fleischer, "A Evolução do Bipartidarismo Brasileiro, 1966–1979," *Revista Brasileira de Estudos Políticos* 51 (1980): 155–85.

[2] For the best discussion of the gradual transformation of elections into popular "plebiscites," see Bolivar Lamounier, "O Voto em São Paulo, 1970–1978," in *Voto de Desconfiança; Eleições e Mudança Política no Brasil, 1970–1979*, ed. Bolivar Lamounier (Petrópolis: Vozes; São Paulo: CEBRAP, 1980). On why Mexico's hegemonic party system inspired regime ideologues in Brazil, see especially Thomas E. Skidmore, *The Politics of Military Rule in Brazil, 1964–1985* (New York: Oxford University Press, 1988), pp. 165–66. For an early and quite prescient analysis of why such a system was doomed to failure in the Brazilian context, see Juan J. Linz, "The Future of an Authoritarian Situation or the Institutionalization of an Authoritarian Regime: The Case of Brazil," in *Authoritarian Brazil: Origins, Policies, and Future*, ed. Alfred Stepan (New Haven: Yale University Press, 1973).

gime's policies. Popular responsiveness to Guimarães's efforts led the opposition party to reevaluate its electoral strategy and actively seek the votes of those citizens who opposed the social and economic policies of the regime.

And in 1974, the MDB staged its first electoral upset—it conquered 48 percent of the valid congressional votes nationwide. In São Paulo and other urban-industrial centers, the MDB overwhelmed the government party electorally, capturing 71 percent of the valid votes in the county of São Paulo. As Bolivar Lamounier notes, "studying the growth of the MDB in São Paulo is the same as studying a process of conversion of an urban vote into an opposition vote into an *emedebista* [MDB] vote."[3]

While the government party retained control of the Chamber of Deputies and the Senate, the election results showed conclusively that by 1974 it was losing its hold over civil society. By framing the illusion of democratic competition within a two-party system, "the regime also created an opposition party which would wind up effectively transforming itself into a thermometer of the regime's legitimacy."[4] Widely acclaimed as "plebiscitary elections" in which the citizens of Brazil confirmed their rejection of the military regime, the 1974 elections led both the opposition party and emergent social movements to reevaluate the role of parties and elections in the struggle against military authoritarian rule.

After 1974, the MDB was hailed as the *sigla magica* (the magical acronym), capable of uniting diverse social sectors and political tendencies in electoral opposition to the regime. The opposition discovered a new and unexpected arena of struggle—electoral competition. And the government was forced to develop new mechanisms to thwart the MDB's electoral ascent.

In anticipation of the 1976 municipal elections, the Geisel administration introduced the first of a series of defensive reforms aimed at combating the MDB's growing electoral "magic." On July 1, 1976, the government promulgated Decreto-Lei No. 6,639, signed by then minister of justice, Armando Falcão, which came to be known as the *Lei Falcão*. The decree prohibited paid electoral propaganda on TV and radio and thus diminished the possibility that the MDB's critique of the regime's policies would reach the majority of the electorate.

Ironically, the *Lei Falcão* forced the MDB to escalate its mobilizational efforts among the popular classes—among those sectors of the population least likely to be reached by the print media and who the 1974 electoral results showed to be the most *emedebista*, the inhabitants of the urban periphery.[5] As

[3] Lamounier, "O Voto em São Paulo, 1970–1978," p. 15.

[4] Maria D'Alva Gil Kinzo, "Novos Partidos: O Início do Debate," in *Voto de Desconfiança*, ed. Lamounier, p. 228.

[5] In "O Voto em São Paulo, 1970–1978," Lamounier shows conclusively that the poorest urban neighborhoods in São Paulo were the most consistently *emedebista* after 1974. See especially pp. 55–63.

Shiguenoli Miyamoto suggests, "the impossibility of access to the means of communication led candidates to try to mobilize large numbers of groups in their quest for support."[6] Whereas prior to 1974 the MDB had little contact with organizations of civil society, candidates now targeted groups like the *Sociedades de Amigos de Bairros* (Societies of Friends of the Neighborhood), *Comunidades Eclesias de Base* (Christian Base Communities or CEBs), religious and professional associations, mothers' clubs, student groups, and charity organizations.[7]

The 1976 electoral results confirmed the opposition's growing strength. The government elected the majority of the municipal legislators; but the opposition showed further gains in the popular vote over 1974.[8] The government feared that a continuation of such a trend in the 1978 legislative elections might compromise its parliamentary majority and once again reshuffled the electoral rules, stacking the results in its favor.

A parliamentary impasse over an executive-initiated reform of the judicial system afforded a convenient pretext. Geisel closed Congress in April of 1977 and passed a series of executive decrees dubbed the April Package (*O Pacote de Abril*). The package indefinitely postponed the direct election of governors, previously scheduled for 1978. It ensured government control over the legislature by creating what in popular parlance became known as the "bionic Senators,"[9] to be elected "indirectly" by the same electoral colleges that rubber-stamped the national executive's choices for governor in each state. And the package further stacked the electoral deck by altering the mechanisms for determining the number of seats in the Chamber of Deputies—now favoring the government electoral strongholds of the North and Northeast and decreasing

[6] Shiguenoli Miyamoto, "Eleições do 1978 em São Paulo: A Campanha," in *Voto de Desconfiança*, ed. Lamounier, p. 117.

[7] An incisive analysis of the lack of effective links between political parties and civil society is provided by Fernando Henrique Cardoso in, "Os Partidos Políticos e a Participação Popular," in *Os Partidos Políticos no Brasil*, vol. 2, ed. David Fleischer (Brasília: Editora Universidade de Brasília, 1981). On the lack of social reach of Brazilian political parties before 1964, see Gláucio A. D. Soares, "A Formação dos Partidos Nacionais," in *Os Partidos Políticos no Brasil*, vol. 1, ed. David Fleischer (Brasília: Editora Universidade de Brasília, 1981); and Olavo Brasil de Lima, Jr., "O Sistema Partidário Brasileiro, 1945–1962," in *Os Partidos Políticos no Brasil*, vol. 1, ed. David Fleischer. For the most comprehensive and compelling analysis of the Brazilian party system of the Second Republic, see María do Carmo Campello de Souza, *Estado e Partidos Políticos no Brasil (1930–1964)* (São Paulo: Alfa-Omêga, 1976).

[8] For a discussion of the 1976 municipal elections and the gains made by the political opposition in Brazil's major urban centers, see Fábio Wanderley Reis, "O Bipartidarismo nas Eleições Municipais de 1976," in *Os Partidos Políticos no Brasil*, vol. 1, ed. David Fleischer. Several detailed case studies of voter realignments throughtout urban Brazil are contained in Fábio Wanderley Reis, ed., *Os Partidos e o Regime: A Lógica do Processo Eleitoral Brasileiro* (São Paulo: Edições Símbolo, 1978).

[9] These senators were seen as "artificial" representatives, manmade replicas of real men, like the cyborg hero of the then popular television series, "The Bionic Man."

the representation of the more *emedebista* urban-industrial states of the South and Center-South.

In spite of the severe limitations imposed by the *Lei Falcão* and the April Package, and in some measure because of them, the opposition continued to gain force throughout the late 1970s. And its strength was derived in large part from the increased outreach of the MDB to organized sectors of civil society. As Miyamoto's study of the 1978 electoral campaign in São Paulo shows, government maneuvers to control electoral results intensified the opposition's mobilizational efforts.[10] Fernando Henrique Cardoso argues that because

> the MDB included people linked to some of the so-called grassroots or "base" movements, there was a greater symbiosis between popular movements and the electoral campaign [in 1978]. Thus, there were candidates supported by sectors of the student movement, candidates supported by union leadership, by feminist movements, by movements in defense of the urban squatters, by the movement against the rising cost of living, by the Black movement, etc. Some of the candidates of this type (almost all of whom were elected) were themselves leaders of the above-mentioned movements.[11]

Cardoso himself, as a candidate for a Senate seat in São Paulo, was among those supported by social movement organizations, including both feminist and feminine groups.

The *Movimento Feminino pela Anistia* (the Feminine Amnesty Movement), under the leadership of Therezinha Zerbini, also mobilized support for those candidates who hoisted the banners of the movement, regardless of whether those candidates belonged to ARENA or the MDB. Irma Passoni and Aurelio Peres, leaders of the Cost of Living Movement, garnered considerable support among the CEBs and mothers' clubs in São Paulo. And the rising cost of living and the demand for political amnesty, issues politicized by mothers' clubs and women's associations since the early 1970s, became central axes of the MDB campaign in São Paulo. The MCC's dual emphasis on the regime's regressive wage policies and the cost of living became the focal points of then Senator Franco Montoro's campaign, whose victorious reelection consolidated support within the MDB for his 1982 gubernatorial nomination in São Paulo.

The feminist movement in São Paulo also rallied around opposition candidates willing to endorse feminist issues.[12] Many of these candidates developed campaign materials specifically aimed at the female electorate and carried out considerable recruitment efforts among feminist and feminine movement organizations. And some explicitly acknowledged the specificity of women's

---

[10] Miyamoto, "Eleições do 1978," pp. 117–18, 140–50.

[11] Cardoso, "Os Partidos Políticos e Paticipação Popular," p. 59.

[12] See "Carta dos Direitos da Mulher" *Brasil Mulher* special issue, 1978. Candidates supported included Fernando Henrique Cardoso, Eduardo M. Suplicy, Airton Soares, Marco Aurelio Ribeiro, Geraldo Siqueira Filho, Fernando Morais, Alberto Goldman, and Antonio Rezk.

oppression. Cardoso's senatorial campaign, for example, stressed the need for "strengthening of civil society." He declared that "the MDB must run quite a bit before it can catch up with society. By this I mean that today there is a very profound sense of autonomy, of identity. The workers in their social movements say: I am a worker, I am not a student. And what do the women say? There is a feminine question. I am a woman." His platform included a call for "freedom of political and cultural expression, valorization of Blacks and other racial minorities, equality of rights for women" to move Brazil in the "direction of a society without exploiters and exploited."[13]

The MDB's "Feminine Department" also gained visibility during the 1978 campaign. Mostly made up of nonfeminist, female party militants, the department predictably "called on women to undertake a struggle next to their men, so that women can achieve political representation . . . struggling against the historical discriminations against women." During the 1978 campaign, MDB women concentrated on promoting women's participation in the electoral campaign and pressuring the party to nominate women for office.[14]

Most feminists did not participate directly in the MDB's organizational infrastructure and chose instead to work on the campaigns of individual candidates sympathetic to the movement. And unlike 1976, when the feminist press merely urged women to vote "generically" against the military regime,[15] in 1978, both *Brasil Mulher* and *Nós Mulheres* urged women to vote "genderically" as well. In 1976, the feminist movement did not believe that the elections represented anything other than the "approval of the official policies of the situation party with your vote or the manifestation of your discontentment, giving your vote to the opposition, with no other alternatives."[16] The feminist press made no reference to how candidates and elections might advance the struggle for women's rights. However, by 1978, the feminist press urged women to support the "popular" MDB candidates, "some of whom are women who will strengthen the struggle for women's emancipation. . . . [T]hey hope to conquer the political right that women have to play a decisive role in the construction of a more just society."[17] After 1978, many feminists came to view participation in electoral politics not just as an opportunity for educating and mobilizing the electorate around the movements' political banners; the electoral success of the MDB suggested that the opposition actually might be able to influence public policy and hence, support feminist policy initiatives.

Despite government maneuvers to quell the rising opposition tide, the MDB once again captured nearly half the popular vote nationwide in 1978 and its

[13] Miyamoto, "Eleições do 1978," pp. 128–29.
[14] *Nós Mulheres* 7 (March 1978).
[15] See *Brasil Mulher* 1, no. 4 (1976) and *Nós Mulheres* 2 (1976).
[16] *Brasil Mulher* 1, no. 4 (1976): 3.
[17] *Brasil Mulher* 3, no. 14 (November 1978).

electoral hold over the urban-industrial centers was further consolidated. In São Paulo, for example, its percentage of the valid votes grew from just over 30 percent in 1970 to 71 percent in 1974 to 77 percent in 1978.[18]

From the government's perspective, the 1965 two-party system had reached a definitive impasse. The bipartisan system unintentionally had evolved into a bipolar one—"the artificial simplification of [political] options had permitted the clear crystallization of certain basic tendencies," providing an "institutional mold for simplistic counterpositions" along the lines of "the government" versus "the people," "the rich" versus "the poor," and so on.[19] In the aftermath of the 1978 elections, the principal ideologues of the regime's controlled political opening sought to surmount this institutionalized electoral impasse. As Maria Helena Moreira Alves argues,

> By 1979 the civil-military coalition in power perceived in the electoral growth of the MDB a substantial threat. Studies carried out by the SNI [the National Intelligence Service] and other governmental agencies indicated that, in spite of the new electoral regulations, it was likely that the opposition would win control of the Congress, the state assemblies and even many of the municipal governments in the next elections. Hence, it had become necessary . . . to attempt to divide and fragment the opposition and to control more carefully the organization of political parties.[20]

A Party Reform Bill, masterminded by the principal ideologue of *abertura*, General Golberey do Couto e Silva, and implemented by the Figueiredo administration in December of 1979, thus forcibly dissolved both ARENA and the MDB and established strict rules for the creation of new political parties—rules that, as in the past, were intended to ensure the military regime's political hegemony.[21]

The new legislation required that, within a year of its passage, new parties hold regional conventions in at least nine states and municipal conventions in at least one-fifth of the municipalities in each of those states. Furthermore, municipal conventions could only be held in counties where parties had a minimum number of registered members. In order to become permanently registered with the Supreme Electoral Tribunal, each new party would have to re-

---

[18] Bolivar Lamounier, "O Voto Em São Paulo," p. 39.

[19] Fábio Wanderley Reis, "O Eleitorado, os Partidos, e o Regime Autoritário Brasileiro," p. 75.

[20] Maria Helena Moreira Alves, *State and Opposition in Military Brazil* (Austin: University of Texas Press, 1985), p. 212.

[21] See Alves, *State and Opposition*, pp. 212–20, for a concise description of those rules and their effects on the resulting new party system; for further information on the post-1979 party system see Maria D'Alva Gil Kinzo, "Novos Partidos: O Início do Debate," in *Voto de Desconfiança*, ed. Lamounier, p. 228; Gláucio A. D. Soares, "El Sistema Político Brasileño: Nuevos Partidos y Viejas Divisiones," *Revista Mexicana de Sociología* 44, no. 3 (July-September 1982): 929–59; and David V. Fleischer, "De la Distensión a la Apertura Político-Electoral en Brasil," *Revista Mexicana de Sociología* 44, no. 3 (July-September 1982): 961–98.

ceive 5 percent of the popular vote in the next congressional elections and at least 3 percent of the vote in each of the nine states in which it was formally organized.

While the regime intended these rules to guarantee the predominance of its new official party, the PDS (*Partido Democrático Social* or Democratic Social Party),[22] one unintended consequence was that the rules forced "various opposition sectors to engage actively in party organization at both the formal and grass-roots levels, an activity that involved the efforts of thousands of party militants over the next two years."[23] Thus, this new legislation, like the 1976 *Lei Falcão*, actually bolstered the political opposition by pushing it to strengthen its ties to civil society.

After 1979, the Party Reform Bill spurred contentious debates within the oppositon as to what kind of strategy would be most effective in countering the regime's hegemonic offensive while simultaneously addressing the concrete demands of diverse social groups and classes. And those debates seriously fragmented the opposition and bred strategic confusion within *both* political *and* civil society.

Alves neatly summarizes the substance of the ensuing debate among the various sectors of political society.

> Major opposition sectors defended the "democratic front" alliance, arguing that the sole alternative was to remain together in the only political party, which had been reborn "like the phoenix" from the extinct MDB. More conservative sectors of the opposition, however, viewed with interest the new possibility of acting as a transition government. The military government carefully wooed these sectors with the offer to negotiate a "new social pact" and allow the formation of transition conservative civilian governments. . . . Finally, working-class sectors of the opposition saw a new opportunity to build a grass-roots party more identified with labor and class concerns and open to the participation of workers.[24]

The first opposition tendency Alves identifies congealed into the *Partido Movimento Democrático Brasileiro* (Party of the Brazilian Democratic Movement or PMDB). The second formed two parties: the *Partido Popular* (Popular Party or PP), the party of Tancredo Neves, which brought together sectors of the bourgeoisie who had become disillusioned with the military regime's management of economic policy, and the *Partido Trabalhista Brasileiro* (Brazilian Labor Party or PTB), the revived Vargista party of the populist era. The

---

[22] The new *Lei Orgánica* required that "Partido" be included in the new names of all political parties. The purpose of this stipulation was two-fold. First, it would ostensibly require the old *Movimento Democrático Brasileiro* to abandon its "magical" acronym. Second, the renaming of the official party (PDS) was intended to dissociate the old ARENA from the policies of the military regime prior to 1979.

[23] Alves, *State and Opposition*, p. 214.

[24] Ibid.

third tendency identified by Alves also formed two parties, founding the *Partido dos Trabalhadores* (Workers' Party or PT), an outgrowth of the most politicized sectors of the new union movements of the 1970s, and the *Partido Democrático Trabalhista* (Democratic Workers' Party or PDT), a neopopulist, social-democratic party under the leadership of former governor of Rio Grande do Sul, Leonel Brizola. The PP later merged with the PMDB.

Political debates among varying sectors of the party opposition had direct repercussions within organized social movements. Like MDB party militants and elected officials, participants of social movement groups disagreed as to which strategy would be most appropriate for confronting the new political conjuncture. As the new parties scrambled to consolidate bases of support, opposition sectors within both political society and civil society basically aligned themselves behind two distinct, and often antagonistic, strategies: (1) the continued unity of an ideologically varied opposition "front" with the pragmatic, short-run objective of defeating the regime electorally in 1982 and thus ensuring the transition to liberal democracy; or (2) the creation of ideologically distinct opposition parties whose programs would address the substantive concerns of diverse social groups and classes and thus articulate the already certain, but still programmatically diffuse, oppositional tendencies characteristic of civil society.

Among social movement groups in São Paulo, the two competing strategies outlined above congealed into support for either the PMDB, the "democratic front" that became the direct political heir of the MDB, or the PT, the Workers' Party, a new political party with roots in the "new trade unionism" of the late 1970s, a party that attracted the allegiance of many of the popular MDB candidates discussed above.[25]

With the emergence of concrete partisan alternatives, the women's movements' "unity of purpose," already tenuous in the aftermath of the 1980 Congress, was further fragmented. No longer was party identification predicated upon support for or opposition to the military regime. After December 1979, it increasingly would be premised upon one's "larger" worldview. Moreover, with the direct election of state governors scheduled for 1982, and the concomitant strengthening of executive power at the state level, women's movement groups who supported particular parties, for the first time since the Goulart years, could expect some direct political payoffs.

Figueiredo's *Pacote de Novembro* (November Package) of 1981 further polarized both movement organizations and political parties. For the present

[25] Movement polarization differed in other Brazilian states where the PT did not emerge as a significant political force. For example, women's movement allegiances were divided among the PMDB, PT, and PDT in both Rio de Janeiro and Rio Grande do Sul; the PP, which later was incorporated into the PMDB, also exerted considerable influence in Minas Gerais; in most other states, the polarization between MDB and ARENA was largely transposed to support for their renamed political reincarnations—PMDB versus PDS.

analysis, the most significant features of the new package of electoral reforms were: (1) the prohibition of party coalitions in the selection of gubernatorial candidates; and (2) the establishment of a system through which voters were obliged to vote for candidates from the same party for each of the electoral offices under dispute in 1982—from municipal legislators (*vereadores*) to governor, referred to as the *voto vinculado* (straight-ticket voting, literally linked vote). These measures further prevented electoral coalitions among opposition parties and forced the voters to choose *one* party to represent their interests from the local through the national levels.[26]

FEMINISM, PARTIES, AND ELECTIONS

The 1981–1982 electoral conjuncture debilitated and partially demobilized the politically heterogeneous feminist movement in São Paulo. Just as an adamantly independent sector of the Paulista feminist movement had "come into its own" after the First and Second Women's Congresses and the Valinhos Meeting, the emergence of new partisan options and the 1982 electoral campaign revived many long-standing political and ideological differences among independent feminists.

As shown in chapter 5, in 1980–1981, many feminists in São Paulo asserted a political identity and purpose distinct from that of the orthodox Left, vehemently distinguishing their own goals from those women whose primary loyalties remained with the sectarian Left. Independent sectors of the feminist movement also consolidated links to popular women's associations and achieved wider public acceptability (reflected in more favorable media coverage of the movement). As several of my interviewees suggested, it finally seemed as if feminism, as a distinctive transformational project, had the potential to become a mass-based, cross-class political movement.

Just as 1980 was a peak mobilizational moment for the women's group at Jardim Miriam and other neighborhood-based feminine groups like the *Movimento de Luta por Creches*, it was a peak year for feminist mobilizations as well. But by late 1981, partisan rivalries had exacerbated a number of underlying political tensions within feminist organizations. Ideological and strategic differences generated splits in some groups and even facilitated the eventual dissolution of others.

Most of my interviewees noted that new divisions among feminists were not based on differing conceptions of feminism. Significant portions of the movement in São Paulo had achieved consensus on the need to focus the feminist project on the politics of the private sphere. But with the enforced fragmentation of the political opposition and the upcoming elections, independent fem-

---

[26] According to Alves, the new package was implemented because an SNI study predicted that the PDS was likely to lose the gubernatorial races in all but four states (*State and Opposition*, p. 223).

inists now disagreed, sometimes virulently, as to what would be the most appropriate short-term strategy for advancing gender-based social change.

Some argued that liberal democracy must first be consolidated before any further gains could be made in securing women's rights, that feminists could foster significant change only from within a democratically elected state government. These women tended to support the PMDB in São Paulo. As the political heir of the electorally successful MDB, the PMDB appeared to be the most "useful" or pragmatic vehicle through which to complete the democratic transition, enabling feminists to advance a concrete policy agenda in the short term.

Women who came into the movement through professional or academic networks were among the principal feminist supporters of the PMDB in São Paulo. Among them were those who saw political democracy as a necessary prelude to social and economic democracy (where democracy of both sorts includes women's equality). This was particularly the case for the women affiliated with the various communist parties. Brazilian Communists long had stressed the need to participate in a democratic front which, upon taking power, would permit the legal reorganization of the Left, and in turn, complete the democratic revolution, thus setting the stage for socialist revolution.

Other feminists in São Paulo, many of whom had previous political experience in the militant Left and student movements of the late 1960s and early 1970s, saw the PT as the potential expression of social movements at the level of institutional politics, as the "*retomada dum sonho*" (the resurgence of a dream) of class struggle that was crushed by the repressive apparatus of the State during the early 1970s.

Still other feminist movement participants deeply mistrusted either partisan option, fearing that the women's movement's goals would be subordinated to the goals of parties, and fiercely defended the absolute political, ideological, and organizational autonomy of feminine and feminist movements. According to many of those who engaged in party politics, a significant number of these women were nonetheless active sympathizers of either the PT or the PMDB.

Even before the new parties' conventions were held, tensions arose among independent feminists who sympathized with different parties. For example, when some women from the *Associação das Mulheres* suggested that São Paulo feminists gather again at Valinhos to develop a unified platform for the 1982 political campaign, rumors that some PMDB women were orchestrating the event as a forum from which to declare their candidacies for political office defeated the idea. São Paulo feminists also disagreed as to whether the movement should promote and support "feminist candidates" and if so, who those candidates would be. Moreover, the lines between what did or did not constitute a feminist platform were drawn differently by the various tendencies within the independent Paulista feminist movement.

As political rivalries among would-be feminist candidates and their supporters intensified, several feminist movement organizations began to feel the strain. Some groups, such as the *Centro da Mulher Brasileira*, *Frente de Mulheres Feministas*, and *Sociedade Brasil-Mulher* were almost completely demobilized and partisan tensions contributed to the total dissolution of other groups like the *Associação das Mulheres*. The feminist organizations most adversely affected by partisan rivalries were those "generic" feminist groups described in chapter 4 as "federations" or umbrella organizations for a wide variety of political activities, each informed by distinct political/ideological conceptions of "general social transformation."

Feminist groups with specialized projects or with a single-issue focus, such as *Centro Informação Mulher*, *SOS-Mulher*, *Grupo Ação Lésbica-Feminista*, and *Sexualidade e Política* weathered partisan competition somewhat more successfully. These groups seem to have been better able to resist polarization along party lines as a consequence of shared, concrete organizational goals— such as combating violence against women in the case of *SOS-Mulher* or fighting against heterosexism in the case of *Grupo Ação Lésbica-Feminista*.

The polarization of most feminist group participants into either the political camp of the PT or the PMDB also led the few feminist organizations that remained active throughout the campaign to defend adamantly the movement's autonomy. The insistence on absolute autonomy by some segments of the movement stemmed in part from earlier experiences of partisan manipulation and instrumentalization of the feminist agenda. But it was also rooted in an increasingly widely shared perception that the "cultural transformation" side of the feminist struggle might be jeopardized if feminists were forced to translate their political project into a set of programmatic items to be included in party platforms. Some also were concerned that as more feminist activists flocked to the PMDB or the PT, fewer continued earlier efforts to promote a critical gender consciousness among women in the urban periphery. Feminists' immersion in the 1982 campaign reduced their outreach efforts and contacts with poor and working-class feminine organizations, as those contacts increasingly were restricted to party-sponsored "women's events" and rallies for women candidates.

The demobilization of some feminist groups, then, was also a consequence of the fact that many feminists abandoned movement activism altogether to engage almost exclusively in feminist work within party organizations. In this sense, the long-standing question of double militancy began to be redefined. Whereas in the mid-1970s some feminists "pushed their party's line" in the feminist group in which they participated, now they pursued a "feminist line" in the party organizations in which they were active.

Ultimately, partisan rifts among São Paulo feminists also prevented them from coming together to propose a united platform of feminist demands to be endorsed by the political opposition, as they had in 1978.[27] In short, the au-

---

[27] Feminist organizations in Rio de Janeiro did come together to propose the *Alerta Feminista*

tonomous sector of the feminist movement in São Paulo was initially weakened rather than strengthened by the 1982 electoral conjuncture.

THE SECTARIAN LEFT STEPS IN: THE CREATION OF WOMEN'S FRONT GROUPS IN 1980 AND 1981

As contacts diminished between feminist and feminine groups, the MR-8 and the Communist Party of Brazil (PCdoB) seized the opportunity to promote their own partisan agendas among women in the urban periphery. In 1980, the MR-8 founded the *Federação das Mulheres Paulistas* (the Federation of São Paulo Women), an umbrella group that claimed to "represent" the "women's movement" in São Paulo. As the MR-8 now was harbored within the PMDB, independent feminists immediately denounced the Federation as a "phantom" women's front, said to have few actual contacts with long-standing feminine groups, and created for the sole purpose of advancing the political fortunes of the MR-8 within the PMDB electoral coalition. Not to be outdone by the MR-8, in 1981 the PCdoB (also lodged within the ideologically heterogeneous PMDB) decided it too would form a "mass women's organization," the *União de Mulheres de São Paulo* (Union of São Paulo Women), another umbrella organization that also claimed to represent the women's movement. But others in the women's movement quickly decried the Union as yet another instrumentalist sham.

While independent feminists continued to battle one another as a consequence of divergent partisan loyalties, the hostility between all "independent" feminists and the women who founded the Federation and the Union once again came to a head during the 1981 International Women's Day celebrations. In March of 1981, *two* Women's Congresses, each claiming to "represent" the women's movement as a whole, were held in São Paulo.

One, held in the Pacaembu Sports Stadium, was organized by women linked to the Federation of Paulista Women, the Union of Women of São Paulo, women from the PCB (the Brazilian Communist Party or *Partido Comunista Brasileiro*, also harbored within the PMDB), and other PMDB party activists and stressed women's participation in the "general struggle" for democracy. In a widely circulated document, the coordinators of that Congress unambiguously condemned the efforts of independent feminists to center the Third Congress's agenda on social relations of reproduction and the specificity of women's oppression within class relations and accused such women of being self-obsessesed, bourgeois, man-haters.

(Feminist Alert), a document that enumerated the political demands that candidates must endorse in order to receive the support of the women's movement. In Rio and Porto Alegre, feminist loyalties were divided between the PMDB, the PDT, and the PT. In most other areas of the country, where the electoral contest remained essentially bipartisan (PMDB vs. PDS), the electoral conjuncture did not prove as divisive for feminist movement organizations.

In reality, the resistance of these bourgeois ladies (*grá-finas*) to taking on the struggle against the rising cost of living, unemployment, mass sterilization and for democracy is due to the fact that for them, the principal source of the problems which today afflict Brazilian women is not the reactionary and anti-popular policies of the dictatorship but rather their husbands and male relatives. That is why they want . . . to transform the lamentable [incidence of] marital violence, the fruit of the despair and tyranny to which the people [are] subjected, into mere police cases. . . . In truth, the distancing of those ladies does not occur solely in relation to the problems of women of the popular classes, but in reality, in relation to their own condition as women. And that is why what they present as "specific [women's] problems" which should deserve the exclusive attention of the [Third] Congress, are in fact a direct negation of the feminine condition.[28]

The fact that such a hostile and unmistakably antifeminist posture was assumed by women who formed part of the PMDB irrevocably alienated many Paulista independent feminists from that party.

The "second" Third Congress, promoted by feminine and feminist groups who now came to be known as the *autonomistas* (autonomists),[29] was held at the Catholic University, and reiterated the gender-specific demands raised by the First and Second Congresses. In response to the accusations made in the document cited above, the organizers proclaimed that:

We lament the behavior of these *companheiras* and also the positions taken by the newspaper *Hora do Povo* after the [Second] Congress, wagering on the division of the women's movement, slandering and distorting the facts. The principal lesson we learned from these incidents is that we must struggle for the unity of the Women's Movement. A broad, mass movement where white women, black women, Catholics, Protestants, housewives, factory workers, etc. can participate. The differences that exist among us do not divide us, but on the contrary, enrich our movement.

We respect those differences and try to promote that which unites us: we are women and this determines much of our lives, we are women and because of this we are discriminated against, humiliated, silenced, isolated in our kitchens or op-

[28] Reproduced in Maria Carneiro da Cunha, "Contra o Dogmatismo e o Maniqueismo," *Movimento* (February 9–15, 1981).

[29] The organizations that sponsored this Congress included: *Sociedade Brasil Mulher*, *Associação das Mulheres*, *Departamento Feminino da Favela do Uirapuru*, *Centro da Mulher Brasileira*, *Coordenação da Campanha pela Legalização do Aborto*, *Associação das Donas-de-Casa*, *Serviço Orientação da Família (região sul)*, *Servico Orientação da Família (região leste)*, *Movimento Contra a Carestia*, *Movimento de Luta por Creches*, *Grupo de Estudos da Mulher*, *Departamento Feminino dos Bancarios*, *Sindicato dos Jornalistas (Comissão de Mulheres)*, *Associação dos Empregados em Entidades Sindicais*, *Centro de Cultura Operaria (zona sul)*, *Associação Popular de Saude*, *Acão Lésbico-Feminista*, *Sindicato dos Texteis*, *SOS-Mulher*, *Sindicato dos Arquitetos*, *Grupos de Rua COHAB-Itaquera*, *Grupo de Mulheres da Favela Nova Jaguare*, *SAB A.E. Carvalho*, and *Frente de Mulheres Feminista*.

pressed in factories and offices, we are women and we want to modify our role in society and in the family.[30]

The organizers of this Congress insisted that the women's movement must remain autonomous of political parties: "The Women's Congress is without a doubt a political event, but not a partisan event. We don't want women to divide themselves in support of one or another opposition party."[31] Referring to the partisan disruptions of the Second Congress (see chapter 5), the coordinators decried the positions taken by those organizing the Pacaembu Congress:

> A group which spoke in the name of the PMDB, in spite of the fact that it did not represent the positions of that Party with regard to women's struggle, saw our Congress as an opportunity to disseminate their [partisan] positions, not respecting the decisions of the majority, wanting to impose their proposals, causing commotion and dividing the women's movement.[32]

As this statement makes clear, the *autonomistas* no longer considered the *companheiras* who organized the Pacaembu Congress to form part of the women's movement; after 1981, women from groups like the Federation of Paulista Women were cast out definitively from the feminist fold.

POLITICAL PARTIES, ELECTIONS, AND NEIGHBORHOOD WOMEN'S ORGANIZATIONS

Legal and sectarian parties alike remained primarily the turf of middle-class women with greater class-based access to male-dominated, elitist, party forums; some of these women had long-standing ties to the MDB or clandestine political parties. While independent feminists battled one another and women from the MR-8 and the PCdoB scrambled to find new recruits for their party-linked women's mass organizations, women in the urban periphery remained relatively marginal to partisan internecine warfare.

Party identification in the urban periphery in 1982 remained largely bipolar—the PMDB seemingly inherited the MDB's "magical" appeal among the popular classes of urban Brazil.[33] Political polarization was thus somewhat less acute among popular women's organizations than among feminist groups, despite the efforts of the MR-8 and the PCdoB to influence women's vote in the urban periphery.

Nevertheless, in São Paulo, there was a great deal of elective affinity be-

[30] Reproduced in *Movimento* (February 16, 1981).

[31] Ibid.

[32] Ibid.

[33] Bolivar Lamounier and Judith Muszynski, "São Paulo, 1982: A Vitória do (P)MDB," *IDESP Textos* 2 (1983).

tween the PT and many urban movement organizations.[34] Many of those organizations professed to have developed a new political ethic and proclaimed a new style of "doing politics," focused on the resolution of immediate community needs and committed to fostering the practice of direct democracy among members of the community. The new urban movements of the 1970s mistrusted "old style" politicians whose clientelistic style and empty campaign-time promises clashed with the self-proclaimed "authenticity" of neighborhood direct democracy.[35] That mistrust was reinforced by the overt support of some sectors of the progressive church for an alternative approach to politics—an approach ostensibly embodied by the PT in São Paulo.[36]

The lines between "old style" and "new style" politics were clearly drawn at Jardim Miriam, where I was able to observe closely the final months of the 1982 campaign. The PT was the only party with a visible presence there, whereas the PDS, PMDB, and PTB all worked primarily through conventional party structures and less visible mobilizational methods.

The PT organized party nuclei (*núcleos*) throughout São Paulo's urban periphery. At Jardim Miriam and other neighborhoods for which I have primary and secondary data, the *núcleo* was organized by the same core of mobilizational agents who were instrumental in generating neighborhood movements, especially those linked to the progressive Catholic church.

During the electoral campaign in Jardim Miriam, it seemed as if the electoral contest were solely being held between the PT, supported by most community movements, especially those associated with the Roman Catholic church in the neighborhood, and the government's PDS, supported by the more traditional neighborhood associations, like the *Sociedade de Amigos de Bairro* and religious groups linked to the local "Brazilian" (conservative) Catholic church. Residents were highly mobilized during the campaign—innumerable PT rallies took place in the central plaza and *petista* campaign propaganda enveloped the urban landscape.

The core organizers of the local women's and day-care groups also enthu-

---

[34] While the PT organized many more *núcleos* in São Paulo's urban periphery than did the PMDB and also received the outright support of progressive sectors of the church in some regions of the city, the electoral "roll-back" of its grassroots political organizing proved quite limited—in 1982, it received only 14.3 percent of the vote in the city of São Paulo and only 7.6 percent in the interior of the state, for an overall 9.9 percent of the total state vote. Ibid., p. 10.

[35] Teresa Pires do Rio Caldeira, "A Luta pelo Voto em um Bairro da Periferia," *Cadernos do CEBRAP* (1984): 10–11.

[36] Cardoso notes that many of the new social movements had no previous experience in party politics and therefore viewed it with distrust: "During elections, say the critics, the politicians come and ask for the vote. Later they manipulate power without rendering accounts to the electorate and, worse, use politics for their own personal profit. . . . In this attitude, there frequently exists a super-estimation of the 'grassroots movements' and a sub-estimation of the political function of parties." Fernando Henrique Cardoso, "Os Partidos Políticos e a Participação Popular," in *Os Partidos Políticos no Brasil*, vol. 2, ed. David Fleischer, p. 59.

siastically supported the PT. These women were attracted by the *petista* emphasis on organizing a working-class party "from the base up" and by the PT's insistence that it would guarantee the political autonomy of social movements. The party professed a desire to become the direct "institutional expression" of social movements, a mere conduit for grassroots demands. Given earlier conflicts with the parish over the issue of the women's group's ideological autonomy (see chapter 5), this posture was particularly appealing to the core organizers of the Jardim Miriam women's group.

The core organizers of the women's group made "politics and elections" the focus of the sewing course's theoretical section during 1981–1982. At the beginning of each semester of the course, organizers would ask new and returning students what topics they wished to discuss during the theoretical portion of the classes. I was told that in 1981, the students wanted to discuss political parties and the upcoming elections since most expressed a lack of information about "this party business." The group invited PT and PMDB candidates, mostly women, to speak to the student/participants in the course. Contacts with those candidates were made by the middle-class feminists who worked closely with the neighborhood group, once again highlighting the centrality of extralocal agents in community organizations.

Throughout much of 1982, the group's classes featured educational slide shows and films, distributed by the church, on the meaning and importance of "the people's vote" in the upcoming elections. Core organizers promoted discussions among student/participants as to the various political options represented by each of the new parties, always signaling out the PT as "the only party that really belongs to the workers" and "the one which is most responsive to our community's needs." And when none of the PT's local *chapas* (lists of candidates) included women candidates or candidates explicitly committed to "women's issues," the women's group endorsed its own list, composed entirely of women candidates, all of whom had addressed the group over the course of the preceding months, and all of whom worked closely with feminist or feminine organizations or women's departments of the unions.

For election day, the group designed its own *dobradinha* (a complete list of candidates from governor to municipal legislator), which they distributed at polling places throughout the neighborhood. The women's *dobradinha* included Lula and Jacó Bittar (the PT's candidates for governor and senator); Janete Rocha, a Black woman metalworker from nearby Osasco who worked with union women, for federal deputy; Clara Charf, the candidate endorsed by the PT's women's commission and widow of guerrilla leader, Carlos Marighela, for state assemblywoman; and Irede Cardoso, feminist activist and journalist for *Folha de São Paulo*, for the municipal assembly.

After election day, the group's core organizers engaged in internal discussions that revealed a number of tensions between its avowed purpose of mobilizing neighborhood women "around their specific interests" and the group's activities during the electoral campaign. It is important to recall that 1980–1981 was a peak mobilizational moment for the women's group in the neighborhood. Group discussions and events congregated hundreds of local women. Discussions of sexuality and reproductive rights, for example, attracted women by the dozens, like no other previous local mobilizational efforts among women—and it was precisely at this time that the campaign took hold of the neighborhood.

The core organizers of the women's group noted that student attendance at the course's theoretical discussions fell off dramatically when the focus was on political parties and elections. Whereas discussions of sexuality, reproduction, women's health, differential education, and so on attracted large numbers of neighborhood women (including some who were not enrolled in the sewing course), attendance at these explicitly "political" discussions was quite limited.

I attended several of these discussions during the final weeks of the campaign. And though election day was imminent and neighborhood mobilization at its apex, the women student/participants seemed somewhat indifferent to this generalized electoral fervor. In spite of the core organizers' insistence that politics *was* women's business, many of the student/participants expressed feelings of inadequacy when it came to "formal" politics ("I don't understand anything about parties," "politicians only come around here when there are elections and they confuse me even then") or insisted that politics was "men's business" ("I don't fool with politics, my husband does").[37] Whereas many of these student/participants successfully mobilized neighborhood women for protests at the *prefeitura* to demand day care or health care from local government agencies, the elections constituted a form of political participation alien to them as women and as residents of the urban periphery.[38]

With little prior experience in electoral participation, the local women's group and other community organizations were unable to draw the line between party militancy and movement militancy. As Teresa Pires do Rio Caldeira notes in her analysis of the impact of the campaign on social movement groups in Jardim das Camelias, the campaign confounded the division of "po-

---

[37] Most of the discussion of neighborhood women and party politics is drawn from my field notes from Jardim Miriam, October 1982 to March 1983. A study of six peripheral neighborhoods during the electoral campaign, conducted by a CEBRAP research team, also showed this tendency among women when it came to partisan politics. For a preliminary analysis of their findings, see Ruth Corrêa Leite Cardoso, "Em Matería de Eleições nem Tudo que Reluz da Ouro," in *A Periferia de São Paulo e o Contexto da Ação Política, Realtório Preliminar de Pesquisa, São Paulo*, CEBRAP, 1983 (Mimeograph). See also Teresa Pires do Rio Caldeira, "Mujeres, Cotidianidad y Política," in *Ciudadanía e Identidad: Las Mujeres en los Movimientos Sociales Latino-Americanos*, ed. Elizabeth Jelin (Geneva: UNRISD, 1987).

[38] Some of the core organizers also noted that several of the students told them that they, or other student/participants, were "put off" by the organizers' overt endorsement of the PT during the campaign.

litical labor'' among neighborhood groups.[39] At Jardim Miriam, most of the more politicized community organizations "took sides" (*tomaram partido*) and worked actively to turn out the vote. But the local PT, the would-be conduit of grassroots demands, also assumed for itself many of the organizational and mobilizational functions previously performed by social movement groups. This may seem to be a positive, democratizing development. However, parties are not adequate substitutes for the politicizing effects that local social movement organizations can have on the day-to-day lives of the community. And this is especially true with regard to women's mobilization, as local women's organizations provide vital forums wherein women can develop critical consciousness about their gendered oppression.

In a study of female social movement participants in six peripheral neighborhoods in São Paulo, Caldeira notes that most of the women did not view their participation in community activities as "political." Politics was something politicians did, an activity that was often portrayed by the women in rather pejorative terms—self-serving, self-interested, and unethical. What women did within the women's associations or other neighborhood groups was viewed as something done in the interests of their community, their families.[40]

Significantly, Jardim Miriam women did not participate actively in the creation and organization of the PT *núcleo*. The core organizers of the local PT were almost exclusively male, mostly men who participated in the parish's *Pastoral Operaria* (the only parish group with a predominantly male membership). In the case of Jardim Miriam, moreover, it was not just a lack of familiarity with historically elitist, male-dominated party politics that kept some of the more gender-conscious local women from participating more actively in the PT; the group's postelectoral discussions also suggested that the local PT *núcleo* did not prove to be a very hospitable place for women from the group. Though the core organizers of the women's group repeatedly stressed the need for local women "to have a voice within the PT," attendance by group participants to party meetings or events was quite irregular; this in spite of the fact that the PT held its weekly meetings in the hall rented by the women's group, free of charge, and the fact that two middle-class male PT leaders (who were among the core organizers of the local health group) regularly appeared at women's group meetings to announce PT events and mobilizations to be held in the neighborhood. The women's group finally designated representatives to accompany the work of the PT in the neighborhood and report back to the group on a regular basis. But even so, the representatives' attendance at PT meetings was highly erratic.

Some of the women felt that male party colleagues lacked respect for their

---

[39] Caldeira, "A Luta pelo Voto em um Bairro da Periferia."
[40] See Caldeira, "Mujeres, Cotidianidad y Política."

group, that their demands were trivialized, and that women were not treated as equals within the party organization. Furthermore, it appears that the "feminist" stigma with which participants of the group had been branded also had repercussions within the PT. The work that the women did was perceived as "apolitical" or "divisive" and was therefore deemed either "frivolous" or even "dangerous."

PARTISAN TENSIONS WITHIN CITYWIDE POPULAR WOMEN'S MOVEMENTS

At Jardim Miriam, partisan options did not divide the women's group participants as occurred in some other peripheral neighborhoods. The core organizers took a firmly *petista* stance and supported PT candidates with established links to popular women's movement organizations. However, the group's involvement with the PT campaign did divert it temporarily from other, gender-specific political objectives and demobilized many of its student/participants.

In the case of neighborhood-based feminine movements with regional or citywide organizational instances, party allegiances were far more disruptive. The *Movimento de Luta por Creches* (MLC or Struggle for Day Care Movement) is a case in point. Though the MLC remained unified during the electoral campaign, much of its leadership was divided in support of either the PT or the PMDB. For example, the women who were PCdoB party members (who were always very influential among some neighborhood MLC groups in the urban periphery) followed their party's directive and supported PMDB candidates during the election. The PCdoB-linked leadership of the MLC was also instrumental in creating the *União de Mulheres de São Paulo*, an umbrella organization of dozens of neighborhood-based women's groups, which openly endorsed the PMDB in São Paulo and also actively engaged in organizing women in the *periferia* to demand day care.

Other leaders of the MLC supported the PT. In the case of the Jardim Miriam *creche* group, for example, the director (who was also active in the leadership of the citywide day-care movement) and some local leaders of the MLC were active in the neighborhood PT.

During the campaign, there were few manifest tensions between *petistas* and *pemedebistas* in the MLC, as both the PT's and the PMDB's party platforms and a number of candidates from both parties expressly supported the extension of the day-care network in the city. But crucial differences in the content of the two parties' support for day care became evident immediately after the November elections.

Though these differences will be discussed at length below, it is useful to raise them briefly here. One of the MLC's key demands was that government day-care centers be directly funded and administered by local government agencies with the participation of neighborhood residents. But after the elections, the PMDB's support for the day-care issue was qualified by an important caveat. The new administration would need to search for alternatives to "direct *creches*," proclaimed the new PMDB mayor and the new Municipal Secretary of Social Welfare, as these were "administratively unfeasible"— too costly given the financial crisis in which the PDS administration had left the city. And this new angle on PMDB support for the MLC's long-standing demands generated considerable conflict between the PT and PMDB supporters within the day-care movement—conflicts which, according to movement participants, led to the total disarticulation of the movement at the regional or citywide levels by 1984.

MLC *petistas* maintained that the government must honor the grassroots demands made by neighborhood day-care groups for "direct *creches*," regardless of cost considerations, and pointed to the administrative and pedagogical inefficiencies of day-care centers administered by charitable organizations or other private entities (the so-called indirect *creches* that the PMDB administration seemed to be promoting in 1983). The *pemedebistas* within the MLC in turn contended that the new political conjuncture called for a different strategy for the day-care movement—one focused on negotiation and lobbying with the "opposition" government instead of the previous movement strategy of protest marches, sit-ins, and other extrainstitutional tactics. The differences in strategy proved irreconcilable and the movement's citywide coordination was dissolved in 1984—leaving the issue of day care to PMDB feminists working in the local State apparatus and to dispersed, neighborhood-based day-care groups.

CONCLUSION

Popular women's associations remained relatively marginal to party politics, even when they strongly favored a particular party, as was the case in Jardim Miriam. This was, in part, attributable to participants' own feelings of inadequacy vis-à-vis formal political institutions of any sort and their professed rejection of "politics as usual" in favor of community-based forms of direct action. Polarization along party lines was not as acute among most popular women's groups, even though some groups were temporarily diverted from their community consciousness-raising activities.

But the military authoritarian regime's divide-and-rule strategy, aimed primarily at the opposition party, nevertheless spilled over into other sectors of the São Paulo women's movement. The women's movement's putative unity, already belied by divisions manifest during the Second Congress, was further shattered as activists confronted ideologically distinct alternative strategies for "general" social change, represented by competing parties of the progressive opposition.

By 1982, many feminist organizations (like other organized sectors of civil society) had become demobilized and divided on partisan issues during the trajectory of the campaign. Left-wing women's fronts were created for the avowed purpose of mobilizing women for greater participation in the campaign process. Many women activists, including independent feminists, had left movement militancy to engage solely in party militancy—political society had temporarily swallowed up sectors of civil society.

Many individual feminists in fact "took sides" and sometimes worked on the campaigns of candidates who were the electoral rivals of the candidates supported by other participants in their own group. Some feminist groups split up as party preferences accentuated existing personal and political tensions within movement organizations. Others remained distant from party competition, furiously defending the movement's political autonomy and fearing the instrumentalization of the movement by party organizations. As Ruth Cardoso points out, "Instead of the movements strengthening the political parties, as many had hoped, party militancy often weakened the movements. . . . 'Taking party' implies breaking the consensus created by a common *vivência* [lived experience or identity]."[41]

The channeling of feminists' political energy into parties and electoral campaigns also detracted from the movement's cultural work and consciousness-raising activities in society at large—in the media, the arts, and especially the urban periphery, even as feminists successfully pressured parties to endorse many of the movement's historical banners, as we shall see in chapter 7. This dynamic tension, which characterized women's movement politics in Brazil after 1982, presaged a seemingly inevitable trade-off between the achievement of the movement's policy goals and the continuation of a feminist "revolution in day-to-day life," a trade-off which became a central point of contention among feminists who chose to work in parties and the State and those who did not. But, as chapter 7 will show, the movement of independent feminists into political parties also had some salutary effects. As more feminists moved from movement organizations into parties, they successfully pressured opposition parties to introduce gender-specific and gender-related issues into their platforms and programs.

[41] Ruth Cardoso, "Movimentos Sociais Urbanos: Balanço Crítico," pp. 237–38.

CHAPTER SEVEN

Dubious Allies in the Struggle for Women's Rights: Parties and Gender Strategies in the 1982 Campaign

THE ASCENT of party politics rekindled divisions among feminist, feminine, and nonfeminist women's groups, and resulted in new forms of ideological struggle *within* and *among* ever more divergent sectors of the women's movement, as shown in the preceding chapter. But as this chapter will demonstrate, the electoral conjuncture also benefited women's movements in significant ways. As legal parties of the recently divided opposition scrambled to secure votes for the 1982 elections, there was renewed partisan struggle *over* the organized constituencies and electoral capital represented by feminist and feminine movements.[1] Competition for the organized female electorate led all newly formed parties to include at least some generic demands in their programs and platforms.

Parties thus served as new vehicles for advancing women's movement demands. During the 1982 electoral campaign, the new opposition parties addressed many of the issues politicized by movement organizations during the 1970s. Movement banners made their way into campaign slogans, party platforms, and nationally televised debates. And among those banners were the "private" issues named as political by neighborhood feminine groups and feminist organizations. In this sense, parties and elections played a key role in the further politicization of gender in Brazilian society—sometimes translating feminist *protests* and neighborhood *carências* (needs) into concrete, programmatic policy proposals and would-be legislative reforms.

But such politicization brought with it new contradictions for women activists. As elsewhere, parties and women's movement organizations in transitional Brazilian politics proved to be "strange bedfellows" in the struggle for women's rights.[2] I have already documented the strained alliances between clandestine parties and women's movement organizations during the 1970s. Those tensions, as seen in the preceding chapters, made many feminists wary

---

[1] This crucial distinction regarding struggles "over" and struggles "within" social movements in the Brazilian context is developed by Margaret Keck in her incisive analysis of the dynamics of the new trade unionism of the 1970s. See her "The New Unionism in the Brazilian Transition," in *Democratizing Brazil*, ed. Alfred Stepan (New York: Oxford University Press, 1989).

[2] For a comparative, historical perspective on the relationship between women's movements and political parties in Latin America, see Sonia E. Alvarez, *The Politics of Gender in Latin America: Comparative Perspectives on Women in the Brazilian Transition to Democracy* (Ann Arbor, Mich.: University Microfilms, 1987), chapter 2.

of dealing with male-dominant political parties that appeared to be invariably manipulative and instrumentalist. Now those same "independent" feminists had to weigh the costs and benefits of securing allies among conventional parties pursuing an electoral, rather than revolutionary, path to power. Would legal parties of the opposition also manipulate and instrumentalize women's movement organizations? Was a shift to more conventional forms of interest articulation warranted by the new electoral conjuncture? Were male-dominant and sexist political parties capable of aggregating and articulating women's gender interests? Whose gender interests? Would the relative benefits of electoral participation and the institutional legitimation of a feminist political agenda outweigh the costs of potential instrumentalization? Would the "cultural transformation" side of the feminist struggle be neglected if autonomous feminist activists joined political parties and reduced their demands to a "feminist laundry list" to be included in party platforms and programs?

Until the November 15, 1982, elections, I spent most of my time closely observing the different strategies developed by each of three of the five legal political parties, the PDS, the PMDB and the PT, to mobilize and recruit women voters in São Paulo and the strategies developed to "court" the organized female constituencies. I looked closely at the gender politics of the PT and the PMDB since in São Paulo both feminist organizations and neighborhood women's groups had divided their loyalties between these two opposition parties. The PDS's platform and strategies were also of particular interest as that party articulated the regime's official position on women's issues.

Each of the parties elaborated a specific mobilizational strategy aimed at female constituencies. All included gender issues in their national platforms. This chapter analyzes the differing strategies adopted by parties vis-à-vis organized female constituencies during the 1982 campaign, the role of feminist pressure groups within and outside the party organizations in shaping those strategies, and the impact of the so-called "women's movement candidates' " campaigns on the politicization of gender-specific issues within parties and among the electorate at large. The contradictions resulting from the party mobilization of women during the 1982 electoral conjuncture are stressed, highlighting both positive and negative effects of such mobilization for the further politicization of gender in Brazilian society.

WOMEN IN THE GOVERNMENT PARTY

The *Partido Democrático Social* (PDS or Democratic Social Party, the reconstituted, pseudoliberalized official government party, previously ARENA) included some general references to women's participation and equality in its national platform. Unlike the pre-1982 ARENA platform, which made no specific reference to women, the new PDS platform stated that the party would promote the "right of women to participate in political, economic, and social life, in accordance with the principle of equal rights and *in accordance with women's own specific life possibilities.''*[3] This reference to women's "life possibilities" reflected the party's attempt to "feminize politics" in seeking women's electoral support. As is typical of conservative parties, the PDS presented women's participation as completely consonant with women's roles in the private sphere, as a mere extension of those roles into the political arena.

In São Paulo, ARENA had had a "Feminine Department" since 1971, long before the establishment of an MDB equivalent. This feminine branch of the government party was presided by the same woman during the ensuing eleven years, Guiomar Sartori, who also worked in the ARENA political infrastructure in the state assembly. In an interview conducted in 1983, Sartori asserted that "our department is in no way feminist," that its purpose was to "prepare women for politics . . . to develop in them the capacity to participate in politics." This was necessary because "the participation of women was not seen as very elegant. There was a series of restrictions on women being very involved in politics and it was therefore important to show that women could be ladies, could be refined, and at the same time could collaborate in politics." Women must be organized within the party because they "play a very important role within their family, their community" but it was also crucial to do so in a way that did not threaten women's "special place" in society.

I believe that women must secure all that they have worked for over the centuries, with so much astuteness. Women conquered a little place for themselves; thus men open car doors for them. Our feminine situation which we conquered so subtlely we must not now give up . . . and at the same time we must add that which we consider our right: to participate in politics. Because of that [participation], we do not give up our femininity, our gracefulness, our maternity, our children, our home, our beauty.[4]

Sartori explained that during the campaign the Feminine Department had canceled its weekly lectures (usually proffered by "learned men" or prominent male party leaders) and focused instead on mobilizing women in support of PDS candidates. It established feminine departments in most PDS directorates in almost all the municipalities of Greater São Paulo as well as in the interior of the state. A Central Commission (composed of a president, a supervisor for Greater São Paulo, a supervisor for the capital, and a supervisor for the interior) was responsible for organizing feminine departments within local party directorates and for turning out the women's vote for the PDS.

During 1982, the PDS's vague political platform and its conservative approach to female participation in political life, so vividly described by Guiomar Sartori, was translated into equally vague and sex-stereotyped mo-

---

[3] Quoted in Fanny Tabak, "A Questão da Autonomía do Movimento Feminista," in *Mulher e Democracia no Brasil*, ed. Fanny Tabak (Rio de Janeiro: Pontífica Universidade Católica do Rio de Janeiro and Núcleo de Estudos da Mulher, 1987), p. 73, emphasis added.

[4] Interview with Guiomar Sartori, president of the São Paulo MMDS, São Paulo, June 21, 1983.

bilization and recruitment strategies vis-à-vis the female electorate. Since most women's movement organizations identified with the opposition to the regime, the PDS made little effort to tap those groups as potential sources of support. Instead, the PDS fortified its own "women's movement," the *Movimento de Mulheres Democráticas Sociais* (Movement of Democratic Social Women or MMDS), instituted at the national level by Senator Eunice Michiles (with the collaboration of then national PDS president, José Sarney) to recruit support among women voters. The PDS launched twenty-four women candidates in the county of São Paulo (more than any other party), none of whom had any prior experience in autonomous women's movement organizations.

In pursuit of a new legitimacy formula involving "neopopulist" concessions (often no more than cosmetic changes) to limited demands made by organized civil society for better living conditions, improved urban infrastructure, and so on, many PDS candidates developed a new political discourse on women and women's issues. For example, as will be seen in chapter 9 below, former São Paulo mayor, Reynaldo de Barros, the PDS's gubernatorial candidate for state of São Paulo, made the construction of 330 day-care centers during his administration one of the major banners of his political campaign.

But one cannot minimize the role of the MMDS in persuading male party leadership that it was important for them to address "women's issues." Presided by Senator Eunice Michiles,[5] a self-proclaimed feminist, the women's branch of the government party brought issues of gender inequality within the regime to the attention of policy makers. Due in part to the MMDS's lobbying efforts, for example, President Figueiredo appointed Ester Ferraz de Figueiredo (no relation) as minister of education in 1982, making her the first woman to hold a ministerial post in all of Brazilian history.[6] The feminine branch also pressured the PDS to include women in the party's decision-making structures from the national through the local levels (Michiles herself was the sole female member of the party's National Executive) and to present women candidates for all levels of elective office nationwide. The MMDS also mobilized thousands of women throughout Brazil in support of PDS candidates. In the state of Santa Catarina, for example, the MMDS claimed to have recruited seventy thousand female party members in 1982 alone.

Discussions among MMDS leaders who gathered in Brasília in July 1983 for a *Forum de Aperfeiçoamento Político* (Political Refinement Forum) revealed that many women felt discriminated against by their male PDS colleagues and that female candidates received little support from the party ma-

---

[5] Michiles had become Brazil's first female senator in 1981. In 1978, she had been elected "alternate" to the Senate seat from Amazonas and took office upon the death of the incumbent, her husband.

[6] This discussion is based on formal and informal interviews with leaders of the MMDS from several Brazilian states, including Michiles herself, during my participation in the four-day National Meeting of the MMDS held in Brasília in July of 1983.

chine during the 1982 campaign. When Michiles addressed the 1983 Forum, she stressed that part of its purpose was to make clear to the men of the party that ''we want more space; we want to participate; we want to be heard.'' In a speech entitled, ''The Participation of Women in National Life,'' the PDS senator from Amazonas asserted that ''women now hold positions of distinction in all areas of human activity,'' which disproves ''the myth of feminine inferiority.'' She went on to suggest that

> for fifty years now women have been electors, but they are still second class electors, they are only regarded as voters, but as candidates or elected officials, much less so. . . . If someone asked me is there discrimination against women in Brazil today, I would point to this flagrant lack of female representation in politics. . . . We [women] must have a more expressive voice in this country's political decisions at all levels. . . . You cannot structure a country solely on male thought . . . if it is women who know the most about running a home, managing prices and food supplies, then why not place women in . . . COHAB, or even the BNH. . . . Women are just as capable, or more so, than men.[7]

The ensuing discussion among Forum participants further suggested that the PDS women party militants were not merely ''appropriating'' feminist discourse, however ''mild'' that discourse might seem when compared to that of opposition-linked sectors of the feminist movement. The women of the MMDS appeared legitimately to be dissatisfied with how their party had dealt with women and saw the MMDS as an organization capable of rectifying their party's discriminatory practices. However, they, of course, framed demands in ways consonant with the the PDS's larger commitment to the political status quo. For example, Michiles's speech also criticized the fact that ''there [were] no women 'indirect' Senators . . . no women mayors of the national security areas'' without for a moment questioning the ''indirect'' election of senators nor the existence of national security areas as such.[8]

Several MMDS women noted that unless the PDS took some concrete steps toward incorporating women into the party and toward promoting greater equality between the sexes, the opposition would ''win over'' the female electorate. They were clearly worried about the fact that all of the opposition parties had more complete statements about gender-related issues and that women's movement groups of all types were solidly in the opposition's camp.

WOMEN IN THE POLITICAL OPPOSITION

Indeed, there could be no question as to the women's movement's allegiance to the various new parties of the opposition. And during the 1982 electoral

---

[7] ''A Participação da Mulher na Vida Nacional,'' tape recorded speech by Senator Eunice Michiles, Brasília, July 22, 1983.

[8] Ibid.

campaign, the opposition parties as a whole paid significantly more attention to the female electorate and to organized female constituencies. This can be attributed to three principal factors: (1) most women's movement organizations had identified themselves as part of the broad-based opposition to the regime since the early 1970s and thus were perceived by the parties as potential (and untapped) sources of political support; (2) the female electorate had proven to be no less supportive of the opposition than the male electorate in 1974, 1976, and 1978[9] and (3) many feminists and other women's movement activists joined the ranks of these parties and pushed male party leadership into including women's issues in the official party platforms. In São Paulo, this was particularly true in the case of the PT and the PMDB, though both the PTB and the PDT also included gender-specific demands in their party platforms and programs.

PARTIDO MOVIMENTO DEMOCRÁTICO BRASILEIRO

In 1982, the PMDB (official "heir" of the MDB, the only legal opposition party in the pre-1979 two-party system established in 1965) had perhaps the most extensive statement on women's rights of any of the parties, the inspiration for which can be traced clearly to demands raised by São Paulo feminists and women's Congresses. As the MDB, the party was relatively responsive to women's movement organizations and several candidates and legislators (especially after 1978) expressed support for gender-specific demands, though the party platform made no direct reference to women's rights. The 1982 PMDB party program, on the other hand, addressed a number of specific demands raised by women's movement organizations.

> [T]he PMDB is opposed to anachronistic legislation which impedes the complete exercise of citizenship and civil rights by Brazilian women. The Party defends the guarantee of legal equality in the direction of the marriage union, as well as the legal protection of single mothers, and under any hypothesis, the protection of children. The Party also defends full rights for women workers, is against the discrimination in salaries of which women are victims, for the abolition of any type of discrimination in employment and hiring of married women, pregnant women, and women with children; will struggle for mandatory day-care centers in the workplaces and

---

[9] Fábio Wanderley Reis, "Classes Sociais e Opção Partidaria: As Eleições de 1976 em Juiz de Fora," in *Os Partidos e o Regime: A Lógica do Processo Eleitoral Brasileiro*, ed. Fábio Wanderley Reis (São Paulo: Edições Símbolo, 1978). Several voting studies show that sex was not a significant variable in party preferences for these election years. In fact, the studies showed that sex differences in voting tended to disappear altogether when other variables such as educational or occupational status are controlled. A study of the 1976 municipal elections in Juiz de Fora, conducted by Fábio Wanderley Reis, for example, found that women were slightly more likely than men to have voted for the MDB.

places of residence, to be maintained by private enterprises and by the State and to be administered under the direct control of those interested. . . .

The PMDB recognizes the existence of discrimination against women, is in solidarity with their struggle for equality of opportunity with men, and supports the revindications of women for an equal division of domestic work.[10]

The party's progressive position on women's issues was the result of extensive lobbying of male party leadership by feminist activists within the PMDB's electoral coalition. One PMDB activist told me that this last clause regarding the party's support for the equal division of domestic labor, for example, was included at the insistence of feminist party activists present during the National Executive's early discussions of the party platform.[11]

The PMDB endorsed many long-standing demands raised by both feminist and feminine organizations: the extension of workers' benefits to all categories of women workers; the eradication of discrimination against women in the workplace; the extension of day-care services, subsidized by the State and the private sector and administered by parents and community members (an essential demand of the Struggle for Day Care Movement); and the reform of the Civil Code to provide for greater equity between husband and wife in marriage. And as an expression of solidarity with non–policy-related feminist demands, the PMDB even took a programmatic position on the desirability of a more equitable division of domestic labor between spouses.

However, as several PMDB feminists I talked to noted, the party shied away from endorsing political claims that radically challenged prevailing ideologies of gender in Brazilian society. Women's movement demands deemed more "controversial" or potentially "disruptive" to existing gender power arrangements or which would promote gender role *change* rather than simply gender role *equity* did not make their way into the PMDB's platforms or programs. For example, in spite of feminist pressures, PMDB party leadership refused to endorse the movement's demand for the decriminalization and/or legalization of abortion.

Discussion of how best to mobilize and recruit women began shortly after the founding of the "new" party in 1980. PMDB women and men disagreed over whether or not to create a "women's branch"—a discussion repeated among activists in other opposition parties. There were those who argued that a women's branch would isolate female party militants from the "larger" policy issues and others who felt that some sort of "women's division" was essential for attending to gender-specific demands and recruiting "apolitical women" such as housewives and church women. The difference in approaches was particularly pronounced due to the electoral front-like nature of the party—political tendencies from the Far-Left to the Center-Right were

[10] Partido Movimento Democrático Brasileiro, "Programa Nacional," 1983.
[11] Informal interview with Ruth C. L. Cardoso, December 12, 1982.

grouped under the PMDB banner, and each of those tendencies had its own analysis of the "woman question" and thus its own proposals for recruitment and mobilization. This resulted in a rather mixed party strategy vis-à-vis the female electorate and organized women's groups.

A group of liberal professionals and academic women (mostly former participants of feminist groups, most prominently, the *Frente de Mulheres Feministas*, and feminist research centers) constituted themselves as a *Grupo de Estudos da Situação da Mulher* (Study Group on the Situation of Women), joining the ranks of the multiple study groups on specific issue-areas that operated for nearly two years prior to the 1982 PMDB campaign in São Paulo. This group did not direct its activities at mobilization and recruitment, but rather focused on the formulation of a specific "Proposal of PMDB Women for the Montoro/Quercia government," widely distributed in pamphlet form during the final months of the electoral campaign. The proposal included four basic areas of action to be implemented and supervised by a *Conselho Estadual da Condição Feminina* (literally, the State Council on the Feminine Condition, hereafter referred to as the Council) if the PMDB came to power in the state of São Paulo. This Council would "serve as an instrument for a *global politics* destined to eliminate the discriminations suffered by women."[12] The four principal areas of concern to the Council would be: (1) women's work and the elimination of salary and employment discrimination, (2) women's health and reproductive rights, (3) *creches*, and (4) the protection of women against violence. The women who made up this study group and those who supported their work within the PMDB tended to come from the ranks of the more professional-based feminist groups in São Paulo—the *Frente de Mulheres Feministas, Pró-Mulher*, and the *Casa da Mulher Paulista*. Arising from the women's professional and academic networks discussed in chapter 4, these groups had concentrated on raising women's issues in the mainstream media, academia, and the arts. On the whole, the PMDB also was able to recruit significant support among women from the "new middle class" who had been sensitized to gender inequality.

Women militants from the clandestine or illegal parties (such as MR-8, PCdoB, PCB, and others) also formed part of the PMDB. As seen in chapter 6, some of these women created their own women's fronts to recruit women for the PMDB campaign and for the partisan platforms of their own political organizations—thus founding the *Federação das Mulheres Paulistas* (Federation of Paulista Women, linked to the MR-8) and the *União de Mulheres de São Paulo* (Union of São Paulo Women, linked to the PCdoB).

During 1982, the MR-8 (Eighth of October Revolutionary Movement or *Movimento Revolucionario 8 de Outubro*, named in commemoration of the

---

[12] Grupo de Estudos da Situçào da Mulher, "Proposta das Mulheres do PMDB para o Governo," 1982 (Mimeograph).

date of the assassination of Ché Guevara in Bolivia), promoted the organization of state-level women's federations throughout Brazil. They argued that the women's movement should be centralized so that "women's struggles" could be better coordinated. These federations need not be composed exclusively of women's groups—the MR-8 wanted to "federate" party organizations, community groups, and labor unions, regardless of whether or not these groups worked specifically with women or addressed gender-specific issues. As one movement activist from Salvador, Bahia, noted, "In the planning of the March 8th celebrations where the proposal for the Women's Federation was to be discussed, the women of *Hora do Povo* [the MR-8 newspaper that served as its legal front] wanted the agenda to center on 'unemployment, the cost of living, and the constitutional assembly.' We insisted that the agenda focus on women's issues, namely 'day care, violence against women, and reproductive rights.' "[13] Most independent feminist activists shared this woman's feeling that the MR-8 wanted to centralize the movement in order to impose its partisan agenda on the women's movement—an agenda that in 1981 and 1982 centered upon consolidating support for the MR-8–linked candidates within the PMDB's electoral front.[14]

In São Paulo, as we saw in chapter 5, tensions between the MR-8 and other women linked to the sectarian Left and women participating in the independent feminist movement exploded during the Second Congress in 1980. The split between these women and *autonomista* feminists turned into an ever-wider and seemingly unbridgeable chasm during the 1982 electoral campaign.

The *União de Mulheres de São Paulo* was not organizationally linked to the PCdoB to the same extent that the *Federação* was to the MR-8. Instead, much of the Union's leadership, including its founders, were active PCdoB militants. The *União* proclaimed simply that the "worker's struggle and the women's struggle" were inextricably linked (a position that few independent São Paulo feminists would disagree with) and that therefore "the political struggle interests us and that struggle must be widely discussed at the core of the women's movement. We don't want to be left alienated, outside of politics."[15]

---

[13] Participant at the Third National Feminist Meeting, held in Brasília, July 23–26, 1983, from my tapes of the discussions.

[14] This information on the Federation's activities at a national level is derived from tapes of the proceedings of the National Feminist Meeting held in Campinas in July 1982 and from the proceedings of the National Meeting of PT Women, held in São Paulo that same year. Both sets of tapes of the proceedings can be found at the women's movement archives, *Centro Informação Mulher*, in São Paulo. For more information on the MR-8 position on gender issues, see also Comissão Executiva da Coordenação do III Congresso da Mulher Paulista, *Resoluções do III Congresso da Mulher Paulista* (São Paulo: Editora Quilombo, 1981); and Movimento Revolucionario 8 do Outubro, *A Mulher e a Revolução Brasileira, Resoluções do MR8 sobre o Trabalho entre Mujeres* (São Paulo: Editora Quilombo, 1981).

[15] See União de Mulheres de São Paulo, "Programa," pamphlet distributed at one of the two March 8 celebrations held in São Paulo in 1982. Much of my information on this group is drawn

Nevertheless, the founding of the *União* amid the partisan rivalries that riddled the movement throughout 1981–1982, coupled with the PCdoB's known participation in the PMDB electoral front, led many São Paulo feminists to equate it with the *Federação*; both were pegged as party fronts that intended to instrumentalize and manipulate the women's movements.

The PMDB launched twelve women candidates (one of whom, to the chagrin of many São Paulo feminists, was the president of the above mentioned *Federação das Mulheres Paulistas*).[16] Among the PMDB women candidates were three self-proclaimed feminist candidates (Silvia Pimentel, Ruth Escobar, and Ida Maria Janscó) who conducted a joint campaign centered on issues such as women's legal rights, equal pay for equal work, the elimination of discrimination against married women in the Brazilian civil code, and aimed at organized feminists, neighborhood women's groups, and the female electorate at large. The three women candidates called themselves the *trinca feminista* (feminist triad) and their campaign unquestionably sensitized thousands of people, especially in the interior of the state, to gender-specific issues.

This was especially true in the case of Ruth Escobar's campaign for state assemblywoman. The reknowned actress and entrepreneur was one of São Paulo's "historic feminists" and became the PMDB's "official feminist" during the 1982 campaign. Escobar was often invited to speak to women and women's groups on behalf of male candidates and was widely known for her considerable irreverence and defiance of established norms of "candidate-like" behavior. In her campaign speeches and discussions with women throughout the state of São Paulo, Escobar never failed to raise those gender-specific issues considered politically taboo by many, issues not necessarily endorsed by the PMDB. For example, she openly supported the decriminalization of abortion, even when speaking to church-linked mothers' clubs in the interior of the state, arguing that "illegal abortion is not a crime, it's violence against women."[17]

The *trinca feminista*'s campaign materials also went further than the PMDB party platform in raising some strategic gender issues. For example, one of their leaflets stated that "[w]omen continue to die and suffer the drama of clandestine abortion. We can't wait any longer. Women want laws to resolve this problem and want the State to take responsiblity for women's health."[18]

---

from several extensive interviews with its president and from participation in several group meetings, conferences, rallies, and other events.

[16] PMDB women I interviewed explained that the relatively small number of women candidates was the result of the fact that nominations for the various elective offices were hotly contested within the PMDB, the largest of the opposition parties in 1982—especially given the fact that all of its diverse political factions demanded to be proportionally represented.

[17] Interview with Jacira Melo and Maria Aparecida Schumaher, both of whom worked on Ruth Escobar's São Paulo campaign, São Paulo, August 16, 1983.

[18] Campaign leaflet (October 1982).

In spite of the efforts of organized feminists within the party, however, the sectors of the PMDB who had wanted a "feminine" branch also eventually implemented their strategy, creating the *Comité Feminino Pró-Montoro* (Feminine pro-Montoro Committee) in August of 1982, headed by the candidate's wife, Dona Lucy, and his daughter, Gilda. This "women's auxiliary" did not address gender-specific issues but rather focused on mobilizing relatively "apolitical" middle- and working-class housewives for work in the Montoro campaign—a common party strategy for female recruitment and not unlike that implemented by MMDS or other Brazilian political parties earlier in the twentieth century. A new middle-class feminine group, the São Paulo Housewives' Association, created in 1982 to organize consumer boycotts to protest rising inflation, avidly participated in the PMDB's feminine department; the president of the association was launched as a candidate for municipal councilwoman by the PMDB.

The PMDB's gubernatorial candidate, Franco Montoro, specifically targeted the *donas de casa* (housewives) of São Paulo during the final months of the campaign. He made frequent appeals to "the housewives of São Paulo who have their feet firmly on the ground and will therefore vote for the PMDB since they know better than anyone that what São Paulo needs is change."[19] In a speech reproduced in *Folha de São Paulo* during the final days of the campaign, Montoro expressed confidence that the PMDB would receive the immense majority of female votes throughout Brazil. According to the candidate, one of the reasons for this, was "the fact that *donas de casa* know how to evaluate the consequences of the dramatic unemployment index and of the constant rise in the price of food, clothing and education, with a great deal of realism. The PMDB is strong among *donas de casa* because they are the ones who feel the tragedies that the federal government imposes on the Brazilian people, who are tired of seeing prices rise because of our leaders and members of the PDS."[20] Montoro thus clearly invoked "militant motherhood" in his quest for support among female voters.

THE PARTIDO DOS TRABALHODORES

But perhaps the most direct (if electorally, less effective) appeal to the "common woman" and the organized women's movement came from the *Partido dos Trabalhadores*. As a party "born of popular struggles" and drawing its primary support from urban movement organizations in which women have been key participants, the PT's ranks included the largest proportion of women members (estimated at over 40 percent in the county of São Paulo) and launched the second largest number of women candidates (23 to PDS's 24).

[19] *Folha de São Paulo*, November 6, 1982.
[20] Ibid.

The party's 1982 national program expressed "support for movements in defense of the rights of women, Blacks, and Indians" and supported the creation of "public *creches* in workplaces and places of residence." In the national platform, the support for the struggle against discrimination was reiterated.

> Woman is treated like a second class being. The worst jobs and lowest salaries are reserved for her, besides being submitted to a double workday, since she is responsible for all household chores as well. She is constantly subjugated and humiliated, oppressed not only as a worker, but also as a woman. . . . We demand equality in the laws that rule the family, labor, and society. The right to employment, to professionalization and the extension of worker's rights to all women workers, such as domestic workers, and respect for equal pay for equal work. Women must possess the means to choose whether or not to have children, which implies the recognition of the social function of motherhood, the supply of safe and secure contraceptive methods, and permanent medical care at all stages of women's lives.[21]

An addendum to the party program declared that "the PT considers that discriminations are not secondary questions as the problems of women workers, segregated in the factories, in the fields, and also in the home, are not secondary."[22]

As in the case of the PMDB, feminist movement participants active in the PT were instrumental in pushing male party leadership to endorse feminine and feminist movement political claims. When none of the speakers at the party's founding convention addressed the specificity of women's oppression within class relations, *petista* feminists immediately caucused to develop a "women's platform" and presented it to the National Executive, demanding that the party subsidize a national PT women's convention before the elections.

Feminists were also an organized presence at the PT's 1982 nominating convention and the party's electoral program incorporated many of the issues politicized by feminine and feminist movement organizations during the 1970s and early 1980s:[23] the elimination of all legal discrimination against women; the extension of publicly funded day care; professionalization and extension of workers' rights to all women workers, including domestic workers; and the right to equal pay for equal work.

The ideological recognition of the social rather than "natural" function of motherhood and the PT's endorsement of "reproductive rights" for all women reflected the significant impact that women's movement organizations had had on political society's gender discourses by 1982. In spite of the PT's endorse-

---

[21] Partido dos Trabalhadores, "Plataforma Nacional," 1982 (Mimeograph).

[22] Silvia Pimentel, "A Necessaria Participação Política da Mulher," *Revista do PMDB* 1, no. 3 (August/September 1982): 22.

[23] Interview with Regina Stella Duarte, PT activist, São Paulo, August 10, 1983.

ment of some *strategic* gender issues, however, the PT's links to the progressive Catholic church kept it from endorsing the decriminalization of abortion, for example.

Though the PT was also an electoral front constituted by various Left and Center-Left political tendencies, from Trotskyists to the progressive church, its political discourse on women and mobilization and recruitment strategies toward them were somewhat more uniform than the PMDB's. Again, this was in no small measure the result of effective feminist lobbying within the PT organization.

The women's movement activists who joined the *petista* ranks came mostly from grassroots feminist and neighborhood feminine groups and from women's sections of some of São Paulo's trade unions. Unlike their PMDB counterparts whose feminist activities centered around ideological dissemination and mass media exposure of women's issues, PT women tended to come from community-oriented groups providing direct services and technical or political advice to low-income women. They engaged in female-led neighborhood struggles for day care and urban improvements, and promoted popular education on women's issues in peripheral neighborhoods. They included many former members of the militant opposition and student movements of the late 1960s and early 1970s whose political networks had served as a basis for early feminist organizing, whereas PMDB feminists tended to come from the professional and academic networks that also subsequently had been mobilized around feminist issues. Given earlier conflicts with male comrades in the militant Left and feminists' ideological reevaluation of that Left's economistic focus and vanguardist political strategy, the former were drawn by the *basista* ("base-oriented" or grassroots) orientation of the PT.

That is, the PT's avowed purpose of "building a national worker's party" from the base up and its nonvanguardist discourse appealed to the politicized neighborhood women's groups who had come to mistrust the São Paulo "political class" as a whole and to grassroots-oriented (if still predominantly middle class) São Paulo feminist groups—such as *Centro Informação Mulher, SOS-Mulher*, and *Sexualidade e Política*—who had become disenchanted with the theory and practice of the orthodox Left in Brazil.

Soon after the PT was legally constituted, PT feminists began discussing whether to create a "women's division," linked to the Party Secretariat for Popular Movements. The women's division, it was agreed, would advise the executive committee of the party on women's issues, educate party militants on the "specificity of women's oppression," and promote PT participation in women's movement activities, while respecting the autonomy and self-determination of existing women's organizations.[24] A document issued by the PT

[24] Partido dos Trabalhadores, Comisão da Mulheres, "O Porquê da Comisão de Trabalho sobre a Questão da Mulher," 1980 (Mimeograph).

Women's Commission for the International Women's Day celebrations in 1981 declared that

> we feel the need to discuss the participation of women in the PT, in the sense that we are perhaps the only party which did not constitute a feminine department. And if we don't have a feminine department, it is not because we don't grant importance to women's struggles. On the contrary. It is because we conceive of women's participation in the party differently. In the first place, we understand that women should be shoulder to shoulder with the men in our party, and not separate from them. . . . In the second place . . . there is a [women's] movement which is growing, assuming its own forms of organization. . . . We are a Party which is born with the registered mark of respect for the entities, the forms of organization of the working people. It would be absurd if we had a feminine department or any other instance which would swallow the movement, instead of strengthening it.[25]

PT also launched the largest number of women candidates with organic links to women's movement organizations—Luiza Erundina de Souza, Tereza Lajolo, Clara Charf, Janete Rocha, and Irma Passoni, linked to urban movement groups and feminine organizations; Irede Cardoso and Caterina Koltai, supported by several feminist and gay groups in São Paulo.

Charf's campaign materials proclaimed that "the women's struggle is also the struggle of workers and the workers' struggle is also the struggle of women," and her political campaign, in which many São Paulo feminists participated, took both "feminine" and "feminist" issues to women of the popular classes.

> Today, the word of women is in the streets. . . . To spread the words of women who struggle. . . . We have been struggling for years: against the rising cost of living, in our neighborhoods, in the amnesty movement. Here in São Paulo we organized Women's Congresses. Together we discovered that we are exploited and discriminated against. That we are not heard, that we have not had a chance. But we also discovered our strength. . . . That is why the elections are important for us. Let's talk about our struggle and our movement. . . . We want the right to decide about the society in which we live. For us, women, this is new. Because many times we let others speak for us while we remain quiet. Many times we struggle but we let others decide. Now we will talk, decide and participate in politics.[26]

Erundina, Lajolo, Rocha, and Passoni similarly encouraged the women who had been active in neighborhood movements to participate in their party and in national, state, and local politics. They, more than any of the PT male candidates, consistently addressed all of the practical gender interests that had

---

[25] Partido dos Trabalhadores, Comissão da Mulheres, "A Participação do PT no III Congresso da Mulher Paulista," 1981 (Mimeograph).

[26] Campaign leaflet (October 1982).

been the focus of feminine movement organizations throughout the preceeding decade. And feminists who had continued to work with women in the urban periphery were especially active in their campaigns.

Irede Cardoso, who had been a central figure in promoting feminist issues in both the print and electronic media for many years, also made feminist and feminine demands the center of her platform in her successful campaign for municipal councilwoman.

> We want women to be happy, women who can choose and exercise their profession. We want women who will not let violence reign in this country. We want women to feel fulfilled whether or not they have children. Maternity is not the essence of women. We want women to know that their bodies are being used by an unjust system and to struggle to modify that fact.[27]

Caterina Koltai went much further than other PT or PMDB feminist candidates in calling for a radical restructuring of gender power relations in her electoral platform. A highly controversial leaflet, entitled *"Desobedeça"* (Disobey), was widely distributed by feminist and gay movement activists who supported her campaign for municipal councilwoman.

> Disobey the order that your body is not yours, but belongs to "others." Abortion should be your choice, struggle for its legalization. . . . Disobey the order that only with persons of the opposite sex is love permissible and that you should participate in the oppression of all who are "different." Any form of love is worthwhile.[28]

Koltai's "advocacy" of homosexuality, legal abortion, and other "irreverent" demands (such as the legalization of marijuana) led the Regional Electoral Tribunal to ban the distribution of *"Desobedeça"* and to prosecute Koltai for offenses against "morality" in 1983.

These PT women candidates, along with the PMDB *trinca feminista* and feminist pressure groups within both parties, promoted an unprecedented statewide debate on women's rights. And several of these women-centered campaigns were successful: Ruth Escobar (PMDB) was elected to the state legislature; Luiza Erundina, Tereza Lajolo, and Irede Cardoso (PT) were elected to the municipal legislature (making up three out of five PT members in the municipal assembly); and, Irma Passoni and Bette Mendes (PT) were elected to the national legislature. The PTB also elected one woman to the state legislature and one to the national legislature (this latter was Ivette Vargas, the national president of the PTB); neither of these women had any connections to women's movement organizations.

[27] Campaign leaflet (October 1982).
[28] Campaign leaflet (October 1982).

CONCLUSION

When the new multiparty system was installed in 1980–1981, the relationship between political parties and organized sectors of civil society, including women's movement organizations, changed dramatically. All the parties had to seek new social bases of political support or reconsolidate old ones. And in so doing, parties introduced women's issues into national political discourse and policy debates, lending legitimacy to many of the generic claims raised by women's organizations during the 1970s.

Thus many issues previously considered "private," such as violence against women, day care, contraception and sexuality, and many others voiced by women over the previous decade, were, for the first time in Brazilian history, prominently included in the platforms and programs of many individual candidates and national political parties. For the first time since the Brazilian suffrage movement in the 1920s and 1930s, gender became the basis for widespread electoral mobilization and gender inequality the object of generalized political debate.

For women's movement activists who worked in PT and PMDB campaigns, the electoral conjuncture brought other important gains, despite the demobilization and disarticulation it generated within some Paulista feminist groups. National party networks greatly facilitated the articulation of the movement on a national level, improving networks for exchange of information, organizational resources, and political solidarity among women's groups throughout the country.

However, most of the new parties reproduced some aspects of gender inequality in their platforms and organizational infrastructures. The political "courtship" of recently mobilized female constituencies sometimes perpetuated or reinforced power imbalances between the sexes by replicating and institutionalizing unequal gender power arrangements within the party organizations themselves. Both the politically conservative PDS and Center-Right sectors of the PMDB, for example, assigned women a "special place" within party ideologies, platforms, programs, and organizational infrastructures—a place quite compatible with prevailing stereotypes of women's proper roles in Brazilian society. Women's branches were created for the sole purpose of mobilizing the female electorate, not to provide gender-specific input into party policy and programs. Both the PDS and the more conservative factions of the PMDB also appealed to women's "mothering" roles or "special intuition" in seeking their electoral support.

The "feminization of politics" that typified these "feminine branches" of the parties, however, was tenaciously resisted by organized feminists within the PMDB and the PT. Both the PMDB's *Grupo de Estudos da Mulher* and the PT's *Comissão de Mulheres* struggled with male party leadership and persuaded them to support some *strategic* gender interests politicized by women's movement organizations over the course of the previous decade. The historical tendency for parties to manipulate or instrumentalize genderic issues thus was partially counteracted by the significant presence of women's movement activists within the party organizations themselves (including "conservative" feminists within the PDS).

Predictably, feminist activists could not persuade party leaders to endorse more radical genderic demands. Both the PT and the PMDB feared that incorporating such demands would alienate important sectors of their larger constituencies, for example, the staunchly moralistic "progressive" Catholic church. On the other hand, this cautious approach did not seem to factor into party discourse on class, as both the progressive wing of the PMDB and the PT as a whole incorporated a fairly radical critique of prevailing social relations of production yet seemed far less willing to challenge social relations of *re*production. The endorsement of gender-related political claims by progressive parties of the opposition, thus, remained a qualified one.

Parties' responsiveness to both practical and strategic gender interests, as will be shown in chapters 8 and 9 below, receded significantly after organized female constituencies ceased to be perceived as prized electoral currency. The PMDB, the resounding victor in the 1982 gubernatorial races in São Paulo and eight other Brazilian states, took the initiative in mobilizing women's support for the new "democratic" government of São Paulo, again, due to the successful lobbying of PMDB feminists active in the new ruling party.

CHAPTER EIGHT

Approaching the Authoritarian State: Women's Movements and Population Policy in Transitional Brazilian Politics

As opposition parties began making overtures toward organized female constituencies and professed a greater commitment to some of the women's movement's historic claims, women's groups of all types faced complex dilemmas as to whether, when, and how to advance their claims through male-dominant party channels. As shown in chapters 6 and 7, the increased significance of parties and electoral competition widened existing schisms among independent feminists and bred considerable strategic confusion within most women's movement groups, even as new party programs and platforms lent political legitimacy to some generic claims. Once viewed as inaccessible and irrelevant to women's efforts to redress gender inequality through public policy, after 1980, parties became important arenas for gender struggle.

Focusing on the discourses and policies of family planning, this chapter addresses two key questions: (1) why, during the latter stages of political liberalization, the State was transformed into a crucial, if still highly problematic, arena for gender struggle; and, (2) how various sectors of the women's movement responded to this transformation. Rapid developments in the realm of population/family-planning policy and feminist responses to those developments in the mid-1980s illustrate important changes in feminist strategies over the course of the regime transition.

I will show that the economic and political crises confronted by the Brazilian military authoritarian regime after the mid-1970s forced it to contend politically with some of the very social movements its policies had engendered. As the opposition grew in strength and the economy careened into crisis in the late 1970s and early 1980s, Brazil's rulers donned a more "popular" and "democratic" facade, sometimes appropriating opposition discourses and appearing to respond to some societal demands. In seeking a new hegemonic strategy in the face of the ever greater strength of organized civil society, the ruling coalition tried to cement new electoral linkages among those social sectors most adversely affected by earlier authoritarian development policies. In an effort to prop up its eroding legitimacy, the Democratic Social Party (PDS) administration in São Paulo suddenly appeared anxious to respond to the Struggle for Day Care Movement's (MLC) long-standing demand for publicly financed day care (see chapter 9).

At the state and federal levels, new pressures from international lenders and regulatory institutions, such as the International Monetary Fund (IMF), prompted the previously pro-natalist regime to propose a national family-planning program. In an effort to buttress its democratic facade, the regime's proposed program appropriated many historic feminist claims about family planning, abruptly transforming the military authoritarian State into a dubious ally of women's movement organizations who sought "reproductive rights" for all women.

New developments in the realm of population policy at first confounded Brazilian women's movement strategies. Generally in liberal democratic contexts, feminists have turned to the State to seek changes in women's status; however, the exclusionary and repressive nature of the Brazilian political system had made the vertical articulation of feminist demands for safe, accessible, noncoercive family-planning appear futile, if not absolutely ludicrous. Moreover, Brazilian feminism's roots in the militant Left led many feminists to equate any State-sponsored family-planning initiatives with coercive, neo-Malthusian population control. Demands for reproductive choice were articulated horizontally instead. That is, Brazilian women's movements initially pushed parallel social movement groups to assume some of their political banners; and it was only after 1980 that feminists pressured parties to do the same.

But when the federal government initiated plans to implement a comprehensive national "family-planning" program, feminists had to reassess their stance vis-à-vis State policy. Aware that the authoritarian regime was capable of coercively enforcing a policy aimed at population control, some feminists set out to influence government policy formulation so as to prevent reproductive rights abuses and to gear the proposed program toward Brazilian women's very real need for safe, accessible birth control. What made feminists think that such influence was feasible? I will argue that, during the latter stages of regime transition, feminists strategically took advantage of new fissures that appeared in the ruling civil-military coalition at the federal level and gained limited access to the policy arenas in which the government's program was being formulated. And in the state of São Paulo, I will show that the post-1983 PMDB (Party of the Brazilian Democratic Movement) opposition administration provided new access points through which feminists were able to fashion a family-planning program that was quite responsive to feminist demands for reproductive choice.

CHANGING STATE DISCOURSES ON POPULATION POLICY

While family-planning and reproductive rights have long held a prominent place in Brazilian feminist politics, feminist activists most certainly would not have turned to the State to attempt to secure women's reproductive rights during the 1970s. Though sectors of the women's movement, most notably the day-care movement, always focused their demands for social services on the State, most feminists adhered firmly to the the notion that the State could never be trusted to provide women with access to non-coercive family planning. As neo-Malthusian "family-planning" programs were the order of the day throughout Latin America in the 1960s and 1970s, Brazilian feminists argued that any such government program would ignore women's health needs; promote medically unsound, unsupervised, and arbitrary distribution of birth control pills and other unsafe contraceptive methods; and force poor and working-class women to be sterilized against their will.

Moreover, throughout much of the 1970s, feminists did not have to contend with State initiatives in the realms of population and reproduction. Subimperialist, expansionist ideology—the Economic Miracle's vision of *O Grande Brasil*—appears to have led the regime to resist the implementation of a nationwide family-planning program in the 1960s and 1970s when most other Catholic Latin American nations were doing so. In the 1960s and early 1970s, Brazil's authoritarian rulers insisted that the vast, underpopulated Brazilian territory, with its rich, largely untapped natural resources could accomodate an infinite level of population growth. A declaration by Planning Minister Delfim Neto aptly summarized the dominant government position in the mid-1970s: "The question of population control should not occupy our attention in the present phase of Brazilian development. If we are 'condemned' to have to grow at a rate of 9 or 10 percent a year there is no point in wasting our time in speculation. . . . Control will come in time and will be executed by each individual, insofar as we overcome the educational problems of our people."[1]

Nevertheless, from 1965 on, the authoritarian regime allowed the Society for the Welfare of the Family in Brazil (BEMFAM, *Sociedade Civil Bem Estar Familiar no Brasil*), a privately funded branch of International Planned Parenthood, to set up clinics throughout Brazil and approved the private distribution of birth control in several Brazilian states—primarily in the economically depressed Northeast where population control was seen as a panacea for the lack of federal investment in industrial and agricultural development in the area.[2]

Coupled with this expansionist component of the regime's ideology in its early stages was a firm ideological commitment to "the family." Indeed, as discussed above, bourgeois civilian supporters of the 1964 military coup that installed the regime had mobilized thousands (primarily women) against Gou-

[1] Cited in Theirry Linard de Guertechin, "O Controle da Natalidade: Uma Questão Demográfica e/ou Um Problema Político," in *Controle da Natalidade x Planejamento Familiar no Brasil*, ed. Theirry Linard de Guertechin et al. (Rio de Janeiro: Achiamé, 1987), p. 28.

[2] For an excellent discussion of the activities of BEMFAM and other private agencies and their contracts with government agencies in some states, see Raquel A. Pego and Arnaldo Chain Richa, "Estado e Instituições de Planejamento Familiar," in *Controle da Natalidade x Planejamento Familiar no Brasil*, ed. Guertechin et al.

lart, whose radical populist policies allegedly threatened the Brazilian family. During the early 1960s, the Right organized marches throughout Brazil in the name of "Family, God, and Liberty" (the now infamous *Marchas da Familia, com Deus, pela Liberdade*). The family, writ-large and abstractly, thus became a cornerstone of the new authoritarian regime in Brazil, just as it has often functioned as the bulwark of conservatism elsewhere in Latin America. Brazilian pronatalist policies of the 1960s and early 1970s were significantly shaped by the regime's ideological focus on the family. However, these policies were highly contested within the regime.[3]

In the heyday of the Economic Miracle, the regime refused to endorse the neo-Malthusian tide sweeping international politics during that period.[4] Yet from the first authoritarian government on, competing perspectives on the "population problem" were represented by different factions within the regime, obstructing the consolidation of a consistent policy on population.

Among those who positioned themselves in favor of State action directed at reducing [Brazil's] rhythm of demographic growth [during the Castelo Branco administration], two currents can be identified: one, alleging that uncontrolled demographic growth is one of the most important agents threatening national security. They defended the diminution of births among middle and lower classes, so that the increase in population would not signify a constant threat to political stability. The second current, grounded in a technical, economic discourse, justified population control on the basis of the necessity of increasing national savings. With fewer Brazilians, the country would have greater savings and investments and fewer social demands to be satisfied. . . .

During the government of General Emílio Médici, some positions contrary to State population control policies emerged. . . . [A]ccording to these, the fertility index was not an obstacle to [Brazil's] development, as they believed that the growing evolution of the economy, and particularly of industrialization, would in itself reduce the rhythm of demographic growth without direct State interference.[5]

---

[3] Maria Inacia d'Avila Neto explores some of the psychosocial dimensions of the relationship between authoritarianism and the subordination of women in *O Autoritarismo e A Mulher: O Jogo da Dominação Macho-Fêmea no Brasil* (Rio de Janeiro: Achiamé, 1980). It should be noted that the military government has always kept the profamily, anti–artificial contraception church abreast of all policy matters concerning "family planning," reassuring the otherwise increasingly progressive CNBB that any State policies would not undermine the Brazilian family.

[4] For a discussion of neo-Malthusian ideology and population policy in Latin America, see Bonnie Mass, *Population Target: The Political Economy of Population Control in Latin America* (Toronto: L. A. Working Group and Women's Educational Press, 1976), and Karen L. Michaelson, ed., *And the Poor Get Children: Radical Perspectives on Population Dynamics* (New York: Monthly Review Press, 1981).

[5] Pego and Richa, "Estado e Instituições," pp. 36-37. The ambiguity of Brazilian population policy was again manifest at the 1974 International Population Year Conference in Bucharest. The Brazilian regime held to its apparently pronatalist position while simultaneously declaring itself to be unilaterally opposed to any type of policy aimed at controlling population size.

It was not until 1977 that the federal government made its first feeble attempt to institute State-sponsored family-planning. Through a Ministry of Health program called the Prevention of High-Risk Pregnancy (*Programa de Prevenção de Gravidez de Alto Risco*), the government approved the limited distribution of contraceptives (primarily birth control pills) through the public health system for women whose health would be threatened by pregnancy. But as Raquel Pego and Arnaldo Chain Richa point out, critics of this program maintained that it was "synonymous with population control . . . they argued that close to 50 percent of high-risk pregnancy cases are caused by malnutrition and that, therefore, instead of distributing pills it would be sufficient to provide food."[6]

In 1978, President Ernesto Geisel became the first Brazilian head of state to proclaim that the State had a responsibility to provide citizens with birth control methods, arguing that family planning was a means of elevating the quality of life in Brazil as it promoted "a necessary conciliation between demographic growth and satisfactory provision of employment, education, health care, housing and other social opportunities which are fundamental to a worthy life for all citizens."[7] However, Geisel emphasized that "we believe that the limitation of fertility should not be imposed. It should be the discretion, the desire, the will of the couple."[8]

Early in his administration, President Figueiredo and his Social Development Council (composed of ministers involved in "social welfare" issues, including, of course, the military ministers) also expressed concern over the population problem. In 1980, a federal health program entitled *Prev-Saúde* (Preventive-Healthcare) included an extensive section on family-planning under the rubric of "maternal-infant care," aimed exclusively at the distribution of birth control pills to fertile women (ages 15–49). However, neither of these programs was ever implemented effectively on a national scale.

While BEMFAM had five clinics functioning in the state of São Paulo by 1978 and in the capital Dr. Milton Nakamura established several "maternal-infant care" clinics, which distributed birth control pills to "indigent" women, it was not until 1980 that the São Paulo state government began promoting government-sponsored family-planning. Governor Paulo Salim Maluf instituted the Mobilization of Community Resources for Family Planning Program (*Programa de Mobilização de Recursos Comunitarios para o Planejamento Familiar*), and later promoted in 1981 the controversial Pro-Family program (*Pró-Família*).

Each of these state programs, like the federal ones that preceded them, targeted low-income populations, proclaiming that family planning was a "hu-

---

[6] Pego and Richa, "Estado e Instituições," p. 38.

[7] Walter Rodriguez, *Painel sobre Planejamento Familiar, presentado na Escola Superior de Guerra* (Rio de Janeiro: BEMFAM), p. 64.

[8] Ibid., p. 65.

man right" denied to poor populations because they lacked the economic means to purchase contraception and the public health facilities at which to obtain birth control methods. Funded by Japanese and American private family-planning organizations and entrusted to the governor's wife, Silvia Maluf, *Pró-Família* involved training community volunteers to distribute birth control pills to women in peripheral neighborhoods in the capital and in rural areas elsewhere in the state, with limited or no medical supervision. The governor's *Grupo de Assessoria e Participação* (Participation and Advisory Group, known as GAP), a special *Malufista* organ created by the PDS in São Paulo to advise the executive branch on community issues, further suggested that people of color should be the primary targets of state population policy—or else the Black population would come to predominate electorally and otherwise in the state of São Paulo.[9]

POPULATION CONTROL OR FAMILY PLANNING? WOMEN'S MOVEMENTS RESPOND TO FEDERAL AND STATE POLICY INITIATIVES IN THE REALM OF REPRODUCTION

The overtly neo-Malthusian, racist targeting of low-income and Black populations for birth control by the State elicited an immediate response from both the São Paulo women's movement and the opposition-controlled state legislature. Labeling the *Malufista* family-planning programs *controlista* (antinatalist or coercive), the São Paulo legislature passed *Projeto Lei* No. 244 in 1980, sponsored by MDB State Assemblymember Antonio Resk,[10] attempting to prohibit the "implementation of any family-planning program which seeks to, directly or indirectly, control population size, without the previous approval of the State Assembly." The legislative project was promptly vetoed by Maluf.

The Paulista women's movement also responded firmly and rapidly to these overtly coercive State policy initiatives. In 1980, all activists could easily agree that State discourses on population policy in no way addressed the health care and contraceptive needs of Brazilian women. The first statewide meeting of São Paulo feminist groups, held in Valinhos in June of 1980 (see chapter 5), created a special commission to study the government's past and present

[9] *Folha de São Paulo*, August 11, 1982. The extent to which *Pró-Família* was actually implemented during the final months of the Maluf administration is still unknown. Relevant public documents are "missing." My own extensive search uncovered little information regarding policy implementation. I could not track down any related documents in any of the several state government organs involved in either population policy formulation or implementation. It is now suspected that the *Pró-Família* program may have been the victim of corruption and health-related abuses and the PMDB administration established a special legislative commission (*Comissão Especial de Inquérito*) to investigate these and other *Malufista* abuses of State power.

[10] Significantly, Resk was among the candidates endorsed by the feminist movement during the 1978 campaign.

population control/family-planning policies and to propose a feminist alternative "which would express the real interests and needs of Brazilian women." The commission released an extensive document for internal discussion within the movement in late 1980, a pamphlet-length version of which was distributed widely during the 1981 International Women's Day celebrations throughout the state of São Paulo. Proclaiming that "women's right to control their own bodies has long been one of the great banners of feminism" and that "both natalist and antinatalist politics have utilized sexuality, the body of woman, as a social patrimony, denying her rights and her individuality," the documents vehemently opposed the "ambiguous official proposal for intervention in the 'regulation of fertility' of women" and argued for the "right to have the necessary conditions to opt freely for maternity."[11]

This feminist position differed markedly from that of the male-dominant parties of the Left and Center-Left. Agreeing with the Left that "it is not the demographic explosion which is causing hunger, misery, and the *aggravation* of our historical situation of oppression but rather the unjust distribution of national wealth and the lack of democratic freedoms which are there to preserve the privileges of a minority, to the detriment of the overwhelming misery of the majority,"[12] this document went on to argue, in a dramatic break with feminism's own earlier anti-State discourse, that the State should be held responsible for providing women with safe, accessible, noncoercive methods of birth control.

> Today we struggle to have the conditions with which to exercise the right to opt freely to have or not have children, how many to have, and the spacing between one pregnancy and another. This is for us a legitimate and democratic demand because it contains a series of aspects which are essential to the advance of the liberation of women such as: the strict respect for the free exercise of our sexuality; the demand that motherhood and domestic work be assumed as social functions; the battle against any and all forms of utilization of our bodies as a social patrimony, above our individual right to choose.[13]

Feminists denounced the government's programs for isolating women's reproductive function from other health issues of concern to women. Moreover, in emphasizing reproductive choice as an essential precondition for women's liberation, this historic document introduced a new, gender-specific element into the Brazilian pronatalist versus antinatalist debate—proclaiming that the heretofore "personal" control of fertility *was* an issue for public, political debate and State action, not to be dismissed solely as an "imperialist plot" to

[11] Comissão de Estudos sobre Planejamento Familiar das Entidades Feministas de São Paulo, "Controle da Natalidade e Planejamento Familiar," São Paulo, Brasil, 1980 (Mimeograph).

[12] Ibid., p. 4.

[13] Ibid., p. 8.

"kill future *guerrilheiros* in the womb," as much of the Brazilian Left historically had contended.

It must be stressed that this position on reproductive freedom marked a significant departure from earlier feminist objections to State-sponsored family-planning. In the mid-1970s, most feminists had merely echoed the Left's objections to the neo-Malthusian content of State population policy proposals, criticizing the government in the "generic" discourse prevalent among other sectors of the progressive opposition. By 1980–1981, feminist discourse on population policy already reflected the movement's newfound emphasis of gender-specific struggle, on strategic as well as practical gender interests. Many feminists now insisted that women had a "right" to control their fertility and that the State had an "obligation" to provide the means for women of all social classes to exercise that right.[14] Still, some sectors of the women's movement, especially those tied to MR-8 and the Catholic church, continued to view any State family-planning initiative as invariably *controlista*.

A feminist-sponsored public meeting to protest *Pró-Família*, held in late 1981, was to generate a massive campaign against Maluf's proposed family-planning program. But in 1982, the partisan polarization of women's movement (discussed in chapters 6 and 7) and disagreements among movement activists as to whether a State family-planning policy would potentially be liberating or intrinsically coercive prevented such a campaign from being effectively carried out.

But when in 1983 the previously ambivalent federal government suddenly started talking about promoting a comprehensive national "family-planning" program, all sectors of the women's movements urgently had to reassess their strategies and remobilize their constituencies. Facing the 1982–1983 debt crisis and consequent renewed negotiations with the IMF and other international lenders, the authoritarian regime suddenly declared family-planning to be one of its policy priorities in March of 1983.

This was no coincidental development, especially if one considers the regime's previous vacillations on the subject of population policy. Population control policies in the Third World often have gone hand-in-hand with strict monetarist policies imposed on national governments by the international aid community.[15] The official justification for such policies is that controlling the "exaggerated" population growth rate in underdeveloped nations is a quick, cost-efficient solution to the inequitable distribution of national resources. This neo-Malthusian idea is fairly straightforward: government policies should

---

[14] Raquel Abrantes Pego provides an excellent account of the evolution of Brazilian feminist thought on reproductive rights in "A Luta das Mulheres pela Livre Concepção," in *Controle da Natalidade x Planejamento Familiar no Brasil*, ed. Guertechin et al.

[15] See Carmen Barroso, "UN Population Policies and Women," 1984 (Mimeograph), for an excellent discussion of the relationship between UN population control initiatives and its efforts to promote improvements in the status of women (as these are thought to reduce fertility).

be aimed at decreasing the number of people who need to be housed, fed, schooled, and employed, rather than at redistributing wealth or augmenting State investments in housing, social welfare, education, and other services.

Shifting political pressures from the international aid community for the adoption of population control measures, then, must be seen to be at least partially responsible for the regime's sudden change of heart on this issue. Before the 1982 debt crisis, the regime was in a much stronger position to resist the international aid community's ardent advocacy of population control.

But in 1982–1983, the economic and political crises propelled by the largest foreign debt in the Third World tied the Brazilian regime more rigidly to the policy dictates of the international aid and financial communities. The pressures of international lending agencies, combined with the emergence of antinatalist ideologies within the ruling coalition, led the Brazilian regime to formulate a policy of State intervention in women's fertility as a means of balancing its key national resource—population—with other, ever more scarce national resources. Since the Brazilian population growth rate has in fact decreased significantly over the past three decades, one cannot attribute the sudden shift in State population policy (from natalist to antinatalist) to economic considerations alone—sociopolitical contradictions arising from the regime's increased dependency on central capitalist nations and their lending institutions must be seen as at least partially responsible for this shift.

In his address to the newly elected National Congress on March 1, 1983, President Figueiredo declared that: "In Brazil, during the last 40 years, demographic growth has surpassed 50 million inhabitants. This human growth, in explosive terms, devours, as has been observed, economic growth. [As] the agent of instability, population growth causes social, economic, cultural and political disequilibriums which call for profound meditation. . . . A wide debate on this subject, especially by the National Congress, will contribute to the fixing of objective, fundamental directions in this regard."[16] The National Congress followed suit, immediately creating a special commission to study population problems, the Senate Parliamentary Inquiry Commission on Population Growth (*Comissão Parlamentar de Inquérito sobre Aumento Populacional*) in March 1983. The Commission was addressed by leading politicians and private citizens, including some nationally known Brazilian feminists, and concentrated on the issue of "family planning" rather than demographic imbalances as such.

Family planning suddenly attained a prominent place on the floor of the national Senate as well. Former Planning Minister and then PDS Senator Roberto Campos stressed the need to curb population growth in his first official address to the Senate.

---

[16] *Folha de São Paulo*, March 2, 1983.

A negligence of demographic issues is manifested in our timidity, if not our inertia, before the population explosion. In the last decade, we evolved from a position of antipathy to family-planning, to a sympathetic apathy, and now, an apathetic sympathy. The last census, of 1980, sets the population growth rate at 2.49 percent, declining in relation to 1960 and 1970, but even so, it is enough to condemn us to relative poverty and to pockets of absolute poverty. . . . The country must exorcise the demographic taboo. . . . In the south, due to the combined effect of education, income growth, and urbanization, there is already spontaneous family-planning. All that is called for is to give the poorer classes and regions the opportunity to practice responsible paternity, impossible today due to lack of information and the inaccessibility of preventive instruments.[17]

"Responsible paternity" became the catchword of antinatalist arguments in 1983. PDS Senator Eunice Michiles, the only woman in the national Senate and president of the *Movimento de Mulheres Democráticas Sociais* (MMDS), the feminine branch of the PDS, made it her primary political banner. In a speech before the Senate on April 28, 1983, the "women's Senator," combined neo-Malthusian arguments with women's rights arguments to propose the creation of an Interministerial Department for Family Planning (*Departamento Interministerial de Planejamento Familiar*) to be directly linked to the presidency and to be directed by a woman "due to her natural affinity with the program." After blaming a score of national ills on the "population problem," Michiles added that:

The important fact is that women have been systematically omitted from the discussion of family-planning; one cannot omit the fact that it is woman who is the principal agent of human reproduction, the one who spends nine months carrying a child, protecting it with her own body, the one who gives birth with all the joy and suffering that involves . . . the understanding of contraceptive methods opens the doors to feminine independence, in the sense that a woman can decide *how many* children she will have, *when* she will have them, giving her the sensation of control over her destiny, allowing her a greater utilization of opportunities for education, and employment.[18]

The executive branch of the federal government also began its own plans for implementing a national family-planning program, independent of the deliberations of the National Congress. The Ministry of Health elaborated a new program called the Program for Integral Assistance to Women's Health (*Programa de Assisstência Integral à Saúde da Mulher* or PAISM), which, like Michiles's proposal, also appropriated the "reproductive rights" discourse developed by the Brazilian women's movement, an ideological emphasis no-

[17] *Folha de São Paulo*, June 9, 1983.
[18] Brasil, Senado Federal, "Palestra da Senadora Eunice Michiles sobre Planejamento Familiar," April 28, 1983 (Mimeograph), emphasis in the original.

tably absent from the pre-1983 State population policies. The PAISM called for a holistic approach to women's health in contrast to the way in which "traditionally a woman has been attended by the health system almost exclusively during the period in which she crosses the cycle of pregnancy and childbirth, leaving other aspects or phases situated outside that cycle on a secondary plane."[19] On paper, the program indeed seemed more all-inclusive than previous health programs aimed at women, and clearly appropriated aspects of feminist discourse, though its emphasis remained on the female reproductive role. The ministry's recommendations were explicitly *anticontrolista* in rhetoric, professing to repudiate "isolated vertical actions of family planning" which would interfere directly in "women's right to choose" maternity or which would be solely preoccupied with the "reproductive aspects of women and not with their general health."[20]

A FEMINIST FAMILY-PLANNING PROGRAM IN THE STATE OF SÃO PAULO?

In June of 1983, the Ministry of Health directed all state health departments to begin discussing state-level implementation of the PAISM. But in São Paulo, the discussion of a possible family-planning program had already been initiated within the PMDB regime. At the urging of the State Council on The Feminine Condition, created by the recently installed Montoro administration at the behest of PMDB feminists, the Department of Health, under the leadership of left-leaning Secretary José Yunes, was already contemplating a comprehensive health program that would respond to demands of organized women in São Paulo. Elaborated by a special working group of leading PMDB feminists, representatives of the Council on the Status of Women, and health and demographic specialists, the *Programa da Saúde da Mulher* (Women's Health Program) was even more in tune with women's movement demands than the federal program.

The Women's Health Program exemplified the newfound clout that some sectors of the feminist movement acquired within the post-1983 São Paulo opposition administration. Openly feminist in orientation, the text of the proposed program addressed issues of women's equality, women's sexuality, sex education, reproductive rights, and other issues first politicized by the Paulista women's movement.

Facing, in a general sense, adverse conditions in the workplace (where the worst paid and least gratifying functions are customarily reserved for them), women accumulate domestic obligations in a toilsome double shift which consumes their physical and mental health. As housewives who dedicate themselves integrally to unpaid

[19] Brasil, Ministério da Saúde, "Assistência Integral á Saúde da Mulher. Subsídios para uma Ação Programática," June 1983 (Mimeograph), p. 4.
[20] Ibid., p. 20.

domestic labor, they also suffer the consequences of carrying out uninterrupted, repetitive, isolated and socially devalued activities.

Besides the specific conditions of women's work, the role of women in reproduction requires special attention, since pregnancy, childbirth, and lactation are processes that demand their biological, psychological, and social involvement. Women's psycho-social involvement with maternity assumes larger proportions in our society, where the sexual division of the labor of childcare determines that this responsibility falls exclusively on the shoulders of women, without the participation of their companions and without the provision of nurseries, day-care centers, or other services by the State.[21]

The Women's Health Program addressed the general health conditions of women in the State of São Paulo and professed to want to contribute to the "demystification of antinatalist and natalist fallacies . . . and clearly disassociates itself with a demographic policy, that is, does not seek to interfere in fertility, either to reduce it, maintain it, or increase it."[22]

The São Paulo Program thus clearly embodied a new feminist approach to State-promoted reforms. The PMDB feminists who helped elaborate the program in the state of São Paulo argued that given that the federal government was going to implement a population program anyway, feminists had to make every effort to make such a program as noncoercive and as beneficial to women as possible. Though these women hardly embraced the State as a trustworthy ally, they chose to work to ensure that, at least at the level of São Paulo, family-planning did not become coercive population control. Moreover, many women insisted that such a program, if inspired and closely monitored by feminists, could respond at least partially to needs articulated by poor and working-class women in particular. As discussed above, feminine group participants with whom feminists had worked consistently expressed a desire to have greater control over fertility. In short, many feminists in São Paulo maintained that the federal government's population control initiatives could and certainly should be subverted to provide women with improved access to family-planning.

But even the seemingly "women-centered" federal and state family-planning programs elicited distrust on the part of other Brazilian women's movement activists, left-wing opposition parties, and the church. This reaction was hardly surprising given that the military authoritarian State had proven itself to be a staunch opponent of social justice and could hardly have been transformed overnight into a trustworthy ally of those seeking reproductive rights and gender justice. Some groups, like the MR-8's *Federação* and the PCdoB's *União*, as well as some women PT activists in São Paulo, continued to claim

[21] Estado de São Paulo, Secretaría de Saúde, "Programa da Saúde da Mulher," 1983 (Mimeograph), p. 5.

[22] Ibid., p. 6.

that State initiatives in family planning merely masked more sinister population control motives.

Most of the Left and sectors of the progressive church denounced both federal and state family planning as genocidal and imperialist-imposed. The PT in São Paulo, for example, publicly proclaimed its wariness of even the State Health Department's feminist-inspired Women's Health Program as potentially *controlista*.

Many individual women's movement activists and autonomous women's organizations outside the ruling PMDB coalition in São Paulo shared this wariness. They argued that the scarce funds likely to be allocated to these programs (estimated at only C R $11 million or approximately U.S. $20,000 for the federal program in 1983) would lead merely to the arbitrary distribution of birth control pills (and not other, more expensive, but safer methods) and to sterilization abuse among low-income populations, rather than in comprehensive health care for all women.

Women's movement consensus on how to interpret and respond to State family-planning/population control initiatives proved more elusive still as no clear federal or state population guidelines were established and the implementation stage awaited some sort of consensus within the governing coalition at both the national and state levels. While Figueiredo, Campos, Michiles, the Ministry of Health, and other key government sectors endorsed a national family-planning program (for differing reasons), opposition to such a program emerged elsewhere within the State apparatus and among the ranks of the governing party. Key political figures such as then Minister of Social Welfare Helio Beltrão, Minister of Education Ester Figueiredo, Minister Jarbas Passarinho, and some sectors of the *Escola Superior de Guerra* (Superior War College) and the Armed Forces continued to espouse natalist opposition to family-planning or advocated a more balanced approach to population control, arguing that increased State outlays in education and health care would lead to a natural reduction of the national birth rate.

As divisions among State factions fostered policy vacillation and immobilism, the various sectors of the São Paulo women's movement remobilized around reproductive issues, attempting to anticipate the content of the state and federal government family-planning programs and to develop a movement counterproposal more in tune with women's needs. At a June 22, 1983, meeting at *Casa da Mulher* in São Paulo, representatives of *Centro Informação Mulher, SOS-Mulher, Frente de Mulheres Feministas, Grupo Ação Lésbica-Feminista, União de Mulheres de São Paulo*, and the State Council on the Status of Women's Study Group on Women's Health, elaborated a feminist proposal addressing women's health needs as the movement perceived them.

This document, however, poignantly illustrated the new strategic dilemma confronted by women's movement activists as many of its recommendations strongly resembled the São Paulo Health Department's proposal. Points of departure included support for free, publicly funded abortion on demand, the formation of discussion groups for men and women on sexuality and reproduction at public health posts throughout the state, special precautions against sterilization abuse and unnecessary gynecological surgery, and the provision of medical and psychiatric assistance to women victims of rape and battery.[23] The feminist proposal was broadcast on national television during feminist Martha Suplicy's segment of *TV-Mulher*—a program viewed daily by over six million Brazilian housewives.

Autonomous women's groups abruptly were caught in a bind vis-à-vis State initiatives in reproductive politics. Suddenly the male-dominant, military authoritarian State, heretofore perceived as their primary adversary, was espousing a politic that approximated their own. And women's movement activists expressed an urgent need to distinguish their own proposals for reproductive freedom from State attempts to intervene in the control of fertility—a difficult task given that the women's movement was the first to introduce the notion of State responsibility for the provision of birth control to all women.

Brazilian Feminists Rethink Their Approach to the Authoritarian State

An incipient feminist reformulation of the question of how to deal with the State on this issue began to surface in mid-1983. Reproductive politics headed the agenda at the Third National Feminist Meeting held in Brasília in July of 1983. Participants from over twenty women's groups from São Paulo, Rio de Janeiro, Belo Horizonte, Salvador, Recife, Fortaleza, Goiânia, Curitiba, and Florianópolis, elaborated a document specifying a national feminist position on birth control, abortion, and family planning to be widely distributed to the press and to leaders of opposition parties. Those present also agreed to form state-based movement commissions that would monitor the implementation of state- and federal-level programs in an effort to prevent abuses such as the indiscriminate distribution of pills or forced sterilization.

At the Brasília meeting, Rio feminists also advanced their proposal for a National Abortion Rights Campaign to be launched on September 22, 1983. Though the idea for this campaign grew out of a national meeting on Women's Health, Sexuality, Contraception, and Abortion, held in Rio on March 4-6, 1983, and financed by the Pathfinder Fund, many of the women now gathered in Brasília refused to endorse such a campaign as they feared that a stress on abortion would be problematic at a time when the government had antinatalist intentions that politically could compromise a demand for abortion rights.

[23] Entidades Feministas de São Paulo, "Carta ao Conselho Estadual da Condição Feminina," May 25, 1983 (Mimeograph).

Some participants asked, "did the feminist movement want abortion to be legalized as a further State measure to control population size?"

Immediately preceding the feminist meeting in Brasília, the women of the government party held a national meeting of their own there. Called by MMDS president, Senator Eunice Michiles and alternate federal deputy from Minas Gerais, Ana María Mendoça, general secretary of the MMDS, the agenda of the meeting was family-planning, "responsible paternity," and the mobilization of support for Michiles's proposed Interministerial Department for Family Planning. The appropriation of feminist discourse also was evident in the MMDS's discussions of family-planning. The meeting endorsed Michiles's neo-Malthusian program, couched rhetorically in proclamations of "woman's right to control her own body."[24]

Still in late 1983, State-sponsored family planning remained at the level of discourse and policy formulation. The regime's internally generated succession crisis and the opposition-led mobilizations in support of direct elections, and, later, in support of the indirect candidacy of Tancredo Neves, slowed plans to implement a federal family-planning program on a national scale.[25]

Undaunted by these delays, many feminists continued to view the regime's proposed program as an opportune vehicle for making birth control more widely accessible to Brazilian women. Feminists then working in the Ministry

[24] A further outcome of the meeting was the MMDS's coordination of the First National Brazilian Congress on Maternal Infant Protection and Family Planning, held in Brasília on September 23–25, 1983, timed to coincide with the feminists' September 22, "National Abortion Rights Day." Organized by an MMDS-related group called *Pró-Família* (unrelated to Maluf's program by the same name), the Congress included representatives from the Ministries of Health, Education, Interior, Labor, Justice and Social Welfare, the Brazilian Legion of Charities (LBA), several federal universities, the government of the Federal District of Brasília, state governments, various political parties, the CNBB, feminine organizations, and, of course, the MMDS. International participants included representatives from UNICEF, the UN, the O.A.S., the World Health Organization, the Pathfinder Fund, and International Planned Parenthood. Closing resolutions endorsed neo-Malthusian interpretations of Brazilian demography cited above and the consequent need to immediately implement a nationwide State-financed family-planning program.

[25] For a journalistic account of the 1984 nationwide mobilizations in favor of direct elections, see Ricardo Kotscho, *Explode um Novo Brasil: Diario da Campanha das Diretas* (São Paulo: Brasilense, 1984). On the PMDB shift to a strategy of "beating the regime at its own game" by seeking to defeat the PDS's candidate within the Electoral College, see Gilberto Dimerstein et al., *O Complō que Elegeu Tancredo* (Rio de Janeiro: Editora JB, 1985). For more analytical treatments of strategic realignments both within the government and within the opposition, see Bolivar Lamounier and Marcus Faria Figueredo, "A Crise e a Transição para a Democracia no Brasil," *IDESP Textos* 5 (1984); Scott Mainwaring, "The Transition to Democracy in Brazil," *Journal of Interamerican Studies and World Affairs* 28 (May 1986): 149–79; and Maria Helena Moreira Alves, "Dilemmas of the Consolidation of Democracy from the Top: A Political Analysis," *Latin American Perspectives* 15, no. 3 (Summer 1988): 47–63. Francisco Weffort's *Por Qúe Democracia?* (São Paulo: Brasilense, 1984) provides the most incisive and compelling analysis of why progressive sectors within the political opposition aligned themselves behind the seemingly "bourgeois" cause of reestablishing political democracy in Brazil.

of Health's bureaucracy greatly influenced the content of PAISM; therefore, the program's stated goals, argued some independent feminists, made it feasible for feminists to insist that PAISM include health and sex education outreach dimensions that would reduce the risk of coercive population control. Throughout 1984, some in the national feminist movement consistently pressured the Ministry of Health and other policy-making arenas within which the PAISM was being developed to ensure that the regime remain true to its *anticontrolista* discourse. Official family-planning policy was rendered more vulnerable to such organized pressure precisely because it had incorporated so much of the reproductive rights discourse articulated by women's movements over the previous decade.

At the federal level, some State factions continued to push for the immediate establishment of a national council on population that would implement a nationwide population control program. Appropriating the oppositon slogans most prevalent during the 1984 direct election campaign, centered on the end to military rule *now* ("Direct Elections Now!," "Tancredo Neves Now!," "Constitutent Assembly Now!"), *controlista* segments of the ruling party and the State began advocating "Family Planning Now!" (*Planejamento Familiar Ja!*).[26] The chief of the *Estado Maior das Forças Armadas*, General del Aire Waldir de Vasconcelos, made population control his principal political concern during most of 1984. He traveled extensively throughout Brazil, meeting with prominent politicians, industrialists, and community leaders, arguing that curbing population growth was essential to Brazilian economic growth and prosperity and therefore must be seen as a crucial component of "national security." Michiles's MMDS also engaged in a massive, nationwide propaganda campaign to promote its own neo-Malthusian brand of "feminist" family planning.[27]

Independent sectors of the national women's movement launched a counteroffensive of their own. In July of 1984, the Fourth National Feminist Meeting, held in São Paulo and attended by ninety-seven women from thirty-three feminist organizations, focused on the issues of women's health and family-planning in an attempt to further elaborate a consensual movement position on reproductive rights through which to contest *controlista* policy proposals at the state and national levels. And such a position began to take definitive shape during the remaining months of 1984.

It would occur to no one to suggest that the federal Program of Integral Assistance to Women's Health is what women aspire to in terms of a public health policy. This

[26] Interview with Margaret Arilha, then coordinator of the São Paulo State Council on the Status of Women's Commission on Women's Health and member of the Council's Executive Committee, São Paulo, August 22, 1985.

[27] Movimento de Mulheres Democráticas Sociais, "Planejamento Familiar Ja!," 1984 (Mimeograph).

program, created by the military regime in recent times, however, contains some of the demands that feminists have been making. In spite of this, we believe that the bureaucratic manipulation of this program could result in few advances [for women] and for this reason, we have decided to participate more actively in its implementation, monitoring it, demanding forums and debates with institutional organisms, participating in conferences and other activities proposed by these organisms.[28]

In September and October of 1984, follow-up regional meetings were organized in Rio and in São Paulo. And in November of that year, several women's groups in São Paulo organized the First National Meeting on Women's Health, held in the city of Itapecirica and attended by over four hundred women from nineteen Brazilian states.[29]

After three days of discussing government family planning/population control initiatives in different Brazilian states, participants elaborated a joint set of resolutions, to be included in a public letter addressed to federal and state level government agencies responsible for the implementation of the PAISM. The *Carta de Itapecirica* called for "the participation of women's groups in the elaboration, execution and monitoring of women's health programs, sex education for all the population, the reclaiming of popular and feminist wisdom against the excessive medicalization [of women's health] and a revalorization of natural forms of life and health."[30]

In short, significant portions of the feminist movement reformulated feminism's historically "antistate" posture and exacerbated the contradictions inherent in State family-planning initiatives. In this sense, then, the Brazilian feminist movement successfully mobilized against those State factions who promoted *controlista* solutions and "beat" the outgoing authoritarian regime "at its own game." That is, the State's attempt to mask population control efforts beneath the veil of "reproductive rights" backfired. Organized sectors of civil society, spearheaded by women's movement organizations, and feminists active in opposition parties, leading their respective women's divisions, pushed the regime to confront its own internal contradictions regarding the formulation and implementation of population policies and made PAISM more susceptible to feminist influence.

Organized opposition to State factions who advocated *controlista* or neo-Malthusian formulations of family-planning policy thus had a significant impact on the regime's formulation of the PAISM. Such intervention by civil society in the regime's policy process was possible due to conjunctural vari-

[28] Coletivo Feminista Sexualidade e Saúde, "Brasil: Mujeres y Salud," in *La Salud de las Mujeres: La Experiencia de Brasil, Reflexiones y Acciones Internacionales*, ed. ISIS International (Santiago, Chile: ISIS, 1985), p. 11.

[29] Organizing groups included *Casa da Mulher de Bela Vista*, *Casa da Mulher de Grajau*, *Coletivo Feminista Sexualidade e Saúde de São Paulo*, *Serviço Orientação Família*, and *Centro Informação Mulher*.

[30] Coletivo Feminista Sexualidade e Saúde, "Brasil: Mujeres y Salud," p. 13.

ables at play in the final stages of the Brazilian regime's transition to civilian rule. In its last attempts to restore its eroding hegemony in the face of widespread opposition, even from among its previous allies (sectors of the National bourgeoisie and the PDS, which defected to the Liberal Front over the issue of direct elections), some factions within the regime, and apparently within the Ministry of Health in particular, appear to have become more receptive to demands emanating from civil society.

Some feminists discovered that the transitional authoritarian State was not a seamless monolith. Indeed, the Ministry of Health proved an unusual point of access through which the Brazilian women's movement could influence the authoritarian State apparatus.[31] The bureaucratic team to which the Ministry's PAISM was entrusted was presided by feminist-identified, progressive health professionals who were exceptionally responsive to women's movement demands for "reproductive rights" and who actively combated the efforts of General Vasconcelos, the MMDS, and other sectors of the ruling coalition to wrest the State's would-be family-planning program from the purview the Ministry of Health. To counter Vasconcelos's pro–population control crusade, the ministry launched its own educational campaign in favor of noncoercive family planning. The women and men responsible for the PAISM within the ministry also toured Brazil, appearing in public debates, radio and television programs, and even directly debating General Vasconcelos on a few occasions.[32]

The dramatic crisis of legitimacy suffered by the military regime after 1983 made the authoritarian State more pliant, less hermetically sealed off from civil society. By late 1983, it was clear that the presidential succession, a key element in regime stability that on previous occasions had stirred significant conflict within the ruling civil-military coalition, was escalating into a fullscale political crisis. Having promised to turn the presidency over to a civilian in 1985, President Figueiredo gradually lost control of the succession process as different wings of the ruling party openly battled one another for control of the federal government.[33]

The ensuing schisms within the ruling coalition and the political opposition's united decision to accentuate those rifts by initiating a massive campaign for direct presidential elections to be held in 1985, resulted in consid-

[31] I am indebted to Margit Mayer for having drawn my attention to differential "access points" within the State apparatus. See her "Urban Social Movements and Beyond: New Linkages between Movement Sectors and the State in West Germany and the United States" (Paper presented at the Fifth International Conference of Europeanists, Washington, D.C., October 18–20, 1985).

[32] Interview with Margaret Arilha, São Paulo, August 22, 1985.

[33] See Thomas E. Skidmore, "Brazil's Slow Road to Democratization, 1974–1985," in *Democratizing Brazil: Problems of Transition and Consolidation*, ed. Alfred Stepan (New York: Oxford University Press, 1989). See also Scott Mainwaring, "The Transition to Democracy in Brazil."

erable policy immobilism at the federal level, thus enabling the Ministry of Health to proceed with its more coherent proposal for family planning. This crisis increased the opportunity space available to sectors of civil society who both opposed any *controlista* policy proposals, and wanted to promote safe, noncoercive, State-sponsored family-planning and thus increase women's contraceptive options. That space was immediately seized by those feminists who were able to reformulate the movement's historically antistate posture and thus take advantage of an unprecedented point of access to the authoritarian State's policy-making process.

CONCLUSION

During the latter stages of regime transition, women's movement activists in São Paulo were faced with new dilemmas about how best to approach the local and national State. First, as the military regime's eroding legitimacy prompted it to disguise population control initiatives under the rubric of "family planning" and to appropriate the "reproductive choice" discourse developed by Brazilian feminists, activists confronted the question of how to react when the authoritarian State began articulating a policy disturbingly similar to that which the movement had been advocating.

In this instance, some women's movement activists managed to take advantage of, and ultimately subvert, the indisputably nonfeminist motives behind these State policy initiatives. In the process, women's movement strategies kept the federal government true to its *anticontrolista* discourse, at least in the policy formulation stage.

After 1983, the women's movement in São Paulo also had to figure out how best to approach democratic "opposition" governments that professed to be addressing gender interests as articulated by the movement. Here the movement confronted a more complex situation: how to adapt strategies to a more democratic context while advancing women's gender interests within a still male-dominant State. The feminist-inspired Women's Health Program in São Paulo, on paper at least, was very much in tune with movement demands for reproductive choice. Though some in the movement still believed that any State intervention in the realm of family-planning would be inevitably *controlista*, the decision of major sectors of the feminist movement to monitor family-planning policy developments eased those fears and enabled the movement to face the State from a united stance.

This chapter has shown that State policies affecting women's status are sometimes quite contradictory and feminist strategies can often exacerbate those contradictions by taking their struggle into the heart of the State apparatus. The avenues available to women's movement activists who seek to influence State policy appear to be more fluid than a "State as ultimate patriarch" view might lead us to believe.

Though regime transition brought about rapid changes in State-society relations and bred considerable strategic confusion among movement activists, in the case of family-planning policy, the patriarchal barricades were momentarily lowered and women's movements gained access to limited areas of policy planning and formulation. Chapter 9 examines a political development that would further confound movement strategies while increasing women's access to State policy making: the creation of a State Council on the Feminine Condition in the PMDB-controlled state of São Paulo.

CHAPTER NINE

Taking Feminism into the State: Gender Policy and the PMDB's Councils on the Status of Women

THE PMDB "opposition" state government, elected in November 1982 and headed by former Senator Franco Montoro, professed a commitment to greater popular participation in public policy formulation. At the urging of feminists in the PMDB (Party of the Brazilian Democratic Movement), the new government created the *Conselho Estadual da Condição Feminina* (literally, the State Council on the Feminine Condition or CECF), a "women's space" in the state administration. The PMDB women who proposed the CECF envisioned it as serving two principal purposes: it would provide São Paulo women's movements with a direct avenue of access to policy making and implementation and it would represent women's interests within the state administration.

Thanks to the efforts of PMDB feminists, the new ruling party's electoral platform also committed it to advancing some of the women's movements' long-standing policy goals. But the installation of democratic PMDB administrations in the state and county of São Paulo also bred confusion and sparked further fission among the various sectors of the women's movement, even as the new opposition administrations introduced some important gains for women in the realm of family-planning and day-care policy. My analysis will focus first on how women's movements in São Paulo responded to these rapidly changing State discourses and policies, as the local State appeared to metamorphose from "women's worst enemy" into "women's best friend."

Though many non-PMDB women's movement participants viewed the Council as an instance of State cooptation and "institutionalization" of the independent Paulista women's movement, I will show that the CECF succeeded in influencing the policy process in significant ways, ways that made both family-planning and day-care policy more responsive to the demands of some sectors of the women's movement. However, movement access to State policy-making arenas remained mediated by questionable representatives—white, middle-class PMDB-affiliated women appointed by the governor and thus, in many respects, beholden to the PMDB administration and not to the movement constituencies they ostensibly represented.

THE CREATION OF THE SÃO PAULO COUNCIL ON THE FEMININE CONDITION

From the outset, the creation of the CECF posed many questions of strategy for São Paulo women's movement activists. Should all movement claims now be channeled through the Council? Was the Council a legitimate conquest of the women's movement as a whole? Would it represent the demands of the diverse sectors of the women's movement before the new administration? Or would the Council become an instrument of top-down mobilization of women that would promote a partisan PMDB "women's agenda"?

The answer to the last question appeared obvious to many non-PMDB feminists in São Paulo. Discussions of how the Council would be constituted, whether a *Secretaría da Mulher* (Women's Department) would be preferable to a Council, and which areas of government policy toward women would be prioritized under the new administration remained a closed partisan discussion among PMDB feminists. It seemed clear to many that some sectors of the women's movement (those who had supported the PMDB during the campaign) were now in power and the "opposition" women (especially members or sympathizers of the Workers' Party, the PT) and nonpartisan women's movement activists saw themselves as marginalized from the decision-making process that was to define the new administration's policy toward women.

The result was that even before the PMDB had officially announced its plan of action vis-à-vis women, strong opposition to the Council was already brewing among the ranks of some feminist groups, neighborhood women's groups, and sectors of the day-care movement. This incipient opposition viewed the plan for the Council as a possible instance of "institutionalization" of the women's movement. In keeping with *basista* discourses prevailing within the PT and among sectors of the people's church (a position that equated movement "autonomy" with direct democracy and viewed representation as suspect), any form of incorporation by or concession from the State was viewed as intrinsically co-optative. Women who adhered to this notion of movement autonomy regarded those sectors of the movement involved in policy planning as "unrepresentative" of the women's movement as a whole, since all were movement activists who had opted for the PMDB after 1980. However, the women's movement "as a whole" was so disarticulated after the 1982 electoral conjuncture that it was unable to present a concrete, alternative plan of action for confronting the more organized and cohesive PMDB plan for women.

Tensions were further aggravated when the PMDB Women's Study Group, discussed in chapter 7, presented a proposal to governor-elect Franco Montoro on March 8, International Women's Day, for an executive decree creating the Council, without having previously consulted with local women's movement organizations as to its content, requesting that it be the governor's first executive decree when he took office on March 15. The actual decree was signed by the governor on April 4, 1983, and was a significantly altered version of the PMDB women's original proposal.

The Council was granted broad "advisory" powers, but had no executive or implementation powers of its own, nor did it have an independent budget, being totally dependent on the Governor's Civilian Cabinet for financial and technical assistance. The decree made no mention of the State Program in Defense of Women's Rights, developed and proposed by PMDB feminists. Instead, the Council was given the power to "*propose* measures and activities which aim at the defense of the rights of women, the elimination of discrimination which affects women, and the full insertion of women into socio-economic, political and cultural life"; it was to "incorporate preoccupations and suggestions manifested by society and *opine* about denunciations which are brought before it . . . *support* projects developed by organs, governmental or not, concerning women, and *promote* agreements with similar organizations and institutions."[1]

The avowed purpose of the CECF, according to both the governor and the PMDB women who proposed it, was to grant the women's movement a voice within the state government and give women influence over several areas of the state administration rather than isolate women in a separate "women's department." The original structure of the Council was fairly innovative in this regard, as its members included "representatives of civil society," ostensibly linked to women's movement organizations of various types, and official representatives of several state-level executive departments. The idea was to create direct access points to those departments, thus enabling the Council, and, through it, the women's movement, to influence the formulation of gender-specific and gender-related public policies and monitor their implementation. However, since the Council was given *no* executive power, its influence over policy was necessarily somewhat limited—though its very creation unquestionably represented an advance for women relative to the previous PDS administration.[2]

The Council's "representativeness" also proved to be an enduring point of contention among women's movement participants in São Paulo. All fifteen of the original councillors were members of the PMDB. Given the disarticulating and divisive consequences of the 1982 electoral conjuncture, this fact did little to heal existing partisan rivalries within and among women's movement groups. From the outset, the CECF openly admitted to its partisan composition, stating that "the criterion for supra-partisan representation [within the Council] is still a dream, [that was] unviable at the time of the Council's

---

[1] Governo do Estado de São Paulo, *Diario Oficial*, Decree no. 20892, April 5, 1983, emphasis added.

[2] Montoro appointed *no* women to any of the twenty-four posts in his first State Cabinet and only two were apppointed to the municipal cabinet—in posts that have "traditionally" been held by women in liberal democracies, the *Secretaria Municipal da Família e BemEstar Social* (Department of the Family and Social Welfare) and the *Secretaria Municipal de Educação* (Education Department). In 1986, at the urging of PMDB feminists, Montoro appointed Alda Marco Antonio, the first vice-president of the CECF, a state Secretary of Labor.

creation.''[3] Yet, the women who made up the original CECF also seemed aware of the problematic nature of the Council's relationship both to the male-dominated PMDB State apparatus and the independent women's movement. In one of its earliest official publications, Eva Blay, the first president of the CECF, addressed the precariousness of the Council's position within the State administration:

Another question to be profoundly considered refers to the political-administrative form chosen [to represent women's interests within the new government]; a Council. Social movements, and among them, women's movements, desire and should guarantee their autonomy vis-à-vis the State. To be part of the State apparatus in order to be able to utilize it from within but at the same time maintain the freedom to criticize it is an extremely complex question. Nevertheless, this difficulty must not constitute an obstacle which paralyzes the participatory process. The [political-administrative] form devised to avoid the reproduction of vices typical of the traditional [political] structure is the creation of a Council which has a majority representation of sectors of civil society. The mechanisms of selection [of said representatives], have yet to be defined as it is hoped that organized groups or independent feminists will pronounce their opinions on the subject. . . . Created within an opposition party, due to the initiative of a study group, the Council on the Status of Women now belongs to all women, who can and should manifest themselves as to its future direction.[4]

But the problem posed by the CECF itself as to which women's organizations were to be represented within the Council and which women were to represent them immediately generated a great deal of conflict between the Paulista women's movement and the new PMDB administration. The July 1983 appointment of fifteen PMDB party women,[5] predominantly from the more liberal, professionally based feminist organizations in São Paulo to the Council,[6] led some PT-affiliated women and independent women's groups, under

[3] Governo do Estado de São Paulo, Conselho da Condição Feminina, untitled newsletter, 1984. In an interview conducted in August 1985, Council President Eva Blay reiterated the notion that a ''nonpartisan'' Council was unviable given the pronounced and continuing conflicts between the ruling PMDB and the opposition PT in São Paulo.

[4] Governo do Estado de São Paulo, Conselho da Condição Feminina, untitled document, Fall 1983.

[5] Due to the lobbying efforts of the São Paulo Black Women's Collective and the United Black Movement, the Council later added a black woman to its group of ''representatives'' of civil society. It is important to note that people of color are extremely poorly represented in the New Republic and that race-specific political claims are among the most difficult to articulate within institutional arenas, due in large part to the continuing myth of racial democracy upheld by even the most progressive white Brazilians. Black women have been dissatisfied with the extent to which the predominantly white feminist movement has confronted race issues in women's lives and have formed their own, separate feminist organizations in recent years. See chapter 10.

[6] The representatives of civil society appointed to the Council were mostly women who entered the feminist movement through academic or professional networks as opposed to women who

the leadership of *petista* municipal councilwoman Irede Cardoso, to accuse the Council of being "undemocratic" and "unrepresentative." These women argued that the Council was an entirely partisan organism, that the PMDB administration was trying to co-opt the women's movement through the creation of the Council, and that the PMDB women who composed the CECF had failed to consult the broader women's movement in the establishment of its political priorities and its organizational structure and composition. The CECF in turn maintained that its strength and effectiveness depended on the strength and effectiveness of women's movement organizations, and that it needed the support and collaboration of those organizations in order to gain clout within the state administration. Some independent women's organizations indeed recognized the CECF as a legitimate conquest of the women's movement (and particularly of organized feminists within the PMDB) and chose to approach the new institution from a cautious, but supportive perspective.

The creation of the CECF in and of itself remobilized and strengthened the women's movement in São Paulo. Confronted with a new "women's institution" created by an administration theoretically sympathetic to women's claims, São Paulo feminist and feminine movement organizations had to concretize and redefine their political priorities so that they could be channeled effectively through the CECF, or else risk having those priorities manipulated by the new administration for its own political gain.

A few independent women's groups called a public forum in May of 1983 to discuss the movement's potential relationship to the Council and this forum was established as a monthly event to discuss relevant developments within the PMBD administration and to plan unified movement strategies in response to those developments. These monthly forums were the first instance of ongoing, unified feminist and feminine political action since the 1981 International Women's Day celebrations. This movement response to state policy initiatives is a clear illustration of the dialectical nature of the relationship between social movements and the State.

The CECF itself acknowledged the importance of sustained political pressure on gender-specific issues from outside the State and claimed that it hoped "to serve as an instrument for the dynamization and reinvigoration of the autonomous women's movement."[7] But by late 1985, many feminist activists were concerned about the fact that the CECF seemed to be absorbing, even preempting, many of the movement's independent mobilizational initiatives. After 1983, the São Paulo Council assumed many of the activities that previously had been the purview of autonomous women's movement organizations. In 1984 and 1985, for example, the International Women's Day celebrations

---

came into feminism through experiences in the militant opposition or the student movement. See chapter 6.

[7] Governo do Estado de São Paulo, Conselho Estadual da Condição Feminina, untitled document, 1984.

in São Paulo, previously peak mobilizational moments for the independent women's movement, were transformed into political showcases for the CECF's conception of "women's interests," mobilizing women in support of the PMDB's local and national political projects. In 1984, the theme of International Women's Day was "*Direitos, Diretas e Paz*" (Rights, Direct Elections, and Peace), a theme reflecting not only the concerns of the independent women's movement (couched in more acceptable or politically palatable rhetoric) but also the PMDB's efforts to promote direct presidential elections during 1984.

The danger in this CECF's strategy was that, however unintentionally, the Council also to some extent preempted the mobilization of gender-conscious political pressure from outside the PMDB administration. The Council's activities at least temporarily absorbed the initiatives of organized female constituencies within civil society. This tendency towards absorption and institutionalization of autonomous, nonpartisan women's movement political demands could eventually jeopardize progress toward the eradication of gender-based inequality by preempting organized, gender-conscious political pressure from outside the State, which is critical for mediating the State's propensity to co-opt women and women's issues to suit the wider goals of a given incumbent administration.

The CECF's mobilizational capacity as an organ of the local State thus was deployed not only to promote the eradication of gender inequality, but also to support the larger interests of the PMDB coalition in power in the state of São Paulo. And this fact, in part, accounted for the continuing skepticism of sectors of the women's movement outside the ruling coalition as to where the primary loyalties of the CECF lay.

COUNCIL INTERVENTION IN FAMILY-PLANNING/POPULATION CONTROL POLICY

Despite tensions between the Council and some segments of the São Paulo women's movement, the CECF had a considerable, if hardly uncontroversial, impact on public policies affecting women during the first two years of the PMDB administration. In the realm of family-planning policy, the CECF's intervention proved critical for ensuring that safe, accessible, and noncoercive family planning be made available to women through the state's public health network. As noted in chapter 8, the Council played a leading role in the formulation of family-planning policy at the state level. But the danger of co-optation and manipulation of women's demands for reproductive freedom is greatest at the implementation phase. The historical tendency in Latin America and elsewhere in the Third World has been for State-sponsored family planning to consist of the arbitrary distribution of birth control pills and the encouragement of sterilization, especially among women of color and poor women. Thus, the existence of a gender-conscious mechanism, within the State apparatus, to supervise and monitor the implementation of State-sponsored family planning was crucial for mediating this historical tendency.

While divergences within the PMDB administration and in civil society delayed the implementation of the São Paulo Women's Health Program, the Council consistently insisted that "conception and contraception, with information about and access to all of the contraceptive methods" must remain integral components of the Program. The CECF sponsored several public forums on reproductive rights and family planning and one of its subcommittees, the Women's Health Commission, worked closely with the São Paulo Department of Health in the further elaboration of the Program. Many feminist and feminine activists attended these forums and collaborated closely with the CECF's efforts to fashion a Program that legitimately reflected feminist demands for reproductive choice.

In promoting the feminist-inspired content of the Program, the Council had to combat progressive factions of the PMDB administration who viewed any such program with suspicion. The Left, or *auténtico*, wing of the PMDB predominated in the state Department of Health and, as we saw above, the Left in Brazil historically has equated family-planning policy with imperialist population control initiatives. Though this view is partially warranted given the neo-Malthusian content of family-planning policies proposed by the Right and the international aid community, the CECF maintained that the Women's Health Program was also a legitimate need of Paulista women. The Council's Commission on Women's Health argued that if the Program was properly administered and accompanied by popular education, it would advance the status of women by enabling women of all social classes to make informed reproductive choices. In short, as Margaret Arilha put it, "the Council had to combat the ghosts of population control" among left-wing sectors of the PMDB administration and other progressive sectors of civil society.[8]

During 1985–1986, the Council exerted constant pressure to get the São Paulo Health Department to begin the implementation phase of the Program. Its access to the department's policy process was facilitated by the fact that a representative from the Health Department sat on the Council. The Council's structure and membership, combining representatives from civil society and the State, thus proved especially effective in the area of family-planning policy. Council members directly lobbied the secretary of health, the directors of the department's seventeen regional subdivisions, and other key policy planners throughout 1984 to convince them of the worthiness and the urgency of implementing the Women's Health Program. It also launched an extensive propaganda campaign to dispel fears of population control among progressive sectors of civil society. As a direct consequence of the Council's sustained

[8] Interview with Margaret Arilha, São Paulo, August 22, 1985.

efforts, the department made the Women's Health Program one of its programmatic and budgetary priorities in 1985.

After months of discussion and deliberation in the Council, it was agreed that family-planning representatives, trained and supervised by the Department of Health in conjunction with the Council's Commission on Women's Health, would supervise the implementation of the Program for Women's Health in all seventeen subdivisions in the state of São Paulo. The Council also facilitated the women's movements' access to the policy implementation process, urging the Department of Health to hold monthly public "Forums to Accompany the Implementation of the Program for Women's Health." These forums, initiated in early 1985, brought state health policy planners, employees of the public health network, and movement participants active in grassroots sex education, health, and reproductive rights advocacy together to discuss the progress of the Program.[9] The São Paulo Council was also instrumental in generating new access points through which women's movement organizations could impact the federal PAISM, pressuring the Ministry of Health to create a "Commission on Reproductive Rights," which, like the state forums, brought together policy makers, health professionals, and women's movement activists to promote a safe, accessible, and noncoercive federal family-planning policy.

What differentiated the Council's actions within the São Paulo administration, then, from similar administrative organs created throughout Latin America (largely as a consequence of the UN-sponsored Women's Decade), was the pronounced *feminist* presence within the São Paulo CECF from 1983 to 1985. Though nonfeminist women and PMDB party militants were also members of the Council, a feminist position on family planning, largely derived from the contributions of the Brazilian feminist movement to political discourse on population policy, prevailed in shaping CECF policy.

In undertaking the supervision of the implementation of family-planning policy at the state level, the Council accomplished what the independent women's movement could never accomplish on its own due to its structural position outside the pact of domination. And the continued mobilization of women's movement organizations on a national, state, and local level around reproductive rights and family planning unquestionably contributed to the relative success of this gender-conscious family-planning policy.

As shown in the preceding chapter, independent feminists held several statewide discussions on family planning, responded agilely to State initiatives, and closely monitored the Council's and the Department and Ministry of Health's deliberations and policy proposals on this issue. Though some in the women's movement and some women's groups tied to the sectarian Left

[9] Informal interview with Ana Maria P. Pluciennik, coordinator of the Women's Health Program, Secrataria da Saúde, São Paulo, August 21, 1985.

continued to regard the Women's Health Program with suspicion, most movement participants reached a working consensus on the fact that, within the bounds imposed by the military-controlled federal government, the São Paulo Program largely was consistent with historic feminist demands for reproductive choice and merited movement support. And unquestionably, such consistent, consensual, gender-conscious political pressure from within civil society contributed to the São Paulo PMDB's unusual responsiveness to the Council's proposals in this policy area.

COUNCIL INTERVENTION IN DAY-CARE POLICY

As the Council advanced a position on reproductive rights and women's health that reflected the consensus of major segments of the feminist movement, CECF actions in the realm of family-planning policy sparked relatively little controversy in movement circles. In this policy area, the Council indeed appeared to be fulfilling its function as the direct representative of women's movement demands within the State apparatus. But in the area of day-care policy, movement consensus proved more elusive and the contradictions inherent in the ability of an administrative organ of the State to "represent" a divided women's movement rose to the surface.

Day care assumed a prominent place in São Paulo local politics first under a Democratic Social Party (PDS) mayor and subsequently under the opposition PMDB administration. Though since 1943 industrial and commercial establishments employing more than thirty women were required by Brazilian labor law to provide day care for their employees, prior to 1979 the State seldom enforced this legislation nor provided publicly funded alternatives to private day care.[10]

As we saw in chapters 4 and 5, a popular movement for day care developed among women organized in church-linked mothers' clubs in São Paulo's Southern Zone in 1973 and spread to other areas of the city during the 1970s. Isolated groups of poor and working-class women began directly pressuring the municipal Family and Social Welfare Department for publicly funded, community-based, and community-administered day-care centers for their children—initially getting no response from the local State apparatus.

Unlike their feminist counterparts whose Leftist roots originally made them

---

[10] A study conducted in 1979 by the *Delegacia do Trabalho* in the state of Santa Catarina, for example, revealed that out of 593 companies required to provide day care for their female employees by law, only three did so. An enforcement drive led to compliance by 32.8 percent of the firms by 1981. A day-care clause was included in Vargas's 1943 CLT (*Consolidação das Leis Trabalhistas* or Consolidation of Brazilian Labor Laws) thanks in large part to the efforts of first-wave Brazilian feminists. It languished in the books, however, as first-wave feminism faded from the political scene and neither male-dominant unions nor the State saw cause to pursue its enforcement.

reticent to deal with the State at any level, the State was the primary target of day-care movement demands from the outset. The issue of whether the State should make child care available to Brazilian women was not originally a point of contention among day-care movement participants. All urban popular movements in São Paulo addressed the State directly when seeking the expansion of public services, rarely channeling those demands through party organizations.

In March of 1979, at the First São Paulo Women's Congress, isolated groups of neighborhood women and their middle-class feminist allies launched a unified effort to attain State funds for community-based day care. In May 1979, a manifesto was signed by forty-six São Paulo feminine and feminist groups establishing the Struggle for Day Care Movement (*Movimento de Luta por Creches* or MLC). The movement unmasked women's role in the domestic or ''personal'' sphere as politically and economically determined, demanding that the State and private capital assume increased responsibility for the reproduction of the labor force.

> We are workers who are a little different than other workers. . . . [W]e are different, in the first place, because we are not recognized as workers when we work at home 24 hours a day to create the conditions for everyone to rest and to work. This is not recognized, but our work creates more profit that goes directly into the pocket of the boss.
>
> We are different because when we also work outside the home, we accumulate two jobs—at home and in the factory. And they always pay us *less* for what we do. We work more and are paid less. . . . Women are the ones who most feel the problem of lack of day care . . . even though children, since they are not only children of their mothers, are of interest to all of society. It is society which should create the conditions so that these workers of tomorrow can develop good health and with a good education. . . . Day-care centers are our right.
>
> We want *creches* [day care centers] that function full-time, *entirely* financed by the State and by the companies, close to workplaces and places of residence, with our participation in the orientation given to children and with good conditions for their development—we will not accept mere depositories for our children.[11]

This manifesto was followed by dozens of others like it, demanding that ''personal'' child care become ''public day care,'' insisting that the State must assume responsibility for women's domestic burden. It is important to note that the above manifesto expressed a fundamental mistrust in the State's willingness to provide sound education and nutrition for children. Day-care movement participants insisted, as did feminists who advocated free, noncoercive family planning, that State intervention in the realm of reproduction must be

---

[11] Movimento de Luta pela Creche, ''Manifesto,'' March 1979.

closely monitored by civil society and adminstered with the input of those most directly affected by and interested in such policies—Brazilian women.

The day-care movement quickly expanded throughout São Paulo's *periferia* as women organized in neighborhood women's groups and church-linked mother's clubs created *creche* groups or commissions. Adopting strategies typical of other contemporary urban popular movements, the Struggle for Day Care Movement focused on bringing direct pressure to bear on the municipal government, regularly staging sit-ins at the prefecture (*batendo na porta da prefeitura*) and mobilizing popular support for public day care through rallies, assemblies, neighborhood petitions, and surveys.[12]

The MLC's newly reformulated claim that the State must alleviate women's childrearing responsibilities resonated unexpectedly in the co-optative policy initiatives of the PDS-controlled São Paulo county government. This new PDS administration had adopted a legitimacy formula based on neopopulist concessions to the demands of increasingly active popular organizations—a formula inspired by the need to seek electoral support for the PDS in opposition-controlled metropolitan São Paulo. With the Economic Miracle long over and the first gubernatorial elections since 1965 scheduled for 1982, the *Malufista*-led PDS in São Paulo sought new bases of support among São Paulo's poor through the provision of meager social services to peripheral, economically depressed neighborhoods.

In late 1979, the day-care movement took its demands to newly appointed PDS mayor of São Paulo, Reynaldo de Barros. And *creches* rapidly became the social service that featured most prominently in de Barros's neopopulist formula. Despite the fiscal crisis already faced by the county of São Paulo in 1979, de Barros promised a commission of representatives from thirty women's groups from the city's Southern Zone that he would build 830 day-care centers during his administration; and, true to the movement's demands, he promised that these *creches* would be administered by community councils selected and trained by local *Sociedades de Amigos de Bairro* and other neighborhood groups. De Barros requested and was granted a budget of Cr $9 billion (approximately U.S. $2 million) from the *Banco Nacional de Habitação* (BNH or National Housing Bank) for the construction of day-care centers in the county.[13] At the time of de Barros's announcement, São Paulo had 123

[12] Importantly, feminists helped shape the MLC's discourse and strategies. Assuming a banner raised by working-class women's groups as their own, middle-class feminists in the late 1970s hoped to foster the prinicipal goals then prevailing in "the other woman's feminism"—the politicization of feminine struggles and the construction of a cross-class, mass-based women's movement. Several prominent Paulista feminists submerged themselves in the citywide day-care movement, only to emerge years later with few of their goals accomplished.

[13] The grant itself reflected the federal government's encouragement of conservative reforms at the local level as part of its reformulated hegemonic strategy in the face of the growing electoral strength of the opposition throughout urban Brazil.

creches serving 17,055 children, but only three of these were publicly funded.[14]

The construction of *creches* during the de Barros administration followed a clear pattern—day-care centers were constructed first where the organized day-care movement was strongest, in an effort to politically "win over" the extensive day-care movement network. The first seven public *creches* were built in the neighborhoods in the Southern Zone where the movement had the longest history and the greatest mobilizational capacity and *creche* groups in those neighborhoods were given the right to select the day-care workers and administrators for those centers—as stated in the demands of the unified day-care movement.[15]

The relationship between the *creche* movement and the PDS municipal government from 1979–1982 was observably a dialectical one. Movement protests at the *prefeitura* elicited a response from the local State apparatus—the construction of a day-care center in a given neighborhood or a series of centers in a particular region of the city. State concessions in turn fueled the day-care movement on to further mobilizations and protest actions. The movement grew as a consequence, in part, of concrete State responses to day-care movement demands.[16]

De Barros rescinded his promise to allow communities to designate their own day-care administrators in late 1980, decreeing that the prefecture would now appoint the directors of day-care centers. The MLC entered onto a collision course with the de Barros administration thereafter, dashing his hopes of winning the electoral support of the vast day-care movement in São Paulo. By 1981, his 1979 promise of 830 *creches* had dwindled to 330.

By the end of de Barros's administration, 141 day-care centers, the so-called *creches diretas* entirely financed by the municipal government, had been constructed in the county of São Paulo. De Barros, who became the PDS gubernatorial candidate in São Paulo, made *creches* a central rallying cry of

[14] *Estado de São Paulo*, October 21, 1979.

[15] Several activists I spoke with ascribed less than noble motives to the MLC's insistence that the local community must select workers and administrators for centers. They argued that because day-care facilities were used for other purposes, i.e., holding community meetings for local movement groups, control of the centers was a commodity treasured by clandestine parties, such as the PCdoB, who were active in the urban periphery.

[16] Movement access to municipal policy arenas during the PDS administration was secured through contacts with individuals in the local State bureaucracy. Bureaucrats sympathetic to the opposition and to the masses, opposed to the continuation of the military's urban policies, could be found throughout the municipal and state social welfare apparatuses. Some actively sought contacts with local day-care groups to subvert the dominant party's neopopulist strategy. Others were courted by day-care activists and persuaded that the movement's claims were legitimate. In either case, sympathetic social workers and bureaucrats were crucial to the MLC's relative success under PDS rule; many maintained regular contact with the MLC's coordination and neighborhood day-care groups, sometimes urging them to stage timely protests at the mayor's office or SEBES when key policy decisions were at stake.

his political campaign, stating in numerous campaign materials that "when Reynaldo de Barros came into office São Paulo only had three day care centers. Now São Paulo has 333!" The 333 were in the planning stages, at best, though de Barros had further serviced his political aspirations by preappointing the directors of all unconstructed day-care centers.

Despite de Barros's clientelistic overtures, the MLC remained staunchly in the opposition's camp. All opposition parties had endorsed the movement's demand for publicly funded day-care centers and the transition to an opposition government in 1983 made MLC participants hopeful that the State now would attend more fully to their demands. Instead, the centers that had been constructed but had not been put into operation during the PDS administration became the focus of acute conflict between the day-care movement and the 1983 PMDB local government.

In April of 1983, leaders of the day-care movement met with Governor Franco Montoro who vowed to call on all the State's mayors to prioritize the construction of day-care centers. Movement leaders also met with the interim mayor, Altino Lima, and with Municipal Secretary for Family and Social Welfare Marta Godinho, shortly after the PMDB local government was installed. The movement's unusual access to PMDB State officials was in part the consequence of the heavy influence of the *Partido Comunista do Brazil* (PCdoB), a then-illegal party that formed part of the PMDB, within the day-care movement. The PCdoB-linked *União de Mulheres de São Paulo* had assumed much of the political direction of the movement as middle-class *autonomista* feminists left the previously cross-class day-care movement over the years. During the first two months of the PMDB administration, the PCdoB leadership in the *creche* movement expressed its confidence that the "new, democratic government of São Paulo would support the people's demand for free, community-administered day care."[17]

However, movement unity was soon torn assunder when, in sharp contrast to the de Barros administration's neopopulist strategy, the PMDB administration appeared to place more emphasis on the cost of day care, in light of the fiscal crisis confronting the county, than on the potential benefits to be reaped electorally from meeting day-care movement demands. Arguing that municipal coffers had been virtually ransacked by the corruption of the previous administration combined with the 1982–1983 debt crisis, the PMDB rebuffed historic movement demands and decided to make the sixty-eight *creches* built under the de Barros administration indirect, rather than direct, ones. Indirect *creches* had been rejected by the day-care movement as inefficient and pedagogically unsound. Partially financed by the municipal government but administered by private entities (usually charities), indirect *creches* precluded com-

---

[17] Field notes from a citywide meeting of the MLC held in São Paulo in February 17, 1983.

munity participation in the administration of community-based day care—a fundamental demand of the movement since its inception.

The result was open confrontation and acerbic conflict between the new PMDB government and the day-care movement by June of 1983, as both State and movement recalcitrance generated militant protest actions of the sort that had not typified the movement since the early days of the de Barros administration. PMDB's refusal to build new day-care centers and to allow communities to administer existing day-care facilities sparked a massive remobilization of the day-care movement in São Paulo. In interviews I conducted at the time, a number of movement activists pointed to the irony of the situation— under authoritarian rule, they noted, *creches* were conceded by the State; under democratic rule, they were being denied.

Day-care movement participants disagreed vehemently as to what the *Movimento de Luta por Creches*'s strategy should be vis-à-vis the new PMDB municipal government. Underlying partisan conflicts, subsumed during 1982 as both the PT and the PMDB had endorsed movement demands, assumed much sharper dimensions within the citywide movement during 1983–1984. The PMDB sympathizers in the MLC argued for a new political strategy, one that would be sensitive to the new "democratic" conjuncture and attempt to negotiate with the PMDB regime despite its seeming reluctance to honor fundamental movement demands. The *petistas* in the MLC, on the other hand, insisted that the movement had to assume an oppositional or contestatory posture vis-à-vis the local administration and mobilize movement groups throughout the city to delegitimize the new regime's day-care policy by proclaiming it to be "unrepresentative of the popular will."

The movement's citywide and regional coordinations were unable to reach consensus on how to respond to the local government's policy initiatives on the day-care issue. The previously prevailing consensus on how to approach the State was undone as the local State apparatus was now controlled by a partisan opposition rather than by a known adversary, the military-controlled PDS. By late 1984, the MLC's citywide and regional organizational instances had been totally disarticulated by differences over political strategy. All that remained of the previously massive, united, grassroots movement were dispersed, neighborhood-based day-care groups.[18]

The CECF in theory had been fashioned to respond to and mediate precisely this sort of movement-State conflict. Its putative goal was to "represent" and articulate the movement's demands within the State apparatus. But how was it to represent the antagonistic positions of the recently divided day-care move-

---

[18] Much of the above discussion is based on interviews with Maria Amelia Telles de Almeida, coordinator of the Conselho Estadual da Condição Feminina's Day Care Commission and former member of the Executive Committee of the MLC, August 19, 1985; and, with the director of the Jardim Miriam day-care center and former member of the regional and citywide coordinations, August 23, 1985.

ment? And, given that the day-care movement as a whole supported direct over indirect *creches*, would the Council side with the local PMDB administration or the movement on this question?

The CECF had made day care one of its four priority areas for policy action. It elaborated the following position on day-care policy under the PMDB administration:

1. The right to day care should be considered an extension of the universal right to education.
2. Official policy on day care should integrate existing initiatives, guarantee minimal coherence in the actions of the various organs involved [in policy implementation], avoid the dispersion of resources to innumerable programs and organs, and be open to new proposals.
3. In this integrational effort, it is necessary to be clear that the State and society must assume responsibility for the child, guaranteeing it care, protection, and education, principally for the children of working women who constitute that portion of the population most in need of places where they can safely leave their children during working hours.
4. The popular movements, and especially the women's movement, have demanded day care as a right of working mothers and have already accomplished, through their struggles, the recognition of that right through the installation of "direct *creches*" in several cities.
5. Day care policies to be elaborated should integrate the community, parents and professionals, in the process of implementation of the day care center and in the guarantee of popular participation in its functioning.
6. The day care centers should function during periods that correspond to the working hours of mothers.[19]

This statement, issued in late 1984, in the midst of acerbic movement-State conflict, clearly illustrates the CECF's need to juggle the policy constraints imposed by the local administration, which clearly favored indirect *creches*, while representing the sole remaining demand around which the day-care movement, an important segment of the Council's nominal constituency in civil society, remained united—the creation of direct *creches*.

After considerable deliberation, the CECF decided to endorse the regime's contention that the fiscal crisis precluded the creation of more direct *creches*, which required greater State investment in the "means of reproduction" than *indirect* or privately administered *creches*. At the same time, at the urging of PMDB supporters within the day-care movement, the CECF supported the claim that those *creches* designated as *direct* by the previous PDS administra-

[19] Governo do Estado de São Paulo, Conselho da Estadual Condição Feminina, *Mulher* I, September 1984.

tion should be maintained as such as these represented a "right of working mothers" legitimately acquired through "popular struggle."

In a further effort to mediate the conflicting demands of the day-care movement and the local administration, the CECF participated in the preparation, supervision, and coordination of the Special Inquiry Commission on Day Care created in the São Paulo municipal legislature in October 1984. The Commission was presided by PMDB councilwoman and *trinca feminista* candidate, Ida María Jancsó.[20] The CECF refined its position on day care in its testimony before this Commission.

> The municipal chain of direct *creches* constitutes a conquest of the popular movements and the women's movement and as such should be *discussed*. An effort in the sense of *discussion* and adopting a creche policy which perfects the existing chain of direct *creches* is urgent, as [the present system] aside from its high cost (due to inefficiencies and excessive centralization) offers low quality care.[21]

Again, this statement reflects the precarious *structural* position of a "women's space" within the State apparatus that simultaneously claimed to "represent" the interests of women *outside* the pact of domination. On the issue of day care, the CECF, as part of the State apparatus, supported the administration yet also pushed the local government to honor some of the legitimate conquests of the popular-based day-care movement.

The CECF also succeeded in blocking a far more problematic policy initiative in the realm of day care, in this instance, siding firmly with all sectors of the day-care movement in opposing the establishment of a proposed home day-care alternative. Given the clear resistance of some sectors of the state and local administration to the idea and feasibility of direct *creches*, the CECF, in collaboration with some day-care activists, began redefining the long-standing popular demand for day-care facilities.

At the local level, resistance to direct *creches* emanated primarily from municipal Secretary of the Family and Social Welfare Marta Godinho. At the state level, the governor's wife, Lucy Montoro, in particular, pushed for alternative approaches to the "problem" of day care. During 1983 and 1984, Dona Lucy and others in the PMDB actively promoted the idea of "*mães crecheiras*" or day-care mothers—neighborhood women who would be employed and trained by the State to care for the children of other working women and provide these children with a "familial environment"—as an alternative to more expensive, "impersonal," and "inefficient" public day-care centers.

Opponents of this alternative, both within the day-care movement and the

---

[20] Interview with Ana Maria Wilheim, legislative staff of Municipal Councilwoman Ida María Janscó, August 20, 1985.

[21] Município de São Paulo, Camara Municipal, Comissão Especial de Inquérito sobre Creches, "Relatorio Final. Nossos Filhos, Nosso Futuro. Vamos Melhorar Nossas Creches," 1984, emphasis in the original.

CECF, maintained that given the precarious conditions of life in urban, working-class neighborhoods, *mães crecheiras* could not possibly meet children's pedagogical, recreational, and nutritional needs adequately. They also criticized the exploitative nature of the plan, arguing that it merely would transfer the responsibility for child care from one low-income woman to another, paying the second substandard wages and granting her no worker's benefits. Moreover, opponents argued, a *mãe crecheira* policy would reinforce existing patterns of gender inequality by creating *more* low-paying, low-status jobs for women, jobs that merely commodify women's socially ascribed mothering roles.[22]

The CECF chose to combat this traditionalist tendency within the local and state administrations. Thus, the Council increasingly argued for day care in broader terms, appealing to "universal rights" rather that "women's rights" to widen political support for Council day-care proposals within the ruling coalition. Whereas day-care movement organizations had insisted that day care was a "woman's right" or a "mother's right," given women's socially ascribed responsibility for domestic labor and childrearing, the CECF now argued that "the *creche* is a right of children, of workers. . . . [T]he right to day care should be seen as an extension of the universal right to education."[23] This reframing of the day-care issue succeeded in temporarily blocking the day-care mother proposal and eventually persuaded PMDB Mayor Mario Covas to build some new direct *creches*, which were now portrayed as part of his decision to expand public education in São Paulo.

After 1985, the CECF opted to redefine its day-care strategy—focusing now on the *private* provision of day care by enterprises employing more than thirty women, an aspect of the 1943 labor laws (CLT) that had never been enforced by the State.[24] The Council began encouraging unions and government agencies to increase their monitoring of this CLT provision, thus resolving the conflict between the day-care movement and the State by deflecting the demand for, and the costs of, day care onto the private sector.[25] The CECF also began pressuring the Ministry of Labor to revise the CLT's provisions for day care in the workplace. At the state level, it also hoped to promote closer Department of Labor monitoring of commercial and industrial establishments to

---

[22] Interview with Ana Maria Wilheim, São Paulo, August 20, 1985.

[23] Governo do Estado de São Paulo, Conselho da Estadual Condição Feminina, "Creche no Local de Trabalho," 1985 (Pamphlet).

[24] Interview with Maria Amelia Telles de Almeida, São Paulo, August 19, 1985.

[25] Governo do Estado de São Paulo, Conselho Estadual da Condição Feminina, Comissão de Creche, "Levantamento e Caraterísticas dos Bercarios/Creches no Local do Trabalho," 1985. This study found that virtually none of the establishments obligated by law (those that employ more than thirty women) to provide day care for infant children of their employees do so. In the entire state of São Paulo, only thirty-eight businesses maintained day-care services for their employees.

ensure that they provide pedagogically sound and conveniently located day-care services for their female employees.

CONTRADICTIONS OF A "WOMEN'S SPACE" WITHIN A MALE-DOMINANT STATE

The preceding discussion of day care and family planning in São Paulo raises critical questions about how women's diverse gender interests can best be represented in the context of a democratizing, yet still bourgeois and male-dominant State. I focused my analysis on day-care and family-planning policies as these issues have been especially prominent in women's movement politics *and* government policy in recent years.

These two issues are of particular interest due to their class-specific gendered content. Both family-planning and day care are relevant to *all* women as the primary reproducers of Brazilian social relations, but poor and working-class women do most of the reproductive work for their upper- and middle-class "sisters." Thus while many (if not most) middle-class women have domestic servants to alleviate their socially ascribed confinement to reproductive labor, day care is an issue of particular relevance to women who carry the double burden of paid labor (for bourgeois industrialists *or* bourgeois and petit bourgeois women) and unpaid (domestic) labor in their own homes. Similarly, though access to safe contraception is limited for all Brazilian women, women of the popular classes lack both the information and the capital with which to acquire the means of contraception more readily available to middle- and upper-class women.

Though women of the popular classes formed the backbone of the day-care movement during the 1970s and early 1980s and many supported the opposition PMDB in São Paulo, their access to the State under the PMDB administration remained mediated by questionable "representatives"—the middle-class professional and academic PMDB women who were granted limited political space within the ruling coalition. Our discussion of family-planning policy developments suggests that some of the strategic gender interests of women of the popular classes were being represented by the Council on the Status of Women—the actions of middle-class feminists both within and outside the State blocked the implementation of coercive population control policies that most often have targeted poor and darker-skinned women, and instead, provided women of the popular classes with unprecedented access to safe and informed ways to control their fertility.

However, a clear class bias is evident in day-care policy developments in São Paulo since 1983. Day care is an issue around which primarily poor and working-class women have organized at the community level; the provision of public day-care facilities is of strategic interest to women of the popular classes—not to the middle-class women who have the means with which to employ their working-class "sisters" to care for their children. By deflecting the responsibility for and cost of day care onto the private sector, one could argue that the CECF was not representing the strategic gender interests of low-income women, most of whom are employed in the informal sector or in small-scale industrial and commercial establishments exempted from providing day care by the law. Moreover, it is conceivable that increased State monitoring of those businesses that are required by law to provide day care (those employing more than thirty women) could serve as a disincentive for hiring more female employees, especially at a time when labor supply far exceeds the demands of a private industrial sector in crisis.

By late 1986, many in the São Paulo women's movement had begun to question the concept of representation embodied by the Council. As members of the Council were appointed by the governor, rather than designated by independent women's groups or elected by citizens at large, it seemed to some activists that the movement might have difficulty keeping the CECF responsive to its nominal constituencies. How the Council could represent the divergent sectors of the women's movements in the absence of movement consensus on a specific issue also appeared more problematic in light of old and new divisions among São Paulo women's groups. The contradictory dimensions of this putatively representative women's institution became all too evident in the late 1980s, as will be seen in chapter 10 below.

A further source of concern among many movement participants outside the State apparatus was that the incorporation of some gender-specific demands by the state and local PMDB administrations threatened to "over-absorb" the dynamism of feminism, and women's mobilization in general, as forces for social change in civil society. After all, what distinguishes autonomous social movements from traditional interest groups, political parties, and State-linked women's institutions is that movements have cultural and social, as well as political and policy, goals. They seek normative as well as structural transformations of society more actively than do traditional interest groups or political parties.

The exclusion of the more grassroots-oriented sectors of the women's movement from the Council, its overwhelmingly white and middle-class composition, and its top-down mobilizational initiatives among women in São Paulo indirectly served to suppress or deligitimize some of the generic claims emanating from civil society that, since the mid-1970s, spurred the politicization of many issues previously considered "personal." Feminists working within a male-dominant State apparatus necessarily must couch their generic claims in less radical terms and must be open to negotiation and compromise. Thus, for example, though the CECF could insist on promoting safer and more widely available birth control methods, it could not hope to advance proposals to legalize abortion on its own initiative without jeopadizing its bargaining position within the State.

As David Bouchier notes, in the United States the early radical core of the feminist movement was "written out of history when [the] movement gain[ed] momentum and wider political and commercial considerations [came] into play."[26] In the case of the United States, liberal "feminism [was] more quickly and thoroughly integrated into the upper middle class status quo than any other protest movement in history."[27]

This same quick and thorough integration of the more acceptable or moderate demands of the Brazilian women's movement seems to have been under way in São Paulo since 1983. Thus, the demand for day care was more politically successful when couched in terms of the universal right to education or as an extension of workers' rights, less so when framed as a demand for the State to assume a greater role in alleviating women's domestic responsibilities. The demand for safe, accessible birth control, similarly, is likely to be more politically acceptable than the right of women to choose abortion. These more radical generic demands necessarily emanate from outside the pact of domination represented in the State.

The indirect delegitimation of the more radical core of the women's movement's political claims, through the incorporation of its more acceptable claims—those that do not directly conflict with larger State political or developmental objectives or do not challenge prevailing gender power arrangements—potentially weakens feminism as a force for change within civil society, even as progress toward women's emancipation is made within the State and political society. Furthermore, the likelihood of more thorough co-optation of movement demands is also increased. Bouchier suggests that

> a radical core produces a fruitful and dynamic tension in a social movement . . . [a] mass following of people with moderate views is needed to influence elites. But a radical wing, constantly raising unresolved issues and generating new ones, constantly on the alert for cooptation and retreat, is essential to preserve the oppositional movement from a gentle slide into the prevailing hegemony. They also, quite unintentionally, help give the more moderate wings of the movement an appearance of relative acceptability which they might not otherwise achieve.[28]

THE BENEFITS OF A WOMEN'S INSTITUTION: TAKING GENDER STRUGGLE INTO THE HEART OF THE STATE APPARATUS

Despite these contradictions, the creation of the Council enabled Paulista women's movements in effect to pursue a two-pronged political strategy. The women who won minimal access to the State through PMDB party activism

---

[26] David Bouchier, "The Deradicalization of Feminism: Ideology and Utopia in Action," *Sociology* 13, no. 3 (September 1979): 392.

[27] Ibid., p. 394.

[28] Ibid., p. 397.

moved to consolidate and institutionalize the gains made during the preelection period. They pursued an interest group–oriented strategy akin to that which typifies liberal feminist pressure groups in the United States and Western Europe. The Council became their principal access point to state and municipal policy-making arenas.

Though a small sector of the organized movement continued to view the Council as an instance of State co-optation, most activists reformulated their policy goals and rethought the movement's relationship to the State and political society. They focused on new strategies for influencing Council policy and preventing State co-optation. During the early phases of democratization at the state and local levels, feminists "outside" the State put pressure on both the Council and the PMDB São Paulo administrations to advance the movement's more radical goals. In the case of family-planning at least, such pressure kept CECF members responsive to a grassroots constituency and indirectly legitimated the claims of women working within the State. Movement activists continued engaging in grassroots-based or movement-oriented politics, relying on protest actions, petitions, rallies, and other forms of autonomous organizing rather than on direct contact with policy makers or politicians. And as a result of this dual strategy, feminism had a subversive impact on some State policies affecting women.

Under the Montoro and Covas administrations in São Paulo, the State Council on the Status of Women pushed the PMDB to attend to some of middle- and working-class women's *strategic* as well as *practical* gender interests. And in some cases, it provided a number of new access points to the State apparatus that would otherwise not have been available to women's movement organizations. For example, the São Paulo Council's Commission on Violence against Women persuaded the mayor to create, in August 1985, the *Delegacia da Mulher*, a police precinct staffed entirely by specially trained female police officers, which processes cases of rape, sexual abuse, and domestic violence.[29] The ground-breaking recognition of this gender-specific aspect of crime by the State is unprecedented in Brazil, and indeed the "women's precinct" structure is unparalleled anywhere in the world. On this issue, the Council's effectiveness in promoting policies that directly addressed the concrete needs of Paulista women was partially derived from the São Paulo women's movements' constant protest actions and public education campaigns around the issue of violence against women.

However, the success of the 1983–1985 CECF was partially determined by four conjunctural phenomena. First, the Council had a firm feminist majority during its first two years in operation and this fact unquestionably influenced

[29] Since its creation, the São Paulo *Delegacia* reportedly has been receiving two hundred to three hundred complaints per day. Similar "women's precincts" have been installed elsewhere in Greater São Paulo and other Brazilian cities.

the nature and content of its fairly radical generic policy initiatives in family planning and violence against women. Second, the PMDB administrations at both the state and local levels were new ones, still invested in transforming their electoral support into solid hegemonic bases of support for the new local "opposition" governments within civil society. Third, both the Montoro state government and the Covas municipal government were ideologically committed to a politics of administrative decentralization and community participation, policies that legitimated women's demands emanating from organized civil society. And fourth, the ruling PMDB remained essentially a coalition of political forces from the Far-Left to the Center-Right of the political spectrum. As we saw in the above discussion of day-care and family-planning policies, different and even competing gender ideologies were represented within different sectors of the State apparatus. Thus, some sectors of the State (such as the state Department of Health) proved more malleable or amenable to gender-specific political claims than other sectors (such as the municipal department of the Family and Social Welfare). In the absence of these conjunctural determinants, the dynamics of the State-Council-Movement relationship would be expected to vary. This changing dynamic will be explored in chapter 10.

Finally, the political influence wielded by the São Paulo Council from 1983 to 1985 was not characteristic of all other such "women's spaces" in different local or state contexts. In states where the PMDB ruling coalition was politically narrower, as in Minas Gerais where Center-Right elements of the PMDB predominated, the range of generic policy initiatives and gender ideologies represented within the administration was far narrower as well. In 1983, Governor Tancredo Neves also created a Council on the Status of Women, but unlike its São Paulo counterpart, the Council in Minas was composed primarily of women PMDB party members with few, if any, links to or experience within autonomous women's movement organizations. Independent sectors of the women's movement in Minas, in fact, remained aloof from the Council, viewing it merely as a bureaucratic ornament, directly subservient to the PMDB's most conservative wing—"a place where deputies' wives [could] be appointed to the government." As will be seen in chapter 10, many of the state and municipal councils created after 1985 did little to promote progressive gender policies and had few organic links to organized female constituencies in civil society.

A NATIONAL COUNCIL ON WOMEN'S RIGHTS IN THE "NOVA REPÚBLICA"

In 1985, the March 8 International Women's Day celebrations coincided with the nation's transition to civilian rule after twenty-one years of military dictatorship. The national women's branch of the PMDB and the State Councils on the Status of Women in São Paulo and Minas Gerais (the home state of Tancredo Neves) marked the occasion by presenting the new administration with a proposal for the creation of a National Council on the Status of Women. Unlike the São Paulo Council, this proposed national body was to have its own budgetary allocations and its president was to be granted ministerial rank.[30]

From the experience of the São Paulo Council, PMDB feminists surmised that unless it was composed of a minimally feminist majority, the National Council might well become merely another democratic ornament, like the Minas Council and so many similar bodies presently in place in other Latin American regimes. The PMDB women who formulated the proposal seemed aware of this danger, suggesting that the National Council be composed of "women representative of civil society whose political social trajectory has been linked to the struggle for equal rights between the sexes in various areas of political action."[31]

In the postauthoritarian *Nova República*, feminists also had reason to expect that women's political claims would receive further endorsement given the importance of women's participation in the opposition since the early 1970s. At the federal level, the new regime owed a considerable amount of its popular bases of support to organized female constituencies.

Autonomous women's movement organizations and women's branches of the principal opposition parties played an important role in the nationwide mobilizations for direct elections in 1984 and in the subsequent mobilization of women's support for the "indirect" presidential candidacy of Tancredo Neves. The parties' women's divisions organized several massive women's demonstrations in major Brazilian cities during the nationwide campaign for direct elections in 1984. The State Councils in São Paulo and Minas Gerais and the Women's Division of the PMDB furnished the organizational infrastructure for these demonstrations. When the PMDB shifted to a strategy of defeating the regime at its own game by organizing a "Democratic Alliance" to support of the candidacy of Tancredo Neves in the Electoral College, the women's division of the PMDB organized a national campaign of *Mulheres com Tancredo* (Women with Tancredo).

The PMDB women who mobilized organized female constituencies in support of Neves's candidacy also sought Tancredo's support for their gender-specific political claims. In June 1984, São Paulo State Assemblywoman Ruth Escobar, elected on a feminist platform in 1982, organized a suprapartisan commission of over sixty women to present the candidate with a *Carta das Mulheres* (Letter from Women), specifying the issues that they felt must be included in the candidate's platform and asking that he consider the creation of a Women's Council or Ministry at the federal level.

[30] *Mulherio*, January-March 1985.

[31] Partido Movimento Democrático Brasileiro, "Terceira Proposta—Minuta, Conselho Nacional da Condição Feminina," March 15, 1985 (Mimeograph).

In November 1984, Escobar organized a national conference, attended by over five hundred women from eighteen Brazilian states, to discuss the organizational form that such a federal "women's institution" should take and the goals that it should pursue the realm of public policy. And in January 1985, Neves officially endorsed the creation of a women's institution and appointed a multipartisan commission of women legislators, presided by Escobar, to elaborate a legislative proposal for the creation of a National Council on Women's Rights.[32]

The *Conselho Nacional dos Direitos da Mulher* (National Council on Women's Rights or CNDM) was installed on September 11, 1985, thanks to the relentless politicking of Escobar and other women legislators who doggedly lobbied for rapid congressional approval of the executive proposal developed by the women's parliamentary commission earlier in 1985.[33] The original CNDM was presided by Escobar and composed of women legislators from the PMDB, the PFL,[34] and the PT, "representatives of civil society" linked to autonomous women's movement organizations, and intellectuals and academics who specialized in the field of women's studies.

Through tenacious and efficient lobbying Escobar secured an initial budget of Cr $6 billion (nearly U.S. $1 million) for the CNDM's first three months of operation alone—an allocation greater than that of many of the smaller executive departments or ministries. The original CNDM also had a solid feminist majority, despite the need to accommodate the multitude of political tendencies within the ruling PMDB-PFL coalition and within the national women's movement itself.

In an interview conducted in late August 1985, CNDM president, Ruth Escobar, outlined some of the principal political and organizational goals of the National Council: "The Council will be a more dynamic organ than a Women's Ministry could possibly be. It will open new spaces, new channels. . . . It will create new groups within the various ministries which will enable us to influence policy more broadly, more effectively." Escobar suggested that the Council structure was a preliminary step toward the creation of a full-scale Ministry on the Status of Women. She argued that women must first "conquer greater political space and strength" within the State apparatus, within policy-making arenas (hence the presence of women legislators on the Council), and

---

[32] Interview with Ruth Escobar, first president of the National Council on Women's Rights, São Paulo, August 26, 1985.

[33] Informal interview with Maria Aparecida Schumacher, member of Ruth Escobar's legislative staff, August 25, 1985.

[34] The PFL or *Partido da Frente Liberal* was created by the dissenting wing of the PDS that left the ruling party in 1984 over the issue of direct elections and joined with the PMDB to create the *Aliança Democrática*, the political coalition that advanced the "indirect" candidacy of Tancredo Neves of the PMDB in 1984. With Tancredo's untimely death on the day before his inauguration as the first civilian president in twenty-one years, his running mate from the PFL, José Sarney, became president.

must prove its mobilizational capacity vis-à-vis organized female constituencies in civil society before such a Ministry can be created. She asserted that "without such a power base, the Ministry would be ineffective . . . like in Venezuela, where a Ministry on the Status of Women was created in the mid-70s and dissolved less than a year later."[35]

Escobar was then confident that partisan rivalries and ideological differences could be overcome within the CNDM—the multipartisan commission that planned the Council had reconciled many partisan tensions, she argued, as she insisted that "women's issues supersede the parties even if they [the parties] don't want them to." However, Escobar's predictions proved excessively sanguine. As will be seen in chapter 10, the ruling coalition of the *Nova República* was extremely disparate and the ascension of Center-Right tendencies and the increased hegemony of President José Sarney's PFL, whose platform on women's issues was little more progressive than that of its "parent party," the PDS, eroded some of the gains made by women's movements during the transition and seriously compromised the CNDM's ability to promote women's strategic and practical gender interests at the national level.

[35] Interview with Ruth Escobar, CNDM President, São Paulo, August 26, 1985.

CHAPTER TEN

Women's Movements, Gender Policy, and the Politics of Democratic Consolidation (1985–1988)

TRANSITION politics temporarily brought down some of the patriarchal barriers that customarily hedge women out of political life. Civil society rose in protest, and women, like men, took to the ramparts in day-to-day opposition to military rule. New progressive oppositional discourses, secular and religious, enjoined women to enlist in the struggle and lent legitimacy to women's quest for greater equality. Competing elites jockeyed for the support of organized constituencies, reaching down into civil society for new allies, and courting the female electorate as never before. The ruling civil-military coalition and the post-1983 opposition state and local governments alike sought legitimacy in elections and participation-based accountability, expanding the structure of political opportunities available to women.

Since the return to civilian rule in 1985, however, some patriarchal barricades have again been erected. Two structural dimensions of gender politics continued to restrict progress toward women's equality in postauthoritarian Brazil. First, political society and the State in the New Brazilian Republic, of course, remained preeminently male domains. And second, Brazil's increased dependence on central capitalist nations placed an important brake on national gender policy developments.

Feminists made inroads into political society and the State during the transition, but those inroads will not necessarily be transformed into permanent paths to effective power and political influence. Even if more solid horizontal linkages with male-dominant trade unions and social movement organizations are effectively forged, the "masculinity" of the State and political society make the vertical articulation of gender interests particularly problematic. And finally, by the late 1980s, Brazil's economic crisis and its intractable foreign debt further limited the State's ability to pursue new initiatives in the realm of gender policy. As State spending was curbed drastically, the burden fell most heavily upon women. Social services that might alleviate women's "reproductive work," such as child care, could easily be considered "luxuries" because, after all, women already performed them; these kinds of State expenditures therefore were the first to be slashed.

Based on fieldwork conducted in June and July 1988, this chapter assesses the extent to which, given these structural constraints, women's movement organizations were able to conquer further political space in the first three years of the new civilian regime and consolidate the gains made during the transition process. Were the women's movement groups that proliferated during the transition merely ephemeral instances of crisis mobilization? What happened to the various sectors of the women's movement in the postauthoritarian political order? Will the political currency represented by organized female constituencies during the transition remain central to the electoral and mobilizational strategies of new political parties operating in the postauthoritarian regime established in 1985? Will the male-dominant parties become effective mechanisms for channeling women's movement political claims into democratic policy-making arenas? Will new women's spaces within the parties and the State prove viable institutions through which to advance the status of women in contemporary Brazil?

SOCIAL MOVEMENTS IN THE NEW DEMOCRATIC POLITICAL ORDER

Before we look at the specificity of post-1985 gender politics in Brazil, we must consider the consequences of Brazil's elite-controlled transition process for social movements in general. Analysts have stressed that the "partyization" of politics and the creation of a vital democratic political culture are the cornerstones of democratic consolidation.[1] But scant attention has been focused on how popular interests, articulated by the grassroots social movements organizations, fare in the aftermath of elite-dominated transitions.[2] Though North American political scientists have been especially silent on this question, their South American counterparts have begun assessing how new social movements might contribute to the consolidation of a democratic political culture and are exploring the ways in which such movements might or might not deepen the scope of democratic politics as usual.[3]

[1] See Bolivar Lamounier, "Challenges to Democratic Consolidation in Brazil" (Paper presented at the American Political Science Association Convention, Washington, D.C., September 1–4, 1988); Bolivar Lamounier and Rachel Meneguello, *Partidos Políticos e Consolidação Democrática: O Caso Brasileiro* (São Paulo: Brasilense, 1986); Juan J. Linz, *The Breakdown of Democratic Regimes: Crisis, Breakdown, and Reequilibration* (Baltimore, Md.: Johns Hopkins University Press, 1978); and Guillermo O'Donnell and Phillippe C. Schmitter, *Transitions from Authoritarian Rule: Tentative Conclusions about Uncertain Democracies* (Baltimore: Johns Hopkins University Press, 1986).

[2] The vast literature produced on new social movements (NSMs) during the 1970s and 1980s, of course, focused on the contributions of such movements to the transition itself. Since the establishment of civilian rule, few studies have examined what has happened to NSMs in the new democratic context.

[3] Scott Mainwaring's "Urban Popular Movements, Identity and Democratization in Brazil," *Comparative Political Studies* 20, no. 2 (July 1987): 131–59, is a notable exception. Unless otherwise indicated, the ensuing discussion of NSMs draws on Ilse Scherer-Warren and Paulo Krischke, eds., *Uma Revolução no Cotidiano? Os Novos Movimentos Sociais na America do Sul* (São Paulo: Brasilense, 1987); Ruth Corrêa Leite Cardoso, "Isso É Política? Dilemas da Participação entre o Moderno e o Pós-Moderno," *Novos Estudos do CEBRAP* 20 (March 1988): 74–80; Elizabeth Jelin, ed., *Movimientos Sociales y Democracia Emergente*, 2 vols. (Buenos Aires: Cen-

The new social movements (NSMs), according to many who studied them in the 1970s and early 1980s, developed an alternative model of democracy. NSMs seemed to be breaking out of the clientelistic mold, rejecting party politics narrowly focused on conquering State power, proclaiming a suprapartisan or autonomous political stance, and refusing to fall prey to political instrumentalism on the Left or cooptation on the Right. Encouraged by new progressive ideologies such as liberation theology, NSMs were said to foster "new ways of doing politics," based on the politicization of daily life, the practice of consensus politics and direct democracy, community-building and consciousness-raising.

Many observers thus heralded the NSMs as the harbingers of a new, transformed democracy in postauthoritarian Brazil, the "last, best hope" for true and profound democratization. In short, much of the literature on NSMs suggested a rather hopeful prognosis for the impact that these movements would have on the politics of the New Brazilian Republic.

The conservatizing dynamics of the final stages of the Brazilian transition and the early stages of democratic consolidation, however, engendered a new pessimism among social movement scholars and activists. During 1983 and 1984, Figueiredo's inability to control the presidential succession process and the massive nationwide campaign to hold direct presidential elections in 1985 gave rise to new tensions within the ruling civil-military coalition. The direct elections initiative, which brought an estimated twenty million Brazilians into the streets and was supported by over 90 percent of the electorate, was ultimately defeated, as was the PDS's "indirect" presidential candidate, Paulo Salim Maluf. In the end, moderate and conservative sectors of the PMDB joined with PDS dissidents (who later founded a new Center-Right party, the PFL), to form the Democratic Alliance (*Aliança Democrática*), a politically and ideologically disparate coalition that supported the successful indirect candidacy of Tancredo Neves and ushered in the New Brazilian Republic.[4]

---

tro Editor de América Latina, 1987); Ruth Corrêa Leite Cardoso, "Os Movimentos Populares no Contexto da Consolidação da Democracia," in *A Democracia no Brasil: Dilemas e Perspectivas*, ed. Fábio Wanderley Reis and Guillermo O'Donnell (São Paulo: Vértice, 1988); Rafael de la Cruz, "Os Novos Movimentos Sociais: Encontros e Desencontros com a Democracia," in Scherer-Warren and Krischke, *Uma Revolução Contidiano*; and Eunice Ribeiro Durham, "Movimentos Sociais: A Construção da Cidadania," *Novos Estudos de CEBRAP* 10 (October 1984): 24–30.

[4] A full discussion of the political dynamics that led to the civilianization of Brazilian politics is beyond the scope of the present project. On the final stages of the Brazilian transition, see William C. Smith, "The 'New Republic' and the Brazilian Transition: Elite Conciliation or Democratization?" (Paper presented at the XIII International Congress of the Latin American Studies Association, Boston, Mass., October 23–26, 1986); Fábio Wanderley Reis and Guillermo O'Donnell, eds., *A Democracia no Brasil: Dilemas y Perspectivas* (São Paulo: Vértice, 1988); Alfred Stepan, ed., *Democratizing Brazil: Problems of Transition and Consolidation* (New York: Oxford University Press, 1989); Alfred Stepan, *Rethinking Military Politics: Brazil and the Southern Cone* (Princeton, N.J.: Princeton University Press, 1988); Scott Mainwaring, "The

Brazil's transition has been characterized as a "transition from above," initiated by regime leaders who closely monitored and tightly controlled an incremental democratization process.[5] Such transitions are said to result in the greatest degree of continuity in authoritarian personnel and policy. A number of leading figures in the authoritarian regime could be found at the helm of Brazil's new democracy in 1985. And little was done to increase popular participation in policy making or redress egregious social and economic inequalities.

The prominence of leaders from the "ancien régime" from 1985 to 1989 portended a bleak future for Brazilian democracy. Conciliatory pacts made with regime hard-liners and the elite-orchestrated transition strategy dashed the hopes of progressive forces for more thoroughgoing democratization in the short run. Indeed, scholars agree that postauthoritarian Brazil was one of the least progressive and least democratic of the civilian regimes installed in the Southern Cone in the mid-1980s. While the Sarney government restored basic civil liberties and institutionalized some procedural norms, these were extremely fragile, especially given the considerable influence retained by the military in "national security" matters. Leftist parties were legalized, illiterates enfranchised, and neopopulist emergency relief food and housing programs put into effect. After over nineteen months of deliberation and acrimonious debate, a Congressional Constituent Assembly elected in November 1986 issued a relatively progressive Constitution in September 1988, but direct elections for the presidency were delayed until November 1989.

And the leadership of the old regime continued to reign in the first years of the New Republic. After twenty-one years of military rule, Tancredo Neves's untimely death on the eve of his inauguration made the Center-Right PFL's (Party of the Liberal Front) José Sarney the first civilian president of the *Nova República*. And Sarney, former president of the Democratic Social Party (PDS), and many of his PDS-PFL conservative ministers, were recent converts to the cause of democracy, to be sure. The military retained six Cabinet posts in the Sarney administration and de facto veto power over a number of key policy areas.

The Democratic Alliance nevertheless held together for the first two years of the New Republic, with the PMDB (Party of the Brazilian Democratic Movement) exercising a hegemonic role within the coalition government. The Alliance coalition parties (PMDB and PFL) conquered all but one of the state governments and the overwhelming majority of the Congressional Constituent Assembly in the 1986 elections.

Transition to Democracy in Brazil," *Journal of Interamerican Studies and World Affairs* 28 (May 1986): 149–79.

[5] For a comparative typology of regime transitions in the Southern Cone, see Eduardo Viola and Scott Mainwaring, "Transitions to Democracy: Brazil and Argentina in the 1980s," *Journal of International Affairs* 38, no. 2 (1985): 193–219.

But the Democratic Alliance was torn assunder soon thereafter, as the Center-Right and Right increasingly squeezed the progressive wing of the PMDB out of power. The regime's shift to the right began in the immediate aftermath of the dismal failure of Sarney's much-touted heterodox stabilization plan, the *Plano Cruzado*.[6]

As the Constituent Assembly began its deliberations in 1987, a conservative hegemonic bloc was further consolidated. When progressive legislators advocated reforms deemed to represent "excessive concessions" to the working classes, conservative sectors of the PMDB, PFL, PDS, and PTB (Brazilian Labor Party) coalesced into a solid voting bloc, dubbed the *Centrão* or "big center," and defeated many of the Left and Center-Left's initiatives in the realms of social and labor policy. The "coalition government" moved so far to the right in the eyes of some Center-Left PMDB founders that, in August 1988, they withdrew from the ruling PMDB in protest to form a new opposition party, the *Partido da Social Democracia Brasileira* (Brazilian Social Democratic Party or PSDB).

The November 1986 elections also brought a number of Center-Right PMDB and PFL governors to power, and they often sided with Sarney and the *Centrão* in shaping the conservative politics of the early years of the New Republic. In São Paulo, as will be seen below, the 1986–1988 state and municipal administrations reversed many of the gains made by NSMs under Montoro and Covas. The expanded political opportunity space generated by the post-1983 state and local administrations appears to have been transitory and conjuncturally determined.

In short, the foundational project of the postauthoritarian regime, shaped by a conservative and exclusionary transition process, did not seem to augur well for NSMs and the interests they articulated. In 1988, NSMs were seldom heralded as harbingers of change by political analysts; indeed, many social movement activists shared in this pessimism. And there appeared to be an emerging consensus among social scientists that social movements, and especially popular, grassroots movements, were on the decline in the late 1980s.

Analysts argued that NSMs seemed to be unable to move from the crisis mobilization and confrontational tactics of the transition period to strategies of negotiation and compromise necessitated by democratic political rules of the game. NSMs were incapable of developing effective links to political parties, it was claimed; "communities" fostered by shared needs and opposition

---

[6] For an excellent discussion of the Cruzado Plan and its Argentine counterpart, the Austral Plan, see William C. Smith, "Heterodox Shocks and the Political Economy of Democratic Transition in Argentina and Brazil" (Paper presented at the XIV International Congress of the Latin American Studies Association, New Orleans, March 17–19, 1988); see also Rui Affonso, Plinio Samapio, Jr., and Gilson Schwartz, "Política Econômica e Democratização: O Impasse Brasileiro," in *A Democracia no Brasil: Dilemas e Perspectivas*, ed. Fábio Wanderley Reis and Guillermo O'Donnell (São Paulo: Vértice, 1988).

to military rule were shattered by partisan rivalries. And movement groups failed to come together to form peak organizations that would better represent their interests vis-à-vis parties and the State.

The foundational politics of the New Republic indeed posed difficult questions for social movements born under authoritarian rule. NSMs were faced with a regime that professed a commitment to democracy, that intially proved receptive to grassroots demands, and promised to bring "the people" back into Brazilian politics. Movements had to decide how best to advance their claims in the context of a democratizing, but ever-more conservative civilian regime.

BRAZILIAN WOMEN'S MOVEMENTS IN THE LATE 1980s

Contrary to the assertions of many movement scholars and feminist activists I talked with in the summer of 1988, women's movements and other popular and liberation movements hardly appeared to be "fading away." Though some sectors of the women's movement, especially the more radical, socialist-feminist currents, were less visible, dispersion rather than disappearance would be a more acurate way to describe the state of the movement in the late 1980s.

The arenas of gender struggle in fact multiplied in postauthoritarian Brazil; "feminisms" proliferated and women from a variety of social classes and races, urban and rural, espousing differing class ideologies (from Trotskyism to neoliberalism), claimed feminism as their own.

Most of the founding members of the first feminist groups of the 1970s who I interviewed again in 1988 nonetheless expressed concern about the future course of the movement. I repeatedly heard that "institutions have swallowed up the movement," that many movement militants had been "conservatized" or "neutralized" by their participation in parties and State institutions, that there was "little left of the militant feminism of the late 1970s and early 1980s."[7]

Indeed, the radical core of the movement that, as seen in the preceding chapters, was so critical for organizing gender-conscious pressure at the base during the latter stages of the transition, did appear to have dissipated in the late 1980s. Most of the historic groups, such as *Frente de Mulheres Feministas*, no longer existed; and many of my interviewees maintained that this was because "so many feminists now work exclusively in parties or for the government."

However, if radical socialist-feminism was dispersed or absorbed by polit-

[7] The ensuing discussion is based on over twenty-five formal interviews and innumerable informal conversations with long-time movement activists, in São Paulo and Brasília, during June and July 1988. Unless otherwise noted, quotation marks indicate citations drawn directly from my field notes from that period.

ical society and the State, it did not merely fade away. Many of the key organizers of the massive feminist events of the late 1970s and early 1980s turned
to a kind of life-style or cultural feminism, focusing their energies on building
alternative families, organizations, and communities, putatively free of sexist
oppression. Many among the first generation of second-wave feminists were
now paying increased attention to how oppression is manifest in their day-to-
day lives, an emphasis notably absent in the days of the "other-woman's-
feminism." And this, it could be argued, may be a salutary development for
individuals who have "burned out" after years of political struggle. It may
also, as I will suggest below, have rather negative consequences for Brazilian
gender politics in the long run.

Others were pursuing feminist activism in new arenas, taking feminism into
the arts, the media, the universities as never before. In São Paulo and other
major cities, feminist film and video collectives, women's writing groups, and
other cultural activities blossomed in the late 1980s. By 1988, feminist research centers and women's studies programs could be found in over a dozen
universities, where only one such program existed in 1981. In short, it appears
that many feminists took the slogan "the personal is political" a step further—
they moved beyond the confines of politics as conventionally defined (e.g.,
parties and grassroots organizing) to engage in activism in nonconventional
arenas that also shape and reinforce gender power arrangements (i.e., academia, culture, film). As one of my interviewees now exclusively working in a
women's research group at the University of Brasília explained, "I no longer
have patience with consciousness-raising groups or organizing large women's
events. I want to do something different, something that will shake up the way
we think about the world, about literature, about men and women."[8]

Autonomous middle-class feminist organizations of the "umbrella group"
variety that prevailed in the late 1970s had been replaced by service-oriented
groups such as *Sexualidade e Saúde* (Sexuality and Health) and *Centro Informação Mulher* (Women's Information Center) in São Paulo. Such groups provided alternative health care, legal, educational, consulting, or other services
to women in an effort to overcome the limitations of government or private
services.

Still other individual feminists had chosen to take their message to parallel
organizations of civil society and political parties. Some women formerly active in autonomous women's groups developed a new conception of "double
militancy," an issue that sparked pugnacious polemics within feminist movement organizations during the 1970s. Now, these women argued, feminists
must take their struggle into trade unions and progressive political parties,
rather than forcing their "party line" onto feminist groups. While they almost

---

[8] Interview with Ana Vicentine, former member of *Brasília-Mulher* and current member of
Núcleo de Estudos da Mulher at the University of Brasília, Brasília, June 29, 1988.

230 · Chapter Ten

always encountered resistance in male-dominant organizations that still viewed gender inequality as secondary to the "larger" struggle, individual feminists and women's caucuses were building new horizontal links with organized sectors of civil society that might facilitate the articulation of gender-based claims and widen the electoral appeal of feminist issues. Indeed, many unions, especially those organized under CUT, the PT-dominated *Central Única dos Trabalhadores* (Central Union of Workers), now have fairly militant women's departments. And some feminists in professional associations, such as the Brazilian Bar Association, had created semiautonomous women's divisions.

One of the most visible developments in the women's movement in the late 1980s was the growth of a nationwide, self-defined "popular feminism." Popular feminism was in many ways the outgrowth of the politicization of feminine groups and mothers' movements discussed above. In Greater São Paulo, groups with overwhelmingly working-class membership, such as *Rede Mulher* (Women's Network), *Comité de Mulheres de São Bernardo do Campo* (São Bernardo do Campo Women's Committee), and *Casa da Mulher de Grajaú*, were advancing strategic claims that encompassed their class, race, *and* gender interests as "women at the bottom of the bottom." *Rede Mulher* had affiliates throughout the state of São Paulo and contacts with other working-class women's networks throughout Brazil, as did the "new" *União de Mulheres de São Paulo*, which, as shall be seen below, broke with the PCdoB. The *Comité* in São Bernardo boasted over 350 members and international women's day celebrations organized by the group in 1987 and 1988 drew between six and seven hundred neighborhood women.

Whereas the feminine movement groups discussed in the preceding chapters focused exclusively on issues pertaining to women's socially ascribed roles (i.e., urban services, running water, cost of living, and so on), these new popular feminist organizations worked to transgress those roles and stressed the specificity of women's oppression within class relations. They were nevertheless often quite critical of the women they called "historic feminists." As one of the core organizers of the *Comité* in São Bernardo explained, popular feminists believed "historic feminists" (the founding members of groups such as *Nós Mulheres* in the 1970s) "were sexist and did not pay enough attention to class issues . . . though they played an important role in the women's movement because they were the first to raise the woman question."[9] As seen above, early middle-class–based feminist groups, if anything, were in fact primarily concerned with the "general struggle," focused on working with grassroots women's movements for day care and other urban services, and reticent to raise issues such as sexuality or abortion for fear of dividing

[9] Interview with member of the executive committee of the *Comité de Mulheres de São Bernardo do Campo and Casa da Mulher Nora Astorga*, São Bernardo do Campo, July 4, 1988.

the struggle against the dictatorship or losing key allies on the Left. But as feminists gradually moved out of the day-care struggle and as many ceased working in the urban periphery, focusing instead on creating feminist cultural or service organizations or on influencing elite-controlled institutional politics and policy, the rift between working-class and middle-class women's mobilization widened. In 1988, considerable tensions characterized the relationship between popular feminist groups and middle-class feminists active in the movement since the 1970s.

Many middle-class feminists I talked with were ambivalent about the recent surge in grassroots organizing among working-class and poor women. More than ever, "historic feminists" drew a clear dividing line between *o movimento feminista* (feminist movement) and *o movimento de mulheres* (women's movement or feminine movement). Many middle-class feminists argued that many of the new popular feminist groups were manipulated by the church and the sectarian Left, that such groups had reduced the feminist political project to a mere "laundry list" of demands that could easily be translated into programmatic items for party or union platforms. What was lost, according to some feminists, was that side of feminist struggle that concerned the radical transformation of culture and society, not just of political economy and policy.

But a rather more complex picture emerges if we look closely at the multifaceted women's movement in Brazil at the turn of the decade. Some new women's organizations were indeed no more than women's fronts for the sectarian Left or were bound by the doctrinaire dictates of the Catholic church. More will be said about these below. However, other sectors of the *movimento de mulheres* claimed to be expanding rather than narrowing the feminist agenda, an agenda which, they contended, did not fully respond to the needs of poor and working-class women. One of the core organizers of the São Bernardo Women's Committee insisted on differentiating their popular feminist organization from those controlled by the sectarian Left. Unlike leftist women's front groups such as the MR-8's *Federação das Mulheres Paulistas*, she argued, "we do not think sex and sexuality are secondary contradictions. . . . They think that socialism must come first. We believe that only socialism will create the objective conditions [for women's liberation] but that we have to start today to raise women's issues like sexuality or differential education of boys and girls and make some progress, even if it's only partial."[10]

The kind of feminism practiced by the women of Jardim Miriam in the early 1980s, discussed in chapter 5, can be seen as a precursor of this current in the grassroots women's movement. Indeed, the trajectory of the São Bernardo group in the 1980s was quite similar to that we traced in Jardim Miriam in the 1970s and early 1980s. The group was spawned when local women, in collaboration with feminist PT activists and members of the Grajaú Women's Center

[10] Ibid.

(also discussed in chapter 5), got involved in efforts to bring subsidized milk to the neighborhood. The milk distribution program was one of the Sarney administration's first neopopulist emergency relief measures in 1985 and a *Movimento de Mulheres pela Alimentação* (Women's Movement for Nutrition), reminiscent of the Cost-of-Living Movement of the 1970s, was formed by sixteen grassroots women's groups in Greater São Paulo in an effort to establish community control over the program. According to neighborhood women I talked with in July 1988, women involved in this movement began expressing a desire to explore other concerns they shared as wives and mothers. As in Jardim Miriam, middle-class feminist activists provided key organizational and ideological resources in São Bernardo as well. And as local women residents began identifying the power relations that underlie their socially ascribed roles, group discussions quickly turned to other gender-specific issues such as sexuality. While day care and the cost of living remained at the center of their concerns and mobilizational initiatives, so too did issues like women's health and reproductive rights. And popular feminist groups also actively engaged in consciousness-raising activities aimed at imploding gender power relations in families and communities.

Middle-class feminist ambivalence about this new current in the *movimento de mulheres* was in some ways ironic. After all, in the mid-to-late 1970s, early feminist groups aspired to create a cross-class, mass-based feminist movement. Ties to the church sometimes prevented the leadership of some popular groups from addressing explicitly male domination in the family or the politics of sexuality, contraception, and abortion, the ultimate Catholic taboos. But popular feminist groups were broadening the agenda of working-class gender politics and expanding the arenas of feminist struggle, taking gender-specific claims into local community groups and municipal politics.

Another important development in Brazilian gender politics in the 1980s was the growth of Black feminist organizations. Black women have always been integral participants in the larger Black movement and in Black religious and cultural associations. And individual Black women activists were also among the founders of the predominantly white second-wave feminist movement. In the early 1980s, some began to realize that their needs and concerns were not being articulated adequately by either the male-dominant Black movement or the white-dominated feminist movement. Arguing that racism in the women's movement and sexism in the Black movement necessitated the creation of autonomous Black women's groups, women in Rio organized two Black women's collectives in 1981 and 1982.

In São Paulo, most Black women continued to organize as part of the larger Black movement throughout the 1970s and early 1980s. Though sometimes sympathetic to the feminist movement's political claims, most remained aloof from the movement due to its inattention to the triple oppressions experienced by most Black women and by feminism's lack of analysis of the specificity of racial oppression within class and gender relations.[11]

However, in 1983, fifteen white women were appointed to the newly installed State Council on the Feminine Condition (CECF) in São Paulo, and this glaringly racist "oversight" on the part of a putatively democratic state government led Black women in São Paulo to mobilize to attain representation on the Council, according to Black feminist activists, Edna Roland and Sueli Carneiro. One Black representative and an alternate were added to the Council shortly thereafter, and a CECF Black Women's Commission was formed. But the women who mobilized for representation decided that they should remain organized, founding the São Paulo Black Women's Collective in early 1984. The creation of the Collective again highlights how State policies sometimes shape or inform the strategies and tactics of social movement organizations.

The Collective organized a number of cultural and political events in the late 1980s and collaborated closely with the CECF's Black Women's Commission. A similar Black feminist group was active in the coastal city of Santos. The first Black Women's Conference was held in São Paulo in July 1988; statewide conferences were planned in Rio and other states as well in preparation for the First National Black Women's Conference, held in December 1988.

By 1988 the Black women's movement, like the Brazilian women's movement as a whole, was ideologically quite diverse. Many active in Black women's groups rejected the feminist label. Their repudiation of feminism, according to Black activists I talked with, stemmed from a variety of sources: some Black women feared losing key allies among some Black men in the movement who, like some white men on the Left, viewed gender as a "secondary contradiction" and believed that feminism was a bourgeois, white woman's issue; others believed that Black women must work "side-by-side" with Black men to eradicate racial oppression, that race takes precedence over gender in defining the oppressive conditions of Black women's lives; and for many, the racism operative within Brazilian feminist groups had irreparably damaged feminism's credibility. Many found early feminist groups inhospitable and even hostile to Black women's insistence that feminism must account for how racism permeates the social construction of gender in Brazilian society.

[11] This discussion is based on formal and informal interviews with Black women active in early feminist groups and the MNU (United Black Movement) in São Paulo during 1982, 1983, and 1985 and retrospective formal interviews with two Black women active in Black feminist organizations in São Paulo today: Edna Roland, member of the São Paulo Black Women's Collective and of the Black Women's Commission of the São Paulo State Council on the Status of Women, São Paulo, June 24, 1988, and Sueli Carneiro, also a member of the Collective and director of the Black Women's Program of the National Council on the Status of Women, Brasília, June 29, 1988.

Still other Black women were reclaiming feminist banners and wanted to expand the boundaries of feminist struggle, arguing that there could be no hierarchy of oppressions, that race, class, and gender shape the lives of Black women in inseparable ways, making their struggle distinct from that of Black men *and* white women. This latter position prevailed among women who work in the CECF's Black Women's Commission and in the CNDM's (National Council on Women's Rights) Black Women's Program. In a 1988 document launching the latter program, coordinator and movement activist, Sueli Carneiro, summarized the position of this feminist current within the Black women's movement.

> The problematic of Black women is situated at the intersection of two social movements, the women's movement and the Black movement. And the political task emerging from this strategic point is, on the one hand, to sensitize the women's movement to the fact that the sexual identity of women does not necessarily lead to racial solidarity, and on the other, to sensitize the Black movement to the fact that racial identity does not "naturally" result in sexual solidarity among Blacks.
>
> This lack of understanding has in general determined that the conquests of the women's movement tend to benefit white women as a consequence of the racial discrimination which weighs upon Black women. In a similar fashion, the few conquests of the Black movement tend to privilege Black men as a consequence of the sexual discrimination which falls upon Black women.[12]

The diversity of perspectives on race and gender politics represented in Black women's groups sometimes led white feminists to deny them a place within the "feminist fold," to "dismiss" the new Black feminist collectives in São Paulo as part of the *movimento de mulheres*; perhaps this is one more sign of the racism that most Black women have experienced in the feminist movement over the past two decades.

In short, in 1988 Brazil was clearly witnessing a fairly widespread diffusion of feminist ideas. But feminist ideology was being taken to task by many women whose strategic gender interests, they believed, were not represented by the feminist groups of the late 1970s and early 1980s. The many new currents that flourished in the Brazilian women's movement in the late 1980s provided ample evidence of the multiplicity of practical and strategic interests manifest in racially and culturally stratified class societies. And these interests were being voiced and politically articulated by ever-more diverse and sometimes antagonistic women's groups.

Given these multiple conceptions and articulations of strategic gender interests, it was not surprising that the Brazilian women's movement had "failed" to form peak associations to represent women's interests within the civilian

---

[12] Conselho Nacional dos Direitos da Mulher, "Programa da Mulher Negra, Centenario de Abolição," March 1988 (Mimeograph).

regime. But this was not necessarily a sign of weakness, and may instead prove to be a source of strength.

After 1985 tensions among Brazilian feminisms, on the one hand, and between feminists of all types and women militants of the sectarian Left, on the other, exploded in a number of national and international feminist forums. Contentious debates about who was a feminist and what constituted a feminist political agenda characterized all national movement meetings and conferences.[13] With the rapid expansion of popular feminist groups after 1985, national feminist meetings were attended by hundreds of women. The Eighth National Feminist Conference, held in Rio in 1986, was attended by close to eight hundred women. The Ninth, held in the interior of the Northeastern state of Pernambuco in 1987, attracted over one thousand participants, whereas at the Third National Feminist Conference (discussed in chapter 8), held in Brasília in 1983, there were only thirty or forty women in attendance.

The differences and conflicts among feminisms no longer revolved around whether the *general* struggle must take precedence over the *specific* struggle for gender equality. As one long-time feminist activist told me, "today, the debates revolve around how to carry forth both struggles simultaneously." The line between feminists and nonfeminist or antifeminist partisan women's groups could thus more easily be drawn: feminists according to most activists I interviewed, whether they were involved in "historic," popular, or Black feminist groups, were those who do not prioritize one form of struggle over the other. But from there, the distinctions *among* feminists became blurred.

Several historic feminists I interviewed in 1988, however, argued that the feminist message was not only being broadly diffused, it was also being diluted. For these women, many of them veterans of the conflict-ridden Paulista women's congresses, the translation of the feminist transformational project into neat categories and a list of policy demands was a betrayal of the revolutionary feminist cause.

These continuing conflicts among women's organizations, of the feminist, feminine, or antifeminist variety, made the creation of a single peak women's organization a questionable goal. New "Coordinations" of the feminist movement were established in the state of São Paulo and in the ABCD region (including Santo André, São Bernardo do Campo, São Caetano, and Diadema) of Greater São Paulo. Composed of many of the new popular feminist organizations, such as *Rede Mulher*, the São Bernardo Women's Committee, and the Black Women's Collective, as well as the Women's Division of the PT, these coordinations seemed aware of earlier problems generated by the 1980–

---

[13] For an analysis of how these debates have developed in the Latin American women's movement as a whole and how tensions have been manifest in Latin American and Caribbean feminist *Encuentros* or regionwide conferences held every two years since 1981, see Nancy Saporta Sternbach, Marysa Navarro, Patricia Chuchryk, and Sonia E. Alvarez, "Feminisms in Latin America: From Bogota to Taxco" (forthcoming).

1981 Coordination and sought to overcome them organizationally. Participants in the São Paulo "precoordination," which met weekly after early 1986, argued that though a coordination should not claim to "represent" the interests of all women's groups in the state and should not become a political entity in itself, it was vitally important to create organizational instances that would facilitate joint mobilization around consensual issues or demands. They aspired to create an ongoing forum for exchange of information about movement activities, the planning of key celebrations like International Women's Day, and the coordination of joint actions to bring pressure to bear on parties and the State.[14]

These coordinations differed markedly from renewed partisan attempts to create "representative" organizational instances. The MR-8 and its *Federação das Mulheres Paulistas* had long been interested in promoting a "Confederation" of Brazilian women, a nationally-based umbrella group which, like the *Federação*, would serve as a vehicle for partisan mobilization and as a transmission belt for the party's political line. The MR-8 gained considerable clout in Sarney's New Republic, given its long-standing support for the PMDB. In the city of São Paulo it also aligned itself with the conservative, neopopulist PTB administration of Jânio Quadros, which came to power in March of 1986. With the support of their new patrons in power, the MR-8 was finally able to found a National Confederation of Brazilian Women, made up of federations they organized or were then in the process of organizing in seventeen states.

The organizing principle behind these state federations and the national confederation was similar to that adopted by the Federation of Paulista Women in 1980: any neighborhood group, association, or union, regardless of whether they worked exclusively or primarily with women, was urged to join. Thus, an anomalous mass of four thousand women, with few organic links to either the federations or other women's movement groups, and mostly from apolitical mother's clubs in the urban periphery, were assembled in São Paulo for the gala founding convention of the Confederation of Brazilian Women on July 1 and 2, 1988.

The MR-8 organizers presented participants with a preestablished agenda and a set of resolutions, approved by the "general assembly" by unanimous acclamation on the second day of the convention. Participants heard speeches from male politicians supported by the MR-8 who applauded the Confedera-

[14] Some activists I spoke with shunned these new coordinations, viewing them as "PT fronts." That is, though the groups involved in the Coordinations were all independent of the PT, all were said to be active sympathizers of that party. And, indeed, breaking with feminism's putatively nonpartisan tradition, both Coordinations endorsed the successful candidacy of Luiza Erundina, long-time activist in urban popular movement groups, who was elected mayor of São Paulo in November of 1988.

tion's goal of promoting "a more just and feminine Brazil." They were also treated to a "women's fair," where Center-Right politicians endorsed by the MR-8 displayed campaign materials, commercial establishments promoted products for the household, and the São Paulo *Federação*'s "Fashion Department" sponsored an ongoing fashion show.

In talking to several of the working-class women in attendance, reviewing the Confederation's founding documents, and observing several preprogrammed workshops, it was readily apparent to me that many present had never taken part in any ongoing feminine or feminist struggles and that many of the state federations were made up of phantom organizations with few if any organic links to women's groups in their region. The "parent organization," the MR-8, was able to secure over U.S. $50,000 to stage the event from its patrons in state and local government: the Jânio Quadros administration provided free office space to the organizing commission as well as considerable funding, as did the PMDB Center-Right state government in Minas Gerais. It is important to note that, in contrast, the autonomous women's movement historically has refused to accept direct government or party funding for any of its conferences or events.

Thus, some sectors of the State either deliberately or inadvertently contributed to legitimizing this pseudorepresentative organizational initiative. Likewise, much of the press celebrated the founding of a "truly" national women's confederation. But most sectors of the women's movement viewed the event as so unrepresentative that not a single member of any of the major independent women's groups in São Paulo was present at the founding conference. And both the CECF and the CNDM decided not to send official representatives; in fact, the National Council on Women's Rights lobbied governors and ministers to turn down the organizers' invitiations to the gala event.[15]

In sum, the attempt at forming a single confederation of Brazilian women is quite illustrative of the problems inherent in creating peak associations to represent "women's interests." Women's interests, as I have argued, are hardly uniform; instead, they vary by class, race, sexual preference, religion, and so on, are couched within in a wide variety of class and gender ideologies, and given political expression by an ever-larger and more diverse set of women's groups.

Perhaps women's groups need not create permanent umbrella organizations in order to effectively advance their goals. A variety of political action arenas, loosely coordinated by conjunctural coalitions, may prove to be the best way to advance the multiple goals of socially, politically, and ideologically heterogeneous movements such as the women's movement in Brazil. Moreover, a

[15] Informal interview with Maria Aparecida Schumaher, executive secretary of the CNDM, São Paulo, July 16, 1988.

decentralized structure leaves the movement less vulnerable to State encapsulation or partisan manipulation.

THE REPRESENTATION OF WOMEN'S INTERESTS IN THE NEW REPUBLIC

If the formation of truly representative peak organizations was neither possible nor perhaps even desirable, then how should women's interests be represented in democratizing Brazil? Political parties, as we have seen, have increasingly pitched special appeals to organized female constituencies; an improvement in the historically strained relationship between male-dominant parties and women's groups, in theory at least, might provide one channel for the political articulation of gender interests.

After the liberalization of party legislation and the enfranchisement of illiterates in 1985, over thirty parties vied for the support of the greatly expanded Brazilian electorate in the late 1980s. And most new parties added "women's issues" to their platforms and created women's branches or caucuses. There is some evidence that parties also allotted more slots to women candidates; fifteen times as many women ran for office in the state of São Paulo in the 1986 congressional elections than did in 1982.[16]

But feminist activists still faced sexist obstacles within party organizations, according to female party militants I interviewed in 1988. Most contended that the parties remained ideologically resistant to the feminist political agenda and still viewed women's organizations only as "electoral fodder." Many women also complained that parties were reluctant to fully support feminist-identified candidates and failed to grant real power to women's caucuses or divisions. In new and old party organizations alike, the political space conceded to women and women's issues remained miniscule.

The *Partido da Social Democracia Brasileira*, a social democratic offshoot of the PMDB, the third largest in 1988, illustrated the continuing barriers confronted by women party activists when trying to channel gender-specific claims through male-dominant party organizations. According to Cristina Masagão, former vice-president of the São Paulo CECF, long-time PMDB activist, and founding member of the new PSDB, women members of the new party pushed for the creation of a women's commission, arguing that women's concerns would not otherwise be represented adequately by the party. Some party founders, led by former São Paulo senator and governor, Franco Montoro, proposed that 50 percent of the new party's collegial executive be reserved for representatives of social movements: women, Blacks, ecologists, and so on. Both proposals were defeated at the PSDB's founding convention, however. The majority of party members, said Masagão, maintained that this

[16] *Mulherio* (December 1986—February 1987).

new party was to be "so modern, so advanced, that women's issues would be discussed in all local party directorates" and that there was therefore no need for a separate women's commission or for representational quotas at the national level.[17]

Several of my interviewees noted that it was now "in vogue" for politicians and parties "to pay lip service" to issues of gender inequality, that speaking of women's concerns conferred "democratic legitimacy" on politicians in the New Republic; party organizations were too often invested merely in reaching out to women's organizations in order to shore up electoral support.

The marginalization of women and women's issues and their manipulation for electoral purposes characterized the full political spectrum from Left to Right. Little progress has been made toward the true integration of women and their strategic gender claims. At a June 1988 statewide meeting of Workers' Party (PT) women, I heard many of the same complaints expressed by women PT activists in the early 1980s: "too many activists view the woman question as secondary"; "the Party does not support or subsidize the women's movement"; "the women's comission is not consulted on key programmatic issues"; "the Party must create a space for political reflection of feminist issues and train cadres on the specificity of gender oppression."[18]

New tensions emerged within communist parties as well. The leadership of *União de Mulheres de São Paulo*, all of whom were veteran PCdoB activists, were accused of being "man-hating," "bourgeois," and "divisionist" for leading a drive for the decriminalization of abortion in 1987 and raising other radical gender issues; three women, one of whom had been a member of the party for twenty-seven years, were expelled from the Albanian-inspired *Partido Comunista do Brasil* (PCdoB) for "refusing to make the *União* an arm of the Party" and criticizing the party's executive committee for trying to manipulate the autonomous women's movement.[19] The *União* later severed all ties with the PCdoB and began militantly advancing a "popular feminist" political agenda. In response, in late 1987, the PCdoB created a new, more manipulable "nonfeminist" women's front group, the *União Popular de Mulheres*. And not to be outdone by the MR-8, the PCdoB also held a national convention in August 1988 to officially launch its own "Union of Brazilian Women," which, like the MR-8's *Confederação*, claimed to "represent" the women's movement.

Many female party activists had come to view these sexist barriers and manipulative tendencies as insurmountable. By the turn of the decade many his-

[17] Interview with Cristina Masagão, São Paulo, June 27, 1988.

[18] This discussion is based on participant-observation at the *Encontro Estadual das Mulheres do PT*, organized by the *Comissão de Mulheres do PT*, São Paulo, June 25, 1988.

[19] Interview with Maria Amelia Telles de Almeida, president of the *União de Mulheres de São Paulo*, São Paulo, June 22, 1988.

toric feminists, some of whom had engaged in "double militancy" for decades, had withdrawn from party activism altogether, choosing instead to
engage in feminist advocacy work in other arenas. Zuleika Alambert, long-
time core member of the Moscow-line Brazilian Communist Party, for example, left the party, wrote a theoretical treatise critical of communist understandings of the "woman question," and collaborated on a Marxist-feminist
book on women's history with Maria Amelia Telles de Almeida, former member of the PCB's archrival party, the PCdoB.[20]

In 1988 most parties still were ineffective in establishing organic links to
social movement organizations of all sorts, in spite of the efforts of movement
activists to influence party organizations and platforms. The Workers' Party
and, to a lesser extent, the Social Democratic Party were the only partial exceptions to this rule. Women's groups must continue, of course, to educate
the electorate on gender issues so as to increase their bargaining power within
parties. Yet analysts of democratic consolidation too often place the burden of
forging those vital links exclusively on the shoulders of social movement
groups. Instead of pointing to the "failure" of movements, one might argue
that remaining obstacles will be overcome only if parties themselves become
more programmatic, more ideological, and if they create more democratic
structures for effective citizen participation in party affairs.

The political currency represented by organized feminine and feminist constituencies was no longer as valuable to the PMDB/PFL coalition that controlled all but one of the state governments after 1986. Far fewer women and
an insignificant number of feminists or feminist-sympathizers ran for public
office in the municipal elections of 1985. Nationwide, a total of sixty-three
women were elected or reelected in the 1986 congressional elections—one
vice governor, one alternate to the Senate, twenty-six to the Chamber of Deputies, and thirty-five to the state assemblies. But unlike in 1982, most of those
elected had had little or no contact with women's movement organizations.
Since the Congress elected in 1986 also formulated the new Brazilian Constitution, this fact did not bode well for the future of interest-group feminism in
democratic Brazil. While the twenty-six elected female constituents surpassed
the total number of women who had ever served in the national Congress,[21]
eleven of the twenty-six gained office through family ties to male politicians.
Also, most of the congresswomen elected in 1986 came from the less politically powerful states of the North and Northeast where the women's movement was still in its incipient stages. Proportionately fewer women were

[20] Interview with Zuleika Alambert, former president of the São Paulo Council on the Status of
Women and former member of the PCB state executive, currently special advisor to the current
CECF president, Ida Maria Jancsó, São Paulo, June 27, 1988.

[21] Fatima Jordão, "A Bancada Feminina na Constiuinte: Maior e Melhor do que Parece," *Mulherio* 7, no. 27 (December 1986-February 1987): 13.

elected in precisely those states where feminine and feminist movements were most advanced.[22]

MEDIATING THE RELATIONSHIP BETWEEN WOMEN'S MOVEMENTS AND THE STATE? NEW CONTRADICTIONS OF WOMEN'S INSTITUTIONS IN POSTAUTHORITARIAN BRAZIL

If parties were still less-than-effective vehicles for channeling women's demands, then how will the women's movement secure further gains in democratizing Brazil? As suggested above, one strategy that proved relatively successful after 1983 was the creation of new "women's institutions" at the state and federal levels. These theoretically would supersede political parties and establish direct links between women's movements and the State.

In the effusive period of reform that followed the installation of the first civilian federal administration in twenty-one years, it seemed as if these newly created "women's spaces" could ensure further progress toward the eradication of gender inequality. And during the latter half of the 1980s Brazilian feminists indeed consolidated some of the gains made during the *abertura* process. After the installation of eleven opposition-led state governments in March 1983, feminists promoted several important and innovative public policies and secured more women's spaces within the opposition-led government structures. As of mid-1988, State Councils on the Status of Women had been established not only in São Paulo but also in Minas Gerais in 1983 and subsequently in twenty-three other states and municipalities. On December 19, 1986, the São Paulo State Assembly voted to institutionalize the State Council on the Feminine Condition, making it a permanent organ of the state government.

In late 1985 and throughout much of 1986, the National Council intervened in favor of women in federal agrarian reform deliberations, promoted a national day-care policy, implemented antisexist educational reforms, expanded its outreach to women in civil society through its access to government-controlled media, and developed a "Women's Proposal" for the new Brazilian Constitution. The Council initially remained true to the goals of Brazilian feminism, calling for an expanded definition of democracy that encompassed the democratization of both public and private life.

> For us, women, the full exercise of citizenship means, yes, the right to representation, a voice and a role in public life, but at the same time, it also implies dignity in daily life, which the law can inspire and should ensure, the right to education, to health, to security, to a family life free of traumas. Women's vote brings with it a double exigency: an egalitarian political system and a non-authoritarian civilian life.

[22] Ibid.

> We, women, are conscious of the fact that this country will only be truly demo-
> cratic and its citizens truly free when, without prejudice of sex, race, color, class,
> sexual orientation, religious or political creed, physical condition or age, equal treat-
> ment and equal opportunity in the streets, podiums, workshops, factories, offices,
> assemblies, and palaces, are guaranteed.[23]

In short, in 1985–1986, the National Council on Women's Rights and some state and municipal Councils worked to strengthen the autonomous women's movement, providing direct and indirect subsidies to independent feminine and feminist organizations, coordinating national educational and mobiliza-tional campaigns on women's issues, and providing the movement with new access points to State policy-making arenas. The National Council itself be-came the principal stage for the practice of a 1980s brand of Brazilian interest-group feminist politics. During this early posttransition period, the CNDM advanced a fairly radical and successful policy agenda. The Council was es-pecially active in the areas of family planning, day-care, and violence against women.

At the National Council's recommendation, the Ministry of Labor promised to enforce compliance with feminist-inspired CLT day-care provisions, re-quiring that all establishments employing more than fifteen women provide day-care facilities for female employees. In late 1986, the National Bank for Social Development (BNDES) approved a resolution requiring all projects and programs seeking bank loans to conform to CLT day-care provisions. The CNDM later began pressuring other national and state banks to adopt the same requirements.[24]

The Council also promoted ongoing debates, conferences, and educational and media campaigns around family planning and abortion rights. In October 1986, the CNDM and the Ministries of Health and of Social Welfare cospon-sored the First National Conference on Women's Health and Women's Rights. Held in Brasília and attended by over twelve hundred women representing state and municipal health departments, public hospitals and clinics, political parties, and autonomous women's groups, the Conference reaffirmed the women's movement's staunch opposition to population control and its fervent support of women's reproductive freedom. Conference participants agreed to create local "Committees for the Defense of Women's Health" to "act effec-tively in the planning, implementation, and execution of health programs."[25] After protracted debate, participants also endorsed a more radical proposal—that abortion be legalized under the new Brazilian Constitution. Arguing that

---

[23] Conselho Nacional dos Direitos da Mulher, "Carta das Mulheres aos Constituintes de 1987," December 1986 (Pamphlet).

[24] *Informe Mulher* (Bulletin of the National Council on Women's Rights), Brasília, 1986, p. 5.

[25] Brasil, Ministério da Saúde, *Boletim Informativo da 8a Conferencia Nacional de Saúde*, December 1986, p. 4.

"the conditions under which it occurs in the country, abortion constitutes a serious problem for women's physical and mental health," the Conference's final recommendations called for a national plebiscite on abortion and urged lawmakers to give serious consideration to legalization, or minimally, decriminalization.[26]

A national campaign against violence against women headed CNDM President Jacqueline Pitanguy's political agenda in 1986–1987. The Council compiled a "national dossier on the impunity with which violence against women is cloaked"[27] and in mid-1986, launched a "Say No to Violence against Women" campaign, with television spots featuring renowned actors transmitted on government air time.

The reformist euphoria of the first two years of the civilian regime, however, gave way to widespread disillusionment in the late 1980s. New women's councils and forty-six women's police precincts were created throughout Brazil. But these new institutions proved sources of disappointment, frustration, and strategic confusion for Brazilian feminists, even for some of the "founding mothers" of the Councils.

According to feminists who have served on or worked in the CECF and CNDM as of 1988, many of the new women's institutions were profoundly partisan.[28] Most had few if any links to independent, nonpartisan women's organizations and instead were created as electoral gambits by mayors and governors, providing these with a newfound source of democratic legitimacy. To the dismay of the feminists who conceived of the councils as institutions that would channel women's demands into policy arenas and monitor policy implementation, many of the new councils instead served as mechanisms for the top-down mobilization of women.

The São Paulo Municipal Council on the Status of Women, created by Jânio Quadros in 1987, was one of the most disturbing examples of how opportunistic governments and antifeminist groups distorted some of these new women's institutions. Created at the behest of women active in the antifeminist *Federação das Mulheres Paulistas*, the Municipal Council served primarily as a staging ground for that organization's sectarian mobilizational agenda. Con-

---

[26] "Aborto descriminalizado," *Mulherio* 6, no. 2 (September/November 1986): 18. Several studies have estimated the number of illegal abortions performed in Brazil each year to exceed 3 million and that over 400,000 women die in Brazil each year of post-abortive complications.

[27] *Informe Mulher*, 1986, p. 2.

[28] The ensuing discussion is based on a thorough review of 1985–1988 council documents; the feminist print media; formal interviews with Maria Amelia Telles de Almeida, former coordinator of the CECF day care and women and work commissions, June 22, 1988; Edna Roland, member of the CECF Black Women's Commission, June 24, 1988; Zuleika Alambert, former president of the CECF, June 27, 1988; Cristina Masagão, former vice-president of the CECF, June 27, 1988; Ida Maria Jancsó, then CECF President, July 14, 1988; and informal interviews with Maria Aparecida Schumaher, executive secretary, CNDM, July 16, 1988; Vera Lucia Soares, technical director, CNDM, June 28, 1988; and Ruth Cardoso, former CECF councillor, July 7, 1988.

servative São Paulo mayor, Jânio Quadros, serviced his neopopulist coalition in creating this local women's council and its purpose, according to one staff member I spoke with, was quite different than that proposed by the feminists who conceived the councils: the new administration thought that women were "politically backward" and needed to be encouraged to "bring their special qualities" to politics; they have special needs, defined by "their unique roles," which the Council should advance.[29] Just how these "special needs" were to be advanced was unclear. Under Quadros, the Municipal Council had no independent budget, a minimal staff (only two part-time secretaries), no specific legislative or policy agenda, no apparent links to either the municipal legislature or other policy arenas and no ties to any local women's groups except the *Federação das Mulheres Paulistas* whose founding convention swallowed up most of the Municipal Council's limited 1988 budget. Indeed, most of the São Paulo women's movement activists I spoke to had never contacted Quadros's Municipal Council and some believed it did not actually exist.

Of even greater concern to many of the feminists who originally supported the establishment of the São Paulo CECF and the National Council on Women's Rights was that these institutions also appeared to have fallen prey to partisan manipulation or lost much of their already limited political clout after 1987. The structure of political opportunities changed dramatically in the late 1980s, resulting in decreased leverage for the CECF and CNDM, both of which, as discussed above, played a decisive role in advancing a fairly radical, feminist-inspired policy agenda.

The original PMDB ruling coalition in São Paulo experienced serious rifts and the national ruling coalition shifted radically to the Right after the end of 1986. In the state of São Paulo in 1986, the Center-Left PMDB administration of Franco Montoro, oriented toward decentralization and popular participation, was replaced by the Center-Right administration of Orestes Quercia whose power was based on centralization and the allegiance of small town mayors. Quercia dismantled or deactivated many of the participatory mechanisms established under Montoro.

Feminist PMDB activists scrambled to secure the institutionalization of the CECF in late 1986 for fear that Quercia would close the women's space created by Montoro. Their fears appear to have been well-founded. Though Quercia did not try to dissolve the CECF, its clout within his administration dwindled significantly. One CECF staff member summarized the governor's attitude as follows: "leave the girls at the Council to their little games but don't give them any resources or real power."[30]

[29] Telephone interview with staff member of the São Paulo Municipal Council on the Status of Women, July 15, 1988.
[30] Informal interview with Beatriz de Mattes, June 21, 1988.

Since the original councillors' terms were to expire under Quercia, several strategy sessions were convened during the final months 1986 to determine who should head the CECF under the new administration. It was ultimately decided that the president must come from Quercia's wing of the PMDB or else the Council would lose its limited political clout within the state administration. The new governor did indeed service his own power base in appointing new councillors to the CECF: feminists and women linked to the *movimento de mulheres* were in minority in Quercia's reconstituted state Council. Of the twenty-three councillors he appointed, according to one of my interviewees, only ten had any experience in the movement, the rest were dubbed *fisionómicas* (physiognomical or women who "appear" to be representative).[31] And though the National Council on Women's Rights retained a solid feminist-identified majority, a similar danger loomed large as the original councillors' terms were due to expire. The future of the CNDM troubled many staff members I talked with in 1988. Their worst fears came true in September of 1989. After the last of many Sarney Cabinet reshufflings, the new Minister of Justice, in whose ministry the CNDM is formally lodged, was charged with appointing new councillors. Ignoring the recommendations of the CNDM president and current councillors, he appointed six conservative women to the Council. In response to such overt disregard for the CNDM's putative "autonomy" within the federal bureaucracy, the original councillors and much of the CNDM staff resigned in protest. Thus, even these feminist-designed women's institutions appeared to be becoming part of traditional clientelistic politics, spaces to be filled on the basis of favors owed to male politicians by appointing "their" women from patronage networks.

These developments were especially problematic for two reasons. First, much of the CECF's and CNDM's legitimacy vis-à-vis the women's movement was originally based not on their "representativeness" but on fact that the majority of council members were widely recognized to be long-time feminist activists, even if all came from the PMDB. Second, as argued in chapter 9, successful institutional mediation of the relationship between women and the male-dominant State is possible only if a gender-conscious, feminist-identified majority prevails within the Council, the Council facilitates movement access to the State apparatus and policy-making arenas, and the Council does not preempt autonomous women's movement activities.

As a consequence of the turn to the Right at both the state and federal levels, by mid-1988, both the CECF and the CNDM exerted little leverage either within the State or within civil society. Whereas in 1985, the São Paulo Council was a veritable "hotbed of feminist subversion," in mid-1988 it had only one active commission (the Black Women's Commission) and, as one staff

---

[31] Interview with Maria Amelia Telles de Almeida, São Paulo, June 22, 1988.

member told me, "had to scramble for funding for paper clips, let alone women's programs."[32]

The National Council's political effectiveness, some feminists argued, also waned after early 1987. Though the CNDM retained a sizable budget and maintained a solidly feminist staff, several movement activists and Council staff members I talked with believed that "it functions more as an educational institution, disseminating information on women's issues and women's programs" and "exercises little influence in most government ministries."[33]

By mid-1988 many feminists had begun rethinking the nature, structure, and purpose of these women's institutions in the New Brazilian Republic. One problem cited by several women interviewed was the "hybrid structure" of most Councils, that is, the fact that Councils were composed of "representatives" of civil society and of relevant municipal, state, or federal departments. This mixed structure was still praised by some; but others argued that such a structure confounds feminist practice. The latter maintained that the women's movement should "call the State a State," that the movement must recognize the limitations inherent in working in a State institution, even a nominally feminist one, and that the mixed composition of the Councils confused some movement cadres who were still asking "is this the State or is this feminist activism?."[34] I also witnessed another dimension of this confusion during heated discussions about the nature of the CECF and CNDM at a São Paulo PT women's meeting in late June 1988. Though both institutions had been around for several years, many movement and PT activists were still uncertain as to the role these "women's spaces" played in relation to the movement. Some argued that "the councils are completely harnessed to the State," while others retorted "but they *are* the State."

This same confusion plagued the movement's relationship to women's police precincts. Many feminists were disappointed with the ways in which some of the precincts replicated many of the sexist practices of regular precincts in dealing with the victims of violence. Initially, some feminist activists viewed the *delegacias* as potential arenas for combating violence against women and providing women-centered legal and psychological counseling for female victims. Though in some cases feminist scholars and activists were brought in to train female police personnel at these specialized precincts, feminists were marginalized from most, as the selection and training of staff was entrusted to

---

[32] Interview with Zuleika Alambert, former president of the CECF, June 27, 1988.

[33] Interviews with Lia Zanotta Machado and Ana Vicentine, former members of the autonomous feminist group *Brasília-Mulher*, who participated in discussions about the goals and structure of the CNDM with founding president Ruth Escobar and others prior to the installation of the Council in late 1985, Brasília, July 1, 1988; and with seven CNDM staff members, June 26-July 1, 1988.

[34] Interviews with Edna Roland and Beatriz de Mattes, São Paulo, June 24, 1988; and Vera Lucia Soares, Brasília, June 28, 1988.

local police forces. Indeed, it would seem especially hard for feminists to influence effectively the coercive apparatus of the militaristic Brazilian State. In contrast to the United States, where grassroots feminists run rape crisis centers and shelters for battered women and are brought in to advise victims and police, there was little ongoing collaboration between feminists and the new *delegacias*.[35]

This situation was further complicated by the fact that most feminist groups dedicated to combating violence against women had broken up by 1985. The creation of new "women's spaces" within the coercive apparatus of the State seems to have contributed to the deactivation of the ten or twelve autonomous *SOS-Mulher* groups. Feminist pressure outside the State, which might have helped keep the *delegacias* more closely in line with feminist principles, declined markedly.[36] The problem, of course, is that the existence of the *delegacias* will not in itself bring an end to rape and domestic violence. As Raquel Moreno, one of the founding members of *SOS-Mulher* in São Paulo, the first feminist group to dedicate itself to combating violence against women in the early 1980s, compellingly argues, "Women continue to be beaten, and will continue to be beaten as long as machismo is not extirpated, as long as the structure and ideology that tolerates, permits it, and benefits from the atomization of power remains in place, so that the most impotent of men still feels aggrandized by the perception of the existence of someone—his woman—whom he has power over and even beats."[37] Moreno insists that, with or without *delegacias*, feminists must continue to undermine the foundations of male violence and domination manifest at all levels of civil society. The danger, in her view, is that the partial insitutionalization of this and other issues central to the feminist agenda sometimes leads to movement complacency and might indirectly compromise feminist efforts to transform the politics of male supremacy in daily life.

Another troublesome aspect of the Councils on the Status of Women was that these institutions drew in many women who were key organizers in the women's movement, stripping the movement of its best cadres. Some claimed that former activists had been "transformed by the institutions," becoming bureaucrats in the service of the State, and not of the movement.

The issue of who serves on the Councils also posed another pressing question for Brazilian feminism. Were these new women's institutions to become mechanisms of "neocorporatist representation?" Through 1988 councillors had been appointed by the local, state, and federal executives, with little or no

[35] See Brasil, Ministério da Justiça, Conselho Nacional dos Direitos da Mulher, *I Encontro Nacional de Delegadas Lotadas em Delegacias de Defesa da Mulher* (Brasília, 1986).

[36] Interview with Nilce Gomes, former coordinator of the CNDM's Commission on Violence and founding member of *SOS-Mulher* in Rio de Janeiro, Brasília, June 28, 1988.

[37] Raquel Moreno, "De Feminismos, de Feministas, de Mulheres," in *A Condição Feminina*, ed. Nanci Valadares de Carvalho (São Paulo: Vértice, 1988), pp. 46–47.

input from the women's movement organizations they purportedly "represent." Thus, many women argued that the Council structure was inherently nonrepresentative and some suggested that the goal of representativeness should be abandoned altogether.

Several of the women interviewed in 1988 advocated the creation of non-partisan "women's institutes" to replace the hybrid Council structures. The idea would be to create a permanent organ of State administration responsible for monitoring gender policy developments and compiling information on the status of Brazilian women, where appointments would be civil service- and merit-based and not designated by presidents, governors, or mayors. Such a structure, proponents of this alternative argued, would be less dependent on the correlation of political or partisan forces in power or the good will of changing administrations; it would make "women's spaces" part of the State, not part of local, state, or federal administrations, making them less susceptible to patronage politics or top-down manipulation.

The opportunity space available for the articulation of gender issues in policy arenas, which greatly expanded during earlier stages of the transition process, appeared to be shrinking by mid-1988, even as feminism made further inroads into civil society. The temporary "gender opening," characteristic of the latter stages of regime transition, seemed to be closing. And Brazilian feminists were again reformulating their strategies in response to the more conservative political conjuncture.

Gender Policy in Postauthoritarian Brazil

The ascent of the Right, the intransigence of parties, and the partisan manipulation of recently created women's institutions led to policy paralysis and political immobilism and foreshadowed retrogression in the realms of labor legislation, family planning, and other issues critical to the feminist policy agenda. The conservative political climate was hardly propitious for advancing radical gender-specific policies.

In another troubling development, forces on the Right were again engaged in mobilizing middle- and upper-class women in defense of morality, the family, and private property. As early as 1985, upper middle class women began denouncing the "licentiousness" promoted by democratic freedoms, manifest in "pornographic" films and television programs since government censorship was lifted. The Democratic Ruralist Union (UDR or *União Democrática Ruralista*), formed by landowners to resist agrarian reform proposals and known to engage in paramilitary activities responsible for the death of over three thousand peasants since 1985, also boasted a "feminine department," the *UDR-Mulher*. And in December 1987, some of the founding mothers of the right-wing groups who organized women against Goulart in 1964, joined forces with *UDR-Mulher* and the PFL's women's branch to form the Women's

Movement for Free Enterprise (*Movimento de Mulheres pela Livre Iniciativa*).[38]

Some women's organizations also fell prey to the Sarney administration's neopopulist brand of mobilizational and clientelistic politics. For example, when President José Sarney launched his ill-fated heterodox economic stabilization plan in 1986 (the Cruzado Plan), he appealed to the ''women of Brazil'' to help monitor his consumer price freeze. Hundreds of thousands of women whose energies might have been directed at securing day care, better health care, or housing became *fiscais de Sarney* (Sarney's inspectors)—mobilized in the service of the ''fatherland.''

Amidst this surge of conservative mobilization, Brazilian feminists were pushed onto the defensive. Nonetheless, until late 1988 at least, the political inroads made by the women's movement during the transition successfully blocked new antifeminist initiatives and prevented significant setbacks in some critical policy areas.

The feminist-inspired comprehensive women's health and family planning program, PAISM, for example, was stalled after mid-1986. With the aid of the women's health movement and feminist sex education materials, the requisite medical personnel was trained during 1985 and 1986 and the Ministry of Health secured over U.S. $10 million of funding for PAISM from the United Nations Population Fund. In 1985, the CNDM obtained a tripartite accord with the World Health Organization and the Ministry of Health to pursue the implementation of the Program on a national scale. The stage appeared to be set for the fulfillment of the long-awaited feminist goal of providing all Brazilian women with access to safe, noncoercive family planning.[39]

But the deepening economic crisis and the Sarney government's consequent shift to the Right spurred new *controlista* policy initiatives in early 1987. After the November 1986 congressional elections, the federal government finally admitted that the Cruzado Plan had failed and resumed debt rescheduling negotiations with international banks. Not coincidentally, Sarney suddenly announced the creation of an Interministerial Commission on Family Planning, to be supervised by a Council on Social Development (CDS), made up of sixteen ministers from economic planning and social welfare departments, and charged with the immediate implementation of a national family-planning pol-

[38] *Folha de São Paulo*, December 9, 1987.

[39] The ensuing discussion is based on content analysis of federal government and women's movement documents and press coverage of developments in family planning from 1985 to 1988. It also draws on interviews with Dr. Claudio Freitas, director of PAISM, Brasília, June 29, 1988; Dr. Angela Bacha, codirector of the São Paulo Women's Health Program, São Paulo, July 14, 1988; Madalena Brandão, coordinator of the CNDM's Women's Health Commission, Brasília, June 28, 1988; five members of the feminist health collective, *Sexualidade e Saúde* in São Paulo, July 15, 1988; and Carmen Barroso, former member of the Ministry of Health's Commission on Reproductive Rights, São Paulo, July 5, 1988.

icy. The president disregarded the PAISM and excluded the CNDM from policy deliberations. Feminist-designed educational materials on family planning and sexuality, adamantly opposed by right-wing factions in the regime and denounced as immoral by the Catholic church, were to be replaced by new pamphlets that privileged natural birth control methods and depicted family planning as a way of adjusting working-class family budgets and combating poverty.

The feminist response to this assault on reproductive rights was immediate and vehement. Throughout Brazil, women's groups decried the government's new plan and mobilized in defense of the hard-won PAISM. In São Paulo, movement meetings to plan International Women's Day celebrations became forums of protest: "We would like it to be a day of commemorations and not another manifestation of protest. And there will be protests if Sarney does not back down from his population control plan."[40] Feminist health movement activists in São Paulo publicly assailed the plan, reiterating the long-standing feminist position that "family planning must start first with the needs, interests, and desires of woman, because it is upon her body that these policies will act."[41]

The feminists who had conquered limited clout within the regime actively supported movement protests and ultimately forced Sarney to withdraw his controversial proposal. Former CNDM president, Ruth Escobar, argued that "the reasons that move the government of the New Republic and President Sarney to announce the creation of the CDS, 24 hours after having signed an accord with the Paris Club, are of clear-cut *controlista* vocation. . . . It is evident that suddenly committing the entire federal government staff to the implementation [of such a program] is in direct line with the rescheduling of the debt and not the rescheduling of our uteruses, much less of our sexual pleasure."[42] Jacqueline Pitanguy, CNDM president from 1986 to 1989, demanded an audience with Sarney who assured her that in the future the Council would be granted a seat on the CDS and the Interministerial Commission.[43] In São Paulo, the CECF also expressed its outrage at this blatant disregard for the feminist-inspired program, which, after all, had been in the works since 1983. A group of PMDB congresswomen, led by alternate senator and former CECF president, Eva Blay, also publicly voiced their alarm and met with Planning Minister, José Sayad, who promised to try to block *controlista* initiatives. PT Congresswoman Irma Passoni declared that "we will not accept that our uteruses be held responsible for the country's misery," and stated that

---

[40] Albertina Duarte Takiuti, president of *Centro da Mulher Brasileira*, quoted in *Jornal da Tarde*, January 23, 1987.

[41] Simone Diniz, member of *Coletivo Feminista Sexualidade e Saúde*, quoted in *Jornal da Tarde*, January 23, 1987.

[42] Ruth Escobar, "Saias e Combaias," *Folha de São Paulo*, January 28, 1987.

[43] *O Globo*, January 22, 1987.

she would not be surprised if family planning were included in the government's 1988–1989 Goals for Combating Poverty Plan.[44] In sum, feminist inroads into parties and the State bureaucracy made a difference, augmenting the movement's ability to resist retrogressive government policy moves.

Similarly, some of the women's spaces, especially those legitimately conquered by feminist party activists during transitional politics, were critical for securing further gains for women. The CNDM, in particular, served as an effective women's lobby during the drafting of a new Constitution, exerting pressure for the inclusion of key women's movement demands at all three stages of the drafting of the Charter document, introducing gender-specific issues that might never have been considered by the Constituent Assembly, and lobbying key legislators throughout the constitutional debates. The National Council launched a nationwide campaign in November 1985 with the slogan *"Constituinte Pra Valer, Tem que Ter Palavra de Mulher"* (For the Constitution to count, women must be heard).[45] On August 26, 1986, the CNDM sponsored a national conference on Women and the *Constituinte*, charged with elaborating a "Letter from Women to the Constituent Assembly" (*Carta das Mulheres à Constituinte*), later widely distributed to legislators and women's movement organizations.

The *Carta* included pragmatic proposals for changes in labor legislation, family law, health care, and day care, as well as radical proposals that would elevate struggles for the transformation of gender power arrangements to the status of fundamental rights and constitutional imperatives. The document incorporated the full gamut of practical and strategic gender interests raised by the multiple ideological, class-based, and ethnic currents of the Brazilian women's movement. For example, the "women's proposal" stated that:

> All are equal before the law which will punish any discrimination which threatens human rights. No one will be prejudiced or privileged on the basis of place of birth, race, color, sex, marital status, rural or urban work, religion, sexual orientation, political or philosophical convictions, physical or mental handicap or any other particularity of condition. The public authorities, through specific programs, will promote social, political, economic and educational equality.[46]

A broad spectrum of women's groups endorsed the *Carta*. Most congresswomen, several progressive male legislators, and the CNDM's constitutional commission, which acted as the women's movement's de facto official lobby, actively promoted the "women's proposal" in the Assembly. And despite the *Centrão's* virtual control over the *Constituinte*, the vast majority of these proposals made their way into the new Constitution.

[44] *Folha da Tarde*, January 21, 1987.

[45] CNDM, *Mulher e Constituinte*, November 1985 (Pamphlet).

[46] CNDM, "Quadro Comparativo dos Direitos da Mulher na Constituinte," July 1988 (Mimeograph).

However, as predicted by our gender struggle perspective on State power, the issues included in Brazil's new Charter are those that promote *gender role equity*, protect women's maternal role, and do not seriously disrupt existing relations of production and reproduction. Constitutional provisions that promoted *gender role change*[47] or threatened to alter gender power relations or disrupt capital accumulation were excluded from the final Draft Charter, due largely to concerted, well-financed opposition from powerful capitalist, church, and traditionalist lobbies.

Two issues that came before the Constituent Assembly illustrate the limits of gender reforms promoted by dependent capitalist, patriarchal States: proposals for extending maternity and paternity leaves and decriminalizing abortion proved especially controversial, even as formal "equality" before the law was widely acceptable to all but the most reactionary of the Constituents. The new right-wing Christian and capitalist lobbies established in Brasília during 1987 and 1988 mounted formidable campaigns against these and other radical, feminist-inspired reforms.

The extension of maternity leave from 90 to 120 days, argued business and industrial lobbyists, would be unbearably costly for the Ministry of Social Welfare, forcing costs onto debt-ridden Brazilian industry and commerce. The Ministry estimated that the extension would cost the Brazilian State an additional Cz $10.7 billion per year (approximately U.S. $100 million).[48] As soon as the Assembly began debates concerning maternity leave business associations, including the all-powerful Federation of Industrialists of the State of São Paulo (*Federação de Industriais do Estado de São Paulo* or FIESP), threatened to dismiss female employees rather than bear the added costs of the proposed reform.[49]

A proposal to grant an eight-day paid paternity leave, introduced by PFL deputy Alceni Guerra, was judged even more preposterous. The mere suggestion that business should pay for men to be with mother and infant after childbirth, a cost estimated by business lobbies to far exceed the costs of paid maternity leave (Minister Archer set the costs at Cz $49.2 billion or close to U.S. $500 million), and that men should be coresponsible for child care for even this limited amount of time was deemed ludicrous by most members of the Assembly. In fact, Guerra's proposal became the favorite joke of conservative legislators and pundits, frequently cited as one of the prime examples of the "excesses" of the "leftist-controlled" Constituent Assembly.[50]

Brazil's acute economic crisis, fueled by the debt, of course, constrained the ability of either industrialists or the State to extend social benefits to

---

[47] Joyce Gelb and Marian Lief Palley, *Women and Public Policies* (Princeton, N.J.: Princeton University Press, 1982), p. 7.

[48] *Veja*, August 3, 1988.

[49] *O Globo*, March 27, 1988.

[50] See "Luta pela Razão," *Veja*, June 22, 1988.

women workers, or others excluded from the fruits of authoritarianism's version of economic development. From a feminist perspective, however, the cost-efficiency arguments advanced by industrialists were only tenable because women already performed the essential tasks of reproducing the labor force, tasks neither private capital or the State can assume without a radical restructuring of class and gender power relations. Moreover, such arguments are viewed as legitimate in a society where foreign and domestic investors and capitalist development in general have relied on the sexual division of labor and the maintenance of lower-than-low female wages.

Ultimately, a clause specifying a 120-day maternity leave and one establishing the right to paternity leave (for a time period to be specified by law) were included in the final constitutional text. Their inclusion is attributable to the countermobilization and lobbying efforts of union women and the CNDM. In the midst of the Constituent Assembly's heated discussions of labor and social welfare provisions, some São Paulo women's groups and female trade unionists, supported by the CNDM, staged a protest outside FIESP headquarters demanding the inclusion and enforcement of this constitutional provision and denouncing the dismissal of women workers from industrial jobs in anticipation of the reform. The CNDM sent telegrams to thousands of women's groups around the country, urging them to hold similar protests at business and industrial associations throughout Brazil as the constitutional debates on workers' rights were being held in Brasília. Significantly, the Quercia-appointed São Paulo Council on Women's Condition refused to support the movement's militant action, choosing instead to meet with FIESP's president, Mario Amato, behind closed doors, as several hundred working women protesting outside demanded an audience with FIESP leadership.

As the final round of voting on the draft consitution began in Brasília, the CNDM's constitutional commission continued to coordinate movement pressure tactics. Assembly members were met at the main entrance to the Chambers by a CNDM-initiated sit-in, for example. The CNDM's Commission on Women's Work vowed to continue the sit-in until the maternity and paternity leave clauses were voted into the new Constitution.[51] The combined efforts of the CNDM and the movement, then, mobilizing gender-conscious pressure both within and outside the State, succeeded in defeating the usually invincible capitalist lobbies.

The pro-life lobbies, formed in early 1987 and sponsored by traditionalist sectors of the CNBB and the newly influential Brazilian Evangelical movement, in contrast, proved unshakable. The church and the Christian Right packed discussions of family planning, family law, and divorce at the Consti-

[51] Interviews with Nilce Gomes, staff member of the CNDM and co-coordinator of the Council's *Projeto Constituinte*, and Vera Lucia Soares and Sueli Carneiro, also of the CNDM staff, Brasília, June 28, 1988.

254 · Chapter Ten

tutional Subcommission on the Family in early 1987, arguing that feminist-inspired reforms were immoral and threatened the Brazilian family. Zealous pro-life, pro-family lobbyists stalked the halls of Congress throughout the constitutional debates, often engaging in bitter verbal bouts with the CNDM and other progressive lobbyists.

A radical popular amendment[52] on women's health, promoted by *União de Mulheres de São Paulo*, *Coletivo Feminista Sexualidade e Saúde*, and *Grupo de Saúde Nós Mulheres de Rio*, who together gathered 33,338 signatures, called for women's absolute reproductive freedom and "women's right to conceive, avoid conception, or interrupt an unwanted pregnancy up to 90 days after conception."[53] In an impassioned speech to the Constituent Assembly, Maria Amelia Telles de Almeida summarized a long-standing feminist position on reproductive choice—that "we believe that it is not enough to defend life, it is necessary to defend the quality of life."[54]

When, at the urging of feminist constituents, the PT's José Genoino and the PMDB's Cristina Tavares also introduced amendments calling for the decriminalization of abortion, the "otherwise" progressive Catholic church and the evangelicals launched a full-scale frontal attack on reproductive choice. Pro-life protesters held prayer vigils in front of the National Congress. Conservatives in the CNBB added a "dignity of life" provision in a church-sponsored popular amendment that also included far-reaching, progressive, urban and agrarian reforms. And evangelicals resorted to time-honored scare tactics, accusing the Assembly of launching an "assault on the family." Finally, the evangelical bloc in the Assembly introduced an amendment prohibiting abortion even in cases involving rape, incest, or threats to the mother's life, exceptions then allowed by the Brazilian penal code.

These conservative lobbies overwhelmed the efforts of both the CNDM and autonomous women's groups to include more far-reaching abortion reforms in the new Constitution. In a strategic move to prevent a retrogressive develop-

[52] Due to effective pressures from popular movement lobbies and the progressive church, the internal regiment of the Constituent Assembly allowed for popular participation at various phases of the drafting of the constitution. During the early stages, representatives of social movement organizations could testify before any three of the twenty-four Constitutional subcommissions established to prepare drafts of the various sections of the document. After those subcommission drafts were submitted and before the Systematization Commission produced an overall first Draft, any three organizations could sponsor "popular amendments," if they collected at least 30,000 signatures from registered Brazilian voters. One hundred twenty-two popular amendments, signed by 12,277,423 Brazilian citizens, or over 20 percent of the total Brazilian electorate, came before the Assembly in this fashion. Assembleia Nacional Constituinte, Comissão de Sistematização, *Emendas Populares*, vol. 1 (Brasília: Centro Gráfico do Senado Federal, 1987), p. 9. This is especially remarkable as signatures had to be collected in a six-week period and each registered voter could only sign a total of three amendments.

[53] Assembleia Nacional Constituinte, *Emendas Populares*, vol. 2 (Brasília: Centro Gráfico do Senado Federal, 1987), p. 64.

[54] *Jornal Mulher*, official publication of the CECF 2, no. 3 (October 1987).

ment in abortion law, the CNDM and the feminist health movement in the end agreed to withdraw the decriminalization proposal if the "pro-life" amendment was also rescinded.

Other autonomous women's organizations presented popular amendments to the Constituent Assembly. *Rede Mulher* launched its own campaign for the inclusion of "Women's Rights" in the Constitution in December 1985 and over seven hundred grassroots women's groups partook in the elaboration of an amendment, signed by 47,000 people. The amendment, also sponsored by *Serviço de Informação da Mulher* (Women's Information Service) of Matto Grosso do Sul and *SOS-Corpo* of Pernambuco, reiterated most of the CNDM's proposals, though it did not call for the decriminalization of abortion.

But unlike other social movement organizations, the various currents of the women's movement did not establish independent lobbies in Brasília. Predictably, the well-staffed "popular lobbies," supported by left-wing parties and the church, failed to include key women's movement demands on their legislative agendas.

The movement's failure to engage in independent pressure-group activities vis-à-vis the Constituent Assembly is in part attributable to the fact that the CNDM's constitutional commission, claiming to represent the movement, preempted an autonomous feminist lobby; but activists also, in effect, abdicated to the Council, leaving the CNDM, an organ of the State, exclusively in charge of pursuing gender interests in the legislative arena. This preemption-abdication dynamic provides further evidence of how the new institutional women's spaces confounded feminist political practice.

FUTURE PROSPECTS FOR THE BRAZILIAN WOMEN'S MOVEMENT

In spite of the apparent strength of new right-wing movements in defense of "family, God, and private property," the future for the Brazilian women's movement and gender policies does not seem as grim as some historic feminists and movement scholars assert. As of late 1988, the movements' mobilizational initiatives had succeeded in countering the Right's antifeminist offensive. The implementation of important policies and programs, such as the women's health program, were stalled, but feminist pressure within and outside the State had at least prevented further setbacks in the realms of labor legislation and reproductive rights.

Popular feminism and Black feminism were injecting a new vitality into the movement and expanding the scope of gender struggle. The transformative impact of these new feminist currents, however, could be mitigated by the influence of church, the antifeminist Left and Right, or by manipulative parties or governments unless new and historic socialist-feminist activists return to the grassroots and continue publicly to articulate a radical critique of gender power relations. This might be the only way of countering ever-stronger antifeminist initiatives and preventing political manipulation. In this sense, the retreat of some historic feminists into "cultural feminism," the academy or the arts, becomes a kind of self-fulfilling prophecy, a political posture that could have disastrous long-term consequences for the future course of Brazilian gender politics.

In 1988 some feminist voices were now more legitimate, where they were once ridiculed (e.g., in academia and in parties of the Left); but radical feminist voices were increasingly marginalized or silenced as more moderate feminist claims were absorbed by the political mainstream. Some of the basic political claims of the women's movement had been incorporated by the Brazilian State. But many key struggles essential to the eradication of gender inequality will require long-term mobilization and relentless ideological critiques of prevailing sexist social and political assumptions. Only such critiques can ensure that State concessions to women's political claims are not turned into new forms of State control that would ultimately serve the interests of the pact of patriarchal, racist, capitalist domination represented in the State.

In the late 1980s, autonomous social movement organizations were marginalized from decision-making arenas as bourgeois- and male-dominant party politics and formal interest group politics took precedence over cross-class, movement-oriented politics. Though some of the new women's Councils unquestionably secured a number of progressive changes in the status of Brazilian women, women's movement organizations also sometimes were mobilized to advance the larger, partisan goals of the incumbent administration, as we saw above in the case of São Paulo. Many women's movement activists in fact "shed their utopianism" to act like "pressure groups."[55] But the vitality of a radical or utopian, grassroots-based, autonomous women's movement in Brazil during the late 1970s and early 1980s was a crucial ingredient of the Brazilian feminist success story. The decline or disappearance of such gender-conscious political pressure from civil society could threaten further feminist advances. The future success of Brazilian feminism will not only depend on continued collaboration between feminine and feminist groups, but also on effective collaboration between women working for gender-specific social change within *and* outside the State and the party system. The preceding analysis suggests that as the State incorporates or co-opts the political banners of women's movements, groups must develop new political strategies and tactics, a flexible political praxis, or be swallowed up or absorbed by status quo politics.

As to the Councils themselves, their structural position within this still male-dominant, increasingly conservative protodemocratic regime remains precarious at best. A further shift to the political Right by the Sarney govern-

---

[55] Jane S. Jaquette "Introduction," in *The Women's Movement in Latin America: Feminism and the Transition to Democracy*, ed. Jane S. Jaquette (Boston: Unwin Hyman, 1989), passim.

ment's successors could compromise the National Council's effectiveness, especially if feminist councillors continue to be replaced by conservative female party activists or if appointments are doled out in keeping with age-old patterns of patronage politics.

As this book goes to press, Brazilian democracy and the future of women's struggles are at a critical crossroads. Emerging from a transition process tightly controlled and monitored by the military, the postauthoritarian regime installed in 1985 has been a profound disillussionment to Brazil's progressive forces. As we have seen, the first civilian administration in twenty-one years was forged by military-elite pacts and dominated by the Center-Right. Indeed, the Sarney govenment's social and economic policies and institutional parameters differed little from those of its military authoritarian predecessors. By late 1987, conservative civilian forces and their military allies appeared to have established an unshakable hegemony over the process of democratic consolidation.

But Center-Right hegemony began to erode in late 1988. First, thanks to the relentless efforts of Center-Left parties and social movement organizations, the new Brazilian Constitution, promulgated in September 1988, contains some progressive social reforms and provides for increased popular participation in institutional politics. Second, to the bewilderment of many, including the victors, the Leftist Workers' Party (PT), the Center-Left Brazilian Social Democratic Party (PSDB), and the Left-populist Democratic Labor Party (PDT) swept the November 1988 municipal elections, winning in several key industrial areas and state capitals, mostly in the Southeast.

Given the PT's origins in the "new trade unionism" of the 1970s and its close links to most of Brazil's new social movements, including significant sectors of the feminist and feminine movements, the electoral success of progressive parties, at least at the local level, might again occasion a shift in the political opportunity space available to movement groups. In São Paulo, PT Mayor Luiza Erundina de Souza, a long-time activist in urban struggles and two-term municipal councilwoman who won a tight race against conservative PDS candidate and former São Paulo governor Paulo Maluf, vowed to increase popular participation in the municipal administration.

Backed by a "São Paulo Pro-Erundina Women's Committee" and some popular feminist groups, Erundina closed Quadros's "ghost" municipal Council on the Status of Women and, at the urging of feminists in the PT, appointed a seven-woman (5 PT activists and 2 PCdoB militants) commission to develop a plan for an alternative administrative instance to monitor gender policy. In October 1989, a *Coordenadoria Especial da Mulher* (Special Coordination for Women) was inaugurated. Unlike the PMDB-designed Councils, this "women's space" within the municipal government did not purport to be a "representative" instance for civil society. Rather, it was to be made up of a paid professional staff that would respond to movement policy initiatives and make policy recommendations to relevant municipal departments. Whether such an alternative arrangement will resolve tensions that have characterized the often tortured relationship between the movements and previous "women's institutions" remains to be seen. Erundina's administration has little political leverage as opposition parties control the municipal legislature; and many in the movement have long questioned the depth of her commitment to feminist issues.

The would-be hegemony of the Right also appeared to be on the decline at the federal level. Indeed, the Left emerged as a powerful political force in the 1989 Brazilian presidential elections as well. Early in the 1989 race for the presidency, the PT's Luís Inácio "Lula" da Silva and the PDT's Leonel Brizola surfaced as a front-runners in a field of over twenty candidates. Demoralized and delegitimized by the policy failings of their elite-orchestrated "democracy," the Center-Right and Right were unable to produce a viable candidate from within a political class tainted by participation in the "ancien régime" and its inept New Republic offspring, the Sarney administration. Instead, Center-Right forces first fabricated and then lined up behind the candidacy of Fernando Collor de Melo, a young, relatively obscure, conservative governor from the northeastern state of Alagoas who rose precipitously in the polls after midyear. Collor's momentum took a nosedive in the final weeks of the campaign, however, and in the end, he secured only 28.14 percent of votes cast in the first round of voting. The Left surged again during October and November. Lula captured second place (with 16.08 percent of the vote), narrowly edging out Brizola (who tallied 15.74 percent of the vote) and setting the stage for a dramatic second round face-off between the Left and the Right, between a "new" project for democratizing Brazilian democracy and the "old" project of consolidating a restricted one.

Most candidates and parties again included the now customary appeals to women in their campaign materials. But the feminist campaign to legalize abortion, a major focus of mobilization in the politically heterogeneous movement in 1989, also succeeded in pushing candidates to position themselves on this controversial issue. Collor and other right-wing candidates opposed legalization or even decriminalization. Moreover, Collor's platform contained few concrete programmatic items concerning women's equality.

The PSDB and the PDT, at the behest of feminists active in the parties, endorsed the idea of holding a national plebiscite on the abortion issue. The PT national women's commission also persuaded the party to adopt a slightly more liberal if still ambivalent stand on the question of abortion, a major accomplishment given the strong influence of the Catholic Left within the PT. The party officially proclaimed that "the government should launch initiatives for the establishment of legislation that broadens the right to interrupt an unwanted pregnancy and for the implementation of measures that radically reduce maternal mortality caused by the deficiency of health care during pregnancy, childbirth and abortion.''[56] In 1989 the PT also committed itself to programmatic action in five areas affecting women's status—women's work, women's health and reproductive rights, violence against women, education, and the creation of a Ministry or Special Secretariat on the Status of Women at the federal level.

Though Collor narrowly captured the presidency (with 53 percent of the valid votes), Lula's *Frente Brasil Popular* (or FBP, an electoral coalition of the PT, the Communist Party of Brazil or PCdoB, and the Brazilian Socialist Party or PSB) won the support of other Left and Center-Left parties (including the PSDB) and garnered an impressive 47 percent of the valid votes. If the PT and other parties of the Left and Center-Left gain a greater foothold in the Congress in the elections of 1990 or if the PT emerges victorious in the presidential race of 1994, women's rights advocates might again find a more hospitable political climate in which to advance their strategic claims at the federal level. However, as I have argued above, there is little reason to presume that a leftist national government would automatically be more sympathetic or responsive to gender-specific political demands. First, the structural obstacles to the incorporation of women and strategic gender issues in a dependent, patriarchal State and male-dominant party system, discussed throughout this book, would very likely remain in place. Second, the PT's responsiveness to women's issues has always been conditioned by the pressures that feminists brought to bear on the party. If the party's women's commission were to be marginalized from policy formulation and implementation in a PT-led federal administration, or if the Christian Left were to gain a hegemonic position within such an administration, then it seems unlikely that progress in the realm of gender equality would be anything but incremental.

Nonetheless, given the virtual absence of feminist activists and feminist-inspired issues in the Collor campaign, gender policy under a Left-led federal government would undoubtedly be far more progressive than it is likely to be in the next four years. At the time of this writing, even the future of the CNDM itself is in question. During the campaign, Collor vowed to trim down the federal government bureaucracy and eliminate several ministries. The CNDM could well be among the first administrative organs deemed ''extraneous'' by the ''anti–big government,'' conservative president.

[56] Comissão Estadual de Mulheres do PT, Directorio Regional São Paulo, ''Agora, eu sou uma estrela . . . ,'' campaign pamphlet, September 1989.

CHAPTER ELEVEN

Conclusion: En*gender*ing Political Change

The dynamic realignment of social forces and the oscillating political forms of Brazilian authoritarianism in transition has afforded a unique opportunity to unravel the complex relationship between normative, structural, and institutional change and transformations in women's consciousness, gender politics, and policy. I therefore conclude with some reflections on how these Brazilian findings might contribute to further comparative research in the fields of Latin American and gender politics.

THE RISE OF WOMEN'S MOVEMENTS IN AUTHORITARIAN REGIMES

The Brazilian regime's State capitalist foundational project had profound implications for gender, as well as class and race, relations and their political articulation in Brazilian society. Many State policies have gender-specific *consequences*, even when seemingly lacking in gender-specific *content*. Social scientists too often overlook this "hidden," gender-related dimension of political change. They look instead for the presence or absence of "women in politics" or, at best, examine only those aspects of politics or policy that seem to bear directly on women's status (e.g., equal pay legislation or women in development policy).

My analysis of the gender-specific effects of the Brazilian regime's social and economic policies, for example, partially explained the apparent contradiction in the gender politics of authoritarianism in transition. While the official discourse of Brazil's military rulers extolled the virtues of the family and traditional womanhood, the regressive economic policies of the new regime destroyed working-class families' survival strategies and thrust millions of women into the work force, also often propelling them to join community struggles. The massive growth and technocratization of the Brazilian State and the rapid expansion of higher education brought unprecedented numbers of white, middle-class women into male-dominated professions, engendering new contradictions in women's roles. Repressive social and political policies sparked widespread opposition to the regime; women of all social classes defied their historical exclusion from things political and joined the opposition in massive numbers. The regime's own policies, I have shown, heightened the contradictions in women's lives and indirectly helped spark women's consciousness. My analysis of the Brazilian military's foundational project, then, suggests the need for *gender-sensitive macrostructural analyses* of regime change and its implications for women of different social classes.

If we place gender at the center of our macrostructural theoretical frameworks, we might gain new insights into how and why women's movements and gender policies have or have not developed in other Latin American regimes. The State capitalist foundational project of the Peruvian military regime (1968–1980), for example, with its emphasis on developing human resources and its top-down mobilization of the previously excluded, also seems to have generated structural conditions propitious for the development of sizable feminist and feminine movements by the mid-1970s.[1] Indeed, the numerically strongest and politically most effective women's movements in contemporary Latin America can be found in Brazil, Peru, and Mexico, where incumbents have vigorously pursued State capitalist development strategies that brought women into education, production, and politics as never before, thereby generating new contradictions in women's social, economic, and political roles.

Exclusionary authoritarian regimes with neoliberal, antistatist foundational projects appear to have been less conducive to the emergence of gender-conscious movements. Leaving aside for the moment the repressive political context that invariably accompanied neoliberal models, the "deindustrialization" and dismal educational policies of Argentine and Uruguayan military governments, for example, might in themselves account in part for the relatively weaker and numerically smaller feminist movements found in those countries today.[2]

[1] See especially Maruja Barrig, "The Difficult Equilibrium between Bread and Roses: Women's Organizations and the Transition from Dictatorship to Democracy in Peru," in *The Women's Movement in Latin America: Feminism and the Transition to Democracy*, ed. Jane S. Jaquette (Boston: Unwin Hyman, 1989). See also Amy Conger Lind, "Development As If Women Mattered: The Formation of an Autonomous Women's Movement in Peru" (B.A. thesis, University of California at Santa Cruz, 1988); Virginia Vargas, "Movimiento Feminista en el Peru: Balance y Perspectivas," in *Década de la Mujer: Conversatorio sobre Nairobi 1985* (Lima: Centro Flora Tristan, 1985) and her "El Aporte de la Rebeldia de Las Mujeres," in *Jornadas Feministas: Feminismo y Sectores Populares em América Latina*, ed. Coordinación de Grupos Organizadores de las Jornadas Feministas (Mexico, D.F.: Ed. Electrocomp, 1987); J. Anderson Velasco, "The U.N. Decade for Women in Peru," *Women's Studies International Forum* 8, no. 2 (1985): 107–9; and Carol Andreas, *When Women Rebel: The Rise of Popular Feminism in Peru* (Westport, Conn.: Lawrence Hill, 1985).

[2] On Uruguay, see Carina Perelli, "Putting Conservatism to Good Use: Women and Unorthodox Politics in Uruguay, from Breakdown to Transition," in *The Women's Movement in Latin America*, ed. Jane S. Jaquette; Silvia Rodriguez Villamil and Graciela Sapriza, "Mulher e Estado no Uruguay do Seculo XX," *Revista das Ciências Sociais* 1, no. 2 (1987): 209–19; Carmen Tornaria, "Women's Involvement in the Democratic Process in Uruguay," in *The Latin American Women's Movement: Reflections and Actions*, ed. ISIS International Women's Information and Communication Service (Rome: ISIS International, 1986); and "Uruguay," in *Jornadas Feministas: Feminismo y Sectores Populares em América Latina*, ed. Coordinación de Grupos Organizadores de las Jornadas Feministas. On Argentina, see Maria del Carmen Feijoó, "El Movi-

But I have also shown that changes in women's status and macrostructural factors do not tell the whole story of the emergence and development of women's movement organizations, especially in authoritarian political contexts. In spite of extraordinarily repressive political conditions and neoliberal economic policies, for example, Chilean women's movements have flourished in recent years.[3] And in Argentina and Uruguay, the Mothers and Grandmothers of the Disappeared and other organized expressions of militant motherhood, though small in number compared to Brazil's massive feminine movement, played important roles in the opposition to military rule.

Turning our attention to the *micropolitical variables* shaping Brazilian gender politics in the 1960s and 1970s helped explain how new organizational contexts and ideological rationales for female political participation were essential for the development of women's movements. I identified four political developments in particular that fueled nascent feminist consciousness and gave rise to popular women's movement organizations. First, the church urged women to participate in community struggles and fostered the creation of mothers' clubs and housewives' associations among the poor. Second, in the aftermath of military defeats, the Brazilian Left took up intensive organizing among the urban popular classes, leading some women militants to work with neighborhood women's groups. The left-wing opposition's underground and exile networks additionally provided an organizational base for the spread of Brazilian feminism. Third, the regime's protracted process of political liberalization increased the political space available to women's organizations. And fourth, the regime allowed women to organize while still actively repressing other sectors of civil society. Viewing women as intrinsically "apolitical," military rulers appear to have believed women's groups posed lesser threats to national security.

These variables may also provide useful guideposts for further comparative reasearch on gender politics in other political systems, especially in military authoritarian regimes. Let us briefly examine the case of Argentina (1976–1983) along these four dimensions. First, the Argentine church was by far the

---

miento de Mujeres," in *Los Nuevos Movimientos Sociales*, ed. Elizabeth Jelin (Buenos Aires: Centro Editor de América Latina, 1985) and her "The Challenge of Constructing Civilian Peace: Women and Democracy in Argentina," in *The Women's Movement in Latin America*, ed. Jane S. Jaquette; and Silvia Chester, "The Women's Movement in Argentina: Balance and Strategies," in *The Latin American Women's Movement*, ed. ISIS International.

[3] On Chilean women's movements, see Patricia M. Chuchryk, "Feminist Anti-Authoritarian Politics: The Role of Women's Organizations in the Chilean Transition to Democracy," in *The Women's Movement in Latin America*, ed. Jane S. Jaquette and her "Subversive Mothers: The Women's Opposition to the Military Regime in Chile," in *Women, Development and the State*, ed. Sue Ellen Charlton, Jane Everett, and Kathleen Staudt (Albany: State Universtiy of New York Press, 1989); and Julieta Kirkwood, *Ser Política en Chile: Las Feministas y los Partidos* (Santiago: Facultad Latinoamericana de Ciencias Sociales, 1986) and her *Feminarios* (Santiago: Ediciones Documentas, 1987).

most conservative in the Southern Cone, playing a minimal role in the opposition to repressive military rule and more often buttressing the regime's foundational project. It did not actively summon women to participate in self-help community struggles nor did it provide an organizational infrastructure for female participation. Second, the Argentine Left was decimated during the *Proceso de Reorganización Nacional*, rather than "merely" defeated as in Brazil. Few organizational networks remained for the articulation of any alternative political projects, including feminism; the Left in general was brutally butchered by the military in its nefarious Dirty War against internal "subversion"; the political networks of exile, however, did bring some women militants into contact with one another and with women's movements in central capitalist nations. And returning exiles contributed to the surge of feminist organizing in Argentina in the early-to-mid 1980s. Third, the rapid pace of Argentina's "transition through regime breakdown"[4] and the preeminence of male-dominant political society rather than civil society in this transition process restricted the political space available for the articulation of women's movements and their claims. Human rights organizations did play a crucial role in the Argentine transition, however, filling the vacuum left by the church and the Left.[5] And "mothers' movements" and women in general were prominent in the human rights struggle. Here, as in Brazil, female consciousness propelled women to the forefront of the opposition to military rule.[6] Lastly, though the Mothers and Grandmothers of the Disappeared were hardly exempted from the horrors of the Dirty War, these groups originally couched their demands in suprapolitical if not apolitical terms. The ideology of motherhood, explicitly enshrined in the political discourse of the Argentine military regime, legitimated the Mothers' and the Grandmothers' actions in the eyes of Argentine society and may have discouraged the State's repressive apparatus from squelching the movement altogether. The variance along the four dimensions identified in our Brazilian case study, then, sheds light on why the Mothers of the Plaza de Mayo became the most visible and politically effective women's group in Argentina and why fewer feminist groups with comparatively little political clout developed during the Argentine transition process.

In the late 1970s and 1980s, Chile, still under the yoke of Pinochet's unre-

---

[4] This concept is developed by Eduardo Viola and Scott Mainwaring, in "Transitions to Democracy: Brazil and Argentina in the 1980s," *Journal of International Affairs* 38, no. 2 (1985): 193–219.

[5] On the important role of human rights organizations and issues in the Argentine transition, see María Sonderéguer, "El Movimiento de Derechos Humanos en la Argentina," in *Los Nuevos Movimientos Sociales*, vol. 2, ed. Elizabeth Jelin; Susana Wappenstein, "Between Mothers and Military Men: The Struggle for Human Rights in Argentina" (B.A. thesis, University of California at Santa Cruz, 1988).

[6] See Marysa Navarro, "The Mothers of the Plaza de Mayo in Argentina," in *Power and Popular Protest: Latin American Social Movements*, ed. Susan Eckstein (Berkeley: University of California Press, 1989).

lentingly repressive rule, witnessed the rise of hundreds of women's groups. Let us briefly consider how gender-sensitive macrostructural and micropolitical analyses might help us understand this seemingly contradictory political development. On a macro level, as in Brazil, the Pinochet regime's economic growth strategy seriously undermined the survival strategies of poor and working-class families, perhaps contributing to women's significant participation in the grassroots opposition. The absolute impoverishment of the popular classes also seems to have been conducive to the rise of militant motherhood. But again, political variables complete the picture.

First, the Chilean church, like Brazil's, has fostered women's involvement in community struggles. The church's organizational infrastructure for women's participation, in this case, complemented a preexisting network of mothers' centers created by the Frei administration in the 1960s. Thus, Chile, unlike Argentina, had a vast organizational network available for women's mobilization; and as in Brazil, that network provided Chilean feminism with a potential mass base. Second, though the Pinochet regime has manipulated many of the *Centros de Madres*, targeting low-income women for mobilization in support of "Fatherland and Liberty" in a manner reminiscent of the Nazi regime,[7] the Chilean Left, in developing new grassroots-based resistance strategies, also has been working actively among women of the popular classes and encouraging the formation of women's groups in the urban periphery. Third, the stalled nature of Chile's struggle for democracy pushed the opposition to fortify its ties to organized civil society. Their efforts to garner new social bases of support in the uphill fight against the dictatorship led parties to sharpen their appeals to women, generating new opportunities for the articulation of women's demands within political society if not within the State. Finally, the Pinochet regime's strategy of selective repression, like Brazil's, seems to have provided women's groups with more leeway to organize—though again Chilean women have hardly been spared from authoritarian human rights abuses.

COMPARATIVE ANALYSES OF GENDER INTERESTS AND THEIR POLITICAL ARTICULATION

My analysis of Brazilian women's movements also provides insights into how gender interests are shaped and articulated in the context of dependent capitalist, patriarchal social formations. I highlighted the evolution of the Brazilian women's movement's gender discourses over time, discourses constantly modified in response to changing vertical and horizontal strategic linkages and transformations in the structure of political opportunities. Central to the

---

[7] For a compelling, detailed account of Pinochet's reactionary gender strategy, see Norbert Lechner and Susana Levy, "Notas sobre la Vida Cotidiana III: El Disciplinamento de la Mujer," Materia de Discusion, no. 57, FLACSO-Santiago de Chile, July 1984.

evolution of Brazilian feminist ideology was the movement's contradictory relationship to the larger political opposition to authoritarian rule. Brazilian feminist ideology and political practice developed out of the progressive and left-wing opposition to the military regime. I have shown that because that opposition was male-dominant and its praxis sexist, feminism also developed in reaction to the progressive opposition's insistence that gender struggle must be subordinated to the class struggle, or to the so-called "general" struggle for a democratic Brazilian society. The politicization of seemingly "apolitical" mothers' clubs was similarly spurred by progressive opposition forces, both secular and religious.

Middle-class Brazilian feminists voiced some demands distinct from those raised by second-wave feminist movements in advanced capitalist nations. And poor and working-class women, driven by female consciousness, joined neighborhood struggles in a relentless battle to confront deepening crises in the domestic political economy of the popular classes. Whereas in the United States and Western Europe, such grassroots movements have seldom forged organic links with predominantly middle-class feminist organizations, in Brazil, feminists embraced the survival struggles of poor and working-class women and joined forces with the militant opposition. Life-style issues and cultural transformation did not feature prominently in Brazilian feminist politics until recent years. Brazil's exclusionary regime and regressive economic development model led women activists of all social classes to argue that the transformation of gender relations was intimately and inextricably linked to the fate of efforts to restructure radically Brazil's political economy.

Brazil's dependent status in the world economy and the centrality of class and race to the distribution of power no doubt account in part for the women's movement's uniform insistence that *general* and *specific* struggles for women's liberation must be waged. However, there has been ongoing disagreement among and within both middle-class and working-class women's movement organizations as to which struggle is most pressing, whether one must take precedence over the other, and how each struggle should be carried forth strategically.

I am suggesting that the formulation and articulation of gender interests does not flow "naturally" from women's class position, race, or ethnicity, nor is it directly derivative of women's insertion into dependent capitalist relations of production and reproduction. If class, race, or dependency are *constitutive* of strategic and practical gender interests, as my data suggest, they *do not determine* how such interests are ideologically framed or politically advanced. Here, the competing class and gender ideologies and discursive practices prevailing at specific historical conjunctures have been shown to be the key to how gender-based claims are couched and to whether, when, where, and how they are channeled into the political system.[8]

---

[8] In her study of contemporary Italian feminism, Judith Adler Hellman similarly stresses the

Neither feminist or feminine movements formulated their political claims in ideological or institutional vacuums. As we have seen, parties of the Left and male practitioners of liberation theology deeply influenced the movements' genderic discourses, impelling these in a predetermined direction. Moreover, the process of defining gender interests, on the one hand, was initially molded and interpellated by the church's new integrationist theological discourse on women and, on the other hand, by the competing political ideologies informing different sectors of the "larger" opposition to military rule. The sexist obstacles encountered by both middle- and working-class women active in the opposition led some to question the ideological precepts of male allies in the church and on the Left; in the late 1970s, heightened exposure to the ideas of the international women's movement and the expansion of other arenas for voicing "general" opposition to military rule combined to lead women of all social classes to formulate new strategic gender claims. The profusion of genderic claims was accompanied by an expansion of the arenas in which gender struggles were waged: from the factories, to the home, to parallel community groups, to the parish, to the legislatures and the courts. Today, multiple currents of the Brazilian women's movement and hundreds of organizations articulate a wide spectrum of genderic claims, from Trotskyist to neoliberal feminism, and women's demands range from demands for running water to demands for the right to abortion.

The manifold tendencies manifest in different women's movement organizations do not derive mechanistically from the class or racial status of their participants. Thus, women's groups in adjacent poor neighborhoods in Saõ Paulo's urban periphery may well espouse completely divergent ideas about women's struggle and advance radically different, and even competing political claims.

These findings should caution us against making blanket assertions about "Latin American women" and "their interests." Yet North American scholars too often accept the claims of a particular group of women as "representative" of the consciousness and political priorities of Latin American or Third World women as a whole; thus the proclamations of women like Domitila de

---

ways that local political environments and urban regimes shape feminist praxis. Through a nuanced and compelling analysis of local variations in feminist discourses, strategies, and tactics in five Italian cities, Hellman shows conclusively that local regimes and political traditions (especially those of the Left) influenced how women's issues were defined, affected the particular political "path" that led women to the movement, determined the class origins of local activists, shaped the political opportunities available to feminists, and impacted women's definitions of movement success. See her *Journeys Among Women: Feminism in Five Italian Cities* (New York: Oxford University Press, 1987). Studies compiled in *The Women's Movements of the United States and Western Europe*, ed. Mary Fainsod Katzenstein and Carol McClurg Mueller (Philadelphia: Temple University Press, 1987) similarly highlight the centrality of a strong Left, the structure of political opportunities, and the nature of the State to movement dynamics and policy success.

Chungara or Rigoberta Menchú, found in the widely read testimonial literature, are frequently uncritically accepted at face value, as "pure, unfiltered"
Latin American working-class women's consciousness.[9]

Feminist scholars and researchers should be sensitive to the ways in which
competing discourses and practices partially filter and redirect the political
articulation of gender interests in Latin America as elsewhere. Feminist activists, in turn, can also learn a valuable lesson from Brazil—the ideological
resources available to women, independent of social class, race, and ethnicity,
are as critical as organizational resources in fueling women's rebellion. In
Brazil today, a wide variety of feminist understandings of social change rival
antifeminist and nonfeminist gender, ethnic,and class ideologies and provide
women of different class and racial backgrounds with new tools for gendered
resistance.

THE POLITICAL REPRESENTATION OF WOMEN'S GENDER INTERESTS

The diversity of gender interests and the vast array of generic claims evident
in Brazil over the past decade also should prompt us to rethink the concepts
informing our analyses of the "political representation of women's interests."
First, how do we define "women's interests" in a way that would make it
possible to advance strategies or envision political structures that would adequately represent those interests politically? As Maxine Molyneux convinc-
ingly argues, "the concept of *women's interests* . . . is . . . a highly contentious one. Because women are positioned within their societies through a
variety of different means—among them class, ethnicity, and gender—the interests which they have as a group are similarly shaped in complex and sometimes conflicting ways. It is therefore difficult, if not impossible, to generalize
about the 'interests of women.' "[10] My analysis of Brazilian women's movements certainly bears out this proposition. We must be more careful in deploying class-, race-, and culture-specific conceptions of gender interests that
might taint our analyses of the "political representation of women."

Second, the Brazilian case suggests that institutional mechanisms designed
and advanced by feminists in order to influence and monitor gender policy *can*
make a difference, enabling some women to attain greater access to State policy-making arenas and thus impact policy outcomes, potentially pushing gen-

[9] See Domitila Barrios de Chungara with Moema Viezzer, *Let Me Speak!: Testimony of Do-
mitila, a Woman of the Bolivian Mines* (New York: Monthly Review Press, 1978); and Rigoberta
Menchú, edited and introduced by Elisabeth Burgos-Debray, *Rigoberta Menchú: An Indian
Woman from Guatemala*, (London: Verso, 1984).

[10] Maxine Molyneux, "Mobilization without Emancipation?" Women's Interests, State, and
Revolution," in *Transitions and Development: Problems of Third World Socialism*, ed. Richard
R. Fagen, Carmen Diana Deere, and José Luis Coraggio (New York: Monthly Review Press;
Berkeley, Calif.: Center for the Study of the Americas, 1986), p. 283.

der policy in a progressive direction. However, the Brazilian experience demonstrates that such ''women's institutions'' are also highly problematic—riddled by contradictions and prone to manipulation by male-dominant politics. How such institutional mechanisms should be structured and who should chart the avenues of access for women of different racial groups and social classes, then, remain open questions.

The solution proposed by some PMDB feminists in São Paulo in the mid-1980s, the creation of government councils on the status of women composed of ''representatives of civil society'' and government functionaries from various ministries, had proven less than satisfactory to many by the late 1980s. The putative representatives of civil society were deemed ''unrepresentative'' by many in the movement. Moreover, as organs of the executive branch, the councils (and the councillors) were subject to the whims of changing local, state, and federal administrations.

Indeed, many of the councils came to resemble other corporatist mechanisms of interest representation so prevalent in Brazil's twentieth-century political history, institutions designed by the State to control and *de*mobilize citizens, like workers, whose claims undermined the State's hegemonic project. The danger, ultimately, is that these new ''women's spaces'' within the post-authoritarian State apparatus—at the national, state, and local levels—might become female political ghettos, controlled from above and occupied by the most powerful, privileged of women, a dependent capitalist version of what Philippe Schmitter has termed ''societal corporatism.''[11] Under a liberal, democratic regime, such a ghetto might preclude those calling for a more radical restructuring of the politics of gender in Brazil from participating in the regime's policy process, while legitimating those women whose demands for gender-specific reforms are in keeping with the priorities of the still bourgeois, and still male-dominant, New Brazilian Republic.

Some might argue that popularly elected women's councils might curb such neocorporatist tendencies. That is, at least at the local level, women's movement groups or independent citizens could present slates of councillors to be elected for fixed terms by neighborhood or municipal constituencies. But two further hurdles would have to be overcome for such an alternative to be viable. First, women seeking to advance their strategic gender interests would have to develop more effective strategies for influencing public opinion and garnering wholehearted electoral support for their cause. Second, for such strategies to be truly efficacious, women's movement activists would have to secure the support of political parties. Yet two further problems then would have to be confronted. As revealed in my discussion of parties and women's movements,

[11] See Philippe C. Schmitter, ''Still the Century of Corporatism?,'' in *The New Corporatism: Social-Political Structures in the Iberian World*, ed. Frederick B. Pike and Thomas Stritch (Notre Dame: University of Notre Dame Press, 1974), pp. 103–5.

Brazilian political parties remain relatively unreceptive to more radical genderic claims, in no small measure because such claims still lack widespread electoral appeal. Thus, for institutional mediation to be effective, it would be imperative for movement activists to simultaneously promote a progressive gender consciousness and seek to develop larger grassroots constituencies and more effectual tactics for persuading parties to embrace their gender-specific agendas for change.

By the late 1980s, some feminist activists in Brazil were arguing that the pretense of institutional representation of women's interests be abandoned altogether. Many again chose to eschew institutionally based strategies and concentrate on grassroots or cultural feminist work. Others proposed the creation of a women's institute or executive department charged not with representing "women's interests" but with collecting data on women's health, education, and so on, and formulating policy recommendations on the basis of such ongoing research.

The Brazilian case demonstrates that the question of how women's diverse interests should be represented politically is theoretically and strategically a tortuous one. Just what would be the optimal structure, content, and form of institutional instances designed to represent women and their claims is a question that merits far greater attention, and far more complex treatment, from feminist activists, political theorists, and political scientists.

APPROACHING THE LATIN AMERICAN STATE: IMPLICATIONS FOR FEMINIST THEORY AND PRACTICE

The discipline of political science fairly recently has turned its attention back to the study of the State. And as Theda Skocpol suggests:

> As we bring the state back in to its proper central place in explanations of social change and politics, we shall be forced to respect the inherent historicity of sociopolitical structures, and we shall necessarily attend to the inescapable intertwinings of national-level developments with changing world historical contexts. We do not need a new or refurbished grand theory of "the State." Rather, we need solidly grounded and analytically sharp understandings of the causal regularities that underlie the histories of states, social structures, and transnational relations in the modern world.[12]

In the field of gender politics, we similarly must redirect our attention—away from "grand" feminist theorizing on the State and micro-level explorations of female political behavior, and toward "solidly grounded and analytically

[12] Theda Skocpol, "Bringing the State Back In: Strategies of Analysis in Current Research," in *Bringing the State Back In*, ed. Peter B. Evans, Dietrich Rueschemeyer, and Theda Skocpol (New York: Cambridge University Press, 1985), p. 28.

sharp understandings'' of the ''causal regularities'' that underlie the continued intractability of institutional political arenas to women and their multifold practical and strategic gender interests. In short, we need more middle-level analyses of the relationship between women and politics.

The existing literature on women and politics has predominantly focused either on the micropolitical characteristics that affect female political participation (such as education, employment, and fertility) or on the macroanalytical dimensions of women's subordination (such as the interdependence of capitalism and patriarchy, the relative autonomy of class domination from male domination, the relationship between the public and the private, and so on). Yet we have few middle-level analyses that examine how macrosystemic variables influence female political behavior or how women's political participation impacts the political system. That is, we have little understanding of how the institutional and organizational contexts within which women's political participation takes place constrain or facilitate the ''representation'' of ''women's interests'' and even fewer studies of how those contexts help to determine gender-specific policy outcomes.[13]

Our inquiries into the field of women and politics must pay more attention to those political conjunctures which, at specific historical moments, seem to have led the State to act in the interests of particular groups of women. We must examine the instances in which gender-based political claims have the greatest chance of being met by political elites and policy makers. For example, in liberal democratic systems, when women's vote becomes electorally significant, the government and political oppositions may be more responsive to gender-specific demands in order to capture the female vote. In mobilizational regimes, gender-specific demands may stand a greater chance of being met if gender-based mobilization is seen as necessary to solidify regime legitimacy or achieve larger developmental goals.

Feminist theory suggests that State institutions and traditional political arenas (such as political parties) directly contribute to the institutionalization and

[13] Several recent anthologies have begun to fill in this theoretical void in our understanding of ''gender and politics.'' See especially Sue Ellen M. Charlton, Jane Everett, and Kathleen Staudt, eds., *Women, the State, and Development* (Albany: State University of New York Press, 1989); Mary Fainsod Katzenstein and Carol McClurg Mueller, eds., *The Women's Movements of the United States and Western Europe*; Haleh Afshar, ed., *Women, State, and Ideology: Studies from Africa and Asia* (Albany: State University of New York Press, 1987); Carmen Diana Deere and Magdalena León, ed., *Rural Women and State Policy: Feminist Perspectives on Latin American Agricultural Development* (Boulder, Colo.: Westview Press, 1987); Bina Agarwal, ed., *Structures of Patriarchy: State, Community, and Household in Modernising Asia* (London: Zed, 1988); Irene Diamond, ed., *Families, Politics, and Public Policy: A Feminist Dialogue on Women and the State* (New York: Longman, 1983); Sonia Kruks, Rayna Rapp, and Marilyn Young, eds., *Promissory Notes: Women in the Transition to Socialism* (New York: Monthly Review Press, 1989); and Kathleen Staudt, ed., *Women, International Development, and Politics: The Bureaucratic Mire* (Philadelphia: Temple University Press, 1990).

maintenance of women's subordinate status within the family, the market, and the State. This has most certainly been the case in authoritarian and totalitarian political systems.[14] But can the political institutions of capitalist patriarchal States become potential arenas for the promotion of gender-based social change in "liberalized" political systems? Must feminists treat the State as both a source of social control in women's lives and a potential arena for political struggle that might transform at least some aspects of women's lives? This critical question represents a major strategic and theoretical hurdle that must be overcome by those concerned with social, economic, and political equality between women and men.

My analysis of gender politics in postauthoritarian Brazil suggests an alternative to current feminist theories about the State and the bureaucracy. U.S. feminist theorists such as Catherine A. MacKinnon and Kathy Ferguson have portrayed the State and the bureaucracy as immutably masculine.[15] Indeed, for some feminists, the State—whether capitalist, socialist, or dependent capitalist—is inevitably "women's worst enemy." In this view, the State is the ultimate mechanism of social control in women's lives, always acting to "empower men and depower women."[16] Other North American feminists, such as Frances Fox Piven and Barbara Ehrenreich, enthusiastically have embraced the State, in particular the Welfare State, as "women's best friend," viewing women's relationship to the State in the post-depression era as essentially an empowering one.[17]

Evidence from Brazil suggests a need for a more complex, less Manichaean perspective on gender and the State. First, our discussion of Brazilian gender politics points to the importance of political *regimes* and political *conjunc-*

[14] See Claudia Koonz, *Mothers in the Fatherland: Women, the Family and Nazi Politics* (New York: St. Martins Press 1987); Renate Bridenthal, Anita Grossman, and Marion Kaplan, eds., *When Biology Became Destiny: Women in Weimar and Nazi Germany* (New York: Monthly Review Press, 1984); Ximena Bunster Burotto, "Watch Out for the Little Nazi Man that All of Us Have Inside: The Mobilization and Demobilization of Women in Militarized Chile," *Women's Studies International Forum* 11, no. 5 (Summer 1988): 485–91. Cynthia Enloe, *Does Khaki Become You? The Militarization of Women's Lives* (Boston, Mass.: South End Press, 1983) and her "Women Textile Workers in the Militarization of Southeast Asia," in *Women, Men and the International Division of Labor*, edited by June Nash and María Patricía Fernandez-Kelly (Albany: State University of New York Press, 1983).

[15] Catherine A. MacKinnon, "Feminism, Marxism, Method, and the State: Toward a Feminist Jurisprudence," *Signs* 8, no. 4 (Summer 1983): 635–58; Kathy Ferguson, *The Feminist Case Against Bureaucracy* (Philadelphia: Temple University Press, 1984).

[16] Wendy Brown, "Prolegamena for a Feminist Theory of the State" (Paper presented at the Annual Meeting of the Northeastern Political Science Association, Boston, Mass. November, 1986), p. 3.

[17] See especially Barbara Ehrenreich and Frances Fox Piven, "Women and the Welfare State," in *Alternatives: Proposals for America from the Democratic Left*, ed. Irving Howe (New York: Pantheon, 1983); Frances Fox Piven, "Women and the State: Ideology, Power, and the Welfare State," *Socialist Review* 14, no. 2 (March/April 1984): 11–19.

tures. State structures and policies that regulate and mediate gender, race, and class relations of power in society are hardly immutable, especially in the Third World. Changes in political regime—in the institutions that structure the relationship between State and society—may open up new opportunities for some women to influence policy formulation and implementation. Clearly, the State, though still bourgeois and male-dominant, has been far "friendlier" to Brazilian women under civilian rule than under military-authoritarianism. The difference for Brazilian feminists is hardly a trivial one.

There are lessons here for feminists in the United States The Reagan-Bush era has represented far more than a simple change in government. The changes in State-society relations under Reagan-Bush have been far more dramatic: institutional mechanisms designed to monitor gender policy have been dismantled; funding for social services has been slashed; State subsidies to community groups and civil rights organizations have fallen precipitously; advances made by women and/or people of color have been rolled back drastically. The consequences for women are by now well-known: rapid increases in the number of women, especially women of color, and their children who live in poverty; the dismantling of social services that alleviated women's domestic burden; the frontal attack on reproductive choice—the list is endless. Surely, the Reagan-Bush "regime" has been far less friendly to women than its welfare state predecessors. Yet North American feminist theorists still tend to portray the State as either transhistorically patriarchal or unwaveringly benevolent. We too could benefit from thinking about political conjunctures and strategizing more flexibly and creatively about when and how to approach the State.

Second, the Brazilian case highlights the fact that *the State is not monolithically masculine* or antifeminist. If we "unpack" the State and examine its multiple institutional and ideological instances,[18] we may find points of access, points where concerted gender-conscious political pressure might make a difference. Even under authoritarian rule in transition, Brazilian feminists secured new *access points* to State policy arenas, as is suggested in my analysis of family-planning and day-care policy developments. This suggests the need for a selective feminist strategy, one that apprehends the full spectrum of gender ideologies represented within a given political regime, identifies points of gendered bureaucratic resistance,[19] and attempts to impact those policy arenas that are most accessible and amenable to feminist influence at a specific political conjuncture.

[18] Feminist political theorist Wendy Brown identifies four dimensions of the masculinist powers of the State in "Finding the Man in the State: A Theoretical Inquiry into the Masculinist Powers of Postindustrial Liberal Capitalist States," July 1989 (Mimeograph).

[19] Kathleen Staudt develops the concept of gendered bureaucratic resistance in "Gender Politics in Bureaucracy: Theoretical Issues in Comparative Perspective," in *Women, International Development, and Politics*.

In the 1990s, we too would do well to approach different instances of the State more selectively. For example, the Reagan-Bush conservative Supreme Court certainly would seem to make litigation strategies far more problematic, and possibly less efficacious, closing off an "access point" to the State that has been critical to advancing the feminist cause over the past two decades. In this light, it seems not only foolhardy but also dangerous to demand that the State, at the present conjuncture, regulate pornography or determine when and which representations of sexuality are immoral, for instance.

Third, the Brazilian experience points to the importance of a flexible, multidimensional feminist strategy—one that organizes gender-conscious political pressure *at the base*, both within and outside the State. When faced with democratizing conjunctures in state and national politics, Brazilian feminists modified and diversified their political strategies accordingly. Some seized the political space made available to women by parties and the post-1983 state governments and promoted innovative changes from within. Others continued organizing at the grassroots level, fostering a critical, organizationally and ideologically autonomous feminist politics, and indirectly legitimating the actions of women active in male-dominant policy arenas. In spite of continuing conflicts among feminists "in" and "out" of "power," this two-pronged strategy proved surprisingly effective.

In sum, the Brazilian case suggests that feminists should neither dismiss the State as the ultimate mechanism of male social control nor embrace it as the ultimate vehicle for gender-based social change. Rather, under different political regimes and at distinct historical conjunctures, the State is potentially a mechanism either for social change or social control in women's lives. An informed feminist political practice should be principally concerned with discerning the difference, seizing available opportunity space and avoiding excessive "institutionalization" or depoliticization of the feminist agenda. An engaged feminist political theory and political science would help chart the path toward change by examining the varied historical and cross-cultural experiences of feminist attempts to influence State policy "in the meantime," while patriarchal practices and assumptions remain embedded in the structures and policies of socialist and capitalist States.

Finally, this analysis of gender politics in Brazil also has important implications for international feminist practice. The Brazilian case attests to the centrality of international variables in shaping national gender policy outcomes, particularly but not exclusively in Third World States. Brazil's gargantuan debt and acute economic crisis tied it more closely than ever to the policy dictates of central capitalist nations and the regulatory institutions they control, sharply constraining the State's ability to implement the feminist-inspired family-planning program, for example. But feminists outside Brazil could work to reverse the bleak prognosis that Brazilian and other Third World women are doomed to bear the brunt of the failed economic development strategies of Third World States. In the past, international feminist solidarity successfully brought pressure to bear on the international development establishment, indirectly pushing Third World States to open up some political space, however minimal, for the articulation of progressive gender discourses and policies. Renewed international feminist efforts to address the gender-specific consequences of the debt crisis and to support the claims of autonomous feminist movements therefore might enhance the prospects that more thoroughgoing reforms in women's status will be implemented in countries such as Brazil.

Select Bibliography

Affonso, Rui, Plínio Sampaio, Jr., and Gilson Schwartz. "Política Econômica e De-mocratização: O Impasse Brasileiro." In *A Democracia no Brasil: Dilemas e Per-spectivas*, edited by Fábio Wanderley Reis and Guillermo O'Donnell. São Paulo: Vértice, 1988.

Aguiar, Neuma. *Mulheres na Força de Trabalho na América Latina: Analises Quali-tativas*. Petrópolis: Vozes, 1984.

Alambert, Zuleika. *O Marxismo e a Questão da Mulher*. São Paulo: Nobel, 1986.

Almeida, Maria Hermínia Tavares de. "O Sindicalismo Brasileiro entre a Conservação e a Mudança." In *Sociedade e Política no Brasil Pós-64*, edited by Bernard Sorj and Maria Hermínia Tavares de Almeida. São Paulo: Brasilense, 1983.

Alvarez, Sonia E. "Contradictions of a Women's Space in a Male-Dominant State: The Political Role of the Commissions on the Status of Women in Postauthoritarian Brazil." In *Women, International Development, and Politics: The Bureaucratic Mire*, edited by Kathleen Staudt. Philadelphia: Temple University Press, 1990.

———. "Politicizing Gender and Engendering Democracy." In *Democratizing Bra-zil: Problems of Transtion and Consolidation*, edited by Alfred Stepan. New York: Oxford University Press, 1989.

———. "Women's Movements and Gender Politics in the Brazilian Transition." In *The Women's Movement in Latin America: Feminism and the Transition to Democ-racy*, edited by Jane S. Jaquette. Boston: Unwin Hyman, 1989.

———. "Women's Participation in the Brazilian 'People's Church': A Critical Ap-praisal." *Feminist Studies* 16, no. 2 (Summer 1990).

Alves, Branca Moreira. *Ideologia & Feminismo: A Luta da Mulher pelo Voto no Brasil*. Petrópolis: Vozes, 1980.

Alves, Branca Moreira, and Jacqueline Pitanguy. *O Que É O Feminismo?* São Paulo: Brasilense, 1981.

Alves, Maria Helena Moreira. "Dilemmas of the Consolidation of Democracy from the Top: A Political Analysis." *Latin American Perspectives* 15, no. 3 (Summer 1988): 47–63.

———. "Grassroots Organizations, Trade Unions, and the Church: A Challenge to Controlled *Abertura* in Brazil." *Latin American Perspectives* 11, no. 1 (1984): 73–102.

———. *State and Opposition in Military Brazil*. Austin: University of Texas Press, 1985.

Andreas, Carol. *When Women Rebel: The Rise of Popular Feminism in Peru*. Westport, Conn.: Lawrence Hill and Co., 1985.

Avelar, Lucia Merces de. "Perfis do Voto Feminino no Brasil, 1982." Paper presented at the XII International Conference of the Latin American Studies Association, Al-buquerque, N.M., April 18–20, 1985.

Azevedo, Maria A. *Mulheres Espancadas: A Violência Denuciada*. São Paulo: Cortez, 1985.

Bacha, Edmar L., and Herbert S. Klein, eds. *Social Change in Brazil, 1945–1985: The Incomplete Transition.* Albuquerque: University of New Mexico Press, 1989.

Balorya, Enrique A., ed. *Comparing New Democracies: Dilemmas of Transition and Consolidation in Mediterranean Europe and the Southern Cone.* Boulder, Colo.: Westview Press, 1987.

Baquero, Marcelo, and Jussara Reis Prá. "Participação Real e Espaço Imaginário: A Mulher e a Democracia na América Latina." *Revista de Ciências Sociais* 1, no. 2 (1987): 191–202.

Barrett, Michele. *Women's Oppression Today: Problems in Marxist Feminist Analysis.* London: Verso, 1980.

Barretta, Silvio R. Duncan, and John Markoff. "Brazil's Abertura: A Transition from What to What?" In *Authoritarians and Democrats: Regime Transitions in Latin America,* edited by James M. Malloy and Mitchell A. Seligson. Pittsburgh: University of Pittsburgh Press, 1987.

Barrig, Maruja. "The Difficult Equilibrium Between Bread and Roses: Women's Organizations and the Transition from Dictatorship to Democracy in Peru." In *The Women's Movement in Latin America: Feminism and the Transition to Democracy,* edited by Jane S. Jaquette. Boston: Unwin Hyman, 1989.

Barros, Roberto. "The Left and Democracy: Recent Debates in Latin America." *Telos* 68 (Summer 1986): 49–70.

Barroso, Carmen. *Mulher, Sociedade e Estado no Brasil.* Brasília: UNICEF; São Paulo: Brasilense, 1982.

Barroso, Carmen, et al. *Homem-Mulher: Crises e Conquistas.* São Paulo: Melhoramentos, 1987.

Berardo, João Batista. *Guerrilhas e Guerrilheiros no Drama da América Latina.* São Paulo: Edições Populares, 1981.

Blachman, Morris J. *Eve in an Adamacracy: Women in Politics in Brazil.* Ibero-American Language and Area Center Occasional Papers, no. 5. New York: New York University, 1973.

———. "Selective Omission and Theoretical Distortion in Studying the Political Activity of Women in Brazil." In *Sex and Class in Latin America,* edited by June Nash and Helen I. Safa. New York: Praeger, 1976.

Blay, Eva Alterman. "Mulheres e Movimentos Sociais Urbanos: Anistia, Custo de Vida, e Creches." *Encontros com a Civilização Brasileira.* "Mulher-Hoje" Special Issue. 1980.

———. "The Political Participation of Women in Brazil: Female Mayors." *Signs: A Journal of Women in Culture and Society* 5, no. 1 (Autumn 1979): 42–59.

Boff, Leonardo. *Igreja: Carisma e Poder: Ensaios de Eclesiología Militante.* Petrópolis: Vozes, 1982.

———. *The Maternal Face of God: The Feminine and Its Religious Expressions.* San Francisco: Harper and Row, 1987.

Boneparth, Ellen, ed. *Women, Power, and Policy.* New York: Pergamon, 1982.

Bookman, Ann, and Sandra Morgen, eds. *Women and the Politics of Empowerment.* Philadelphia: Temple University Press, 1988.

Boris, Eileen, and Peter Bardaglio. "The Transformation of Patriarchy: The Historic

Role of the State." In *Families, Politics, and Public Policies: A Feminist Dialogue on Women and the State*, edited by Irene Diamond. New York: Longman, 1983.

Borja, Jordi. *Movimientos Sociales Urbanos*. Buenos Aires: Ediciones SIAP, 1971.

Boschi, Renato Raul. *A Arte de Associação: Política de Base e Democracia no Brasil*. São Paulo: Vértice; Rio de Janeiro: IUPERJ, 1987.

Boschi, Renato Raul, and Lícia do Prado Valladares. "Movimentos Associativos de Camadas Populares Urbanas: Analise Comparativo de Seis Casos." In *Movimentos Coletivos no Brasil Urbano*, edited by Renato Raul Boschi. Rio de Janeiro: Zahar, 1983.

Bouchier, David. "The Deradicalization of Feminism: Ideology and Utopia in Action." *Sociology* 13, no. 3 (September 1979): 387–402.

———. *The Feminist Challenge: The Movement for Women's Liberation in Britain and the United States*. New York: Shocken, 1984.

Bourque, Susan C. "Gender and the State: Perspectives from Latin America." In *Women, the State, and Development*, edited by Sue Ellen M. Charlton, Jane Everett, and Kathleen Staudt. Albany: State University of New York Press, 1989.

———. "Urban Activists: Paths to Political Consciousness in Peru." In *Women Living Change*, edited by Susan C. Bourque and Donna R. Divine. Philadelphia: Temple University Press, 1985.

Bourque, Susan C., and Donna Robinson Divine, eds. *Women Living Change*. Philadelphia: Temple University Press, 1985.

Bourque, Susan C., and Kay B. Warren. *Women of the Andes: Patriarchy and Social Change in Two Peruvian Towns*. Ann Arbor: University of Michigan Press, 1981.

Brant, Vinícius Caldeira. "Da Resistência aos Movimentos Sociais: A Emergência das Classes Populares em São Paulo." In *São Paulo: O Povo em Movimento*, edited by Paul J. Singer and Vinícius Caldeira Brant. Petrópolis: Vozes; São Paulo: CEBRAP, 1980.

Bridenthal, Renate, Anita Grossman, and Marion Kaplan, eds. *When Biology Became Destiny: Women in Weimar and Nazi Germany*. New York: Monthly Review Press, 1984.

Brito, Angela Neves-Xavier de. "Brazilian Women in Exile: The Quest for Identity." *Latin American Perspectives* 13, no. 2 (Spring 1986): 58–80.

Brown, Wendy. "Finding the Man in the State: A Theoretical Inquiry into the Masculinist Powers of Postindustrial Liberal Capitalist States." July 1989. Mimeograph.

———. "Prolegamena for a Feminist Theory of the State." Paper presented at the Annual Meeting of the Northeastern Political Science Association, Boston, Mass., November 1986.

Bruneau, Thomas C. *The Church in Brazil: The Politics of Religion*. Austin: University of Texas Press, 1982.

Bruschini, Cristina. *Mulher e Trabalho: Uma Avaliação da Década da Mulher*. São Paulo: Nobel and Conselho Estadual da Condição Feminina, 1985.

Bruschini, Maria Cristina Aranha, and Fulvia Rosemberg. "A Mulher e o Trabalho." In *Trabalhadoras do Brasil*, edited by Maria Cristina Aranha Bruschini and Fulvia Rosemberg. São Paulo: Brasilense, 1982.

———, eds. *Trabalhadoras do Brasil*. São Paulo: Brasilense, 1985.

Bruschini, Maria Cristina Aranha, and Fulvia Rosemberg, eds. *Vivências: História, Sexualidade e Imagens Femininas*. São Paulo: Brasilense, 1980.

Bunster-Burotto, Ximena. "Surviving Beyond Fear: Women and Torture in Latin America." In *Women and Change in Latin America*, edited by June Nash and Helen I. Safa. South Hadley, Mass.: Bergin and Garvey, 1986.

———. "Watch Out for the Little Nazi Man That All of Us Have Inside: The Mobilization and Demobilization of Women in Militarized Chile." *Women's Studies International Forum* 11, no. 5 (Summer 1988): 485–91.

Caldeira, Teresa Pires do Rio. "Electoral Struggles in a Neighborhood in the Periphery of São Paulo." *Politics and Society* 15, no. 1 (1986–1987): 43–66.

———. "Imagens do Poder e da Sociedade (O Mundo Cotidiano dos Moradores da Periferia)." Master's thesis, University of São Paulo, 1982.

———. "Mujeres, Cotidianidad y Política." In *Ciudadanía e Identidad: Las Mujeres en los Movimientos Sociales Latinoamericanos*, edited by Elizabeth Jelin. Geneva: UNRISD, 1987.

———. *A Política dos Outros: O Cotidiano dos Moradores da Periferia e o Que Pensam do Poder e dos Poderosos*. São Paulo: Brasilense, 1984.

Calderón, Fernando, ed. *Los Movimientos Sociales ante la Crisis*. Buenos Aires: Universidad de las Naciones Unidas, CLACSO, IISUNAM, 1986.

Calderón, Fernando, and Mario R. dos Santos. "Movimientos Sociales y Gestación de Cultura Política, Puntos de Interrogación." In *Cultura Política y Democratización*, edited by Norbert Lechner. Buenos Aires: CLACSO, FLACSO, and ICI, 1987.

Calderón, Fernando, and Elizabeth Jelin. "Classes Sociais e Movimentos Sociais na América Latina: Perspectivas e Realidades." *Revista Brasileira das Ciências Sociais* 5, no. 2 (October 1987): 67–85.

Cammack, Paul. "Democratization: A Review of the Issues." *Bulletin for Latin American Research* 4, no. 2 (1985): 39–46.

———. "The Political Economy of Contemporary Military Regimes in Latin America: From Bureaucratic-Authoritarianism to Restructuring." In *Generals in Retreat: The Crises of Military Rule in Latin America*, edited by Philip O'Brien and Paul Cammack. Manchester: Manchester University Press, 1985.

———. "Resurgent Democracy: Threat and Promise." *New Left Review* 157 (1986): 121–28.

Cardoso, Fernando Henrique. "Associated-Dependent Development and Democratic Theory." In *Democratizing Brazil: Dilemmas of Transition and Consolidation*, edited by Alfred Stepan. New York: Oxford University Press, 1989.

———. "On the Characterization of Authoritarian Regimes in Latin America." In *The New Authoritarianism in Latin America*, edited by David Collier. Princeton, N.J.: Princeton University Press, 1979.

———. "La Democracia en América Latina." *Punto de Vista* 23 (April 1985): 1–6.

———. "Os Partidos Políticos e a Participação Popular." In *Os Partidos Políticos no Brasil*, vol. 2, edited by David Fleischer. Brasília: Editora Universidade de Brasília, 1981.

Cardoso, Irede, and José Eduardo M. C. Cardozo. *O Direito da Mulher na Nova Constituição*. São Paulo: Global, 1986.

Cardoso, Ruth Corrêa Leite. "Isso É Política? Dilemas da Participação Popular entre o Moderno e o Pós-Moderno." *Novos Estudos do CEBRAP*, no. 20 (March 1988): 74–80.

———. "Em Matéria de Eleições nem Tudo que Reluz da Ouro." In *A Periferia de São Paulo e o Contexto da Ação Política*. Preliminary Research Report, CEBRAP, São Paulo, 1983. Mimeograph.

———. "Os Movimentos Populares no Contexto da Consolidação da Democracia." In *A Democracia no Brasil: Dilemas e Perspectivas*, edited by Fábio Wanderley Reis and Guillermo O'Donnell. São Paulo: Vértice, 1988.

———. "Os Movimentos Sociais na América Latina." *Revista Brasileira de Ciências Sociais*, 2, no. 5 (October 1987): 27–37.

———. "Movimentos Sociais Urbanos: Balanço Crítico." In *Sociedade e Política no Brasil Pós-64*, edited by Bernard Sorj and Maria Hermínia Tavares de Almeida. São Paulo: Brasilense, 1983.

———. "As Mulheres e a Democracia." *Revista de Ciências Sociais* 1, no. 2 (1987): 287–304.

Carlson, Marifran. ¡*Feminismo! The Woman's Movement in Argentina from Its Beginnings to Eva Perón*. Chicago: Academy Chicago Publishers, 1988.

Carneiro, Sueli, and Thereza Santos. *Mulher Negra*. São Paulo: Nobel and Conselho Estadual da Condição Feminina, 1985.

Carnoy, Martin. *The State and Political Theory*. Princeton, N.J.: Princeton University Press, 1984.

Carvalho, Nanci Valadares de, ed. *A Condição Feminina*. São Paulo: Vértice, 1988.

Castells, Manuel. *Cidade, Democracia e Socialismo*. Rio de Janeiro: Paz e Terra, 1980.

———. *The City and the Grassroots*. Berkeley: University of California Press, 1983.

———. *Movimientos Sociales Urbanos*. Madrid: Siglo XXI de España, 1974.

———. "Urban Social Movements and the Struggle for Democracy: The Citizens' Movement in Madrid." *International Journal of Urban and Regional Research* 2, no. 1 (March 1978): 133–46.

Cava, Ralph Della. "The People's Church, the Vatican, and Abertura." In *Democratizing Brazil: Problems of Transition and Democratization*, edited by Alfred Stepan. New York: Oxford University Press, 1989.

Cavalcanti, Pedro Celso Uchôa, and Jovelino Ramos, eds. *Memórias do Exílio, Brasil 1964–19??* São Paulo: Ed. Livasmento, 1978.

Chafetz, Janet Saltzman, and Anthony Gary Dworkin. *Female Revolt: Women's Movements in World and Historical Perspective*. Totowa, N.J.: Rowman and Allanheld, 1986.

Chalmers, Douglas A. "The Politicized State in Latin America." In *Authoritarianism and Corporatism in Latin America*, edited by James A. Malloy. Pittsburgh, Penn.: University of Pittsburgh Press, 1977.

Chaney, Elsa M. *Supermadre: Women in Politics in Latin America*. Austin: University of Texas Press, 1979.

Charlton, Sue Ellen M., Jane Everett, and Kathleen Staudt, eds. *Women, the State, and Development*. Albany: State University of New York Press, 1989.

Chester, Silvia. "The Women's Movement in Argentina: Balance and Strategies." In

The Latin American Women's Movement, edited by ISIS International. Santiago, Chile: ISIS, 1985.

Chinchilla, Norma. "Women in Revolutionary Movements: The Case of Nicaragua." In *Revolution in Central America*, edited by Stanford Central American Action Network. Boulder, Colo.: Westview Press, 1982.

Chiriac, Jany, and Solange Padilha. "Características e Limites das Organizações de Base Femininas." In *Trabalhadoras do Brasil*, edited by Maria Cristina Aranha Bruschini and Fúlvia Rosemberg. São Paulo: Brasilense, 1982.

Chuchryk, Patricia. "Feminist Anti-Authoritarian Politics: The Role of Women's Organizations in the Chilean Transition to Democracy." In *The Women's Movement in Latin America: Feminism and the Transition to Democracy*, edited by Jane S. Jaquette. Boston: Unwin Hyman, 1989.

————. "Protest, Politics and Personal Life: The Emergence of Feminism in a Military Dictatorship, Chile 1973–1983." Ph.D. diss., York University, 1984.

————. "Subversive Mothers: The Women's Opposition to the Military Regime in Chile." In *Women, the State, and Development*, edited by Sue Ellen M. Charlton, Jane Everett, and Kathleen Staudt. Albany: State University of New York Press, 1989.

Cohen, Jean. "Strategy or Identity: New Theoretical Paradigms and Contemporary Social Movements." *Social Research* 52, no. 4 (Winter 1985): 663–716.

Coletivo Feminista Sexualidade e Saúde. "Brasil: Mujeres y Salud." In *La Salud de las Mujeres: La Experiencia de Brasil, Reflexiones y Acciones Internacionales*, edited by ISIS International. Santiago, Chile: ISIS, 1985.

Collier, David, ed. *The New Authoritarianism in Latin America*. Princeton, N.J.: Princeton University Press, 1979.

Coordinación de Grupos Organizadores de las Jornadas Feministas, ed. *Jornadas Feministas: Feminismo y Sectores Populares en América Latina*. Mexico, D.F.: Ed. Electrocomp, 1987.

Costa, Albertina Gordo de Oliveira. *Política Governamental e a Mulher*. São Paulo: Nobel and Conselho Estadual da Condição Feminina, 1985.

Costa, Albertina Gordo de Oliveira, et al., eds. *Memórias das Mulheres do Exílio*. Rio de Janeiro: Paz e Terra, 1980.

Crummett, María de los Angeles. "El Poder Feminino: The Mobilization of Women against Socialism in Chile." *Latin American Perspectives* 4, no. 4 (Fall 1977): 103–13.

Deere, Carmen Diana, and Magdalena León, eds. *Rural Women and State Policy: Feminist Perspectives on Latin American Agricultural Development*. Boulder, Colo.: Westview Press, 1987.

Deighton, Jane, et al. *Sweet Ramparts: Women in Revolutionary Nicaragua*. London: War on Want and the Nicaragua Solidarity Campaign, 1982.

Diamond, Irene, ed. *Families, Politics and Public Policy: A Feminist Dialogue on Women and the State*. New York: Longman, 1983.

Diamond, Irene, and Nancy Hartsock. "Comment." *American Political Science Review* 75, no. 3 (September 1981): 717–21.

Diniz, Eli. "A Transição Política no Brasil: Uma Reavaliação da Dinâmica da Abertura." *Dados: Revista de Ciências Sociais* 28, no. 3 (1985): 329–46.

Drake, Paul W., and Eduardo Silva, eds. *Elections and Democratization in Latin America, 1980–1985*. San Diego: Center for Iberian and Latin American Studies, Center for U.S.-Mexican Studies, Institute of the Americas, 1986.

Durham, Eunice Ribeiro. "Movimentos Sociais: A Construção da Cidadania." *Novos Estudos do CEBRAP* 10 (October 1984): 24–30.

Eckstein, Susan, ed. *Power and Popular Protest: Latin American Social Movements*. Berkeley: University of California Press, 1989.

Ehrenreich, Barbara, and Frances Fox Piven. "Women and the Welfare State." In *Alternatives: Proposals for America from the Democratic Left*, edited by Irving Howe. New York: Pantheon, 1983.

Eisenstein, Zillah R. *Feminism and Sexual Equality: Crisis in Liberal America*. New York: Monthly Review Press, 1984.

Elshtain, Jean Bethke. *Public Man/Private Woman*. Princeton: Princeton University Press, 1981.

Enloe, Cynthia. *Does Khaki Become You? The Militarization of Women's Lives*. Boston: South End Press, 1983.

————. "Women Textile Workers in the Militarization of Southeast Asia." In *Women, Men and the International Division of Labor*, edited by June Nash and María Patricia Fernández-Kelly. Albany: State University of New York Press, 1983.

Equipe Projeto-Mulher do Instituto de Ação Comunitária, ed. *Mulheres em Movimento*. Rio de Janeiro: Marco Zero, 1983.

Escobar, Arturo. "Social Science Discourse and New Social Movements Research in Latin America: Trends and Debates." Paper presented at the XV International Conference of the Latin American Studies Association, Miami, Florida, December 4–6, 1989.

Evans, Peter. *Dependent Development: The Alliance of Multinational, State and Local Capital in Brazil*. Princeton, N.J.: Princeton University Press, 1979.

Evers, Tilman. "Identity: The Hidden Side of New Social Movements in Latin America." In *New Social Movements and the State in Latin America*, edited by David Slater. Amsterdam: CEDLA, 1985.

————. "Os Movimentos Sociais Urbanos: O Caso do Movimento do Custo de Vida." In *Alternativas Populares da Democracia*, edited by José Álvaro Moisés et al. Petrópolis: Vozes; São Paulo: CEDEC, 1982.

————. "Síntesis Interpretativa del 'Movimento do Custo de Vida,' un Movimiento Urbano Brasileño." *Revista Mexicana de Sociología* 43, no. 4 (October-December 1981): 1371–93.

Evers, Tilman, Clarita Muller-Plantenberg, and Stefanie Spessart. "Movimentos de Base e Estado: Lutas na Esfera de Reprodução na América Latina." In *Cidade, Povo e Poder*, edited by José Álvaro Moisés et al. Rio de Janeiro: Paz e Terra; São Paulo: CEDEC, 1982.

Faria, Vilmar. "Desenvolvimento, Urbanização e Mudanças na Estrutura do Emprego: A Experiência Brasileira dos Ultimos Trinta Anos." In *Sociedade e Política no Brasil Pós-64*, edited by Bernard Sorj and Maria Hermínia Tavares de Almeida. São Paulo: Brasilense, 1983.

Feijoó, María del Carmen. "Alguns Problemas dos Movimentos de Mulheres no Processo de Transição Democrática." *Revista de Ciências Sociais* 1, no. 2 (1987): 153–62.

———. "The Challenge of Constructing Civilian Peace: Women and Democracy in Argentina." In *The Women's Movement in Latin America: Feminism and the Transition to Democracy*, edited by Jane S. Jaquette. Boston: Unwin Hyman, 1989.

———. "El Movimiento de Mujeres." In *Los Nuevos Movimientos Sociales*, edited by Elizabeth Jelin. Buenos Aires: Centro Editor de América Latina, 1985.

Ferguson, Kathy. *The Feminist Case Against Bureaucracy*. Philadelphia: Temple University Press, 1984.

Fleischer, David V. "De la Distensión a la Apertura Político-Electoral en Brasil." *Revista Mexicana de Sociología* 44, no. 3 (July-September 1982): 961–98.

———. "A Evolução do Bipartidarismo Brasileiro, 1966–1979." *Revista Brasileira de Estudos Políticos* 51 (1980): 155–85.

Flora, Cornelia Butler. "Socialist Feminism in Latin America." *Women and Politics* 4, no. 1 (Spring 1984): 69–93.

Flynn, Peter. *Brazil: A Political Analysis*. Boulder, Colo.: Westview Press, 1979.

Fontaine, Pierre-Michel. "Transnational Relations and Racial Mobilization: Emerging Black Movements in Brazil." In *Ethnic Identities in a Transnational World*, edited by John F. Stack, Jr. Westport, Conn.: Greenwood Press, 1986.

Frank, Dana. "Housewives, Socialists and the Politics of Food: The 1917 New York Cost-of-Living Protests." *Feminist Studies* 11, no. 2 (Summer 1985): 255–85.

Fraser, Arvonne S. *The U.N. Decade for Women: Documents and Dialogue*. Boulder, Colo.: Westview Press, 1987.

Freeman, Jo. "A Model for Analyzing the Strategic Options for Social Movement Organizations." In *Social Movements of the Sixties and Seventies*, edited by Jo Freeman. New York: Longman, 1983.

———. "On the Origins of Social Movements." In *Social Movements of the Sixties and Seventies*, edited by Jo Freeman. New York: Longman, 1983.

Frente de Mulheres Feministas. *O Que É o Aborto?* São Paulo: Cortez, 1980.

Fry, Peter, and Edward McRae. *O Que É Homosexualidade?* São Paulo: Brasilense, 1983.

Gelb, Joyce, and Marian Lief Palley. *Women and Public Policies*. Princeton, N.J.: Princeton University Press, 1982.

Gerlach, Luther P., and Virginia H. Hine. *People, Power and Change: Movements of Social Transformation*. New York: Bobbs-Merrill, 1970.

Giacomini, Sonia Maria. *Mulher e Escrava: Uma Introdução Histórica ao Estudo da Mulher Negra no Brasil*. Petrópolis: Vozes, 1988.

Gohn, Maria da Glória Marcondes. *A Força da Periferia: A Luta das Mulheres por Creches em São Paulo*. Petrópolis: Vozes, 1985.

———. *Reivindicações Populares Urbanas: Um Estudo sobre as Associações de Moradores de São Paulo*. São Paulo: Cortez, 1982.

Goldberg, Anette. "Feminismo em Regime Autoritário: A Experiência do Movimento de Mulheres no Rio de Janeiro." Paper presented at the XII International Congress of the International Political Science Association, Rio de Janeiro, August 9–14, 1982.

———. "Os Movimentos de Libertação da Mulher na França e na Italia (1970–1980):

Primeiros Elementos para Um Estudo Comparativo do Novo Feminismo na Europa e no Brasil." In *O Lugar da Mulher*, edited by Madel T. Luz. Rio de Janeiro: Graal, 1982.

Gonzalez, Lélia, and Carlos Hasenbalg. *Lugar do Negro*. Rio de Janeiro: Marco Zero, 1982.

Gorender, Jacob. *Combate nas Trevas—A Esquerda Brasileira: Das Ilusões à Luta Armada*. São Paulo: Ática, 1987.

Guertechin, Theirry Linard de. "O Controle da Natalidade: Uma Questão Demográfica e/ou Um Problema Político." In *Controle da Natalidade x Planejamento Familiar no Brasil*, edited by Theirry Linard de Guertechin et al. Rio de Janeiro: Achiamé, 1987.

Guertechin, Theirry Linard de, et al., eds. *Controle da Natalidade x Planejamento Familiar no Brasil*. Rio de Janeiro: Achiamé, 1987.

Guillespie, Charles Guy. "Democratic Consolidation in the Southern Cone and Brazil: Beyond Political Disarticulation." *Third World Quarterly* 11, no. 2 (April 1989): 92–113.

Guillespie, Richard. "A Critique of the Urban Guerrila: Argentina, Uruguay and Brazil." *Conflict Quarterly*, 1, no. 2 (1980): 39–53.

Hagopian, Frances, and Scott Mainwaring. "Democracy in Brazil: Origins, Problems, Prospects." Helen Kellogg Institute for International Studies, Working Paper no. 100. Notre Dame, Ind.: University of Notre Dame, Kellogg Institute, September 1987.

Hahner, June E. "Feminism, Women's Rights, and the Suffrage Movement in Brazil, 1850–1932." *Latin American Research Review* 15, no. 1 (1980): 65–112.

———. *A Mulher Brasileira e suas Lutas Sociais e Políticas: 1850–1937*. São Paulo: Brasilense, 1981.

Handelman, Howard, and Thomas G. Sanders, eds. *Military Government and the Movement toward Democracy in South America*. Bloomington: Indiana University Press, 1981.

Hasenbalg, Carlos. *Discriminações e Desigualdades Raciais no Brasil*. Rio de Janeiro: Graal, 1979.

Hellman, Judith Adler. *Journeys Among Women: Feminism in Five Italian Cities*. New York: Oxford University Press, 1987.

Hernan, Edward S., and James Petras. "Resurgent Democracy: Rhetoric and Reality." *New Left Review* 154 (1985): 83–98.

Hirata, Helena, and John Humphrey. "O Emprego Industrial Feminino e a Crise Econômica Brasileira." *Revista de Economia Política* 4, no. 4 (October-December 1984): 89–107.

Humphrey, John. *Gender and Work in the Third World: Sexual Divisions in Brazilian Industry*. London: Tavistock, 1987.

Jacobi, Pedro Roberto. "Movimentos Populares Urbanos e Resposta do Estado: Autonomia e Controle vs. Cooptação e Clientelismo." In *Movimentos Coletivos no Brasil Urbano*, edited by Renato Raul Boschi. Rio de Janeiro: Zahar, 1983.

———. "Movimentos Sociais—Teoria e Prática em Questão." In *Uma Revolução no Cotidiano? Os Novos Movimentos Sociais na América do Sul*, edited by Ilse Scherer-Warren and Paulo J. Krischke. São Paulo: Brasilense, 1987.

Jacobi, Pedro Roberto. "Movimentos Sociais Urbanos numa Época de Transição." In *Movimentos Sociais na Transição Democrática*, edited by Emir Sader. São Paulo: Cortez, 1987.

Jaquette, Jane S., ed. *The Women's Movement in Latin America: Feminism and the Transition to Democracy*. Boston: Unwin Hyman, 1989.

Jayawardena, Kumari. *Feminism and Nationalism in the Third World*. London: Zed, 1986.

Jelin, Elizabeth, ed. *Ciudadanía e Identidad: Las Mujeres en los Movimientos Sociales Latinoamericanos*. Geneva: UNRISD, 1987.

―――. *Los Nuevos Movimientos Sociales*. 2 vols. Buenos Aires: Centro Editor de América Latina, 1985.

―――. *Movimentos Sociales y Democracia Emergente*, 2 vols. Buenos Aires: Centro Editor de América Latina, 1987.

Jenson, Jane. "Both Friend and Foe: Women and State Welfare." In *Becoming Visible: Women in European History*, 2d ed., edited by Renate Bridenthal, Claudia Koonz, and Susan Stuard. Boston: Houghton Mifflin, 1987.

―――. "Gender and Reproduction, or Babies and the State." *Studies in Political Economy* 20 (Summer 1986): 9–46.

Kaplan, Temma. "Female Consciousness and Collective Action: The Case of Barcelona, 1910–1918." *Signs: A Journal of Women in Culture and Society* 7, no. 3 (Spring 1982): 545–66.

Katzenstein, Mary Fainsod, and Carol McClurg Mueller, eds. *The Women's Movements of the United States and Western Europe: Consciousness, Political Opportunity, and Public Policy*. Philadelphia: Temple University Press, 1987.

Keck, Margaret. "Democratization and Dissension: The Formation of the Workers' Party." *Politics and Society* 15, no. 1 (1986–1987): 67–95.

―――. "The New Unionism in the Brazilian Transition." In *Democratizing Brazil: Problems of Transition and Consolidation*, edited by Alfred Stepan. New York: Oxford University Press, 1989.

Kerbauy, Maria Teresa Miceli. "A Questão Feminina: Mulher, Partido, e Representação Política." Paper presented at the XII International Conference of the Latin American Studies Association, Albuquerque, N.M., April 18–20, 1985.

Kinzo, Maria D'Alva Gil. "Novos Partidos: O Início do Debate." In *Voto de Desconfiança: Eleições e Mudança Política no Brasil, 1970–1979*, edited by Bolivar Lamounier. Petrópolis: Vozes; São Paulo: CEBRAP, 1980.

Kirkwood, Julieta. *Feminarios*. Santiago, Chile: Ediciones Documentas, 1987.

―――. *Ser Política en Chile: Las Feministas y los Partidos*. Santiago: Facultad Latinoamericana de Ciencias Sociales, 1986.

―――. "Women and Politics in Chile." *International Social Science Journal* 33, no. 4 (1983): 625–37.

Klein, Ethel. *Gender Politics: From Consciousness to Mass Politics*. Cambridge, Mass.: Harvard University Press, 1984.

Koonz, Claudia. *Mothers in the Fatherland: Women, the Family and Nazi Politics*. New York: St. Martins Press, 1987.

Koutzii, Flavio, ed. *Nova República: Um Balanço*. Porto Alegre: L and PM, 1986.

Kowarick, Lúcio, ed. *As Lutas Sociais e a Cidade. São Paulo: Passado e Presente*. Rio de Janeiro: Paz e Terra, CEDEC, and UNRISD, 1988.

Kowarick, Lúcio, and Nabil Bonduki. "Espaço Urbano e Espaço Político: do Popu-
lismo à Redemocratização." In *As Lutas Sociais e a Cidade. São Paulo: Passado e
Presente*, edited by Lúcio Kowarick. Rio de Janeiro: Paz e Terra, CEDEC, and
UNRISD, 1988.

Krischke, Paulo J. "Movimentos Sociais e Transição Política: Contribuições da Democracia de Base." In *Uma Revolução no Cotidiano? Os Novos Movimentos Sociais
na América do Sul*, edited by Ilse Scherer-Warren and Paulo J. Krischke. São Paulo:
Brasilense, 1987.

————, ed. *Brasil: do "Milagre" à Abertura*. São Paulo: Cortez, 1983.

Krischke, Paulo J., and Scott Mainwaring, eds. *A Igreja nas Bases em Tempo de Transição*. Porto Alegre: L and PM, 1986.

Kucinsky, Bernardo. *Brazil: State and Struggle*. London: Latin American Bureau,
1982.

Laclau, Ernesto, and Chantal Mouffe. *Hegemony and Socialist Strategy*. London:
Verso, 1985.

Lamounier, Bolivar. "Authoritarian Brazil Revisited: The Impact of Elections on the
Abertura." In *Democratizing Brazil: Dilemmas of Transition and Consolidation*,
edited by Alfred Stepan. New York: Oxford University Press, 1989.

————. "Challenges to Democratic Consolidation in Brazil." Paper presented at the
American Political Science Association Convention, Washington, D.C., September
1–4, 1988.

————. "O Voto em São Paulo, 1970–1978." In *Voto de Desconfiança: Eleições e
Mudança Política no Brasil, 1970–1979*, edited by Bolivar Lamounier. Petrópolis:
Vozes; São Paulo: CEBRAP, 1980.

Lamounier, Bolivar, and Rachel Meneguello. *Partidos Políticos e Consolidação Democrática: O Caso Brasileiro*. São Paulo: Brasilense, 1986.

Latin American Documentation. *Women in the Church*. Lima: LADOC, n.d.

Lavrin, Asunción. "The Ideology of Feminism in the Southern Cone." Wilson Center
Working Papers, no. 169, The Wilson Center, Smithsonian Institution, Washington,
D.C., 1986.

Lechner, Norbert, and Susana Levy. "Notas sobre la Vida Cotidiana III: El Disci-
plinamiento de la Mujer." Materia de Discusión, no. 57. Santiago: FLACSO,
1984.

Levine, Daniel H. "Religion and Politics, Politics and Religion: An Introduction." In
Churches and Politics in Latin America, edited by Daniel H. Levine. Beverly Hills:
Sage Publications, 1980.

Lind, Amy Conger. "Development as if Women Mattered: The Formation of an Autonomous Women's Movement in Peru." Bachelor's thesis, University of California, Santa Cruz, 1988.

Linz, Juan J. "The Future of an Authoritarian Situation or the Institutionalization of
an Authoritarian Regime: The Case of Brazil." In *Authoritarian Brazil: Origins,
Policies, and Future*, edited by Alfred Stepan. New Haven: Yale University Press,
1973.

Linz, Juan J., and Alfred Stepan, eds. *The Breakdown of Democracy in Latin America*.
Baltimore, Md.: Johns Hopkins University Press, 1978.

Lobo, Elizabeth Souza. "Mulheres, Feminismo e Novas Praticas Sociais." *Revista de
Ciências Sociais* 1, no. 2 (1987): 221–29.

Lojkine, Jean. *Estado Capitalista e a Questão Urbana*. São Paulo: Martines Fontes, 1981.

Luz, Madel T., ed. *O Lugar da Mulher*. Rio de Janeiro: Graal, 1982.

Macias, Ana Maria. *Against All Odds: The Feminist Movement in Mexico*. Westport, Conn.: Greenwood Press, 1982.

MacKinnon, Catherine A. "Feminism, Marxism, Method, and the State: An Agenda for Theory." *Signs: A Journal of Women in Culture and Society* 7, no. 3 (Spring 1982): 515–44.

———. "Feminism, Marxism, Method, and the State: Toward a Feminist Jurisprudence." *Signs: A Journal of Women in Culture and Society* 8, no. 4 (Summer 1983): 635–58.

Mainwaring, Scott. *The Catholic Church and Politics in Brazil, 1916–1985*. Stanford, Calif.: Stanford University Press, 1986.

———. "Political Parties and Democratization in Brazil and the Southern Cone." *Comparative Politics* 21, no. 1 (October 1988): 91–120.

———. "The Transition to Democracy in Brazil." *Journal of Interamerican Studies and World Affairs* 28 (May 1986): 149–79.

———. "Urban Popular Movements, Identity and Democratization in Brazil." *Comparative Political Studies* 20, no. 2 (July 1987): 131–59.

Mainwaring, Scott, and Eduardo Silva. "New Social Movements, Political Culture and Democracy: Brazil and Argentina in the 1980s." *Telos* 17, no. 3 (Fall 1984): 17–52.

Malloy, James M. *The Politics of Social Security in Brazil*. Pittsburgh, Penn.: University of Pittsburgh Press, 1979.

Malloy, James M., and Mitchell A. Seligson, eds. *Authoritarians and Democrats: Regime Transitions in Latin America*. Pittsburgh, Penn.: University of Pittsburgh Press, 1987.

Martins, João Roberto, Filho. *Movimento Estudantil e Ditadura Militar 1964–1968*. Campinas, São Paulo: Papirus, 1987.

Martins, Luciano. "The Liberalization of Authoritarian Rule in Brazil." In *Transitions from Authoritarian Rule: Latin America*, edited by Guillermo O'Donnell, Philippe P. Schmitter, and Laurence Whitehead. Baltimore, Md.: John Hopkins University Press, 1986.

Mass, Bonnie. *Population Target: The Political Economy of Population Control in Latin America*. Toronto: L. A. Working Group and Women's Educational Press, 1976.

Mattelart, Michele. "Chile: The Feminine Side of the Coup d'État." In *Sex and Class in Latin America*, edited by June Nash and Helen I. Safa. New York: Praeger, 1976.

McAdam, Doug. *Political Process and the Development of Black Insurgency, 1930–1970*. Chicago: University of Chicago Press, 1982.

McDonough, Peter, and Amaury de Souza. *The Politics of Population in Brazil: Elite Ambivalence and Public Demand*. Austin: University of Texas Press, 1981.

Michaelson, Karen L., ed. *And the Poor Get Children: Radical Perspectives on Population Dynamics*. New York: Monthly Review Press, 1981.

Miyamoto, Shiguenoli. "Eleições do 1978 em São Paulo: A Campanha." In *Voto de*

Desconfiança: Eleições e Mudança Política no Brasil, 1970–1979, edited by Bolivar Lamounier. Petrópolis: Vozes; São Paulo: CEBRAP, 1980.

Moisés, José Álvaro. *Cenas de Política Explícita: Descaminhos de uma Longa Transição Política*. São Paulo: Marco Zero, 1986.

————. "Contradições Urbanas, Estado, e Movimentos Sociais." In *Cidade, Povo e Poder*, edited by José Álvaro Moisés, et al. Rio de Janeiro: Paz e Terra; São Paulo: CEDEC, 1982.

Moisés, José Álvaro, et al. *Contradições Urbanas e Movimentos Sociais*. Rio de Janeiro: Paz e Terra; São Paulo: CEDEC, 1978.

Molyneux, Maxine. "Mobilization Without Emancipation? Women's Interests, State, and Revolution." In *Transition and Development: Problems of Third World Socialism*, edited by Richard R. Fagen, Carmen Diana Deere, and José Luis Coraggio. New York: Monthly Review Press; Berkeley, Calif.: Center for the Study of the Americas, 1986.

————. "Socialist Societies Old and New: Progress Toward Women's Emancipation?" *Monthly Review* 34, no. 3 (July-August 1982): 56–100.

Moraes, Maria Lygia Quartim de. *Mulheres em Movimento*. São Paulo: Nobel and Conselho Estadual da Condição Feminina, 1985.

Moraes Nehring, Maria Lygia Quartim de. "Família e Feminismo: Reflexões sobre Papeis Femininos na Imprensa para Mulheres." Ph.D. diss., University of São Paulo, 1981.

Moreno, Raquel. "De Feminismos, de Feministas, de Mulheres." In *A Condição Feminina*, edited by Nanci Valadares de Carvalho. São Paulo: Vértice, 1988.

"O Movimento de Mulheres no Brasil." *Cadernos da Associação das Mulheres*, Special issue, 3 (August 1979).

"As Mulheres e os Novos Espaços Democráticos na América Latina." *Revista de Ciências Sociais*, Special Issue, 1, no. 2 (1987).

Munck, Ronaldo. *Politics and Dependency in the Third World: The Case of Latin America*. London: Zed Press, 1984.

Muraro, Rose Marie. *Libertação Sexual da Mulher*. Petrópolis: Vozes, 1975.

————. *A Mulher na Construção do Mundo Futuro*. Petrópolis: Vozes, 1966.

————. *Sexualidade da Mulher Brasileira: Corpo e Classe Social no Brasil*. Petrópolis: Vozes, 1983.

Nash, June, and Helen I. Safa, eds. *Sex and Class in Latin America*. New York: Praeger, 1976.

————. *Women and Change in Latin America*. South Hadley, Mass.: Bergin and Garvey, 1986.

Navarro, Marysa. *Evita*. Buenos Aires: Corregidor, 1984.

————. "First Feminist Meeting of Latin America and the Caribbean." *Signs: A Journal of Women in Culture and Society* 8, no. 1 (Autumn 1982): 154–59.

————. "The Mothers of the Plaza de Mayo in Argentina." In *Power and Popular Protest: Latin American Social Movements*, edited by Susan Eckstein. Berkeley: University of California Press, 1989.

Neto, Ana Maria Q. Fausto. *Família Operária e Reprodução da Força de Trabalho*. Petrópolis: Vozes, 1982.

Neto, Maria Inacia d'Avila. *O Autoritarismo e a Mulher: O Jogo da Dominação Ma-cho-Fêmea no Brasil*. Rio de Janeiro: Achiamé, 1980.

O'Donnell, Guillermo. *Modernization and Bureaucratic-Authoritarianism: Studies in South American Politics*. Berkeley: Institute for International Studies, University of California, Berkeley, 1973.

O'Donnell, Guillermo, Philippe C. Schmitter, and Laurence Whitehead, eds. *Transitions from Authoritarian Rule*. Baltimore, Md.: John Hopkins University Press, 1986.

Offen, Karen. "Defining Feminism: A Comparative Historical Approach." *Signs: Journal of Women in Culture and Society* 14, no. 1 (Autumn 1988): 119–57.

Pacheco, Mario Victor de Assis. *Racismo, Machismo e "Planejamento Familiar."* Petrópolis: Vozes, 1981.

Paris Latin American Women's Group. "Why An Autonomous Women's Movement?" In *Third World/Second Sex*, edited by Miranda Davies. London: Zed, 1983.

Peattie, Lisa, and Martin Rein. *Women's Claims: A Study in Political Economy*. Oxford: Oxford University Press, 1983.

Pego, Raquel A. "A Luta das Mulheres pela Livre Concepção." In *Controle da Natalidade x Planejamento Familiar no Brasil*, edited by Theirry Linard de Guertechin et al. Rio de Janeiro: Achiamé, 1987.

Pena, Maria Valéria Junho. "O Estado e a Condição Feminina." *Revista Brasileira de Ciências Sociais* 1, no. 2 (1987): 203–8.

Perelli, Carina. "Putting Conservatism to Good Use: Women and Unorthodox Politics in Uruguay, from Breakdown to Transition." In *The Women's Movement in Latin America: Feminism and the Transition to Democracy*, edited by Jane S. Jaquette. Boston: Unwin Hyman, 1989.

Pimentel, Silvia. *A Mulher e a Constituente: Uma Contribuição ao Debate*. São Paulo: Cortez, 1987.

———. "A Necessaria Participação Política da Mulher." *Revista do PMDB*, 1, no. 3 (August-September 1982): 17–32.

Pinheiro, Ana Alice Costa. "Avances y Definiciones del Movimiento Feminista en el Brasil." Master's thesis, Colégio de México, 1981.

Piven, Frances Fox. "Women and the State: Ideology, Power, and the Welfare State." *Socialist Review* 14, no. 2 (March-April 1984): 11–19.

Piven, Frances Fox, and Richard A. Cloward. *Poor People's Movements: Why They Succeed, How They Fail*. New York: Vintage, 1977.

Portes, Alejandro, and A. Douglas Kincaid. "The Crisis of Authoritarianism: State and Civil Society in Argentina, Chile, and Uruguay." *Research in Political Sociology* 1 (1985): 49–77.

Randall, Vicky. *Women and Politics: An International Perspective*. 2d ed. Chicago: University of Chicago Press, 1987.

Rede Mulher. "Retrato dos Clubes de Mães e Grupos de Mulheres da Zona Leste de São Paulo." Pesquisa-Avaliação dos Clubes e Grupos de Mães da Cidade de São Paulo, Documento no. 3, June 1985. Mimeograph.

Reis, Daniel Aarão, Filho, and Pedro Moraes. *68: A Paixão de uma Utopia*. Rio de Janeiro: Espaço e Tempo, 1988.

Reis, Fábio Wanderley. "O Eleitorado, os Partidos, e o Regime Autoritário Brasileiro." In *Sociedade e Política no Brasil Pós-64*, edited by Bernard Sorj and Maria Hermínia Tavares de Almeida. São Paulo: Brasilense, 1983.

———, ed. *Os Partidos e o Regime: A Lógica do Processo Eleitoral Brasileiro*. São Paulo: Edições Símbolo, 1978.

Reis, Fábio Wanderley, and Guillermo O'Donnell, eds. *A Democracia no Brasil: Dilemas e Perspectivas*. São Paulo: Vértice, 1988.

Rodrigues, Newton. *Brasil Provisório (de Jânio a Sarney)*. Rio de Janeiro: Editora Guanabara, 1986.

Rosemberg, Fulvia, Maria Malta Campos, and Regina Pahim Pinto. *Creches e Pré-Escolas*. São Paulo: Nobel and Conselho Estadual da Condição Feminina, 1985.

Rosemberg, Fulvia, and Regina Pahim Pinto. *A Educação da Mulher*. São Paulo: Nobel and Conselho Estadual da Condição Feminina, 1985.

Rosemberg, Fulvia, Regina Pahim Pinto, and Esmeralda V. Negrão. *A Educação da Mulher no Brasil*. São Paulo: Global, 1982.

Rosenberg, Rena. "Representing Women at the State and Local Levels: Commissions on the Status of Women." In *Women, Power and Policy*, edited by Ellen Boneparth. New York: Pergamon, 1982.

Rowbotham, Sheila, Lynne Segal, and Hilary Wainwright. *Beyond the Fragments: Feminism and the Making of Socialism*. London: Merlin Press, 1979.

Sader, Eder S. "Quando Novos Personagens Entraram em Cena . . ." Ph.D. diss., University of São Paulo, 1987.

Sader, Emir. "The Workers' Party in Brazil." *New Left Review* 165 (September-October 1987): 93–102.

———, ed. *Constituinte e Democracia no Brasil Hoje*. São Paulo: Brasilense, 1985.

———, ed. *Movimentos Sociais na Transição Democrática*. São Paulo: Cortez, 1987.

Saffioti, Heleieth Iara Bongiovani. "Feminismos e Seus Frutos no Brasil." in *Movimentos Sociais na Transição Democrática*, edited by Emir Sader. São Paulo: Cortez, 1987.

———. *A Mulher na Sociedade de Classes: Mito e Realidade*. Petrópolis: Vozes, 1976.

Sandroni, Paulo, ed. *Constituinte, Economia e Política da Nova República*. São Paulo: Cortez and EDUC, 1986.

Santos, Carlos Nelson Ferreira dos. *Movimentos Urbanos no Rio de Janeiro*. Rio de Janeiro: Zahar Editores, 1981.

Sapiro, Virginia. "When Are Interests Interesting? The Problem of Political Representation of Women." *American Political Science Review* 75, no. 3 (September 1981): 701–16.

Sargeant, Lydia, ed. *Women and Revolution. A Discussion of the Unhappy Marriage of Marxism and Feminism*. Boston: South End Press, 1981.

Sarti, Cynthia. "The Panorama of Feminism in Brazil." *New Left Review* 173 (January/February 1989): 75–90.

———. "É Sina Que a Gente Traz (Ser Mulher na Periferia Urbana)." Master's thesis, University of São Paulo, 1985.

Scherer-Warren, Ilse, and Paulo J. Krischke, eds. *Uma Revolução no Cotidiano? Os Novos Movimentos Sociais na América do Sul*. São Paulo: Brasilense, 1987.

Schmink, Marianne. "Women in Brazilian 'Abertura' Politics." *Signs: A Journal of Women in Culture and Society*, 7, no. 2 (Autumn 1981): 115–34.

Selcher, Wayne A., ed. *Political Liberalization in Brazil: Dynamics, Dilemmas, and Future Prospects*. Boulder, Colo.: Westview Press, 1986.

Sen, Gita, and Caren Grown. *Development, Crises, and Alternative Visions: Third World Women's Perspectives*. New York: Monthly Review Press, 1987.

Simões, Solange de Deus. *Deus, Pátria e Família: As Mulheres no Golpe de 1964*. Petrópolis: Vozes, 1985.

Singer, Paul J. "As Contradições do Milagre." In *Brasil: do "Milagre" à "Abertura,"* edited by Paulo J. Krischke. São Paulo: Cortez, 1983.

———. "O Feminino e o Feminismo." In *São Paulo: O Povo em Movimento*, edited by Paul J. Singer and Vinícius Caldeira Brant. Petrópolis: Vozes; São Paulo: CEBRAP, 1980.

———. "Movimentos de Bairro." In *São Paulo: O Povo em Movimento*, edited by Paul J. Singer and Vinícius Caldeira Brant. Petrópolis: Vozes; São Paulo: CEBRAP, 1980.

Singer, Paul J., and Vinícius Caldeira Brant, eds. *São Paulo: O Povo em Movimento*. Petrópolis: Vozes; São Paulo: CEBRAP, 1980.

Skidmore, Thomas E. "Brazil's Slow Road to Democratization: 1974–1985." In *Democratizing Brazil: Problems of Transition and Consolidation*, edited by Alfred Stepan. New York: Oxford University Press, 1989.

———. *The Politics of Military Rule in Brazil, 1964–1985*. New York: Oxford University Press, 1988.

Skocpol, Theda. "Bringing the State Back In: Strategies of Analysis in Current Research." In *Bringing the State Back In*, edited by Peter B. Evans, Dietrich Rueschemeyer, and Theda Skocpol. New York: Cambridge University Press, 1985.

Sloan, John W. *Public Policy in Latin America: A Comparative Survey*. Pittsburgh, Penn.: University of Pittsburgh Press, 1984.

Smith, Brian H. *The Church and Politics in Chile: Challenges to Modern Catholicism*. Princeton, N.J.: Princeton University Press, 1982.

Smith, William C. "Heterodox Shocks and the Political Economy of Democratic Transition in Argentina and Brazil." Paper presented at the XIV International Conference of the Latin American Studies Association, New Orleans, March 17–19, 1988.

———. "The Political Transition in Brazil: From Authoritarian Liberalization to Elite Conciliation to Democratization." In *Comparing New Democracies: Transition and Consolidation in Mediterranean Europe and the Southern Cone*, edited by Enrique A. Balorya. Boulder, Colo.: Westview Press, 1987.

Soares, Glaucio A. D. "El Sistema Político Brasileño: Nuevos Partidos y Viejas Divisiones." *Revista Mexicana de Sociología* 44, no. 3 (July-September 1982): 929–59.

Sorj, Bernard, Fernando Henrique Cardoso, and Mauricio Font, eds. *Economia e Movimentos Sociais na América Latina*. São Paulo: Brasilense, 1985.

Sorj, Bernard, and Maria Hermínia Tavares de Almeida, eds. *Sociedade e Política no Brasil Pós-64*. São Paulo: Brasilense, 1983.

Staudt, Kathleen. "Women, Development and the State: On the Theoretical Impasse." *Development and Change* 17, no. 2 (April 1986): 325–33.

Stepan, Alfred. *Rethinking Military Politics: Brazil and the Southern Cone*. Princeton, N.J.: Princeton University Press, 1988.

———. *The State and Society: Peru in Comparative Perspective*. Princeton, N.J.: Princeton University Press, 1978.

———. "State Power and the Strength of Civil Society in the Southern Cone of Latin America." In *Bringing the State Back In*, edited by Peter B. Evans, Dietrich Rueschemeyer, and Theda Skocpol. New York: Cambridge University Press, 1985.

———, ed. *Authoritarian Brazil: Origins, Policies, and Future*. New Haven, Conn.: Yale University Press, 1973.

———, ed. *Democratizing Brazil: Problems of Transition and Consolidation*. New York: Oxford University Press, 1989.

Sternbach, Nancy, Marysa Navarro, Patricia Chuchryk, and Sonia E. Alvarez. "Feminisms in Latin America: From Bogotá to Taxco." *Signs: A Journal of Women in Culture and Society*. Forthcoming.

Stevens, Evelyn P. "The Prospects for a Women's Liberation Movement in Latin America." *Journal of Marriage and the Family* 35, no. 2 (May 1973): 313–21.

Studart, Heloneida. *A Mulher, Brinquedo do Homem*. Petrópolis: Vozes, 1969.

Tabak, Fanny. *Autoritarismo e Participação Política da Mulher*. Rio de Janeiro: Graal, 1983.

———. *Mulher e Democracia*. Rio de Janeiro: Pontífica Universidade Católica do Rio de Janeiro, Núcleo de Estudos Sobre a Mulher, 1987.

Tabak, Fanny, and Moema Toscano. *Mulher & Política*. Rio de Janeiro: Paz e Terra, 1982.

Tamez, Elsa, ed. *Against Machismo: Rubem Alves, Leonardo Boff, Gustavo Gutiérrez, José Marquez Bonino, Juan Luís Segundo and Others Talk about the Struggle of Women*. Oak Park, Ill.: Meyer Stone, 1987.

———. *El Rostro Femenino de la Teología*. San José, Costa Rica: Departamento Ecuménico de Investigaciones, 1986.

Tarrow, Sidney. "Struggling for Reform: Social Movements and Policy Change during Cycles of Protest." Western Societies Occasional Papers, no. 15, Center for International Studies. Ithaca, N.Y.: Cornell University, 1983.

Tornaria, Carmen. "Uruguay." In *Jornadas Feministas: Feminismo y Sectores Populares en América Latina*, edited by Coordinación de Grupos Organizadores de las Jornadas Feministas. Mexico, D.F.: Ed. Electrocomp, 1987.

———. "Women's Involvement in the Democratic Process in Uruguay." In *The Latin American Women's Movement: Reflections and Actions*, edited by ISIS International. Rome: ISIS International, 1986.

Touraine, Alain. *Le Voix e Le Regard*. Paris: Editions Seuil, 1978.

Trevisan, João S. *Perverts in Paradise*. London: Gay Men's Press, 1986.

Valenzuela, María Elena. *Todas Ibamos a Ser Reinas: La Mujer en Chile Militar*. Santiago, Chile: Ediciones Chile y América, CESOC, ACHIP, 1987.

Vargas, Virginia. "El Aporte de la Rebeldia de las Mujeres." In *Jornadas Feministas: Feminismo y Sectores Populares en América Latina*, edited by Coordinación de Grupos Organizadores de las Jornadas Feministas. Mexico, D.F.: Ed. Electrocomp, 1987.

Velasco e Cruz, Sebastião C., and Carlos Estevam Martins. "De Castelo a Figueiredo:

Uma Incursão na pré-História da 'Abertura'.'' In *Sociedade e Política no Brasil Pós-64*, edited by Bernard Sorj and Maria Hermínia Tavares de Almeida. São Paulo: Brasilense, 1983.

Verardo, Maria Tereza. *Aborto: Um Direito ou um Crime?* São Paulo: Moderna, 1987.

Viezzer, Moema. *O Problema Não Está na Mulher.* São Paulo: Cortez, 1989.

Viola, Eduardo J. "The Ecologist Movement in Brazil, (1974–1986)." *International Journal of Urban and Regional Research* 12, no. 2 (June 1988): 211–28.

Viola, Eduardo J., and Scott Mainwaring. "Transitions to Democracy: Brazil and Argentina in the 1980s." *Journal of International Affairs* 38, no. 2 (Winter 1985): 193–219.

Weffort, Francisco. *Por Que Democracia?* São Paulo: Brasilense, 1984.

Winant, Howard. "The Little Transition That Couldn't." *Socialist Review* 18, no. 1 (January 1988): 111–17.

NEWSPAPERS AND PERIODICALS CONSULTED

Boletim do CIM
Brasil Mulher
Chana com Chana
Cunhary
Em Tempo
Estado de São Paulo
Folha da Tarde
Folha de São Paulo
O Globo
Isto É
Jornal da Tarde
Lampião
Latin American Weekly Report
Latin American Regional Reports: Brazil
Movimento
Mulherio
New York Times
Nós Mulheres
Senhor
Veja

Index

Programa da Saúde da Mulher, São Paulo (Women's Health Program), 188–90, 196, 204–6

progressive opposition: conflicts within, 110, 138, 146; cooptation of women, 126, 134, 159–60, 176–77, 209; and debates over feminism, 90–97; discourses of, 57–58; and electoral politics, 141–43, 145–47; growth of, 11, 77, 178; male dominance of, 10–11, 58, 60, 86, 94, 107, 109, 119, 265–66; mobilization of, 78, 105–6; professional associations, 120; and the State, 189, 194; women's involvement, 11, 20, 57, 81, 91, 122, 135, 165, 220; and women's movements, 100, 104, 108, 111–12, 118, 120, 241, 265

Pró-Mulher (Pro-Woman), 105, 123, 168

pronatalism, 180–82

prostitutes and prostitution, 115, 134

protective labor laws, 20, 29–30

public realm, 28–29, 35

Quadros, Jânio, 236–37, 243–44, 257

Quercia, Orestes, 244–45, 253

racism, 26–27, 52, 134, 183, 201, 232–34, 256

radical feminism, 256

rape, 28–29, 132, 191, 218, 247, 254. See also sexual violence

Reagan, Ronald, 272–73

Recife, 134, 191

Rede Mulher (Women's Network), 230, 235, 255

regime transition (to civilian rule), 11, 14, 78, 195, 219; and electoral politics, 111, 137; and gender politics, 3, 7–9, 12, 14, 36, 59, 83, 91, 115, 178–97, 220–21, 223–24, 248; macropolitical factors of, 41, 56–57, 78, 261–62, 265–73; micropolitical factors of, 41–42, 56, 59, 78, 262, 265–73; and new conservatism, 225–28; and shift in women's strategies, 12, 34; and social movements, 15, 224; theoretical debates about, 14; and women's movements, 9–11, 14, 20–21, 34–35, 60, 106, 120, 136, 228–29, 234–35

reproduction, 29–30, 39–40, 85, 103, 124, 128, 130, 132–33, 198, 249; and capitalist development, 81, 180–81, 185–86, 193; and Catholicism, 64, 67, 81, 128, 184,

190; discourses, 178–97; rights of, 24–25, 28, 54, 70, 100, 108–9, 112, 114, 116, 118–19, 134, 152, 156, 168–69, 172, 180, 187–88, 191, 193–95, 204–6, 232, 242, 250, 254–55, 258–59, 266; State policies, 178–97, 203–7, 215. See also family planning; social reproduction

"responsible paternity," 187, 192

Revolution of 1964. See Right-wing Coup of 1964

right-wing: limitations of theory about women, 4; manipulation of traditional values, 5–6, 8–9; mobilization of women, 5–6; post-transition resurgence, 227

Right-wing Coup of 1964, 3, 5–8, 37, 76, 180; women's participation in, 6

Right-wing Coup of 1968, 8, 37, 62, 73

Rio de Janeiro, 39, 82, 89–91, 117, 119, 121, 138, 147, 151, 191, 194, 232–33, 235

Rio Grande do Sul, 147

Rocha, Janete, 155, 174

Roland, Edna, 233

running water, 39, 46, 104, 107, 124, 132, 230, 266

Saffioti, Heleieth, 89

Santos, Carlos Nelson Ferreira dos, 41

Sarney, José, 164, 221–22, 226–27, 232, 236, 245, 249–50, 256–58

Sartori, Guiomar, 163

Sayad, José, 250

Schmitter, Philippe, 268

schools, 10, 39, 45, 75, 87, 96, 114, 214. See also education

Second Vatican Council (1962–1965). See Vatican II

Secretaria da Mulher (Women's Department), 199

Secretaria Municipal da Família a Bem Estar Social (Department of the Family and Social Welfare), 200, 206, 213

Secretaria Municipal de Educação (Education Department), 200

self-help organizations, 10, 39, 84, 88

service sector, 52

sewers, 39, 45–46, 104, 107, 124

sex discrimination, 9, 90, 93, 122, 200, 234; in education, 128, 156; through marriage, 170; in paid labor market, 48, 92, 105, 166–68, 216, 253; within social movements, 10; in workplace, 114